A CULTURAL HISTORY
OF SEXUALITY

VOLUME 3

A Cultural History of Sexuality
General Editor: Julie Peakman

A CULTURAL HISTORY

OF SEXUALITY

IN THE
RENAISSANCE

Edited by Bette Talvacchia

B L O O M S B U R Y

LONDON · NEW DELHI · NEW YORK · SYDNEY

Bloomsbury Academic
An imprint of Bloomsbury Publishing Plc

50 Bedford Square	1385 Broadway
London	New York
WC1B 3DP	NY 10018
UK	USA

www.bloomsbury.com

Hardback edition first published in 2011 by Berg Publishers, an imprint of
Bloomsbury Academic
Paperback edition first published by Bloomsbury Academic 2014

British Library Cataloguing-in-Publication Data
A catalogue record for this book is available from the British Library.

ISBN: HB: 978-1-84788-802-0
PB: 978-1-4725-5479-6
HB Set: 978-1-84520-702-1
PB Set: 978-1-4725-5480-2

Library of Congress Cataloging-in-Publication Data
A catalog record for this book is available from the Library of Congress.

Typeset by Apex CoVantage, LLC, Madison, WI, USA

CONTENTS

PREFACE

A Cultural History of Sexuality is a six-volume series reviewing changes in sexual attitudes and behavior throughout history. Each volume follows the same basic structure and begins with an outline account of sexuality in the period under consideration. Academic experts examine major aspects of sex and sexuality under seven key headings: heterosexuality, homosexuality, sexual variations, religion and the law, medicine and disease, popular beliefs and culture, prostitution, and erotica. Readers can choose a synchronic or a diachronic approach to the material—a single volume can be read to obtain a thorough knowledge of the body in a given period, or one of the seven themes can be followed through time by reading the relevant chapters of all six volumes, providing a thematic understanding of changes and developments over the long term. The six volumes divide the history of sexuality as follows:

> Volume 1: A Cultural History of Sexuality in the Classical World (800 B.C.E. to 350 C.E.)
>
> Volume 2: A Cultural History of Sexuality in the Middle Ages (350 C.E. to 1450)
>
> Volume 3: A Cultural History of Sexuality in the Renaissance (1450 to 1650)
>
> Volume 4: A Cultural History of Sexuality in the Enlightenment (1650 to 1820)
>
> Volume 5: A Cultural History of Sexuality in the Age of Empire (1820 to 1920)
>
> Volume 6: A Cultural History of Sexuality in the Modern Age (1920 to 2000)

Julie Peakman, General Editor

SERIES ACKNOWLEDGMENTS

This series has been a long time in the making, mainly because it is not an easy task to bring together fifty-four international scholars, even when we were all willing and eager. Every one of us had other commitments—to our universities, other books, and/or to our families. I therefore appreciate those who came together to create this special project. I want to thank the editors of all the volumes; Peter Toohey and Mark Golden, Ruth Evans, Bette Talvacchia, Ivan Crozier and Chiara Beccalossi, and Gert Hekma for their sterling efforts in the face of my continual demands, and for helping to keep their contributors on track, especially when the occasional one dropped out with little warning. Huge thanks also go to all the contributors who freely committed their time and efforts. I also want to thank Tristan Palmer at Berg for all his support and Catherine Draycott from the Wellcome Trust Picture Library for making available the Wellcome images.

Julie Peakman, General Editor

ILLUSTRATIONS

CHAPTER 1

CHAPTER 3

CHAPTER 4

CHAPTER 6

CHAPTER 7

CHAPTER 9

CHAPTER ONE

Introduction: The Look and Sound of Sexuality in the Renaissance

BETTE TALVACCHIA

Statements about sexuality are articulated through the language of culture, both visual and verbal; the declarations, mute and voiced, allow for interpretation because they follow (or challenge) society's construction of what represents the male or the female gender. The promulgation and enforcement of practices that follow inherent or natural female and male behavior are a driving force in societies throughout history, although the definitions of what constitutes nature change remarkably from time to time and place to place. And indeed, the force of cultural practices is such that once particular customs take hold, they are naturalized. They come to be considered normative, straightforwardly evolved from the structure of nature, rather than a regime developed according to particular cultural ideas and social circumstances.

Here the focus will be on the cultural formulations developed to express gender and sexuality during the European Renaissance, along with the strategies that evolved to question the established formulas. Rather than being a given, static, and unalterable element in nature that transcends history, human sexuality has many histories; the one traced in this volume centers on the representations of male and female in Renaissance culture, ranging through the forms sexuality took in medical science, literature, religious and legal texts, and the visual arts—in other words, human culture in its broadest definition. It will take Western Europe as its main focus, with particular emphasis on occurrences in Italy, the core site for the development of concepts that define the Renaissance as a part of early modern history.

We might begin by thinking of the sexual as linked to biological components of the human body and the gendering of biologically male or female bodies as the prescribed and differentiated behavior for each, stemming from cultural strictures. But if this is a tenable general statement, complications and qualifications immediately come into play. For example, do these realms of biology and culture remain separate, or are they interrelated arenas of action from the start? Research carried out by the eminent geneticist Luca Cavalli-Sforza indicates that genetic and cultural developments operate in a similar manner, and that we can learn about one from the other:

> Genetic inheritance determines the structural characteristics of our physical and psychological organism. Cultural patrimony is absorbed throughout life from earliest infancy, and conditions our existence, our choices, and many aspects of our affective life, and at times it inevitably conflicts with what is transmitted genetically.[1]

A fundamental link between genetics and culture, according to Cavalli-Sforza, is that both are transmitted; a fundamental difference is the way in which the transmission occurs. The dynamics of cultural transmission provide an array of patrimonies that can be bequeathed to a multitude of heirs. Cultural transmission through elders, mentors, teachers, and even peers allows the recipients to have some choice in their heritage beyond that of their genetic makeup. Thus cultural transformation can be transmitted by other than parents, and not necessarily from one generation to another, with results that are more effective and quicker to take effect. Positing language as the "motor" of cultural transmission, Cavalli-Sforza refers to the change-inducing choices as "cultural selection" to stress the parallel with Darwinian natural selection. He further elaborates the similarity by stating:

> In the case of biology, that which evolves is the DNA, while in the case of culture, what evolves are ideas, or we can say knowledge, in the sense that our knowledge is composed of ideas that surface in our conscience and which we exchange with each other. Both of them—DNA and ideas—are transmitted, that is, reproduced in our descendents.[2]

The biological model is further stressed in this theory by positing cultural mutations, described by the term "innovations."[3] These brief and simplified indications of Cavalli-Sforza's rich and complex work are intended simply to suggest the many ways in which the genetic processes of the human body can be usefully compared to the cultural practices that produce changes. This is one way of theorizing the mutating attitudes toward sexuality that can be traced through the history of cultural production. The surviving artifacts, texts, and documents help to define the process through which the sexualized body functioned in Renaissance society. The genetic codes stem from nature, while the cultural patterns are constructed by a consensus of what is accepted as natural, in our case specifically rooted in concepts promulgated throughout Western Europe during the mid-fifteenth to mid-seventeenth centuries.

The mainstream understanding of the biological structure of female and male bodies in this period is so different from our own that a precise mapping of this fundamental concept becomes necessary before we can make any

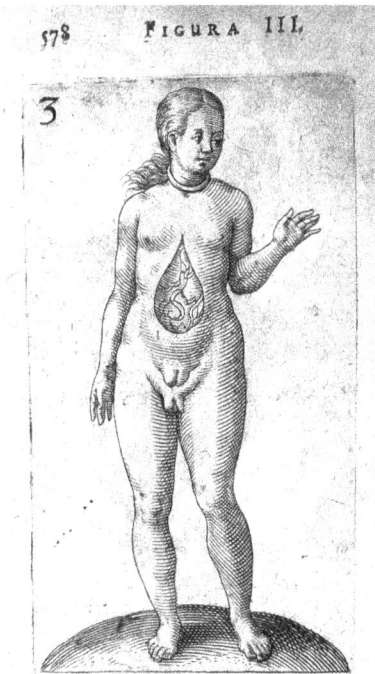

FIGURE 1.1: A hermaphrodite, *De Hermaphroditorum*, 1614. Wellcome Library, London.

FIGURE 1.2: A hermaphrodite, *De Hermaphroditorum*, 1614. Wellcome Library, London.

assumptions about its operation in Renaissance culture. Male biology and female biology were not presumed to constitute mutually exclusive opposite sexes; rather, the distinction could be posited by the degree of heat produced by an individual organism.[4] In order to understand Renaissance assumptions about heterosexuality, therefore, it is crucial to put aside thoughts of binary opposition and replace them with a more elastic system where maleness and femaleness exist within an extensive spectrum of possibilities. The calibrations flow from more to less male, toward thoroughly to barely female, and back again, in advancing or diminishing degrees (see figs. 1.1 and 1.2). This system posits relative, not absolute, differences as the basis for human sexuality.[5]

Ideas that touch upon the interrelation of biology and culture are crucial to the concerns that underlie the study of the representations of sexuality in any given period but have particular significance for the Renaissance. The analogy of procreation and artistic creation held force as a major argument for the nobility of art during this period when study of the human body as a vehicle of knowledge and a means of expression prevailed.

The concept of the male/female continuum was literally embodied in the most innovative examples of Renaissance art, and it was forthrightly glossed by authoritative commentators. Giorgio Vasari, the insider's expert on Florentine art, has left us an analysis of Michelangelo's sculpture of Bacchus, focused on the artist's masterful portrayal of a sort of binomial sexuality. Vasari praises the sculptor's appropriate use of both masculine and feminine attributes to create a compelling representation of the deity, whose iconography incorporates both male and female traits:

> The talent of Michelagnolo was then clearly recognized by a Roman gentleman named Messer Jacopo Galli, an ingenious person, who caused him to make ... a figure of a Bacchus ten palms high, who has a cup in the right hand, and in the left hand the skin of a tiger, with a bunch of grapes at which a little satyr is trying to nibble. In that figure it may be seen that he sought to achieve a certain fusion in the members that is marvelous, and in particular that he gave it both the youthful slenderness of the male and the fullness and roundness of the female—a thing so admirable, that he proved himself excellent in statuary beyond any other modern that had worked to that time.[6]

In this passage Vasari is not making a point about potentially scandalous or scabrous gender ambiguity; rather, the biological fusion of male and female characteristics is taken for granted. Fully aware of classical iconography that imbues the figure of Bacchus with what was defined as the most sexually desirable lineaments—male adolescent litheness and blossoming female softness—Vasari congratulates Michelangelo for coaxing marble to express exactly the right mix.

An ardent study of ancient cultural production was fundamental to Renaissance developments in art and literature. This axiom has been researched and theorized as a cornerstone of Renaissance scholarship, yet the universal impact of classical paradigms beyond the scope of the fine arts has perhaps not yet filtered into a wider understanding of the period's intellectual endeavors and premises. It applies to developments in law, medicine, and science and even touched areas outside of rarified humanist sanctums. For example, a fertile mixture of scientific information from ancient texts with adages from vernacular conventions in the medical codification of sexual identity can be discerned in the early modern period, especially as seen through the prism of anatomical study.[7]

The formulas derived from these studies created (among many other elements) the norms of sexual identity and, conversely, described the lineaments

of marginality. Unorthodox anatomical sexuality resulted in the monstrous, understood as fearsome departures from nature, bodily deformations that could
be called upon to explain behaviors or identities that could call the integrity
of the established models into question. The "monstrous" as a concept could
refer to men or women apparently normal in their corporeality, whose sexuality is called into question by circumstances. These versions allude to the social
and moral disruptions that can be caused by departures from the norm and
often receive cautionary chastisement through prickly humor. A particularly
raucous and very instructive folklore tradition centered on the condition and
adventures of the "pregnant man," whose unnatural physical state linked him
to monstrous races of humanity (fig. 1.3). Stories that describe this unnatural
state of being helped to sublimate suspicion of conception and parturition, uncanny processes for the male, who was normally excluded from the capacity to
procreate. By turning the pregnant man into a figure of ridicule the proper roles
of men and women were reinforced, according to their sexual identity.

A lively study by Roberto Zapperi outlines the origins of the first pregnant
man in the Christian tradition in a mutation undergone in the story of Adam

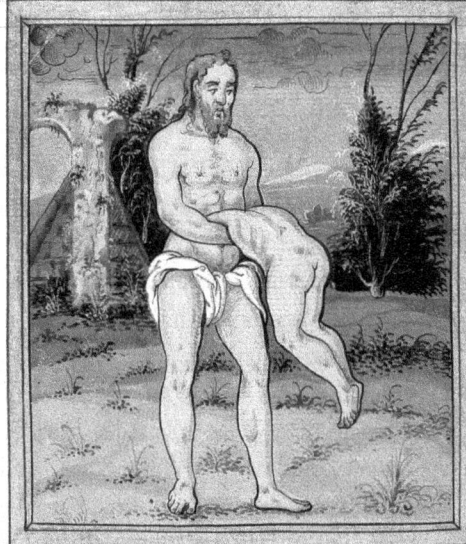

Homme monſtrueux, veu en la Fráce de nře temps.

CELLVS Lucanus Philosophe grec, en
certain opuſcule quil a faiſt de la nature de
L'vniuers traiſtant de la generation nous en-

FIGURE 1.3: A monstrous man, *Histoires prodi-
gieuses*. Wellcome Library, London.

and Eve.[8] Traced in visual arts, the narrative of Eve's creation is encapsulated by a female figure emerging from the side of a sleeping male (fig. 1.4). In this way Adam is portrayed as generating Eve, contrary to the text in *Genesis* that describes the Creator removing a rib from the side of the first man and producing the first woman from it. By giving agency to Adam this misinterpretation provides the ingredients of male parturition. This was a desirable scenario for representing the origins of humankind since it validated arguments in favor of male domination over women. Power was seen to derive from giving birth; the giver of life was owed deference for the supreme favor granted. And while it was deemed unproblematic for parents to rule over their children, a mechanism had to be found to justify a husband's domination over his wife. In describing Eve's emergence directly from within Adam's body, he miraculously gave her birth, providing a paradigm for hierarchy in male/female relationships. The miraculous, nonsexual nature of the event, of course, had to be emphasized in order to avoid any possible reference to incest in the marriage of humanity's first parents. This is one of the Church's teachings that was put into circulation as, we might say, the anatomical or corporeal justification of male authority over

FIGURE 1.4: *God Creating Eve,* fifteenth century. Wellcome Library, London.

female. The fact that in popular legends the laughable figure of the pregnant man is generally a priest is certainly linked to folk expressions of ridicule against authority figures; the effeminized clerics are always shown to be gulled into misconceptions about their ability to conceive a child. However, the link to the clergy also gives the illusion of institutional teaching receiving its just deserts.

The pronouncements of the Catholic Church permeated culture, low and high, during this period, and the narratives of its teaching were rich terrain for symbols and paradigms. The Creator's removal of Adam's rib provides a sacred model for the first dissection, and subsequent practitioners did not operate under the Church's disapprobation, as is often thought (fig. 1.5). Rather, dissection did have its place within religious institutions, in extraordinary circumstances tied to a pious as well as scientific search for signs hidden within the body of exceptional sanctity. Recent work by Katharine Park shows the practice to have been highly gendered, with female bodies privileged in the domain of "holy anatomies," which in many instances were under the direction of female anatomists as well.[9] Far from being solely acted upon in the

FIGURE 1.5: Dissected woman pointing to an extracted uterus. Wellcome Library, London.

anatomical theater of the early modern period, women were active protagonists for at least a portion of its development.

If the look of sexuality was assembled by anatomical theories and scruti-
nized in dissection theaters and interrogated in folktales, the sound of gender
was articulated, by turn with elegance or ribaldry, on the Renaissance stage.
The theater was one of the most compelling venues for examining definitions
of male and female sexuality, acted out before an audience well aware of what
we have come to call the performative nature of gender. With its costumed
bodies (cross-dressed in the English tradition), palpable carnality, and persuasive discourses, the theater was a microcosm of inventions that staged society's
consensus about sexuality at the same time that it was able to flaunt its contra-
vention. The clothing the actors donned to feign a persona was a primary signifier of identity, immediately announcing the character's sex and social status.
The capability of the costume to visually declaim fundamental identification
was especially important when a young male actor played a female role; his
costume manifested what his biology denied. This could function because of
the very strict codes of clothing established in the period, where specific items
were assigned to define the person who wore them. Articles of clothing expressed gender and status and were often regulated by law.

The rigid hierarchies of costumes in real life allowed for their eloquence on
the stage. Indeed the symbiosis was even more complex, as Peter Stallybrass
has argued in outlining the dependence of the commercial theater in Elizabethan England on the clothing trade. In particular, Stallybrass demonstrates
how the structure forced recycling: servants who inherited the fancy clothes of
their masters could make them usable only by selling them to the theaters for
cash, since their rank prohibited them from decking themselves in such finery.[10]
The secondhand luxury of the stage was a reflection of the first-rate opulence
of the audience, who created their own display of sumptuousness that was less
easily policed in the theater setting and was a factor that gave the ambiance a
reputation for dissipation and sexual licentiousness. An Elizabethan observer,
William Harrison, offered a colorfully evocative rant on the situation in the
stalls:

> Few of either sex come hither, but in theyr hol-dayes appareil, and so set
> forth, so trimmed, so adorned, so decked, so perfumed, as if they made
> the place the market of wantonnesse.[11]

That clothes could construct or deconstruct propriety as well as symbolize
power, social standing, and gender was not doubted in Renaissance rituals and

legislation. Carole Frick discusses the "transformational power of clothing," and specifies that in Florence the robes for men of rank were simple but of high-quality fabric, while attention was paid to headdress, which existed in many types, with beret forms usually bedecked with medals and jewels.[12] Framing the face with variety and individuality could certainly be read as a means of insisting on the distinctiveness and social consequence of these men, symbolic of their leadership as heads of civic institutions and households. Women of wealth, on the other hand, wore convoluted outfits, "voluminous multilayered draperies of richly woven and dyed cloth," built up by their various strata of clothing.[13] This system eerily seems to preannounce modern thoughts about how femininity is constructed, layer by layer.

In contrast, however, to the modern ethos that expects only women to be embellished with conspicuous jewelry, the Renaissance extended the right of adornment to rank rather than gender. While men and women generally wore different types of jewels—brides especially were given recognizable betrothal jewels—the splendor of jewelry signified wealth and its positive manifestation of magnificence, appropriate for both men and women of the richest families.

FIGURE 1.6: Agnolo Bronzino, *Portrait of Eleonora di Toledo*, 1544–45. Galleria degli Uffizi, Florence.

Members of the Medici dynasty, for example, were notable collectors and commissioners of important jewels, which they paraded as a tangible sign of their position. If it is predictable to see a mid-sixteenth-century Spanish aristocrat and Medici duchess, Eleonora di Toledo, dripping in pearls in her official portrait (fig. 1.6), it must also be noted that Lorenzo the Magnificent demonstrated his real, if untitled, status in the previous century by wearing fabulous gems along with otherwise unostentatious attire. The wearing of splendid jewels superseded gender differentiation to communicate the brilliance of rank and power.

The instance of jeweled adornment, whose significance worked across gender divisions, is an exception to the otherwise strict codes of dress set apart for men and women. There were many more rules for women's apparel, and they appear to have been more assiduously enforced through legislation that has come to be known as sumptuary laws.[14] Controls that varied through the years and among various locations in Europe show both the importance Renaissance culture gave to clothing as well as the changing standards of judgment about propriety. The enforcement of sumptuary laws was burdened with obstacles, and its very notion was fraught with contradictions in a culture that praised magnificence as a virtue and demanded that social rank be visually attested. Shakespeare pithily summarizes the necessity for sober but sumptuous elegance in Polonius's admonition to his son, Laertes, who is about to return to France:

> Give every man thine ear, but few thy voice;
> Take each man's censure, but reserve thy judgment.
> Costly thy habit as thy purse can buy,
> But not expressed in fancy; rich, not gaudy,
> For the apparel oft proclaims the man,
> And they in France of the best rank and station
> Are of a most select and generous chief in that.[15]

Although Polonius's sartorial adage is not the most often quoted bit of parental advice in this eloquent passage (which concludes with the poignant "to thine own self be true"), its inclusion in the pithy group of maxims bequeathed to his son discloses the crucial import of spending lavishly on clothes in Renaissance culture. This could easily slip into the infringement of sumptuary laws or the social infraction of making a bad impression; at times the latter seems to have been more feared. Coming to the rescue of sartorial uncertainties by establishing the rules by which courtiers were to dress, Baldassare Castiglione provided the particulars for achieving the understated sumptuousness that Polonius recommends. Castiglione's *The Book of the Courtier*, a thorough, highly gendered discussion of how people were to look, behave, interact, and perform in the arena of Europe's courts, was made available to an avid public in at least 110 editions between 1528 and 1619; the sixty editions in Italian were almost balanced by more than fifty in other languages.[16]

The Renaissance recipe of dressing for success calls for enormous portions of black in the male courtier's wardrobe, which allows for variety in other aspects, so long as the garments are not "unusual or inappropriate to his profession."[17] Conservatism is paramount for the courtier; one of the interlocutors in the dialogue, Federico Fregoso, opines that the trick is to eschew anything outlandish. His maxims continue:

> Moreover, I prefer them always to tend a little more toward the grave and sober rather than the foppish. Hence, I think that black is more pleasing in clothing than any other color; and if not black, then at least some color on the dark side. (p. 89)

Castiglione's preference that rich black fabrics and dark, sober colors preside over the gentleman's wardrobe may have also been influenced by the remnants of cultural attitudes that were established in the late medieval period, when the mixture of strong colors carried negative associations. Stripes were especially ill regarded and denoted membership in one of the nefarious professions, such as juggler, clown, or hangman.[18] In a visual tradition that suggests folkloric origin, the ambiguity of St. Joseph's situation was alluded to by his wearing of striped breeches.[19] The implication might be voiced as follows: Although a husband in name only, without the benefit of the usual marital privileges, Joseph took on the burdens of a father without biological progeny who was singularly unable to complain of cuckoldry. The courtier was right to figure the embodiment of probity and manliness encased in black cloth.

Dependence on the severe elegance of black garments, however, was definitely gendered male in Renaissance practice. Aristocratic women flaunted colorful outfits, which if worn by their male counterparts would be open to sneering criticism:

> Yet who of us, on seeing a gentleman pass by dressed in a habit quartered in varied colors, or with an array of strings and ribbons in bows and cross-lacing, does not take him to be a fool or a buffoon?[20]

It should give us pause to note the increasingly strong opposition of male and female fashions as they developed during the Renaissance, in contrast to the more flexible approach to the shared qualities in male and female bodies.

FIGURE 1.7: Cesare Vecellio, A Venetian
noblewoman, *Habiti antichi e moderni,*
1598. Wellcome Library, London.

The contrast is telling: sartorial conventions would be called upon more insistently to reinforce the separation of male and female, stiffening the more
permeable boundaries hypothesized in biological theories (figs. 1.7 and 1.8).

Based on the visual evidence in Renaissance portraiture, we can readily see
that wealthy and aristocratic women wore color, whether in their main garments
or lavish accessories, favoring rich brocades and sparkling jewels (see fig. 1.6).
The fact remains that colorful, ostentatious turnouts were considered appropriate for women, although the painted examples might have on occasion been
exaggerations of the female mode. Many of the bedecked young women are portrayed at the moment of their betrothal, an occasion that customarily demanded
lavish display of family wealth. Further, it has been hypothesized that the portrait medium encouraged an "upgrading" of reality by patrons who requested
painterly fabrication of draperies that the household purse would not permit.[21]

Striking exceptions to this general rule do exist. Widows, for example,
tended to dress severely in black, often assuming the minor vows and garb
of the laypersons who entered the tertiary orders. The third step down in the

FIGURE 1.8: Cesare Vecellio, A Vicen-
tine noblewoman (female costume from
Vicenza), *Habiti antichi e moderni,* 1598.
Wellcome Library, London.

hierarchy of Roman Catholic religious groups, the tertiaries were increasingly,
during the Renaissance period, composed of highly educated noblewomen.
These women built communities as arenas for female spirituality and intellectual activity that was not possible within the restrictive regimes of marriage.

The habit these women wore in the Augustinian tradition was attributed to
Saint Monica, whose legend included sartorial instruction from Mary. Christ's
mother invited Monica and her community of pious women to imitate her own
manner of dressing after the death of her son. This consisted of copious black
garments cloaked by a mantle that was also to be of black cloth, draped over
the white veils that covered the head.[22] These habits signaled a renunciation
of the standard role assigned to females by eliminating frills and appropriating the sober, dark hues that were gendered male. And yet, color apart, the
morphology of the individual garments proclaimed the wearer to be a highly
respectable woman, with no hint of transgressive cross-dressing.

Self-portraits of Sofonisba Anguissola (ca. 1532–1625) show the artist's
use of a similar strategy. Eschewing the vivid textiles and lavish accessories

that her wealthy family's noble status would have permitted, she consistently displays to the viewer a preference for the expensive, strictly unadorned black fabrics recommended for Castiglione's perfect gentleman. Willfully assuming the color code for grave masculinity, Sofonisba signals a request for the male privilege of being taken seriously as a professional. Mary Garrard analyzes the artist's representational strategy as follows:

> In her dress and hair style, Sofonisba Anguissola fashioned herself—presumably in life as well as art—as a dignified, serious, and self-possessed woman. In individual self-portraits painted from 1554 through 1561, she presents herself wearing black or near-black jackets (*corpetti*) with high-necked white lace collars beneath. Her hair is austerely decorous—parted in the middle, pulled back and arranged in braids that conform closely to the back of the head. She looks quite different from other young noble women as they typically appear in portraits of this period. In an age of flamboyant clothing and jewelry and celebrated feminine display, Sofonisba seems to have avoided in the extreme those associations with vanity and luxury traditionally ascribed to women.[23]

We can presume the same intention underlies the appearance of Laura Battiferri as presented in Bronzino's portrait from the 1550s. The figure of Battiferri, who was an accomplished poet and intellectual, actively exploits an attribute of learning to convey her identity. By holding an open book and pointing to a passage from a Petrarchan sonnet, she draws attention to its double significance, alluding to the poet's beloved Laura, her namesake, and her own distinction as a poet. If the ambitions of these serious women dressed in black moved toward upsetting accepted gender behavior, the restraint of their toilette and the undeniable modesty of their costume make them exempla of the virtues demanded of women by their society. Consciously opposed to self-fashioning high status through statements of conspicuous consumption, the subdued appearance of these women would have challenged sexual stereotypes at the same time that it employed virtuous self-discipline. Alas, this sort of moderation was posited as a manly virtue and so was not available as an emblem of female identity.

Renaissance treatises assigned gendered characteristics to notions of propriety, so that dressing properly required clear distinction of male from female usages. If Renaissance culture's social constructions of male and female followed the binary logic of contrariety, it produced from within itself the practices to challenge and overturn the paradigms—for example, through cross-dressing.[24] The tough strictures enabled flagrant transgression. In his dialogue concerning good manners, Giovanni della Casa stipulates, "Everyone must dress well according to his status and age, because if he does otherwise it seems that he disdains other people."[25] The Renaissance classification of indecorous dressing as a social offense tells us an enormous amount about the weight given to appearance in social interactions. It becomes clear why governments found it necessary to regulate the costumes that would assemble tenable proclamations of gender and social standing, marital status, and sexual availability. The central motivation for legal sanctions regarding apparel found in the sumptuary laws is clear: since a person's manner of dress publicly announced his or her status and gender, no false claims were permitted to circulate with impunity. As a corollary, questions of luxuriousness, sexuality, and morality entered from the religious point of view to overlap concerns rooted in questions of civic identity and social order.

Sumptuary laws regulated, among other things, the amount of costly jewels, fabrics, and accessories that could be worn by the different categories of citizens, but there was also legislation regarding vestments that were required to distinguish the identity of certain groups whose deviations from the order imposed by society took place in the sexual arena. For a time in fifteenth-century Venice, obligatory yellow scarves draped the neck of *pubbliche meretrici ed a ruffiani* (common whores and their procurors) as an unmistakable marker of their professions; in other cities a red hood was the indicator.[26] We have seen that striped fabric conferred pejorative connotations on its wearers, so it is not surprising that some examples of sumptuary laws demand that prostitutes wear an article of striped clothing.[27] At the same time, prostitutes were forbidden to dress their hair in the manner of married women. From this type of restriction derived the unique appearance of the high-level Venetian courtesans, whose hair was piled high above each temple, in appearance like fluffy horns. This was one of the few details that visually branded courtesans as different from wealthy matrons, since they rivaled or equaled this group in their luxury fabrics and splendid array.

Another type of very particular sartorial transgression, severely prohibited but clandestinely practiced, became part of sexual commerce in Venice.[28] Some prostitutes introduced the thrill of sexual ambiguity and role-playing into their encounters by wearing men's breeches, fabricated in silk, underneath their properly feminine, voluminous skirts. Apart from documentary evidence, amusing visual records of the effect of the ensemble have come down to us in the form of "flap prints," where a superimposed sheet both covered the image beneath it and allowed for its disclosure. Mimicking both the layering of women's outfits and the necessity for covering up the obscenity, flap prints provided a peep show for the relatively modest price of a print.

An example in the collection of the Metropolitan Museum (fig. 4.1) unmistakably shows a representation of a courtesan, whose hairstyle and elaborate dress mark her profession, while staying within the parameters of the allowable for her station in Venetian culture. Upon lifting the flap that forms her skirt, however, the viewer unveils an illicit thrill. While the exaggerated, high-soled slippers may seem to us to be the kinky element, it was in fact the woman's assumption of pants that was indecent—and highly attractive to certain customers. Since pants were an exclusively male item of apparel in this culture, the breeches might induce the fantasy of homosexual intercourse, or invite an act of sodomy with the prostitute as one of her specialties—an illicit, not to mention sinful, service in this culture. Olwen Hufton has suggested that the flap print engravings, with their interactive component inviting virtual participation, were principally collected by sixteenth-century tourists, who brought home this outré souvenir of the supposed specialization of Venetian prostitutes.[29]

According to Guido Ruggiero's pathbreaking investigation of sexual crime in fifteenth-century Venice, sodomy was a particular concern as an act that crossed the boundaries of accepted sexuality. Although its potential displacement from male-male relations to encounters with prostitutes was seen as a kind of safety valve and a pronounced lesser of two evils, it was still officially noticed and denounced. In Ruggiero's words, "Law and public pronouncements did complain about a growing trend of some prostitutes to hawk their services in masculine garb and with a masculine manner,"[30] yet they were unable to eradicate the transgression that would be revealed only to clients. The situation explains both the valence of the print and its strategy of concealment that is both protection and titillation. The visual thrill was a phantom similar to the experience it implies, a fleeting moment when the reality of the female body was altered imaginatively by the masquerade of male apparel.

Sexuality was very much read on the surface of Renaissance fashions, when clothes were insistently regarded as "second skins" that should properly signify the biological structure beneath. Erasmus applied this concept when he wrote that "clothing is in a way the body's body"—a covering that palpably indicates what lies beneath.[31] The analogy of skin and clothing was a potent vehicle of expression in Renaissance culture, which could function in surprising contexts. The iconography of Saint Bartholomew, for example, conventionally included his flayed skin, the symbol of his martyrdom, as his attribute. Representations of the saint, interchangeable in form with *ecorchée* figures, often show him displaying the inert fabric of skin, removed in one piece as though it had been unfastened and discarded like an unwanted cloak. Looking back to classical iconography of flaying in the myth of Apollo's punishment of

Marsyas (fig. 1.9), Renaissance imagery also found applications relevant to its
scientific interests when it peeled back the skin for observation of the human
body's underpinnings. The flap prints, which we have seen aiming at titillation in exposing the courtesan's breeches concealed under her skirt, were also
employed to instruct more sober observers in the anatomical secrets hidden
beneath the skin. These visual textbooks are fascinating documents, some of
elaborate complexity, that peel away in layers the various systems that construct the male and female human forms (figs. 1.10–1.17). They also could
reveal for inspection the interior mysteries of female sexuality at least with
regard to its reproductive organs.

With its insistent fabrication of metaphorical relationships between mem-
brane and hides, flesh and fabrics, Renaissance fashion could be explicit about
sexuality in a way that our own culture finds embarrassing, as is the case with
the sixteenth-century elaboration of codpieces as a conspicuous feature of male
attire. The codpiece began as a pouch of fabric that covered the genitals (left
exposed by the long hose worn over the legs), which needed draping as doublets rose to shorter lengths. The necessity turned into an embellishment, as
codpieces were elaborately padded and decorated, becoming so unnaturally
roomy that "articles were carried in it and pins affixed."[32] The extravagant

FIGURE 1.9: Melchior Meyer, *Apollo Flaying Marsyas*, 1598. Wellcome Library, London.

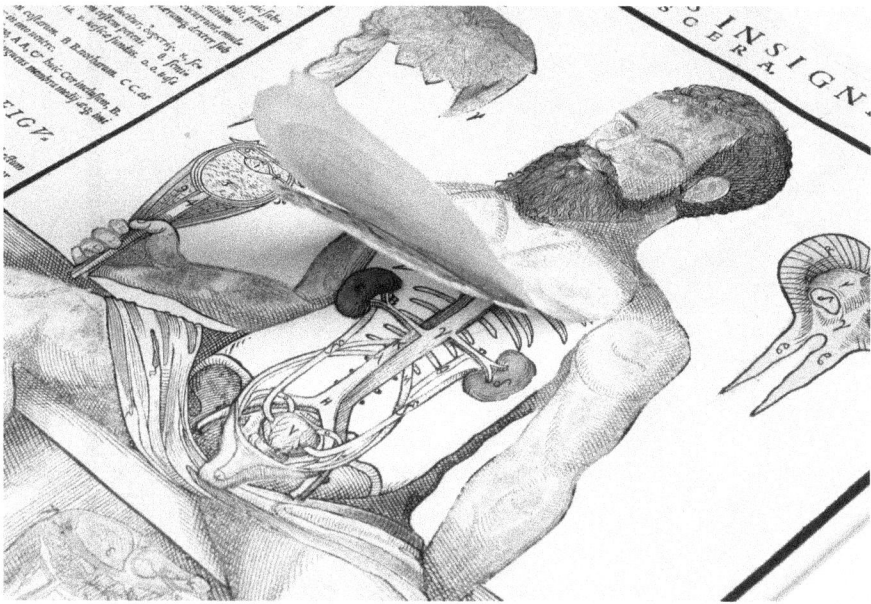

FIGURE 1.10: Male figure (detail), anatomical fugitive sheet, 1573. Wellcome Library, London.

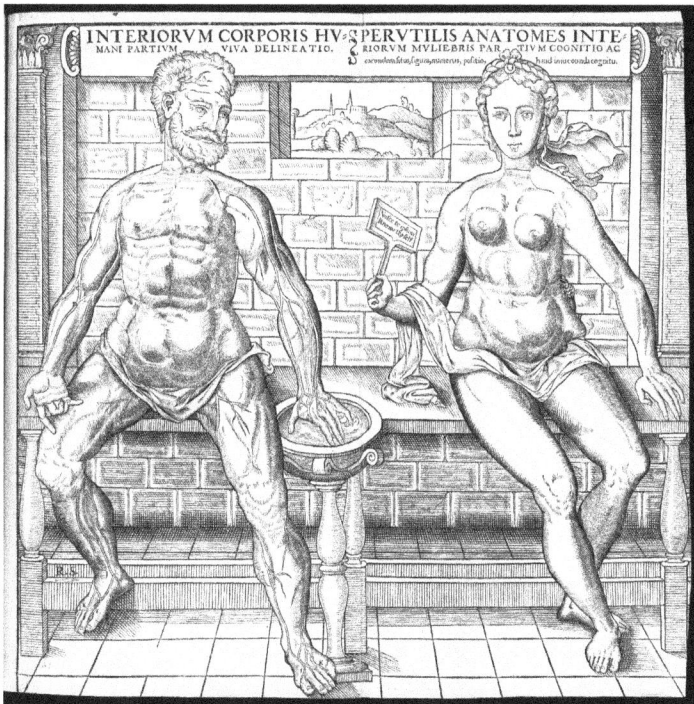

FIGURE 1.11: *Interiorum corporis humani partium viva delineatio,*
ca. 1559. Wellcome Library, London.

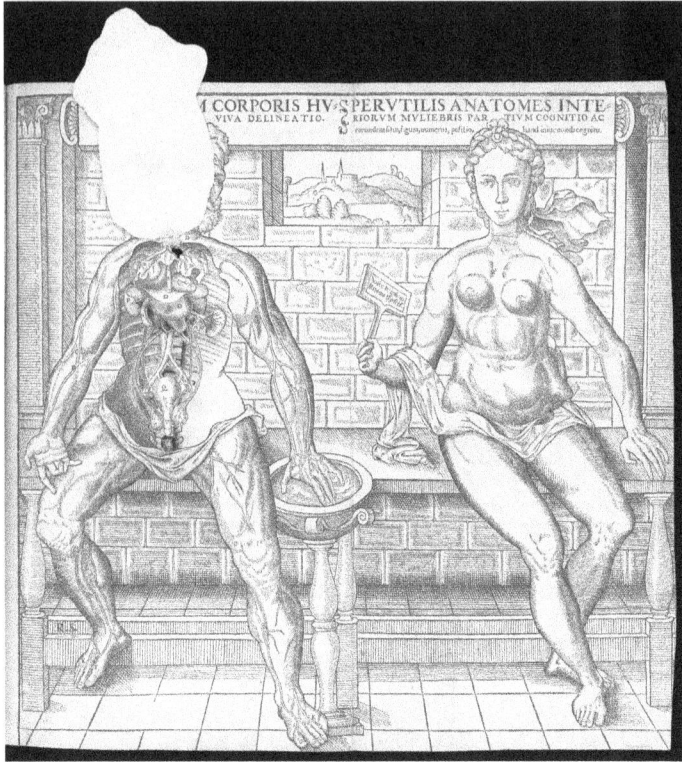

FIGURE 1.12: *Interiorum corporis humani partium viva delineatio*, ca. 1559. Wellcome Library, London.

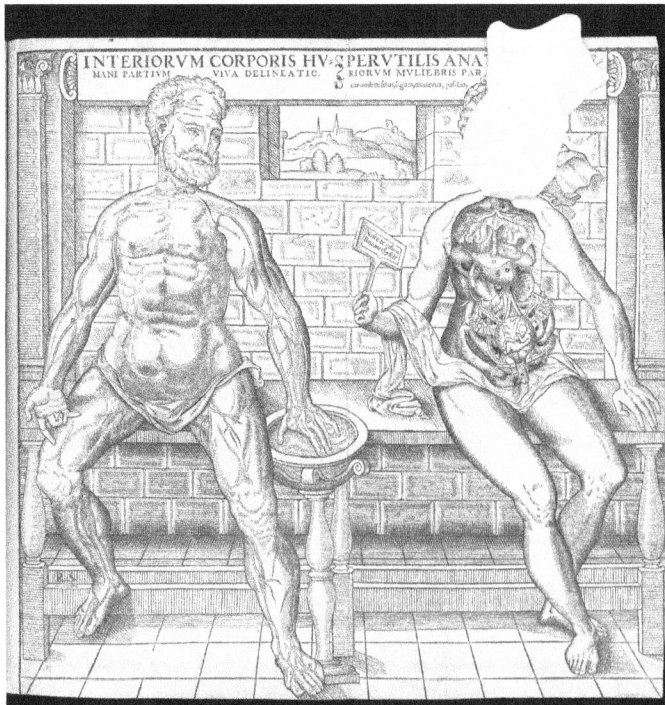

FIGURE 1.13: *Interiorum corporis humani partium viva delineatio*, ca. 1559. Wellcome Library, London.

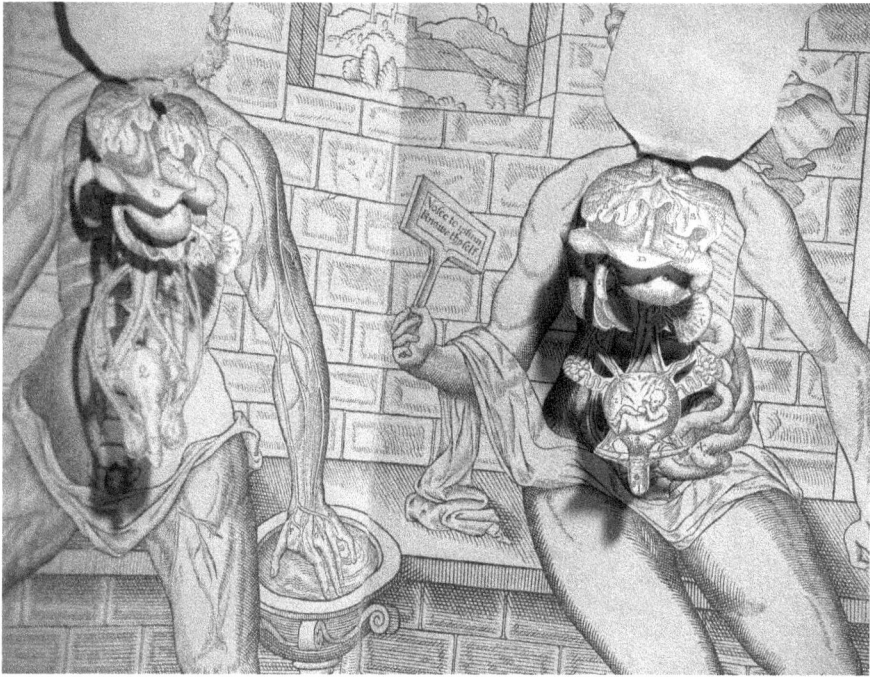

FIGURE 1.14: *Interiorum corporis humani partium viva delineatio*, ca. 1559. Wellcome Library, London.

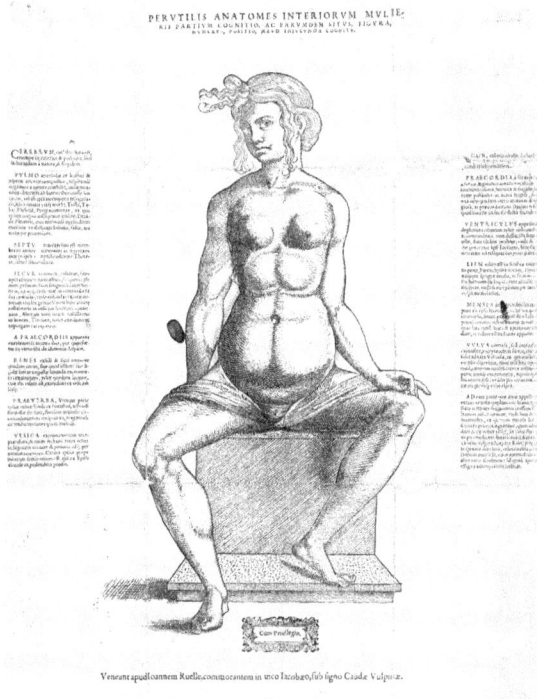

FIGURE 1.15: *Perutilis anatomes interiorum mulieris partium cognitio*, ca. 1540. Wellcome Library, London.

21

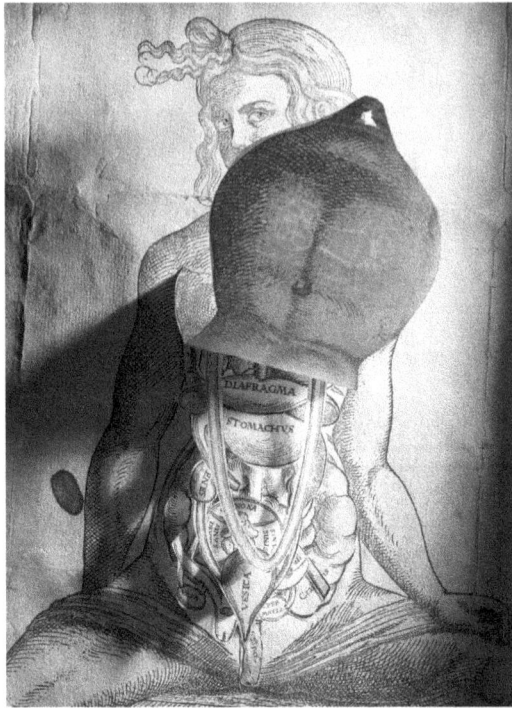

FIGURE 1.16: *Perutilis anatomes interiorum mulieris partium cognitio*, 1540. Wellcome Library, London.

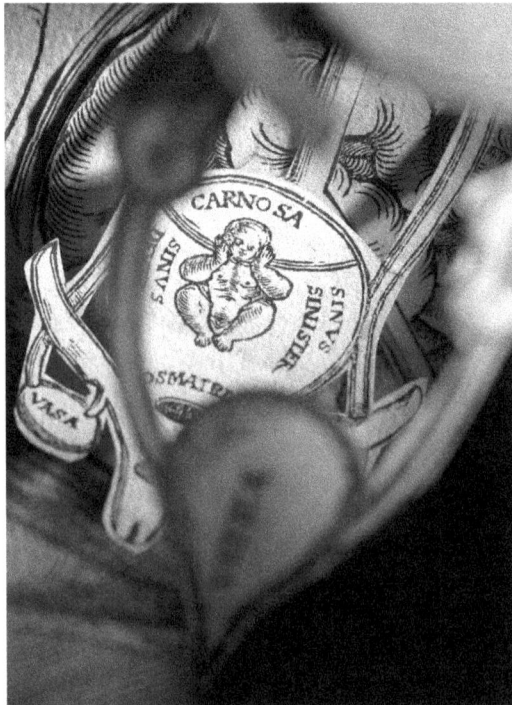

FIGURE 1.17: *Perutilis anatomes interiorum mulieris partium cognitio*, 1540. Wellcome Library, London.

augmentation of the wadding that gave shape to the codpiece produced an amusing neologism, as "bombace," the term for cotton padding, turned into "bombast," inappropriately inflated rhetoric. Although an overblown emblem of virility, the codpiece was clearly worn with earnest elegance, as many portrait paintings demonstrate, and yet the mirth around the mention of codpieces in literature leads us to suspect that the fashion generated a certain amount of hilarity.

Shakespeare puts a saucy pun into the mouth of the maid Lucetta, who advises her mistress on the crucial items of clothing necessary to be convincing in male disguise: "A round hose, madam, now's not worth a pin/Unless you have a cod-piece to stick pins on."[33] In *Love's Labor's Lost*, Cupid is referred to as "Dread prince of plackets, king of codpieces" (III, i, 173), while in *Much Ado about Nothing*, Shakespeare treats us to the sensuously seedy, leering description of "the shaven Hercules in the smirched worm-eaten tapestry, where his codpiece seems as massy as his club" (III, iii, 126–28). Like Erasmus's conceit of the "body's body," the playwright has the piece of clothing become the body part it covers.

FIGURE 1.18: Agnolo Bronzino, *Portrait of Stefano Colonna*, 1546. Galleria Nazionale d'Arte Antica, Rome (Reproduction British Library).

For sheer exuberance, however, nothing approaches the passages devoted
to codpieces in *Gargantua and Pantagruel* by François Rabelais. The author
begins by describing how the codpiece of Gargantua "was fashioned on the
top like unto a Triumphant Arch" and goes on to specify, "The exiture, out-
jetting or outstanding of his Codpiece, was of the length of a yard," a pun in
Sir Thomas Urquhart's 1653 translation that names the penis (= yard) at the
same time that it quotes an improbable, precisely "Gargantuan," length.

Another Rabelaisian character, Panurge, offers a theory that "the Codpiece
is the principal and most especial Piece of Armour that a Warriour doth carry"
(325). His theory is backed by a story of the invention of the codpiece, involving one Lord Humphry de Merville, who, in preparation for an expedition,
tried on his new armor in front of his wife, who astutely noticed a flaw:

> his Lady thereupon in the profound musing of a contemplative Spirit,
> very maturely considering that he had but small care of the Staff of Love,
> and Packet of Marriage, seeing he did no otherwise arm that part of the
> Body, then with Links of Mail, advised him to shield, fence and gabionate
> it with a big Helmet, which she had lying in her Closet, to her otherways
> utterly unprofitable. (329)

Scholars have spiritedly explicated the operations of the codpiece episodes in
Rabelais's text. I will simply comment on the racy, gendered aspect of Lady
Humphry's role as an inventor with a vested interest, superimposed on the
historically accurate link of the codpiece to armor. From the fifteenth century
into the early years of the seventeenth century, men's clothing steadily appro-
priated shapes and silhouettes from plate armor, the quintessential costume of
masculinity.

After the long gowns of the Middle Ages, relatively uniform for both sexes,
Renaissance garments accented the male physique by separating components
that could be manipulated for emphasis, stressing ideals of the body as powerful, virile, potent. According to Anne Hollander's persuasive synthesis:

> Innovations in armor mark the first real modernity in Western fashion,
> showing ways to redesign all the separate parts of the male body and
> put them back together into a newly created shape, one that replaced the
> naked human frame with another one that made a close three-dimensional,
> line-for-line commentary on it in another medium. Male clothing lost the
> unfitted character it had had since antiquity and began to suggest inter-
> esting new lines for the torso, and to consider the whole shape of legs

and arms in its tailoring scheme. Plate armor moreover required an under garment made by a linen-armorer, a close-fitting padded suit that outlined the whole man and protected him from his metal casing, of which it followed the shape. Male fashion quickly aped the shapes created by the linen-armorers, who can really count as the first tailors of Europe.[34]

It is notable that as clothing developed to construct sexual difference, the male paradigm was the soldier. The privileging of a hypermasculine idealization allowed for an unqualified, positive valence for the male sexual attribute, and thus the elaboration of the codpiece. In general this approach contrasted the construction of ideal femininity, where female stomach, womb, and genitalia were safely hidden away under volumes of obscuring, rather than defining, drapery. However, there was an exception to the practice of blurring and shrouding female anatomy, and it was found in dresses that were cut with deep décolletage. The social acceptability of necklines that bared the female neck and breast is another sign that the clarification and presentation of gender identity constituted the most important function of fashion in the Renaissance period.[35]

While to our eyes these open signifiers of sexuality, with their shameless display and featuring of erogenous zones, appear outrageous, they were neutralized in Renaissance culture by their literal, description function. Leaving nothing to the imagination, exaggerated codpieces and plunging décolletage revealed indisputable sexual, and thus gender, identification. Clothes had to be unequivocal in their declaration of the maleness or femaleness of their wearers exactly because the human body partook of both elements. It is easy to understand how these assumptions and practices, calculated for sexual clarity, could cause confusion of another sort. There is an extremely permeable border between provocative clothes that announce sexuality for the legitimate purpose of gender identification, and those that reveal the sexualized body toward commercial gain. Renaissance culture gave itself a lot of work in order to police the difference, especially with regard to the control of prostitution.

At the beginning of the fifteenth century the city of Florence formed a body of officials, the *Ufficiali dell'onestà*, to monitor disruptive sexual activity, particularly of prostitutes. What began as an agenda related to the sumptuary laws, where distinguishing articles of clothing were supervised and limitations of finery controlled, grew to include mandatory registration of prostitutes in addition to the policing of their sexual acts and social visibility. This last concern was addressed by restricting the residence of prostitutes to specific streets within Florence.

The impulse to contain the activity of prostitutes resulted in their confinement to a particular district or street in many European towns and cities. The containment, however, in certain instances went beyond a rather passive acceptance of "red-light districts" to a more active role of landlord on the part of local governments. This became a strategy of control, especially as the role of a middleman came into the equation in the course of the fifteenth century. The machinations of pimps changed the system of selling sexual favors from the relatively straightforward arrangement of an individual woman more or less discreetly renting a room for that purpose, or servicing clients in her home, and keeping all the profits of her employment. The loose arrangements became more tightly knit, with the women less independent and more vulnerable in relation to their pimps, but part of a stronger and more organized force as their business gained a discernable configuration. Eventually the business of procuring was an acknowledged fact of Renaissance society, with procuresses recognized as a subset of workers, and *ruffiani* required to be registered in some cities. Local authorities fought the developing system with their own bureaucratic structures to safeguard against breaches of the social order. Leah Otis has explored the effects and implications of the establishment of recognized brothels in southern France from the late fourteenth to sixteenth centuries, noting that in this period the prostitutes in the region had the same legal rights as other women, and a "relatively positive position in society."[36]

Perceived advantages to the institutionalization of prostitution fueled its development through the Renaissance, until the religious reform movements changed the situation toward the end of the sixteenth century. Throughout the entire period, however, religious and social attitudes toward prostitution and prostitutes were most often in conflict. The positions were often slippery, however; taxes imposed on prostitutes by the Florentine officials were used at one point to support the convents of the *convertite* (reformed sexual sinners), thereby allowing the Church both to exploit the earnings of some prostitutes while managing the conversion of others.[37]

Routinely denounced by the church, prostitution fit in with and complemented other social institutions and practices; it could even function compatibly with ideologies that bound love and sex together.[38] Such emphasis on the positive aspects that could be attached to paying for love and sexual gratification worked to the benefit of societies that delayed the marriage of young men until their thirties but demanded the sexual abstinence of young women, denied marriage to the numerous population of clerics who were men of power and wealth, and defined male sexuality in terms of its active participation in sexual performance.

This definition of legitimate, normative male sexuality was one of the reasons for the social condemnation of homosexuality, beyond the sanctions against it as unnatural, which followed Augustinian ideas elaborated by Thomas Aquinas in the religious sphere. The sexual rapport of two men was seen to undermine the sanctity of heterosexual marriage, both as a fundamental social component and as a means to procreation, the ultimate good that justified sinless sexual relations within marriage. As Nicholas Davidson explains, "Divine and natural law were generally taken to be identical" in the complex discourses that established Renaissance taboos, which operated as a series of injunctions to restrict sexual behavior.[39]

The body of canon law inherited from the Early Christian and later medieval periods vehemently pronounced on the ingredients of sexual sinning, whose various manifestations were collected under the rubric "fornication."[40] The canonistic attitude was rooted in the belief that coitus in itself was always a negative act. It was in every case sinful outside of marriage, which was generally seen as a "cure" for fornication. But even within the bonds of matrimony, if lust was a pronounced component, sinful behavior ensued. And, of course, if pleasure rather than procreation was the objective of a sexual union, fornication was the result. The intrinsic bonds of lust, sexual desire, and pleasure ensured that canon law faced treacherous problems in ruling on the fine distinctions between sinful and guiltless marital relations in their theories. However, one instance of sexual union was determined to be unequivocally sinful and irreversibly criminal: the "unnatural" act of sodomy. This was one of the most grievous transgressions in which a wedded couple could engage; it was all the more culpable when committed not only outside the marriage bed, but outside the bounds of heterosexuality. The multiple deviations charged against homosexual acts stemmed from this line of argument, where sexual activity was suspect even in the most legitimate of circumstances. It was tolerated within marriage only as a corrective to worse temptation, justifiable solely for procreation, and never allowable as a vehicle of unleashed pleasure.

The weight of official opprobrium against sodomy, and especially its practice between two males, is manifest in a plethora of documents, legal stipulations, and social controls of the time. The stern moralizing and religious condemnation, however, were contravened by patterns of behavior throughout the period. And as we have seen for prostitution, another criminal expression of sexuality, there were instances where homosexual structures blended into societal values and institutions. The work of Michael Rocke, founded on thorough archival study, has done much to clarify the societal spaces in which homosexuality operated in Florence. Rocke stipulates the historicity of homo-sexuality and explicates how it functioned in fifteenth-century Tuscany:

> Sodomy in Florence was not limited to any particular social group or to a distinctive and permanent "homosexual" minority. Rather, it was part of the whole fabric of Florentine society, attracting males of all ages, matrimonial condition, and social rank. Indeed, sodomy was so wide-spread, and the policing apparatus for unearthing it so effective in the later fifteenth-century, that in this period probably the majority of local males, at least one time or another, were officially incriminated.[41]

The statistics present a conundrum in the context of a society that ostensibly banned homosexual acts in the most uncompromising terms. The explanation lies in a more expanded and integrated understanding of the cultural opera-tions of homosexual behavior, which offered paths in the maze leading to gen-der identity and avenues of homosociability. Our notion of homosexuality as a determining social and sexual identity is simply anachronistic with regard to the early modern period.

As we have seen, biological theories of this period did not categorize male and female bodies as opposites; similarly, there were no classifications of homosexuality that functioned in opposition to a normative heterosexu-ality. As Rocke eloquently argues, the more usual references to "sodomy" and "sodomite" testify to definition through sexual acts rather than to an all-encompassing sexual identity.[42] Identities were constructed as male or female; partnering with another male in sodomy constituted a sinful sexual act that could be occasional, alternative to heterosexual coupling, or limited to a cer-tain phase of life. In a culture that excluded women from public life, separated the sexes in socializing, customarily allowed huge discrepancies in the mar-riageable age for men and women, and whose professions developed through exclusively male apprentice and workshop traditions, the expansive arena of all-male social spaces resulted in extensive opportunities for homosociability to cross the boundary into homosexuality.

Innovative approaches to the study of homosexuality in the Renaissance place emphasis on its existence within the larger social and cultural patterns of the time. Rather than interrogating it exclusively through the prism of divergence from the norm, such explorations question how it fits into the very rich terrain of same-sex social structures that were a defining aspect of Renais-sance societies. This approach can help to elucidate the eroticism involved in same-sex interactions, for both females and males, searching representations in both literature and art in the separate arenas of socializing carved out for women or populated by men.[43] It is not surprising to find that women's representations of same-sex friendship and passion responded throughout Europe to the dominant cultural valuation of modesty as the prime female virtue. Women thus tended to veil sexual allusions and scenarios in their depiction and imaginative descriptions.

The suspicion, and sometimes terror, with which societies received female expressions of sexuality and the voyeuristic thrill that attended male musings about female same-sex sociability helped to fuel cultural constructs of witches and their witchcraft. Actual or hypothetical manifestations of transgressive female sexuality were reified in the figure of witches, whose supposed violations include the murder of infants (an opprobrious perversion of woman's intended maternal role); their domination of men through love potions; and vituperative sexual insatiability, which sometimes resulted in copulation with the devil. Despite the overblown realm of vicious fantasy that was the terrain of such theories, they were rooted in popular fears of feminine powers or in the beliefs about female biological workings. The misogynistic concept of women's sexual voraciousness was based on medical theories that the "cold" uterus—a fully female component of the body whose makeup was as removed as possible from male "heat"—would shrivel away without the benefit of frequent intercourse.

The exaggeration that took place in designating the characteristics and devilish deeds of witches, and the attendant fear that could be generated about their menacing behavior, eventually led to actual witch hunts and very real persecutions and executions. However, recent research has emphasized that the intense pursuit and brutal condemnation of witches largely postdate the main Renaissance period, reaching their height in the seventeenth century. Indeed, in her distinguished work on the subject, Margaret Sullivan suggests that the approach to witchcraft until after the first half of the sixteenth century was through fantasy, elite humanist responses "more plausible as poetic constructions motivated by artistic goals and fascination with the underside of the ancient world."[44] The sophisticated cultural production in turn had its buttressing effect on the popular view of witches, which later erupted in seeking out and torturing victims.

The 1523 painting by Hans Baldung Grien titled *Two Witches*, according to a recent interpretation, represents precisely a satiric approach to the iconography of women as witches, responding with humor to his society's disproportionate and passionate fear of the alleged phenomenon.[45] The scale and quality of this painting indicate that it was created for the private viewing pleasure of a wealthy and educated patron, who would have been able to discern the

multiple layers of allusions to savor the work's irony, sexual frisson, and relation to folk traditions. The collision of learned and popular culture in instances
such as these, where "high art" mediums fashioned images out of folkloric material, created complex imbrications whose meanings often elude our attempts
at interpretation. Issues of gender and sexuality permeate the iconography of
witches and witchcraft, leading to the sexualization of magic and sorcery and
adding to the interpretive mix of elite and popular elements that must be fused
for us to understand Renaissance treatments of the subject.[46]

Representation of deviant sexual behavior of witches, forming such a large
component of their iconography, was clearly entered into with gusto and imagination by Renaissance artists and writers who made use of folktales and their own
creative fantasy to embody terrifying phenomena. The expressive possibilities of
the transgressive and salacious—all the way to the high impact of obscenity—were
fearlessly exploited during this period, eventually accompanied by reprisals of
varying consequence toward the close of the sixteenth century. The employment
of obscene sexual allusions (and by obscenity I indicate the category of erotic expression regarded as unacceptable[47]) had a forceful tradition in this period.

Not only could the individual body be violated or humiliated in its sexuality, but the social body could also come under attack in sexual terms. Elizabeth
Cohen has coined the term "house-scorning" to describe the rituals carried out
in sixteenth- and seventeenth-century Rome to revenge slights and insults.[48] A
person was shamed by symbolic attacks on their dwellings; obscenities were
yelled through windows, and phalluses or cuckold's horns were inscribed on
facades. This practice indicates a cultural attitude that equated the enclosure
of dwelling space with corporeal integument; each was a personal, protective
layer that had to fend off assaults against illegitimate penetration.[49] The fact
that documents record that known prostitutes were involved in a majority of
these house-scornings further indicates that they were deemed an appropriate
vehicle of vendetta or humiliation against women whose lives were defined by
deviant sexuality. Thus we can deduce that in this instance sexual identity was
registered and broadcast by objects intimately connected with individuals as
well as by their appearance and behavior.

It is no surprise, then, that manners and appetites could be sexualized along
with the bodies that manifest and contained them. Social exchange through
conversation with inappropriate interlocutors could compromise a woman,
symbolically turning her into a prostitute through verbal intercourse. Indeed,
our use of the word *intercourse* continues to express the latent ambivalence of
the activity intended. Given both the fundamental nature of human interaction
through speech and the slippery sexual terrain of conversing, the Renaissance

developed a system to regulate the exchange between various social and gendered groups. The good manners of verbal social intercourse were codified in the last quarter of the sixteenth century by the publication of *La civil conversazione*, by Stefano Guazzo in Brescia.[50] Following the general approach and dialogue format of Castiglione's *Il libro del Cortegiano,* Guazzo's handbook was also a huge international success, with over thirty editions in many languages before the middle of the seventeenth century.

The final example Guazzo offered as a guide for the perfect conversationalist takes place at a fictive banquet offered by the aristocrat Vespasiano Gonzaga in a sumptuous palace in the town of Casale. The scenario places emphasis on the importance of dining as a social setting for conversing and its value in the highest realms of society. There were opportunities for advancement as well as pitfalls for social and sexual transgressions while dining at courtly tables. The accoutrements of this site of interaction could narrate, and at times embody, the sexual tensions that permeated the pleasant assuaging of appetites. Following the esteemed practice of mining classical sources for their erotica, Renaissance artisans produced elaborate tableware with an exotic subcategory whose decoration carried licentious messages.

Pliny lamented the popularity of such dinner service, writing, "The enticements of the vices have augmented even art: it has pleased us to engrave scenes of licence upon our goblets, and to drink through the midst of obscenities" (N.H. 33.2.5).[51] At least one sixteenth-century bon vivant, Pierre de Bourdeille, Seigneur de Brantôme, informs us that he had seen a modern version of such a chalice. He describes the particular use made of it by the owner (an unnamed aristocrat), during his dinner parties: it was set at the place of an unsuspecting female guest, who would then cause general merriment by her consternation at discovering the piquant scenes engraved on her drinking cup.[52] Whether she took the pose of a worldly woman and continued to imbibe or stopped sipping as a sign of her offended modesty, her actions resulted in the hilarity of the other guests. The eroticized vessel became an extension of the woman's own sexual index, publicly announcing her character to be upright or slightly less so; she had no choice but to act in the pantomime.

The association of object with user could function in other ways that were connected with sexual identity and carnal sobriety (or levity). At their first introduction in Venice during the Renaissance, forks were signs of lavish living and sumptuous dining. They came to be associated particularly with the flashy courtesans of this time and place, who disdained having their fingers soiled while indulging in sticky sweets or staining berries, and so were a signifier of intemperate living—or worse. This caused the offending objects, guilty of no misdeed but condemned by association, to be banned by the Church for some time.[53] The evocation of a courtesan feasting, simply by the appearance of an article of flatware, was apparently enough to encourage a context of illicit sexuality in the eyes of religious authorities.

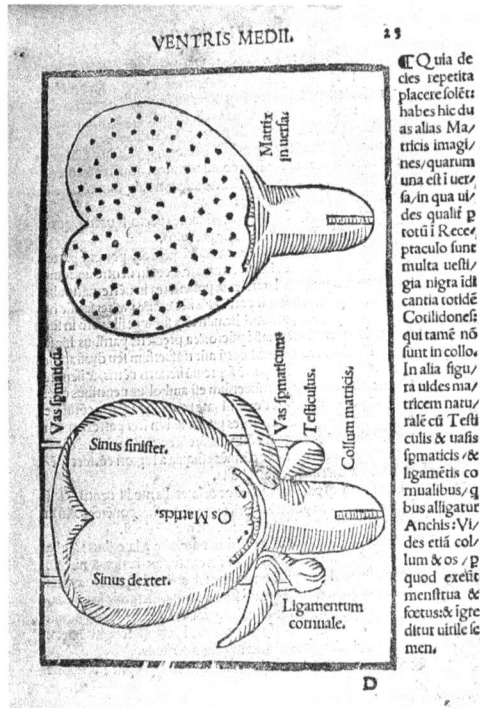

FIGURE 1.19: Jacobus Carpensis Beregarius, Uterus, *Isagoge,* ca. 1522. Wellcome Library, London.

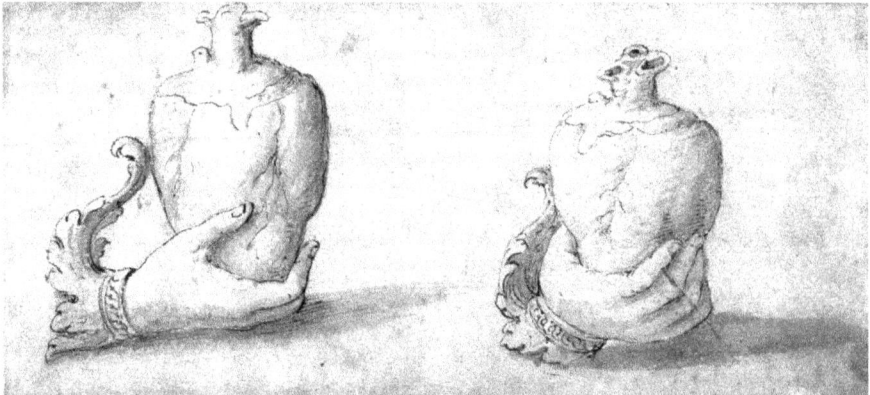

FIGURE 1.20: Giulio Romano (attr.), *Vessel in the Form of a Heart,* sixteenth century. Wellcome Library, London.

Exploration of humankind's physical identity and bodily properties took place across the vast range of cultural endeavors and could be expounded through objects and images as well as verbal discourse. In a very imaginative series of associations, for example, the concordance of the womb with the concept of a vessel, and both with female qualities tied equally to love and service, can be followed in a sequence of drawings where the uterus becomes a heart, and the heart a vessel that pours forth (figs. 1.19 and 1.20). The path that was followed toward the understanding and representation of sexuality during the early modern period willingly branched off in multifarious directions, always with one eye on the alluring remains of the ancient world. The terms for envisioning and then interrogating the definitions and functioning of male and female qualities led to insightful studies of anatomy through dissected corpses; treatises that theorize male and female qualities while pronouncing on proper behavior; literature that explores polymorphous identity; and visual arts that present both the pleasurable and the dangerously seductive sides of sexuality, with newly convincing physicality. All of these cultural activities assembled new and highly nuanced terms of sexual identity and behavior in early modern Europe, in whose reflection we still operate in many ways, either to reinforce the norms or push against them—compelling reasons for furthering our explorations of the cultural legacy of Renaissance Europe in the arena of sexuality.

CHAPTER TWO

Heterosexuality: A Beast with Many Backs

ANN ROSALIND JONES

Two problems arise in applying the term heterosexuality to Renaissance conceptions of sex and the body. The first is that it was by no means generally accepted in the Renaissance that there were two opposite sexes. Although cultural, political, and legal discourses established the differences between men and women in myriad ways, one of the two dominant medical traditions articulated a single-sex model, in which male and female anatomies were not antithetical but homologous.

According to Galen, the second-century Greek physician whose writings were the basis of much of the medical thinking of early modern Europe, men and women possessed the same genital organs, but men's were placed outside the body while women's were contained inside it. In this schema, the vagina was imagined as an inverted penis, while the ovaries corresponded to the testicles and the uterus to the scrotum. The main difference between men and women was one of heat: men were hotter than women. But the difference was relative, not absolute. If a woman became too hot (through running, for instance), her excessive internal heat could thrust her vagina, turned inside out, outside her body, transforming her into a man.[1] This thinking underlay the remark of a student of the Italian physician Vesalius, Baldasar Heseler, who in 1540 stated the single-morphology thesis in reverse form: "If you turn the scrotum, the testicles, and the penis inside out, you will have all the genital organs of the female."[2] In addition, Galen's model of conception, far from defining a simple opposition between male and female, hypothesized a seven-chambered womb, providing seven different possibilities for the development of the fetus according to the placement of human seed, from absolute masculinity through two lesser degrees of it to absolute hermaphroditism, and through two further degrees of femininity before arriving at absolute femininity. The variability of bodily sex led further to the belief that a woman with excessive heat in her body produced male semen and a man with humors too cold might lactate.

An older theory, derived from Aristotle, the Greek philosopher of the third century B.C.E., defined such heat and cold as the sexualizing effect of the four humors. In men's bodies, choler and blood predominated, hotter, drier, and more active than phlegm and black bile, the dominant humors in women's bodies. Hence men's bodies produced greater energy than women's because of the cool, moist humors that predominated in women's bodies. For Galen, this difference was one of quality, not just quantity:

> Now just as mankind is the most perfect of all animals, so within mankind the man is more perfect than the woman, and the reason ... is his excess of heat, for heat is Nature's primary instrument ... the woman is less perfect than the man in respect to the generative parts. For the parts were formed within her when she was still a fetus, but could not because of the defect in heat emerge and project on the outside as men's do.[3]

In intercourse, however, both bodies needed to produce enough heat to convert the blood in their sexual organs into seed to be mixed with that of their partner, because it was the union of the two seeds in the uterus that resulted in conception. Orgasm, the point at which the blood of both partners reached the heat needed for this transformation, was therefore necessary to them both. Accordingly, doctors, midwives, and writers of advice books for married people all suggested ways for the man to stimulate the woman—to heat her up to his higher temperature—so that she would produce seed to join his. Foreplay and the "warming" of the wife's genitals were recommended so that she would have an orgasm. Like doctors, the Dutch moralist Johan van Beverwijck wrote that intercourse was necessary for both sexes because it balanced the humors, thus facilitating pregnancy.[4]

While this call for mutual orgasm worked to the benefit of women as far as sexual pleasure was concerned, its logic also worked against them in the case of venereal disease, a growing concern throughout Europe during this period. An elaborate variation on the humoral theory explained that women, especially prostitutes, communicated such diseases "because in the [sex] act ... the Womb being heated, vapors are raised from the malignant humours, which are suck'd in by the man's Yard [penis]."[5] That is, the heat from many men's orgasms increased the danger of syphilis by combining dangerously in the womb. A late seventeenth-century physician wrote, "After Conversation with so many men, the mixture of so many Seeds does occasion such a Corruption of the Passage of the Matrix that it degenerates into a proper virulent Ferment" (Siena, p. 562). Another reason that the contagion was thought more likely to be transmitted by young women was that their constitutions were thought to be warmer and moister than those of drier, colder old women. The association of excessive heat with the pox was condensed in popular speech when men spoke of being "burnt" by women from whom they had contacted gonorrhea or syphilis.

Further evidence of the way the Galenic model emphasized anatomical parallelism and the potential mutability of the sexes can be seen in early-modern thinking about hermaphrodites. The one-sex model obviously did not hold for people born with the sexual organs of both men and women, so a gender identity had to be established through outer signs, especially sex-appropriate clothing. In a complex judgment made in 1629 in a seventeenth-century settlement in Virginia, the problem was to determine the sex of a young person, Thomas/Thomasina Hall, who had been dressed and brought up as a girl and gone to London to learn how to keep house, but then dressed as a man in order to follow her/his brother to join the British forces in war in France. After this cohort was almost entirely massacred, s/he returned to London and dressed as a woman again, but returned to men's dress in order to travel to Virginia. There, his/her double sexual morphology—a small penis, an only partly formed vagina—was examined, to little avail; the case was solved by defining him as a man because of his history of adventure and work but sentencing him to wear, over his men's clothes, a woman's cap and apron as a visible punishment for his deceptions. His body was so ambiguous that this double clothing was the only way to assign him an appropriately mixed identity—one based on his behavior over time rather than a single-sexed body.

The second problem with applying a later concept of heterosexuality to the Renaissance is that it assumes that a man's sexual attraction to women directly correlates with his virility. While one can certainly find such an association in the Renaissance, it was by no means the norm. Indeed, it was a Renaissance commonplace that the more attracted a man was to women, the more he would become like them. In Baldessar Castiglione's *Courtier*, men at court are warned against imitating and absorbing the physical weakness of the women they consort with; in Shakespeare's *Antony and Cleopatra*, Mark Antony is a model of Roman virility on the battlefield until he falls in love with Cleopatra. But, subjugated by his love for her, he dresses up in her clothes, and Cleopatra, by appropriating his sword, becomes more like him. Far from affirming sexual difference, their love involves a sexual transformation for each of them. The conviction that a man's love for a woman radically subverted his masculinity is articulated by a character in an early seventeenth-century English comedy, who advises a suitor not to imitate (ape) women as he courts them: "Be not too apish female, do not come/With foolish Sonets to present her with,/With legs, with curtesies, congies, and such like:/Nor with pend speeches, or too far fetcht sighes."[6]

Furthermore, the later conflation of normative heterosexuality and married love made the Renaissance concept of uxoriousness (the excessive love of a husband for his wife) increasingly unimaginable. But for John Milton one of the symptoms of corrupt court culture was that it gave power to "Effeminate and Uxorious Magistrates" who in their domestic lives were "govern'd and overswaid" by usurping wives.[7] The English word for a man rendered feminine by his over-intense love of his wife was "cotquean," a frequent term of abuse.

In the Renaissance, the extraordinary proliferation of discourses on the regulation of sexual behavior was governed not by concepts of heterosexuality but by the regulation of sex between men and women in order to assure the production of legitimate children and to prevent bastardy. Wifely chastity was a topic many moralists took up in the interests of husbands wanting to be certain that their sons were genuinely theirs, and thus deserving of their inheritance. This concern underlay Matteo Palmieri's warning in his *Vita civile* (written in 1429, published in 1528): "Wives must exercise the greatest and most extraordinary caution not only not to unite with another man, but even to prevent any suspicion of such filthy wickedness. This error is the supreme disgrace to decency, it effaces honour, destroys unions, renders paternity uncertain."[8] More explicitly, the Spanish humanist Juan Luis Vives, writing a treatise dedicated to Queen Catherine of England in 1532 on the education of women, quoting St. Paul, tells the wife, "A woman does not have power over her own body, but the husband does"; he warns his imagined reader that by being unchaste, "You transfer the heredity from its rightful owner to strangers."[9]

Bastardy, too, was regulated throughout Europe, as much for economic as for religious reasons. One reason, among poorer people, was that their parish or town had to support illegitimate children, so laws not only attempted to prevent the conception of children outside of wedlock but, failing that, to discover the fathers of the children and to make them financially responsible for their offspring. Many trials in England revealed how common it was for maidservants and farmworkers to become pregnant by the men who hired them; in rural Essex in the seventeenth century, over 60 percent of illegitimate births were to farmservants, half of whom testified to having been seduced by their employers.[10]

To avoid punishment (public shaming, imprisonment, whipping, banishment), pregnant women used a variety of subterfuges. The aprons and full skirts that many women wore helped to hide growing bellies; busks, corset stiffeners made of wood, ivory, and sometimes metal, were used for the same purpose. Failing to conceal her pregnancy and sentenced to banishment, a woman in early seventeenth-century France left her town by one gate and immediately came in at another.[11] Women left their own towns and went to midwives in larger cities who offered lodgings or lived temporarily with relatives whose discretion they could count on; they also faked departure for pilgrimages. They also abandoned their infants, sometimes on the father's doorstep or at foundling hospitals, used increasingly throughout Europe in the sixteenth and seventeenth centuries.

The seriousness of such penalties led to an endless search for abortifacients, for which an enormous variety of plants were recommended—as many as a hundred, including dragonwort; hemlock; pennyroyal; rue; laurel; and especially savin, from a small bushy evergreen shrub, *Juniperus sabina*.[12] There may have been some truth in this belief about rue and savin. The logic underlying the recommendation of "hot" herbs, also including calamint and spices like ginger and cinnamon, was that they would make the womb too hot to be hospitable to an embryo.[13] If folk remedies failed, women sought potions from midwives or apothecaries, or faked illness to obtain drugs from physicians. In an extreme case, a Frenchwoman was accused of drinking rat poison.[14] As a last resort, they practiced infanticide, even though it was a capital crime, punishable by hanging, drowning, even impaling or the cutting off of hands.

Marriage was the center of legal control throughout Europe, but the forms of marriage varied according to class and region. In northern Europe the average age of marriage for those outside the elite was the mid-twenties for both men and women; both sexes had to work for a minimum of seven to ten years to save enough to set up a household.[15] Among such couples, it was not unusual to have sex before marriage, nor was premarital sex strongly condemned as long as the couple were seriously courting or had promised to marry each other. Aristocrats and wealthier families, on the other hand, married off their children earlier, sometimes even contracting marriages for them that would be consummated only many years later, if indeed at all. One of many statements of the elite marital ideal was Leon Battista Alberti's *Della Famiglia*, written in Florence in the 1430s, in which men in a prosperous merchant family define the ideal marriage: the man is mature, in his thirties, and his wife is young, in her early teens. One of the speakers, Lionardo, goes on to describe the kind of wife who is physically most suited to childbearing:

> [W]e should try to have in our house a wife well-built for bearing children and strong of body to insure that they will be born strong and robust. ... Physicians say a wife should not be thin, but neither should she be burdened with fat, for the fat are very weak, have many obstructions, and are slow in conceiving. ... They believe that a woman who is tall but full in all her limbs is very useful for begetting many children.[16]

Marriage poems written throughout the period praise new brides and their husbands in romantic terms, but the financial basis of the relationship is more or less explicitly mentioned, as in a sonnet by Moderata Fonte, celebrating Cecilia Pisani's 1588 marriage to Niccolò Sanudo in Venice. The poem begins:

> A rare beauty, always hidden 'til now,
> Guarded like a cherished treasure,
> Suddenly flashed forth like lightning, and the sun
> Seemed dimmer before such a radiant dawn.
> Her loveliness, when she appeared, delighted
> The whole world, and of this rare miracle
> Her charming husband, equal to her in every way,
> Became the lover and the owner.[17]

The husband is a both a suitor and a purchaser of the bride, *amante e possessor*. Why a possessor? As a jealously guarded treasure, the bride is her family's pledge in their creation of an alliance with another highly placed Venetian family. Once married, her role is to participate in the reproduction of these families: she is expected to retreat into their house and produce heirs.

The poem shows that marriage, at least among the upper ranks, was not a romantic but rather a financial and dynastic proposition. Further evidence is the fact that the Florentine patricians Alessandra and Marco Strozzi, in letters discussing the marriages of their daughters, used the word *mercatanzia*, meaning merchandise.[18] The dowry was intended as a guarantee of the bride's financial security, to be returned to her on the death of her husband, though his heirs sometimes refused to meet this obligation, especially if the widow preferred to leave the dead man's household or if she was childless. In any case, a Florentine wife was entitled to live and eat in her dead husband's for only a year after his death. An extreme case ended with a young widow pleading to her stepchildren to provide her with a gown and cloak decent enough to leave their house in: "Date modo ch'io sia vestita! (Let me be clothed!)" By this she meant, "Be generous, for my old trousseau and the clothes and jewels that your father, my dead husband, paid for while he was alive now belong to you."[19] In England, the situation was better: wives of the elite expected, as widows, a dower, as much as one third of what they had brought to the marriage, often including a house on the family estate.

Pregnancy was a state targeted with advice of all kinds. Women were advised not to trust such symptoms as nausea and the cessation of menstruation as proof of pregnancy, because these could have other causes. The sure way to tell was the "quickening" of the child, that is, the movement of the fetus. The woman was advised to avoid looking at anything ugly or terrifying because the sight might produce a child equally repulsive; anger, producing excessive heat, was seen as damaging enough to bring on miscarriage. The birth of a child, especially of a son, was cause for celebration. If a couple wanted a boy, they were advised to make love with the wife lying on her right side, because it was there that the more active masculine seed would gather. Priests insisted that only the missionary position was appropriate for married sex and prohibited sodomy (including oral and anal sex), but they, too, were expected to advise wives on how to arouse impotent husbands. More superstitiously, women wanting boys hung rosaries or charms from their bedposts.

Exhortations to be fruitful and multiply were reinforced from many directions. On the inside lids of the paired *cassoni* (wedding chests) built in Italy to be kept in a new couple's bedroom, painters left tempera images of both a young man and a young woman dressed only in light loincloths; the implication here is that wives as well as husbands would be aroused by visual stimulation.[20] Medical manuals and advice books counseled couples on methods for legitimate copulation: the couple should eat and drink moderately and be in a peaceful frame of mind. Foreplay and the "warming" of the wife's genitals were recommended so that she would have an orgasm. To this end, treatments for a woman having difficulty conceiving included "fomenting her secret parts with a decoction of hot herbes made with muscadine, or boiled in other good wine," and rubbing civet or musk (derived from male animals) into the vagina. Submerge the privates in a warm sitz bath of juniper and chamomile, advises another authority.[21] Childless wives were usually blamed for barrenness, but husbands were blamed for impotence in the form of premature ejaculation. For this problem, a Venetian physician, Giovanni Marinelli, offered the following cure: the couple could tie a string around the man's testicles and release it at the moment the woman approached orgasm, thus mixing their seeds so the woman would conceive.[22]

Popular medicine involved herbal and incantatory treatments for sterility: a Florentine "empiric," as academically untrained healers were called, recommended a poultice to be laid on the belly, though her patients warned that it smelled so terrible that the husband might throw it away.[23] Pharmacists advertised various concoctions guaranteed to make older men feel and perform as if they were decades younger. Bernardino Ochino of Siena, however, speaking for the church, warned wives never to accede to their husbands' requests if they wanted "acts *contra naturam*," that is, practices to prevent procreation.[24]

But the ideologies of proper courtship and family hierarchy were often contradicted in practice by the unruly behavior of men and women of all ranks and by the countercodes and proverbs through which they lived their lives. The transcripts of trials in marital courts suggest that couples found pleasure in many forbidden ways. A man argued that his wife had had sexual experience before their marriage by saying that she showed him how to have intercourse when they were both lying on their sides as well as "with her legs on his back."[25] A young woman testifying at a trial about the impotence of another woman's husband told the judge that the ways she used to excite him had all been useless:

> I told him that if he wanted to sleep with me, I wanted [his penis] in hand, to see for myself. So we began to play, and we proceeded over one [storage] chest and another. And I put my hand down below, and I took his member in hand ... over his trousers. ... We played for more than an hour, and I made a lot of effort [but in vain].[26]

Records suggest that the members and partners of the elite enjoyed pleasures outside marriage more or less freely, even though they offended their fellow citizens by crossing the divisions among ranks in their sexual liaisons. Married noblemen lived in both their family houses and those of their concubines, whom they supported generously. Among ecclesiastics, trial records reveal the frequency with which churchmen were accused of open sexual misconduct. In Burgundy, vicars were fined heavily for seducing unmarried women, and by the 1620s priests were hanged along with their concubines. More comically, fornicating prelates were derided, as in Bernard de la Borderie's ditty:

Le prétre vit de l'autel	The priest lives off his altar,
Et la putain du bordel	And the whore does off her brothel,
mais notre ami Bodeau	But our old friend Bodeau
vit de l'un comme de l'autre	Makes a living from both;
mais notre ami Bodeau	Yes, our old friend Bodeau
est chanoine et maquereau.	Is canon and pimp alike.[27]

As records of public recognition of the outcomes of normative sex, many objects related to the birth of legitimate children have been preserved: recipes for nourishing broths for the mother; elaborately painted Florentine birth trays; presents for the infant, including coral amulets and silver rattles. The father's family often gave cash rewards to the midwife, more for a boy than for a girl, and to the wet nurse. Frequently, painters recorded the importance of birth in lying-in scenes that illustrated Old Testament stories, for example, the birth of the Virgin Mary to her mother, St. Anne. A woman in childbirth was typically attended only by women, especially midwives, who often sat a woman on a hollow-bottomed birthing stool so that gravity would help with her expulsion of the infant. Lacking contraception, a highly born wife typically had many pregnancies, possibly because the giving of newborns to a wet nurse prevented the contraceptive effect of lactation in the mother. On average, a woman of high status could expect to give birth every two years throughout her teens, twenties, and thirties. Men who remarried once or twice might father as many as twenty-four children. Women of lower station, marrying later and nursing their children themselves, might have as few as four, at least those who lived to maturity.

A wife's barrenness or the impotence of a husband could be a justification for the annulment of a marriage, so annulments on this basis were often sought before church and civil judges. The courts authorized doctors and midwives to perform examinations for female virginity and impenetrability and male impotence, though they often came to different conclusions about the same case. Sterility in women was, at the least, a motive for prayers; offerings to the Virgin Mary; and, as a last resort, a turn to magic. The impotence of an old husband, it was recognized, could be the real cause, and also a cause for the wife's infidelity. In Fonte's *Il Merito delle donne,* her character Cornelia quotes a proverb, saying that "a bird in a child's hand and a girl in an old man's both spell danger."[28]

Arranged marriages between aristocratic and wealthy merchant families were celebrated by painters who were commissioned to produce double portraits of the couples and representations of sumptuous banquets such as those on wedding chests and in Veronese's *Wedding at Cana.* Artists also designed and staged wedding pageants on a grand scale. But the patriarchal power and practical financial considerations that determined such alliances also meant that sexuality, separate from fertility and the production of heirs, was usually a topic only insofar as it was illicit.

Sexuality, then, was a topic of official concern largely to the extent that it was related to the norms of marriage. The norms of literary courtship, however, were largely defined in antithesis to marriage. In a single, condensed line, Cressida in Shakespeare's *Troilus and Cressida* asserts the distinction between marriage and courtship: "Achievement is command; ungain'd beseech." What she means is that a woman, either married or having had sex with a man, is subjugated to his command. When he has "achieved" her, she is his to control. But as long as she is unattainable, the male lover is subjugated to her, "beseeching" her for mercy. This is not simply an opposition of gendered power, although it is certainly that. It is an opposition between a discourse of social and political regulation (command) and a discourse of desire (beseech).

Francesco Petrarca was the most influential author of a poetics of desire. He spent a lifetime composing and revising poems to the beautiful, remote Laura, whose inaccessibility he represented as an endless source of imaginative fascination and poetic invention. A typical sonnet from his *Canzoniere,* 159, typifies the idealization of the beautiful *donna* who enslaves and controls the poet:

> What part of Heaven, what Idea/gavethe perfect model in which Nature found/that glad and lovely face where she designed/to show below all she could do above? ... /when has one heart so many virtues bound? although the sum will lead me to the grave. /He seeks in vain where heavenly beauty lies/who has not seen my lady and has still/to see the gentle glancing of her eyes.[29]

The idealism and purity of such love, however, coexisted with vengeful fantasies of punishment and rape even in Petrarch's *Rime Petrose (Stony Rimes),* as in Canzone 4, in which he imagines Love as an ally in a sexually punitive revenge upon Laura:

If I could only see him split her cruel heart/down the middle, for she is quartering mine; ... /Alas, why does she not bark for me,/as I do for her, in the hot pit? ... /If I had grasped her lovely braids, /which I'd made into a lash and whip, /seizing them early in the day, /I'd pass the time with them from sunset into night; /and I'd be neither pitiful nor courteous—/but act like a bear at play, instead; /and if Love whips me with those braids, /I'd take revenge more than a thousand times.[30]

This is a fierce version of the more frankly spoken side of love, and more fiercely framed versions abounded in Renaissance culture. Against the poets' complimentary *blason*, or part-by-part enumeration of the beauties of a beloved woman, satirical writers attacked female ugliness and venality. One of the suitors of Veronica Franco, a member of the literary in-house academy organized by the patrician Venier clan in Venice who protected her, celebrated her beauty, grace, intellect, and eloquence. But this *capitolo* and others like it were undercut by the obscene dialect sonnets of Maffeo Venier, who called Franco "a truly unique whore,/Foxy, flighty, flimsy, flabby, smelly, scrawny, shrimpy," and insulted her as "a grisly spook, a scabby [poxy] ogre, a crocodile ... [and] a knock-kneed mare."[31] The scurrility of Maffeo's attack and its abundance of earthy insults suggests that he was as much a participant in the sexual underground he denounces in his poem as a critic of the women who made their living in it.

Tales of adultery, amorous excess, and murder fill sixteenth-century storybooks, but they are also recorded in the actual lives of women and men. In 1555 in the mountains east of Rome, a father's public slaying of a daughter who had had sex with the local judge and her brothers' murder of the judge were seen as acts of honor, intended to restore the reputation of the family.[32] The nobleman Paolo Orsini could strangle Isabella de' Medici, his adulterous wife, after locking her up in a remote villa on his country estate, and then persuade his fellow citizens that she had died of a stroke;[33] the brother-in-law of Bartolomeo Graziani, who was living away from his wife with his mistress Chiara Matraini in Lucca in 1547, could have him murdered with no damage to himself but gossip.[34]

Trial depositions describe fathers failing to pay their daughters' dowries as they had promised; girls married before the legal age (twelve in most cities; later, thirteen) and being raped by their husbands;[35] men drinking and gambling away their wives' dowries; men infected with gonorrhea insisting that their wives have sex with them nonetheless;[36] wives and husbands beating each other and locking each other out of the house; attempted and successful spousal murders; adulterous liaisons of all kinds; and lovers stabbed, drowned, and exiled. Accusations of these kinds were sometimes exaggerated if not outright false, but the fact that they were recorded and investigated shows that they were at least thought plausible.

Nevertheless, some people were able to pursue their desires outside normative marriage. Historians have concluded from trial records in the sixteenth and early seventeenth centuries that resourceful women and men could escape arranged marriages through legal separation or annulment if they had good lawyers and powerful friends. One justification was nonconsummation because of the husband's impotence or some physical deformation in the wife. In addition, young women or men could explain that they had made a clandestine marriage or run away from an arranged one in order to resist violent coercion from parents or relatives who had tried to make them marry according to family interests. After the Counter-Reformation meetings at Trent, the formula "I said yes with my mouth but not in my heart" was the starting point for an appeal for annulment. Resistance to the regime of sex exclusively within marriage and only for procreation freed wealthy men who had married for profit and propriety, or who, as younger sons, could not afford to marry: they kept concubines more or less openly and sometimes succeeded in legitimizing their daughters by proving that their mistresses were otherwise chaste and faithful.[37] Women whose neighbors and friends gave convincing evidence that their husbands had been excessively brutal, or had dishonored them by turning them into prostitutes or bringing prostitutes into the house, petitioned state and church courts for separation, often because they had found lovers with whom they could live more happily. Divorces, however, the only dissolution of a union that allowed people to remarry, were granted very rarely, and only on the basis of nonconsummation of the marriage or proof that it had been made against the will of one of the spouses. Whatever the Christian or humanist model of marriage might have been, fact and fiction show many evasions of the rule.

The close connection between marriage and economics is implicit in the power of kings and other powerful aristocratic men in many parts of Europe to live outside the sexual regulations that governed their subjects. Charles II, for instance, had twelve children by seven mistresses while having no legitimate heirs by his long-suffering wife, Catherine of Braganza; he openly acknowledged his illegitimate children, many of whom were granted titles and privileges. Indeed, James Croft, the first of Charles's illegitimate children, was created Earl of Monmouth and became a serious rival to Charles's Catholic brother, James, for the throne. Even more strikingly, the most powerful of

Charles's mistresses had significant power as public figures. Barbara Palmer, the Countess of Castlemaine, was given her own suite of rooms in the palace. On the other hand, the double standard was nowhere more extreme than in the sexual behavior expected of a female as opposed to a male monarch. Elizabeth I's relationship with her male subjects was indeed sexualized, but it was framed in the Petrarchan language of courtship, longing, and desire for the unattainable. Her power rested upon her ability to manipulate the discourses and iconography of chastity to her advantage and to use the language of a purified love to establish roles above all for her most powerful, and potentially threatening, male subjects to perform. Yet, despite the double standard, women of sufficiently high status could sometimes live sexual lives outside the norms of marriage. Sir Philip Sidney immortalized Penelope Devereux as the chaste and unattainable Stella of his *Astrophil and Stella* sonnet sequence (1591), although within four years of its publication, while still married to Robert Rich, Earl of Warwick, she began an affair with Charles Blount, Earl of Devonshire, by whom she had four illegitimate children. Although banished from court, Penelope Rich lived openly with Blount, even before her divorce from her husband (a divorce that would have been impossible for anyone of a lower social status).

In Italy married noblemen lived in both their family houses and those of their concubines and supported them generously, as did younger men and clerics, and men of all ranks visited courtesans or prostitutes. Rich noblemen also promoted *virtuose*, professional musical performers and writers of songs who performed in academies and the houses of wealthy men. Although there was no reason to assume that such women accompanied their musical skills with sexual ones, the erotic association that linked the open mouths of women and their seductive voices with seductive sexuality predisposed onlookers to assume that *virtuose* were courtesans.[38] And courtesans, musical or not, occasionally succeeded in marrying noblemen, most famously and scandalously the Venetian patrician Bianca Cappella, who became the mistress and then, in 1579, the wife of Francesco de' Medici, the Grand Duke of Florence.

Widows, too, found satisfactions both social and sexual once their marriages ended. They were expected to spend years in mourning and to dedicate themselves to the memory of their husbands for the rest of their lives. As their portraits suggest, they wore clothing, especially veils, resembling those of nuns.[39] But nunlike behavior was the last thing attributed to them in popular culture. In social expectation, widows were so sexually lively that they were thought to exhaust younger husbands.[40] It was assumed that, driven by lust, they would remarry as soon as they had a chance, and some did, in fact, marry men who had been servants or apprentices in their houses. An English proverb had it that "he who wooeth a widow must go stiff before," in other words, must be physically ready to satisfy her sexual demands.[41] If widows remained celibate, however, they could take over their households and govern them and their children for years. Alessandra Macinghi degli Strozzi (1407–1471) survived her husband by forty-five years and directed the affairs of her exiled sons until their return to Florence years later[42]. If a widow remarried, laws in many regions decreed that she lose her dowry from her first marriage. But many did remarry because they now had the experience to arrange a match of their own choice. The Englishwoman who eventually became the Countess of Shrewsbury married four times, outlived all of her husbands, and ended up one of the wealthiest women in the kingdom, a powerful, independent owner of several country estates, including one that she redesigned according to her own plans.[43]

Literary texts of all kinds are rich in representations of exceptions to the theory of the good marriage. Mockery of husbands unable to control their wives' sexuality abounded: the cuckold was a target of jokes, witticisms, and public satire. Venetians said that when the doge Marin Falier plotted against the nobility in 1355, one reason was his anger at a rhyme put about by young noblemen: "Marin Falier de la bela moier,/Altri la galde e lui la mantien[44] ("Marin Falier's wife is so lovely and nice/Other men lay her but he pays the price"). In France writers composed poems and songs voicing the complaints of a young woman married to a much older man, the songs of *la mal mariée*; another popular genre, the *aubade*, voiced the farewell at dawn of an adulterous couple. And obscene tales, poems, and dialogues were everywhere, in oral as well as written culture. A deliberately shocking example is a story in Marguerite de Navarre's *Heptameron*, in which the narrators claim that every anecdote is truth rather than fiction. A noblewoman at court turns four men, one after the other, into sex slaves, allowing each of them to leave her chambers only after a week; when they discover one another's participation, they confront her, intending to expose her wickedness and destroy her reputation, but she brazens the encounter out with unabashed confidence and no harm to herself.[45]

Scenes persuasively representing the realities of dysfunctional marriages typify the *querelle des femmes*, which continued throughout Europe from the middle fourteenth through the seventeenth centuries. Many polemical and satirical writers throughout Europe joined the fray, including Moderata Fonte, who denounced fathers, brothers, and husbands as irresponsible, venal, and violent. One of her characters, Cornelia, defends prostitutes as the victims of

fathers and brothers who deprive them of a proper inheritance and of husbands who neglect and shame their wives by preferring prostitutes;[46] or, she
adds, it is seduction and rape that lead young women into sex work.[47] Another
such defense was *La Nobiltà e excellenza delle donne coi i difetti e mancamenti degli huomeni* (The Nobility and Perfection of Women and the Defects
and Insuffiency of Men], written by Lucrezia Marinella to refute Giuseppe
Passi, whose venomous and uninspired *Dei Donneschi difetti* (Venice, 1600)
informatively typifies Cinquecento misogyny, including the sexual loathing of
women's bodies. To Passi's all too familiar claim that no women love their
husbands as they should, she responds with a counterargument realistic in its
focus on the mismatched ranks and bodies of a May/December couple in an
image that echoes the court cases of her time:

> Does it seem to you that a husband should marvel if his wife complains
> about him when she is younger, richer, nobler, wiser, and more adorned
> with beauty than he? ... Tell me, would an heiress suit a beggar? ... A
> merry and pleasing young woman a monster, a satyr or a complete wreck?
> A young woman an old man without teeth and with watery eyes and a
> runny nose?[48]

Marinella turns the patriarchal marriage theory articulated by Alberti on its
head, quoting Aristotle's *Politics* to show that a husband and wife's relationship should be one of civil reciprocity. She argues that antiwoman writers are
influenced "by the tyrannical insolence of those many men who make not only
their wives serve them but also their mothers and sisters, showing greater obe-
dience and fear than that [with which] humble slaves and servants serve their
lords and masters."[49] Her work reveals the extent to which nonliterary discussions of gender and sexuality circulated in a disenchanted way around marriage and the proper relations between husband and wife.

That such discussion cannot easily be mapped onto modern concepts of
heterosexuality has been persuasively argued by Henry Abelove.[50] He points
out that we should not collapse early modern sexualities into the normative
regimes of marriage. Such controls were dictated by biological, social, and
economic forces. It was only in the eighteenth century, Abelove argues, that
sex, as opposed to the requirements of begetting children, was mapped onto
marriage in new ways. Heterosexual culture would emerge out of a new hierarchy of sexuality in which the means by which children are conceived (penis
inside, vagina outside, seminal emission, no interruption) was given the sexual
status of "the real thing," against which all other sexual practices ("including

mutual masturbation, oral sex, anal sex, display and watching, and much else besides") were defined as either foreplay or perverse. In contrast to this new norm, a wide range of sexual practices occurred outside marriage, practices that, despite the official decrees of the Church, were focused on everything *but* heterosexual intercourse, with its attendant problems of pregnancy prior to any reliable means of contraception.

To give one example, from the end of the period under discussion: the London diarist Samuel Pepys conducted a wide range of sexual relations with women. Even though he probably knew himself to be sterile, as the result of an operation to remove a stone from his bladder, he rarely practiced heterosexual intercourse (penis inside, vagina outside, seminal emission, no interruption), and when he did, it was with married women. Nor was the bed the privileged space of his sexual activities. On the contrary, most of his sexual activities took the form of mutual exploration and masturbation, usually in his study, in coaches, and in the back rooms of inns. Indeed, the most important sexual relation that Pepys had was with his wife's maid, Deb. But when he was caught in the act by his wife, the act itself was embracing Deb and masturbating her while she combed his hair.[51] Pepys's affairs were invariably with women who were of a lower status than himself, but he was rarely in pursuit of hetero-sexual intercourse with its hierarchy of foreplay and the "real thing" and its restricted range of pleasure.

To conclude, while marriage was central to Renaissance social and eco-nomic structures, heterosexuality as it was defined in the twentieth century is a problematic category for analyzing the range of sexual practices between men and women in premodern Europe. On one hand, a wide range of laws were written to regulate sexuality in terms of biological reproduction; on the other, the celebration of institutional celibacy that remained central to Catholic states, and the sexual forms that were sodomitical in the sense that they were explicitly directed at nonreproductive sex, challenged any attempt to regulate sexuality through marriage. It was above all the illicit forms of sexuality that provided the central topics of Renaissance drama, prose fiction and diary, and poetry.

CHAPTER THREE

Homosexuality: Homosociabilities in Renaissance Nuremberg

HELMUT PUFF

A clothed young man watches six men of different physiques and ages who, with only their genitals covered, pose in an open-air bath in the midst of an urban setting. A highly suggestive choreography of male bodies is on display. The eyes of several men have interlocked; symbolic invocations of lovemaking and the phallic abound; several hands are hidden from view, as if to seduce the viewer into imagining what remains invisible. Only the oldest in the group remains on the sidelines of this sumptuous theater of gazes, gulping down a drink (fig. 3.1).

Carefully executed, printed in a large format, equipped with the artist's monogram, and produced for sale, Albrecht Dürer's woodcut of 1496/97 has frequently been taken to illustrate themes in addition to what it evidently captures, men in a public bath.[1] It has been argued that this composition invokes the five senses and the four temperaments.[2] Critics have also suggested that the facial features are those of well-known humanists from Nuremberg, Dürer's hometown, as well as of Dürer himself: a group portrait in the nude.[3] By comparison, the erotic charge of the image has been mentioned only in passing. Yet

320   *Männerbad*

Abb. 138. Männerbad im Anfang des 16. Jahrhunderts. Aus einem Holzschnitt von A. DÜRER'.

FIGURE 3.1: Albrecht Dürer, *The Men's Bath*,
1496/97, woodcut, 396 × 290 mm. Wellcome
Library, London.

intangible as it may seem, eroticism is crucial to the way in which the woodcut,
with its focus on gazing, engages the viewer.

This chapter seeks to give substance to the soupçon of homoeroticism that
has frequently been linked to the European Renaissances.[4] I argue that between
1450 and 1650 there was a new urgency to representations of erotic scenarios between individuals of the same sex. Such representations originated in
part with circles that sought to reflect on the bonds of their members. The art
and writings of Albrecht Dürer will serve as my window onto the homosocial
sphere of premodern Europe. Through male-authored writings, artifacts, and
representations, we get glimpses of a vast landscape in which women socialized with women and men with men—cultural contexts in which suggestions
of same-sex eroticism surfaced.

Homosociability is my choice of a term to frame the materials presented
here. With its emphasis on dispositions, the term deflects a search for the truth
about sexual actors and sexual acts, pointing instead to the realm of social
structures as well as to that of cultural ideas. For Renaissance Florence, Michael
Rocke has stressed "the typical times, places, and rites of sexual encounters,"

while at the same time carving out "the mutually sustaining links among sexual interactions, other types of social networks, and male sociability."[5] Similarly, homosociability seeks to capture a Renaissance terrain of actual same-sex interactions replete with cultural, emotional, erotic, and representational possibilities.

While homosocial interactions mattered to both sexes in Renaissance Europe, the place of the sexual varied for men and for women, and so did the forms and meanings accorded male and female homosociabilities. As a result, the two parts of this chapter, the first devoted to men and the second to women, are not in symmetry. While the first part focuses on the bonds and idioms that tied a male artist to one of his mentors, the second knows little of historically documented women who bonded with other women. It may be possible to write a history of all-female sociality between 1450 and 1650; writing a history in which eroticism figures at the heart of female same-sex sociability, other than as a history of male visions of sexual excess, proves a difficult endeavor. Nonetheless, analytic gain lies in relating what has rarely been treated as an ensemble, male and female homosociabilities.

Sociability in late medieval and early modern Europe was conducive to same-sex affects and erotic desires. In public squares, inns, and, as Dürer's 1496/1497 woodcut reminds us, in bathhouses, men, whether from the lower classes or the elites, spent time together working, drinking, talking, competing, and carousing.[6] These were not carefree activities but tension-prone, culturally meaningful social pursuits. Males vied to prove their status and their respective masculinities, whether as apprentices, artisans, or councilors. Authorities issued regulations against unruly men—a concern that coexisted with acceptance of male aggressiveness as a fact of social life.[7]

Same-sex sociability flourished in a culture where cross-sex sociability was fraught. As Lyndal Roper puts it poignantly, "Courtships were encounters between two rival sexual groups who (imaginatively at least) inhabited different territories."[8] Several images of cross-sex couples that Dürer produced in the 1490s concur with this vision; they show male-female liaisons as potentially endangering, disorderly, or otherwise charged, as indicated by suggestions of violent scenarios, garish clothes, or the presence of devilish figures.[9] In echelons where property, lineage, or household organization was at stake, families supervised contacts between the sexes. For the less fortunate, livelihood was a concern—a livelihood threatened by unwanted pregnancies. Yet honor was tied to sexual probity with regard to women of all classes. As a result, encounters between early modern men and women were the object of discourses of conduct, oversight, and regulation. Before and after the Reformation, city councils sought to curtail thriving festivities where young men and women socialized.[10]

Traditionally, the social history of early modern Europe has been focused on institutions tied to reproduction: kin, the family, and marriage. Other histories have complemented this anthropology-inspired literature by dwelling on love between the sexes and the rise of domesticity. Focusing on same-sex interactions contributes to ongoing research on bringing the homosocial nexus of early modern life to the fore.[11] As research has begun to show, same-sex sociability constituted a collective terrain marked by rituals, exchanges, investments, and affectivity as well as individual agency. Viewed thus, homosociality was anything but marginal to European societies of the past. Though the homosocial was not a nexus set apart from other social fora, same-sex interactions mattered profoundly. But was eroticism part and parcel of the Renaissance's homosocial fabric?

MALE MEMBERS

Renaissance Nurembergers laid claim to political and cultural preeminence. In an epochal map published in the year 1500, the cartographer and humanist Erhard Etzlaub positioned the free imperial city in the middle of Europe.[12] Nuremberg was a vibrant urban center of Europe-wide trade connections brimming with entrepreneurial activity, artisanal innovations, and intellectual collaborations. The city therefore provides an apt vantage point to tweak a cultural history of sexuality during the Renaissance—a story that has been told mostly from an Italian or English point of view.

The circle of the German "arch-humanist" Conrad Celtis included Willibald Pirckheimer, the scion of a prominent family. Despite his social status and lack of erudition, Dürer, the son of a well-to-do goldsmith, was also a member, mingling with patricians, patrons, and the powerful. In fact, he advanced to a figurehead of Nuremberg humanism in the early 1500s, thanks to widespread local enthusiasm for his art. There and elsewhere, humanists pioneered alliances centered primarily on conviviality or shared scholarly pursuits and less on neighborhood associations, professions, or families. The Celtis circle's interests in the ancients, medieval history, civic life, and religious reform established an erudite arena for, among other expressions, intellectual male bravado. As we will see, eroticisms of many kinds figured potently in this milieu. For our purposes, Pirckheimer's friendship with Dürer illustrates vividly how the homosocial and the homoerotic cohabited in early modern Europe.[13]

Intriguingly, Dürer and Pirckheimer not only acknowledged that men had intercourse; they seem to have bonded over this recognition. A silverpoint drawing Dürer made of Pirckheimer ca. 1503 is among the documents testifying to their tie (whose beginning we cannot date with certainty).[14] Sketched in preparation of a Pirckheimer portrait, the drawing features the inscription "with the man's prick into your asshole" in the Greek language.[15] Though hailed as the new Apelles, the Greek master painter, Dürer had no command of the language. It is therefore unlikely that he wrote the line, jotted down in a Greek cursive. Since the same pencil was used for the inscription as for the drawing, Pirckheimer passes as the inscription's most likely author.[16] Presumably, he was present when Dürer sketched his profile, and over the course of his lifelong studies, he would become one of the most accomplished Hellenists of his generation (fig. 3.2).

"Following the portrait sitting the two men appraise the work together. Pirckheimer asks to use Dürer's pen and adds the line at the top."[17] This is how the art historian Bodo Brinkmann imagines that the drawing and its inscription came into being. The silverpoint pen and the theme of a penetrating

FIGURE 3.2: Albrecht Dürer, *Study for the Portrait of Willibald Pirckheimer,* ca. 1503, silverpoint on paper, 210 × 149 mm. Bildarchiv Preussischer Kulturbesitz/Art Resource, NY.

penis graphically inserted onto the portrait sketch rub against one another. Let us take note, though, that the folio in question was not destined for wide dissemination. Typically, the 1503 charcoal drawing, based on the sketch (let alone the portrait print of Pirckheimer Dürer designed in 1524), lacks this or a similar line.[18] Also, the superscript's language shielded its contents from but a few readers. Command of Greek was a rare accomplishment among Renaissance literati of Dürer's generation. Inserting one of his signature talents into the artist's work as well as leaving a mark on his own likeness, Pirckheimer complemented the drawing with a gesture whose audience was exclusive.[19]

The explanation is not necessarily that Dürer and Pirckheimer tried to keep the true nature of their bond a secret. Dürer's silverpoint drawing contains no personal revelation. Importantly, the superscript does not mention a name, nor are there explicit links to either Pirckheimer or Dürer. After all, the anus could be a woman's or it could be a man's. What is more, the personal pronoun "your" stresses versatility. Even if there were only few viewers, the inscription potentially takes aim at any one of them. If anything, the superscript celebrates phallic exuberance. What matters above all is penetration and the masculine self-assertion associated with it. The sex of the penetrated does not matter; at least it did not merit mention.

It has been argued that the textual add-on constitutes the parody of a motto—small texts that projected a person's presence into a work of art, especially a portrait.[20] Yet it should also be understood as a trace of amical jocularity. The line thus had the potential to signal, perform, and affirm a special bond between two men.

The audacious irreverence of the gesture is hard to escape. Anal sex between the sexes and same-sex sexual acts were punished severely in Nuremberg. Men or women found guilty of such acts faced the threat of capital punishment there and elsewhere in northern Europe, whereas lighter penalties were common south of the Alps. While most German cities including Nuremberg did not have specific laws regarding these delicts, legal thinking and judicial praxis were unequivocal about condemning sex acts defined as the "sodomitical vice" or "crime"—a term that denoted all nonprocreative sexual activity including anal intercourse but was used to refer to male-male sexuality above all.[21] The line thus projected reviled sexual practices into contemporary Nuremberg with its famously strict government. (Notably, Pirckheimer served his native city as a public official over many years.)

Unlike some Italian cities such as Florence and Venice, sixteenth-century Nuremberg experienced sodomy trials only infrequently, however.[22] Magdalena Paumgartner, the spouse of a prominent Nuremberg merchant, found the execution of a weaver and a fruit dealer for "Florentine indecency" noteworthy;

she informed her absent husband of this exceptional event in a letter.[23] The demise of the city of Sodom in the biblical book of Genesis for the deeds of its inhabitants provided a model for purging cities of offenders to the sexual order. Depicting the acts in question by imaging God's wrath was a pictorial convention in medieval and early modern Europe. Dürer used this strategy on the verso of a painting of the Virgin Mary and Christ, now in Washington, when capturing Lot's and his daughters' escape from the city—shown engulfed in flames.[24] Such images potentially issued grave warnings about the destruction that resulted from sexual behavior, but they were elusive on what constituted the essence of the *vicium sodomiticum*.

Whereas we cannot know whether the drawing's superscript reflected sexual experience, there is little doubt that it betrayed sexual knowledge. Such knowledge resulted not only from sexual practice. Demonstrably, it originated with literary horizons. Ancient texts infused the interactions between humanists with opportunities for conspicuous group-fashioning, as was fitting for male circles concerned with philology, poetry, cartography, art, and similarly lofty pursuits. In this case, Lucian's dialogues with their celebration of male companionship and philosophical banter may have offered the themes of erotic love between men and anal penetration.[25] Pirckheimer owned an 1496 edition containing the *Erotes*, then thought to have been authored by Lucian, a debate on the question of whether vaginal intercourse with women or anal intercourse with male adolescents was preferable (with the latter form of erotic love tenuously carrying the day).[26] For the Nuremberg clique, with an artist as its symbolic center, the *Erotes* may have been a particularly appropriate point of reference; an encounter with a sculpture by Praxiteles, the Aphrodite of Cnidus, provided the dialogue's narrative frame. New learned intersections thus may have served as an inspiration for Renaissance homosociability in Nuremberg. If indeed Pseudo-Lucian provided a stimulus in this instance, crude humor entered into the scenario in the process of adaptation.

The Pirckheimer portrait sketch, which may well have been the subject of conversations between friends in the circle, was not the first time that one of Dürer's works explicitly registered sodomy. In 1494, he produced an image after an Italian model. While the latter does not survive, it is safe to assume that it was Andrea Mantegna whose inventions Dürer admiringly copied in two other drawings of the same period. *The Death of Orpheus* depicts the bard as he is about to be brutally slain by women swinging clubs; if we follow the Roman poet Ovid, Orpheus had introduced erotic love between men and adolescent youths to the region of Thrace. It was this twist that inspired his killing in the version of the tale rendered in the *Metamorphoses*.[27]

The drawing in question was more than a copy, as I have argued elsewhere.[28] Among other changes, Dürer added an inscription that could not have been part of the original, now lost, image: *Orfeuß der Erst puseran,* or "Orpheus, the first sodomite," or rather, "bugger." Its language, German, addresses a German audience, and so does the Italian-sounding *puseran,* which, derived from a Venetian swearword, functioned as a foreign-sounding jab in the fifteenth- and sixteenth-century German lands. For everybody to see and hear, this Romance word placed the sexual practice in question nowhere else but in Italy. Reconciling the Orpheus inscription with the thrust of the composition is difficult. Its wording offers an insulting twist on an image that paid homage to Orpheus, the *ur*-artist, and to Orpheus's rebirth in Italian art and literature of the fifteenth century.

Importantly, the 1494 drawing remained just that, a drawing, despite its finished quality, possibly shown to friends or enticing conversations on risqué mythological references. Like the silverpoint sketch of Pirckheimer, it was never transformed into a print—a medium that would have disseminated the image to a viewership beyond Dürer's milieu. In 1494, Dürer was not yet on equal footing with humanists in his hometown, a move up the ladder that would require ambition and fame. Yet he was already soaking up education from many sources, Mantegna among them. The distance in tone between Dürer's 1494 inscription on *The Death of Orpheus* and on the silverpoint drawing of Pirckheimer is remarkable. Comparing the two, we can measure not only the difference between two communicative scenarios but also the terrain Dürer traversed upon his gradual entry into the precincts of humanism. Whether south or north of the Alps, humanists demonstrated their erudite worldliness by, among other things, allusions to sexual practices that were largely condemned outside their milieu (and that they themselves might have condemned in specific contexts).[29]

From the evidence we have, it was Pirckheimer who seems to have taken the lead in encouraging sexual *plaisanteries* between the two men. Given his superior status and university education, this is hardly surprising. Yet neither the artist's mentor nor his mentee readily pass as libertines. Dürer's self-representations in writing, for instance, revolve around religious righteousness; and Pirckheimer was a paragon of the Christian humanism in which the *studia humanitatis* north of the Alps excelled.[30] Sexual explicitness was tied to specific contexts, genres, intimate audiences, and literary-artistic modes of communication. While such expressions benefited from a link to one's self in the manner of the then fashionable *ironia socratica*, they acquired meaning in social settings whose public was limited.[31]

We get a glimpse of the exchanges between the two from the letters Albrecht Dürer, the "servant," wrote to his "lord," Willibald Pirckheimer, from Venice in 1506.[32] Fleeing the plague and leaving his wife behind, Dürer spent more than a year in Italy, basking in the glamour of his rising fame as a visual artist with Europe-wide recognition.[33] The correspondence—only some of Dürer's letters survive—is replete with overtones and undercurrents. Starting with the address, epistolary conventions are both invoked and undermined. Verbal pirouettes may reflect the artifice at the core of this relationship. It appears that the two men's intimacy depended on the performance of proximity in the medium of letters. After all, male-male relations between unequals required great care. Such inequality among men striving to establish a special bond was more common than the classic notion of Ciceronian friendship of the like-minded than its Renaissance adherents would indicate. Humanist friends of the same sex but of different social backgrounds negotiated their intimacy in artful gestures that broadcast an unlikely friendship to others.[34]

In the case of Dürer and Pirckheimer, the idiom of the erotic provided one among many links between the two.[35] First of all, theirs was an epistolary eroticism performed in part for others in on the performance; the letters between Dürer and Pirckheimer were certainly talked about in conversation and occasionally read aloud, one can surmise.[36] While laughter was one of the many aftereffects these communications sought to provoke, business came first. The contents show Dürer acting as Pirckheimer's Venetian agent; he bought precious objects and books for his friend.[37] The opposite also holds true. Dürer asked Pirckheimer to look after his affairs at home.[38] Despite all the work of connecting, however, this relation remained asymmetrical. Dürer calls himself Pirckheimer's "slave," or, rather, *schiavo*. Humorously formulated in an Italian-German hybrid idiom, such macaronic formulae both bridge and stress the distance between their respective locations, Nuremberg and Venice.[39] (Pirckheimer had once been a student in Italy.)

"I am thinking of you often," Dürer writes.[40] He claims to have seen look-alikes of Pirckheimer on the streets of Venice.[41] He expresses mock jealousy after having heard from a common friend that Pirckheimer has gained in good looks whereas he, Dürer claims, has lost them and is suffering.[42] Playful as such comments are, they also convey the sense of a bond whose balance was in flux. It is as if we were entering a hall of mirrors in which identifications and dis-identifications alternated—scenarios whose possibilities were shaped and enhanced by class difference. In this epistolary *imaginaire*, verbal communication has sexual intercourse as its potently binding other. Readily, Dürer engages in long-distance bawdy talk. Misogyny, double entendres, and sexualized slurs connect while the two are in fact separated. In one instance, he asks his friend about sexual exploits by means of pictograms that allude to the names of Pirckheimer's supposed female lovers in Nuremberg.[43] If his epistolary friend doesn't write, love affairs must be the reason. Yet men as well as women merit epistolary-erotic attention. If Pirckheimer were where the letter writer is now, he would find many "courtly" or rather "good-looking Italian mercenaries" (*hüpscher welscher lantzknecht*).[44] Urging his absent friend to come home, Pirckheimer apparently threatened to insert an enema into Dürer's wife if he stayed away any longer. His friend would be permitted to do so, Dürer responds, only if he "loves [i.e., fucks] her to death."[45] At least in fantasy, a friend can take a friend's stead in the marriage bed. The artist's spouse appears as a token of erotic trafficking between men, even to the point where the symbolic death of the intermediary female is taken into account; if only in jest, Agnes Dürer served the epistolary expression of homosocial immediacy.

All the verbal-sexual excess notwithstanding, the letters reinforce difference as much as they at times deny it. The hidden script at their core is submission and mastery, and this may well be why sexual intercourse offered itself as a master plot.[46] Eroticism is not only referred to; the letters themselves enact erotic scenarios: Words do not merely represent acts; they are themselves acts, or purport to be. This is not to suggest that the two Nuremberg men had sex with one another. There is no way of knowing whether they did or did not do it. Mental frisson is what we have evidence for. Scholars who have suggested that theirs was an erotic bond have failed to explicate their reasoning within the historical context.[47] Taking the applicability of modern conceptual categories for granted will in fact detract us from shedding light on the emotional-erotic facture of Renaissance Europe, which differed from today's repertoires in, among other things, interlacing homosocial bonds and eroticism. One could presume that a friendship with sexual benefits would have solidified a complicated bond among unequals. But in ancient literature as well as early modern Europe, sex was imagined to occur mostly between men who differed in age, status, or both; though actual sex acts did not necessarily conform to this notion, we need to keep in mind that the two friends were of roughly the same age. It is precisely the carefully constructed equality of their friendship—in the face of social difference—that would have put this relationship at risk of greater asymmetry, if eroticism had entered into it; after all, during the Renaissance, sex, as a rule, was thought to revolve around asymmetries, whether between members of the opposite sex or the same sex.[48]

Appropriately, there is evidence that Dürer had an erotic interest in an apprentice in his workshop. This is what Lorenz Beheim, another patrician,

intimates to Pirckheimer in a letter of 1507, the year after Dürer had returned from Venice, suggesting that Dürer's carefully trimmed beard vexed
the younger—an affair that appears to have been shared knowledge in the
Pirckheimer and Dürer circle.[49] Interestingly, Beheim deploys the Italian word
gerzone [sic] in a Latin context to describe the apprentice (whose name is not
revealed). To be sure, in Italy and elsewhere, workshops offered ample opportunities for erotic attachments of masters with students or dependents.[50]

From mentions of homoeroticism in the Dürer circle, we can substantiate
the notion that images like the *Men's Bath* integrated male-male eroticism into
their frame. To be sure, such works were part of an expanding imagery that investigated the naked human body. The woodcut of men in a public bath is itself
an archive, with bodies of different ages captured in a variety of poses. These
are not necessarily the eroticized bodies of a later, sexual age. They are replete
with associations ranging from artistry and anatomy to religious devotion and
theology.[51] The investigative representation of especially the male body was
part of a visual theology reminiscent of Christ's beauty as well as the Passion.
Nakedness can therefore not easily be reduced to portraying or provoking lust.
Nonetheless, from early in his career Dürer exploited erotic charge to invest
his images with the power to keep the viewer from averting his or her gaze.
Such scenarios involved a variety of erotic constellations. One may point to the
visual pun of a study of three soldiers in which one figure in the foreground
seems to caress the genitals of another in the background.[52] One could cite the
meaningful glances between a drummer and a piper on the Jabach altarpiece.[53]
In the context of Dürer's heterodox eroticism, Eberlein discusses the drawing
of an executioner casting a lustful gaze at his youthful and naked victim from
behind.[54]

Before and after 1500, German artists developed a growing interest in sexually charged imagery, as the historian Robert Scribner once posited.[55] It would
be erroneous to restrict such eroticism to heterosexual scenarios and to blind
oneself to the range of erotic expressions operative in Dürer's and his follow-
ers' oeuvres, however.[56] In Dürer, erotic charge is present between men as well
as between men and women (less between women, it would seem). These traces
of homoeroticism in imagery do not have to reflect individual psyches or pass
as a general signature of the Renaissance. Such representations arose from an
artistic milieu with interests in challenging pictorial conventions as well as investigating the surrounding world visually. After all, these compositions called
attention to artful images and the virtuosity of their makers.

This moment of homosocial urgency among men, pregnant with artistic,
intellectual, and erotic possibilities as it was, did not last. During his lifetime,

Dürer witnessed how his native city adopted religious reforms in the Lutheran mode, a development he seems to have followed with great interest, in the years after 1517, the beginning of the German Reformation. The spirit of intellectual-moral-aesthetic experimentation as evident in the exchanges between Dürer and Pirckheimer found less favor with a younger generation of confessionalizing humanists who espoused a strict Christian ethic in civic-religious life. Yet we should not assume that Protestant standards of marital fidelity were simply embraced; they were not. As there was no uniform Renaissance culture, there also was no uniform shift from the Renaissance to a confessional society seeking to domesticate the erotic. Whether in cities or in courtly circles, communicative niches in which representations of (homo)erotic scenarios thrived continued to spring up and disappear from sight.

The homoeroticism in the midst of humanist Nuremberg merits our attention not only as a revealing case study about how the erotic functioned and figured between men, but also because Dürer created visual models for depicting homosocial scenes for generations to come—models much emulated, transfigured, and turned upside down.

WOMEN IMAGED AND IMAGINED

When Albrecht Dürer published his large woodcut of a men's bath, he also produced a drawing of a women's bath. Though the two pieces are often described as counterparts, this does not pertain to their medium; his portrayal of naked women was never published. A web of correspondences envelops the two pieces in a dialogue, however: The six women expose themselves in a variety of ways. An old woman to the right has turned away from the scene. The faucets and other utensils remind one of similar elements in the men's bath. A voyeur peeks at the scene from an opening in the back of the room (fig. 3.3).

At the same time, the differences are inescapable. Unlike the men's bath, the women's bath is set indoors.[57] What is more, the women do not seek eye contact among each other. Instead, two of them look outward, inviting the viewer into the scene. Eroticism in this image interpellates a voyeur, or a *voyeuse* for that matter, mirroring the one viewer represented as lurking in the back of the scene. In Dürer's drawing, women are on display, as if on stage.[58]

Male-male and female-female sociability were not analogous. In the *Erotes*, Pseudo-Lucian had one of the interlocutors develop the thought experiment "if males find intercourse with males acceptable, henceforth let women too love each other"—only to have the proposition ridiculed.[59] If homosociability mattered for both men and women in Renaissance Europe, its spaces, practices,

FIGURE 3.3: Albrecht Dürer, *The Women's Bath*, 1496, drawing, 231 × 230 mm. Kunsthalle Bremen—Der Kunstverein in Bremen/ Foto: Karin Blindow.

and representations differed considerably. Women's public image was centered on questions of sexual probity; men's was not, or not in the same way. In certain social contexts, men were called upon to demonstrate their sexual prowess. By contrast, idealized representations or prescriptive literature showed women's lives as centered on the home or homosocial spaces such as this bath. If gender trumped the sexual in the case of women, this representational order also invited highly sexualized images of the female sex.

It comes as no surprise that, viewed from the outside, female spaces spawned erotic suspicions. Since womanhood was tied up with notions of an all-pervasive sexual drive, all-female groups of women lent themselves to male fantasies of unbridled lust. Such representations often link the sexual and the polity's order, betraying a desire for control even where the viewing pleasure seems to have been the primary motive. By contrast, many invocations of female-female love and friendship often downplay or defy erotic innuendo. As a rule, women who claimed self-expression in a male-dominated sphere of art-making and writing labored to fend off the sexualized images projected onto them, their exchanges, or their gatherings.[60]

During a period of increased social disciplining, there was considerable, possibly renewed, interest in representing all-female spaces. Patriarchal authorities and discourses encouraged men to embrace male supervision, if only in the imagination. In his colloquies, Erasmus of Rotterdam composed a dialogue featuring the dispute of two wives over how to realize happiness in marriage—a widely disseminated text that "eavesdropped" on how women communicated among each other.[61] In another part of the same literary work in progress, the *Colloquia*, Erasmus also alludes to the unspeakable doings that went on behind convent walls; one of his characters, Catarina, gives up a life of chaste piety among utterly depraved nuns to lead a worthy secular life instead, though the reasons for her conversion remain unspoken.[62]

But were such representations based on experiential knowledge of a sphere largely inaccessible to men? In the case of Martin Luther, we may consider an interest in analogy as motivating his depiction of an all-female sphere. In a 1522 treatise on marriage, the reformer presented female androphobia as a counterpart to male misogyny.[63] If one advocated matrimony as the appropriate social institution for sexually mature adults, as this religious reformer did, same-sex sociality and its Renaissance corollary, disdain for the other sex, were in dire need of reform. According to Luther, male misogyny and the ready reception of antifeminist stereotypes among men constituted an impediment to escaping the supposedly impure cesspool of nonmarital life. Luther therefore may have rendered male misogyny absurd by supplying it with a female counterpart.

Occasionally, literary imaginings of what women do when they are with other women spell out scenarios of same-sex eroticism. One setting for sexual narratives was the convent, although, in general, the antimonasticism rampant all over Europe during our period centered on heterosexual sex between monks and nuns. In an unpublished novella, the Italian writer Giovanni Sercambi composed a narrative variation of a plot adapted from Boccaccio's *Decamerone*, in which nuns satisfy their sexual lust by means of a strap-on penis until a young man, cross-dressed as a female novice and in love with one of the nuns, enters the institution to provide a superior source of sexual satisfaction.[64] The garrulous chronicler of sixteenth-century French court life, Pierre de Bourdeille, Seigneur de Brantôme, conceived of sexual relations between men and between women through the lens of gender that is asymmetrical in a chronicle that was published only in the seventeenth century. While sexual activities between men occasioned humorous responses just as sex between women did, men risked their status when taunted by accusations of same-sex erotic predilections, whereas women taking sex into their own hands served as a humorous diversion.[65] These gendered discrepancies are why bisexuality as a concept has been misleading with regard to Renaissance culture. It levels the hierarchies and gendered asymmetries as well as the constraints and boundaries of the representations in question.

At any rate, inspired by Dürer's imagistic archive, artists offered explicit accounts of lovemaking between women, at times outdoing their models in graphic detail.[66] While such adaptations reflect long-standing practices among artists, they also hint at modes of reading Dürer's images among connoisseurs. Be that as it may, viewers familiar with both the models and their copies were destined to appreciate the titillating visual resonances at stake.[67]

A small-scale engraving by the Nuremberg artist Barthel Beham serves as an example for such a visual translation (fig. 3.4). It depicts three female nudes and a boy in an enclosed space, strongly reminiscent of, though more intimate than, Dürer's *Women's Bath*. A seated woman reaches with one hand between the legs of a standing female, fondling the woman's genitals while the woman turns around, acknowledging the sensation. A third woman rubs the seated woman's shoulders from behind.[68] Provocatively, the woman reaching into the other's crotch exposes her genitals. In its suggestion of everydayness, the tactile eroticism on show belies the elusive mythological and intellectual fictions that sometimes empowered depictions of erotic love between men or between women.[69] Whether titillation, erotic arousal, satire, moralization, or all of these registers are at stake in Beham's print remains an open question—an intended ambivalence, one suspects, since the artist does little to channel the viewer's response.

In fact, the ceramic stove in an otherwise sparse backdrop may have much to do with the scene's lasciviousness. In the early modern world, eroticism was associated with and thought to be predicated on heat. According to humoral theory, women were cold—one of the reasons why women were constitutionally driven to have sex.[70] As a result, the heat in a bath was thought to incite women erotically.[71]

Barthel's brother Sebald Beham circulated the same image (in reverse), testifying to the scene's appeal. Yet this Dürer-inspired image, *Women Bathing*, also served as the model for a woodcut, published in Augsburg in the early seventeenth century (entitled *Die Badtstuben*, or *The Bathhouse*). As is evident from the print's layout and paratext, this seventeenth-century publication sought to appeal to a popular audience. In keeping with contemporary standards for single-leaf broadsheets, a poem frames our encounter, offering a moral veneer for viewing the image. In fact, the scene is narrated as a family romance gone awry, and the scenery resembles a kitchen more than a bath. Written from the

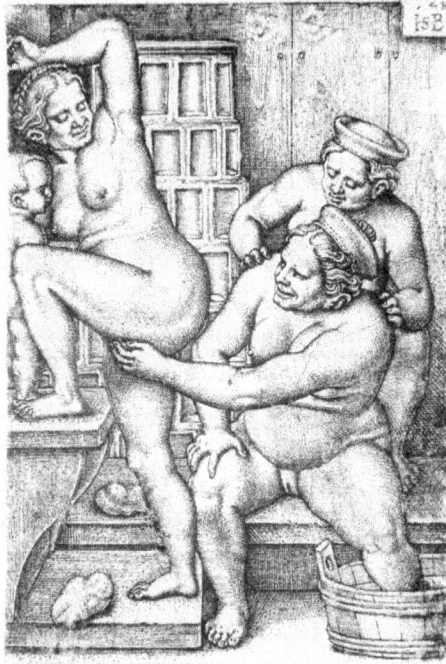

FIGURE 3.4: Sebald Beham (after Barthel Beham),
Women Bathing, 1548, engraving, 83 × 57 mm.
Ashmolean Museum, University of Oxford/
WA1863.3314.

perspective of the boy in the image, the poem praises "pious women's" honor,
an honor code the women depicted overtly defy. The women's actions are said
to have resulted from their being single, a state with which they seem to be content (contrary to what we know about single women's discontents during this
time), since they "laugh for themselves."[72] In fact, they would continue to please
themselves even if they also had sex with a man, the anonymous poet states.

This print thus provides a case study for an image's translation from one
context to another. It has come down to us because Lorenz Schultes, the printer,
was arrested for having published this woodcut without the permission of the
city's authorities. Before the council, he sought to excuse this infraction with
the pursuit of monetary gain. But he acknowledged that the image was "shameful [and] indecent" to view. He was banished from the city in 1626.[73]

Hans Baldung Grien, one of the artists we can tie to Dürer's workshop in
Nuremberg (though we do not know the exact years of their association),[74]
also developed a visual archive of women interacting with women erotically.
Taking his cues from witch motifs circulated by Dürer, he explicated the

eroticism present in the master's inventions when depicting witches in group scenes. His witch representations span a variety of media—woodcuts, drawings, a painting—and his life's oeuvre between 1510 and 1544.[75] These scenes portray a sexualized world of exuberant fantasy. Neither the witch hunts in mid-fifteenth-century Switzerland nor the infamous but during Baldung's lifetime largely neglected *The Hammer of Witches* (*Malleus Maleficarum*) dwelled on witches' orgiastic sexuality other than that they had sex with a male devil or similar such figures gendered as male. In fact, the *Malleus* demonstrated the "sodomitical vice's" utter reprehensibility by claiming that even demons abhorred it (though which sexual practices the passage's author, the Dominican Heinrich Kramer or Institoris, referred to when using the term is unclear).[76] But given the close association of heresy, sodomy, and witchcraft, both linguistically (in German) and conceptually, it is not surprising to find that female witches and heterodox sex acts could at times be conflated.[77]

In his witch-imagery, Baldung produced spectacles of a sexual world upside down.[78] The women-witches seem to have canceled the sexual contract that, as a rule, tied women to men. In the artist's witch scenes, women do not depend on men for sexual satisfaction. Female witches are projected to control their own sexuality as well as that of men: various forms of autoeroticism and eroticism, among them suggestions of women mounting other women, testify to their sexual agency, if not autonomy.[79] They even exert power over viewers whom they engulf with their gazes and the sheer excess of their doings (fig. 3.5).

Contextualizing Baldung's pictorial inventions in the world of Alsatian humanism, the contemporary witch literature, and the witch trials, Joseph Leo Koerner sees them as figments of the "learned imagination."[80] That male spectatorship was intended is likely. An inscription on one of the artist's chiaroscuro drawings suggests that it was a new year's gift for a cleric—a dedication resonant with the caustic wits of anticlerical ribaldry.[81] Such virtuoso images probably served mainly as showpieces for art collectors and humanists, potentially stimulating conversations among cognoscenti, even if, occasionally, women may have had access to them as well.[82] In the words of Charles Zika, Baldung's witch-images "point to a new interest in the erotic among the artistic patrons of early sixteenth-century Europe and to a fascination with the sensualities of lesbian interaction."[83]

We get a glimpse of the intellectual horizon brought to bear on "lesbian-like" women (Judith Bennett) among social and educated elites in a passage from the unpublished mid-sixteenth-century chronicle of Count Froben Christoph von Zimmern. A servant woman named Greta from the count's territory was said to have loved girls. According to the account, she was an unsteady character of undistinguished background, entering into occasional service at

FIGURE 3.5: Hans Baldung Grien, *Witches' Sabbath*, 1510, chiaroscuro woodcut, 374 × 256 mm. Wellcome Library, London.

the market in the Zimmern territory's main stronghold, Messkirch, in the south of Germany.[84] She, a woman, courted "young daughters," buying them small gifts and "[using] gestures and manners as if she had a male affect." The count himself was not called upon as a ruler or judge in this instance. Otherwise he could hardly have afforded a tentative stance—a lack of closure that would have been impossible to maintain in a judicial context. His short paragraph on Greta in his comprehensive chronicle marshals a plethora of explanations potentially relevant to the "problem" he had outlined. In his account, written well after the fact, probably without having met Greta and most likely based on hearsay, Froben Christoph von Zimmern, an educated aristocrat who had studied at various European universities, turned to learned speculation in order to approach this "freak" occurrence in his territory's recent history.

An "inverted, unnatural constellation of the stars at her birth" provided one potential explanatory frame to the count and his family members—a perspective especially appropriate in cases such as this that challenged conventional perceptions.[85] In fact, men or women with rare sexual inclinations, among them women seeking intercourse with other women, were not uncommon as test cases in this field of knowledge.[86]

Alternatively, "historiae" promised guidance on the matter, an explanatory frame for which the count had a particular affinity. Scholars well-read in ancient literatures, he states, report that a "hermaphrodite or androgyne" like Greta was more common in the Greek and Roman past than in the Christian present.[87] We don't know which histories, myths, or narratives—ancient or contemporary—the count referred to.[88] If the descriptor "androgyne" is any indication, the count may, if only indirectly, have referenced Aristophanes's speech from Plato's *Symposium* that lists a third sex, that of a "man-woman," in its myth of origin.[89] Sexual variation intrigued early modern literati. Hermaphroditism in particular attracted a wealth of contradictory images, commentaries, and associations. Since a man-woman embodied both the masculine and the feminine, such a figure was sometimes viewed as ideal in the symbolic realm, while actual "men-women" occasionally faced criminal persecution.[90] "Hermaphroditus" as a term is featured, for instance, in a 1405 *lettre de remission* for a woman named Jehanne who mounted her sixteen-year-old companion, Laurence, moving "her hips" and doing "as a man does to a woman."[91] In short, the "hermaphrodite and androgyne" functioned as a multifarious sign whose median position invited authors to oscillate between sex and gender, body and behavior, literary reference and experientialism.

Clearly, the curious Greta emerged as a sign of a moral crisis. This episode, the count contends, reflected the "evil mores of rotten nations plagued by sins."[92] Notably, the count's is not an exercise in allegory. Froben Christoph places the erotic love of a woman for girls in the experiential world. He applied a variety of discourses to the individual declared to be in need of explanation, ever so slightly probing the explanatory force of various referential systems. It is in this context that the moral reading emerges victorious. With its pragmatic focus, moralism bridges not only between the everyday and the erudite; as a mode of relating to the world, moralizations were omnipresent in early modern culture as well as in the count's chronicle. Yet in the process of his retelling, Greta metamorphosed into a fascinating object of study, a curiosity, a marvel, probably not unlike some of the images discussed here. Most likely, the count recorded her story as an occasion to share stories of similar such phenomena and to incite conversation among kin, both male and female, fellow nobles, or literati—interactions richly documented in his chronicle.

In court trials, rare as they were, the authorities focused on women like Greta or Jehanne who assumed male prerogatives. The accused appear as female offenders not only with a "male manner" but as simulators of masculinity.

Katharina Hetzeldorfer from a well-documented Nuremberg family reinvented herself as a rogue male with a female companion she cared for, making love to her as well as to other women; she was drowned by court order in Speyer in 1477.[93] The farmworker Agatha Dietschi assumed a male role and got married in the Black Forest region—a scheme that worked well until her spouse fell in love with a man and wanted to get married; Dietschi was banned from the city of Freiburg in 1547.[94] Though from different social backgrounds, both Hetzeldorfer and Dietschi were migrants. Otherwise, they could not have lived in couples with another woman as if a man and a woman. There was oversight of female behavior from men as well as from women, and mobility provided one way of freeing oneself, at least temporarily, from such control.

At any rate, in the courts, we rarely get a glimpse of same-sex eroticism among women that did not involve gender realignment. The records of a court investigation against Elisabeth Hertner, suspected of witchcraft and of sodomy in the city of Basel in 1647, offer themselves as a rare illustration. After Hertner (who seems to have been unmarried and young[95]) had been arrested, an interrogation without the use of torture brought to the fore that she had, with the help of devilish ghosts and the magic practices she learned from them, bewitched the marriage of the carpenter Lienhart Müring; she had lain with his wife, a cousin of hers, and the two women repeatedly committed "shameful acts."[96] In the records, the link between the charge of witchcraft and the sexual offense remains underdeveloped.[97] For fear of broadcasting knowledge on either witchcraft or same-sex eroticism, the legal and ecclesiastical consultants involved in the council's investigation argued strongly for covering up the case, seeking to avoid a public outcry in this instance. They feared unrest was inevitable, however, if Frau Müring were prosecuted for sodomy (although, they issued an order to extirpate the superstitions and the "magic booklet," mentioned in passing). As a punishment, Hertner seems to have been put under protective custody.[98]

What Baldung graphically exposes to view, the Basel authorities sought to silence in this case. This tension is emblematic for patriarchal approaches to a female sphere of interaction, approaches that oscillated uneasily between attempts at control and laissez-faire. Yet it was precisely this hesitation to penetrate an all-female sociality that contributed to keeping alive fantasies about what women did behind closed doors. Such a dynamic exposes to plain view that displacing sexual lust onto others, be they women or young men, was a precarious move at best. In representations that collapse the divide between the different homosocial spheres, as in Beham's rambunctious *The Spinning Bee*,[99] Virgil Solis's orgiastic bathhouse scene (known as the "Anabaptists' Bath"),[100] or in the bathing scenes popular in northern European art of the sixteenth century, men *and* women were shown as united in frolic and bawdiness.

In Renaissance Europe, there was a persistent association between same-sex eroticism and the elites. Their interests in the matter surfaced in many of the materials covered in the preceding pages. We know this to be an association that tells only part of the story. Studies of sexuality in history amply demonstrate that across Europe men who stood trial for sexual relations with members of their own sex came from various social stations. Michael Rocke's study of Renaissance Florence sheds light on a vibrant sexual culture among nonelite groups of men. Among the few women who faced court proceedings for having sex with their likes were hardly any members of the elite. To be sure, there were highly visible prosecutions involving male aristocrats and patricians.[101] As a rule, however, unless in highly politicized trials, people of a low or middling class were more likely to be tried for the crime by the name of sodomy. Why then does this persistent association not vanish from sight?

One may cite the fifteenth-century theologian Saint Antoninus of Florence, who posited a causal connection; supposedly, luxuries of all kinds lead to sodomy—*luxuria*, after all, translates as lust.[102] Another Florentine, Benvenuto Cellini, the sixteenth-century goldsmith and artist, corroborates the same nexus from a different angle. Taunted publicly as a sodomite by his artistic competitor, the sculptor Baccio Bandinelli, he claims to have issued the repartee that a "noble art" like sodomy was a pursuit worthy only of Gods or rulers, implying that he, a mortal and artisan, was free of it (something we know not to have been the case).[103] This verbal duel may have happened only in the pages of Cellini's *Vita*. But even if this episode and the laughter that supposedly concluded it in the author's favor did not actually unravel in quite this fashion, this proves a general point. It is precisely in the niches of elite culture where references to same-sex eroticism surfaced most perceptibly in the period between 1450 and 1650. Sometimes such sexual practices were projected onto others—exotic locales, times, peoples, or classes—but the theme asserted a place nonetheless. By means of irony, Cellini cross-referenced the religious and legal condemnation of same-sex eroticism on the one hand to its elevation as a refined pursuit among certain elites on the other.

As we have seen, representations of same-sex eroticism were fueled by an influx of sexually explicit materials across temporal, generic, and geographic borders as well as by contemporary interests in taking up sexual themes or reflecting on the gendered order via narratives of inversions and transgressions. Works of art with suggestions of homoeroticism were the stuff of exchanges that linked elite men with other elite men. Yet Cellini's narrative also sheds light on the fact that such representations occasionally fueled the ire of others—those who may have understood the innuendo but were positioned outside the circles in which such representations flourished.

Renaissance discourses of same-sex eroticism, whether textual or visual, have a precarious relation to the contexts in which these allusions and artifacts came into being. We can almost be certain, however, that the question of how to relate erotic representations and sexual praxis is not ours exclusively. There is evidence that it already haunted conversations among Renaissance literati.

CHAPTER FOUR

Sexual Variations: Playing with (Dis)similitude

FREDRIKA JACOBS

Male and female created He them.

—Genesis 1:27

Sexe is no other thing than the distinction of Male and Female, in which this is most observable, that for the parts of the body, and the site of these parts, there is little difference between them.

—Ambroise Paré, *An Introduction or Compendios Way to Chyrugerie* [1579], 1649

Our Apparell was given us as a signe distinctive, to discern betwixt sex and sex, and therefore one to weare the apparell of an other sexe, is to … adulterate the veritie of his own kinde.

—Phillip Stubbes, *The Anatomie of Abuses*, 1583

Although some qualities are common to both [sexes] and are as necessary for a man as for a woman, there are yet others that befit a woman more than a man, and others that befit a man and to which a woman ought to be a complete stranger.

—Baldassare Castiglione, *Il libro del cortegiano*, 1528

Near the beginning of book 2 of *Il libro del cortegiano*, written in 1516 and first published in 1528, Baldassare Castiglione sets forth a theoretical frame for the ensuing discussion that has as its objective the portrayal of the ideal courtier and, in book 3, the representation of his counterpart, the ideal court lady: "There is no contrary without its contrary." As he goes on to explain, a conjoined opposition (*concatenate contrarietà*) allows one thing, such as a person endowed with virtue (*virtù*), to be defined by its opposite, in this case an individual marked by vice (*vizii*). "Since evil is the opposite of good and good the opposite of evil, it is necessary that, by way of opposition and a certain counter-balance," the essence of one is grasped in comparative relationship to the other.[1] To be sure, this strategy works well with Castiglione's chosen format. Dialogue inherently facilitates a "dialectic abounding in theses and antitheses."[2] At the same time and in accordance with the book's objective, *Il cortegiano* reveals two essential and paradoxical truths about Renaissance culture. First, society generates, and through "incessant and repeated action" enforces, normative identities determined by binary logic.[3] Second, the society producing these identities also challenges, revises, and even inverts them. Regimented by a belief in the biological basis for difference that determined everything from what people wore to what they ate, Renaissance society imposed regulations to keep everyone in her or his proper and readily identifiable place. Yet despite or perhaps because dialogues like *Il cortegiano* reveal the absence of absolutes in their very attempt to present them, gender identity and social order were rendered unstable. During the Renaissance ambivalences, inversions, and transgressions were manifest across class lines, territorial borders, and expressive mediums. Men masqueraded as women and women impersonated men just as goatherds postured as courtiers and courtesans played the part of refined ladies. They did so between the pages of chivalric romances, on theater stages and loges, in city streets, and in rural communities. This raises a challenging question. Was inversion, especially gender inversion, a transgression, or was it instead as normative as the very norms it opposed?

CONTRARIETY

Castiglione's contention that "there is no contrary without its contrary" was neither new nor distinctive. According to Aristotle, all of his philosophical predecessors subscribed to a system for ordering reality known as Pythagorean contrariety. Its structuring principle was simple, yet as is generally the case with dichotomous thinking, its implications were anything but benign. As explained by Aristotle, the Pythagorean system is composed of ten coupled oppositional concepts, including, for example, light and darkness, male and female, good and evil, and right and left. Although each is presented as one component of a pair, the coupled elements are not put forth as either symmetrical or equal. Instead each is placed within a hierarchical (and polarizing) evaluative scheme that rendered any confusion between oppositions unimaginable. First, a positive or negative value was ascribed to each pole. Next, these values were comparatively ranked. The positive pole thus emerged with a higher value, the negative with one that was lower.[4]

Although Aristotle's list of contrarieties was restricted to ten pairs, it is important to note that each concept was weighted by associations. In addition to being evaluated against their respective opposite, each positive component was categorized with all other positives while each negative was conjoined with all other negatives. In this way, female, as an example, not only was juxtaposed with male but was simultaneously affiliated with dark, evil, and other similarly positioned lesser concepts and qualities. By the time Aristotle's list of ten pairs reached the Renaissance it had been both emended and extended. Indeed, as a method for establishing the order of things, the Pythagorean system lent itself to patristic explanations of the relationship of Eve, the privative, to Adam, the positive. It also separated the mind from the body, associating the former with maleness and conceptual enterprise and the latter with femaleness and material accident.

The polarizing effect of the Pythagorean system of contrariety established each component wholly discrete from its defining other. Theoretically there was no room for ambiguity, no way to confuse good with evil, no way, it would seem, to mistake a male for a female, or vice versa. Yet what was true in theory was not always true in actuality, since, as Castglione observes, there are men who "have the appearance of men but who in truth are not."[5] These so-called men, he contends, are like "common whores" (*publiche meretrici*) for they "not only curl their hair and pluck their eyebrows," but are also "in their every act ... so tender and languid that their limbs seem ready to fall apart."[6] Ludovico Ariosto was less harsh but no less damning of such *uomini*. In act 1, scene 22 of *I suppositi*, which was first performed for the ducal court of Ferrara on February 6, 1509, he tells the tale of a buffoonish would-be courtier who receives lessons in what it takes to attain his goal. He is informed that his ultimate objective is to be like a nymph. To this end he must spend hours preening before a mirror, curling and perfuming his hair. Spenser's Britomart is a striking counterpart to Ariosto's clownish courtier and Castiglione's *publiche meretrici*. Like Virgil's Penthesilea who "blazes with battle fury" (*Aeneid* 1:493), she possesses the fearsome capacity to "fight like a man." Significantly, she does so in a battledress that is "alluringly and femininely ornamented." The shrouding of masculine ferocity in feminine dress leads Spenser to conclude that Britomart is a woman "halfe like a man" (*Faerie Queen* 5.5).

As these and any number of other Renaissance texts make clear, gender identity can be brought into question, if not altered, by simply donning the attire of or affecting the behaviors associated with those of the opposite sex. Contrariety, which juxtaposes the "ways, manners, words, gestures, and bearing" of one sex against those of the other in order to clearly define each, detailed the former and thereby described the latter. Thus constructed, gender identity is relational signification and as such depends upon texts like *Il cortegiano* that include reflections on the *regole*, or rules of proper deportment. According to Castiglione, for example, a woman should be "more circumspect" than a man and display "a soft and delicate tenderness, with a manner of feminine sweetness." By contrast, a man should "exhibit a certain solid and sturdy virility to which a woman ought to be a complete stranger."[7] "Corage, feersnes, manlinesse, and strength," the virtues displayed by Edward IV and celebrated by William of Worcester, can be added to Castiglione's characterization of masculinity.[8]

There are two possible ways of reading statements such as these. The first is straightforward. Because gender identity is elucidated so clearly, there should be no way to confuse one gender with the other. A male is or ought to be masculine. A female is or should be feminine. The second way of reading these texts subverts the first. Prescriptive in tone, gender characterizations by Castiglione, Ariosto, Spenser, and William of Worcester are in essence manuals on signification, how-to books providing behavioral guidelines and dress codes. As such they not only direct women and men how to dress and comport themselves as is proper to their gender and class, they also spell-out how to masquerade as the other. In this sense gender is not, as Butler notes, a "substantial thing." It is performative, a subjective representation reflecting the "repeated stylization of the body [through] a set of repeated acts" that coalesce to produce meaning.[9] Generating meaning is not, however, the same thing as constituting identity. As both Spenser's warrior queen and Ariosto's effeminate courtier indicate, veils of disguise are typically woven so loosely as to reveal what is supposedly concealed, and when they do the impossibility of going beyond the "binary limits imposed by the binary of sex" is disclosed.[10] During the Renaissance biological sex is never really thrown into question even as an individual of one sex adopts the gendered mannerisms of the other. Ultimately the values of contrariety remained intact. As "halfe like a man," Britomart is commendable. As a preening fop, Ariosto's would-be courtier is ridiculous. Yet if this is the case, how are we to view any number of factual and fictive examples of gender inversion? The answer depends on the context of the act.

SARTORIAL SHUFFLING, WHORES, AND NUNS

Compelling signifiers, clothes were coded by courtesy manuals and regulated by sumptuary laws. They announced rank and, as the frequently cited passage in Deuteronomy 22 declared, they identified gender.[11] They were not to be abused by misuse: "The woman shall not wear that which pertains unto a man, neither shall a man put on a woman's garment; for all that do so are an abomination unto the Lord our God."[12] Yet the hierarchy promulgated by law and custom was not inviolable. There are records of women wearing the apparel of men and, although fewer in number, men donning the dress of women. Class boundaries were similarly encroached and crossed. Thus as Jean Howard has argued, the meaning of cross-dressing "varied with the circumstances of its occurrence, with the particulars of the institutional or cultural sites of its enactment, and with the class position of the transgressor."[13]

By around 1620, cross-dressed women populated London's streets in numbers noticeable enough to prompt King James I to direct preachers to rebuke the practice from the pulpit. Preachers, he said, should "inveigh vehemently and bitterly ... against the insolency of women, and their wearing of broadbrimmed hats, pointed doublets, their hair cut short or shorn."[14] The confusion "betwixt sex and sex" caused by a switch in clothes as well as that created by violations of class-based sumptuary laws had decades earlier garnered the attention of social commentators who regarded both as disruptive of social order. In *The Anatomie of Abuses in Ailgna* (England) of 1583, Phillip Stubbes denounces the "confuse mingle mangle of apparrell" that makes it difficult if not impossible to distinguish "who is a noble ... , who is honorable or worshipfull from the meaner sort" since everyone flaunts "preposterous excesse," regardless of birth, estate, or station.[15] For a person of one sex to put on the attire of the other seems to have been viewed as an even more flagrant violation of natural law, one that debased the perpetrator of the fraud regardless of his or her sex. In light of this perception it is not surprising that across Renaissance Europe cross-dressing was often entangled with prostitution.

In *The Description of England* of 1587, William Harrison laments the decline of sartorial decorum, observing, "I have met with some of these trulls in London so disguised that it hath passed my skill to discern whether they were men or women."[16] The term "trulle," as Howard notes, is defined in *The Oxford English Dictionary* as "a low prostitute, or concubine; a drab, strumpet, trollop." Several years earlier Stubbes had voiced a similar sentiment. "Honest matrons would blush to go in such wanton and lewd attire as is only proper to man."[17] Records from Bridewell and the Alderman's Court validate Harrison's and Stubbes's observations. Many of the cross-dressed women hauled before London magistrates toward the end of the sixteenth century were charged with prostitution. Dorothy Clayton, who was brought before the Alderman's Court on July 3, 1575, is a case in point. Court documents record that "contrary to all honesty and womanhood [Clayton] goes about the City appareled in men's attire. She has abused her body with sundry persons and lived an incontinent life. On Friday she is to stand on the pillory for two hours in men's apparel and then sent to Bridewell until further order." Johana Goodman, who, "along with her husband, was whipped and sent to Bridewell in 1569 simply for dressing as a male servant so she could accompany her soldier husband to war," was the exception.[18]

In Italy the connection between cross-dressing and prostitution assumed a different form. Venetian courtesans were legendary. Despite attempts by the city's Senate to "curb the excessive expenditure of whores upon their own garments" by forbidding them to wear silk, gold, or silver, Venetian *cortegiane* continued to display the material wealth and adopt the affectations of the social elite, and thus don a mask of decency.[19] Visiting the city in 1608, Thomas Coryat described them, which he said numbered "at least twenty thousand," as "second Cleopatras ... decked with many chaines of gold and orient pearle ... divers gold rings beautiful with diamonds and other costly stones ... [and] a gowne of damske either decked with a deep gold fringe ... or laced with five or sixe gold laces."[20] Cesare Vecellio observed something different. His *Habiti antichi e moderni di tutto il mondo* of 1590 illustrates and comments upon a variety of loose women and their attire. While economic level affects the quality of clothing enabling one to differentiate courtesans (*cortegiane*) from public prostitutes (*meretrici de' luoghi publici*), "nevertheless most of them wear a somewhat masculine outfit."[21] Indeed, a contemporaneous flap engraving affords the viewer the opportunity to see what clients paid for. Lifting the flap reveals, as Vecellio says of raising a courtesan's skirts, "men's breeches" on shapely legs (fig. 4.1). An often cited letter from Pietro Aretino to the courtesan known as La Zufolina written in 1548 documents the double, titillating pleasure derived from the sexual ambiguity of having one's lover enter the room in one guise (*maschio*) only to reveal another (*femina*). One cannot be sure, he jests, whether the enticing presence before him is La Zufolina or Il Zufolino.[22] In light of Aretino's expressed delight it comes as no surprise that in two fictive works, *La cortegiana,* published in revised form in 1534, and *Sei giornate* of 1536, he makes cross-dressing a trick of the prostitute's trade.

FIGURE 4.1: *Venetian Woman with Moveable Skirt,* ca. 1590, engraving. Metropolitan Museum of Art, The Elisha Whittesley Collection Fund, 1955 (55.503.30).

While males no less than females were susceptible to the equation of cross-dressing with prostitution, a point made clear by Castiglione's denunciation of primping males as "common whores," and although androgynous dress was condemned across the board, the sex of the perpetrator seems to have mattered. A woman dressed in man's clothing was viewed as loose, her morality regarded as an ominous threat to society. According to Stubbes, "I never reade, nor heard of any people, except drunken in Cyrces cup or poisoned with Exorcisimes of Medea that famous ... Sorceresse, that ever would weare such kind of attire."[23] Here the implications of cross-dressing are pushed to the extreme. Coupled with the concocting of love potions and visits to graveyards to secure ingredients of human flesh for those potions, sartorial deception is linked to witchcraft. Stubbes was not alone in conjuring this connection. In the second act of Aretino's *La cortegiana* the conniving and now old, ugly, and "French diseased" Alvigia laments the imminent death of the woman who had schooled her in the arts of magic and procuring. Alvigia's skilled mentor is soon to be burned at the stake as a witch.

Whether male or female any individual who put on the clothes of her or his opposite was, depending on the circumstances of the act, viewed with unease, mocked as an abomination of nature, or censured as an affront to society. Yet despite the contemptibility of both, the transgressions of each were at least to some extent seen to be distinctive. While cross-dressed women might be accused of witchcraft, they were not, as was the case with cross-dressed men, accused of homosexuality. That said, both were clearly disparaged as whores. The dispersion reflects a popular perception that was skewed by false assumption. Even in Florence, where nearly 50 percent of the male population was investigated for sodomy between 1432 and 1502, there is no corroborating evidence—as there is for the cross-dressed women brought before the magistrates at Bridewell and the Alderman's Court of London—to substantiate a connection between cross-dressing and prostitution.[24] This is not to say that illicit sexual behavior and cross-dressing were divorced from one another when the offender was a male. The *Mémoires* of Jacques Du Clercq record the following: "On the 17th day in the said month of May [1459] ... in the city of Lille, a man claimed to be a man and a woman and having two sexes he ... [opted] to dress in the habit of a woman, and moreover ... he was sleeping with young males and committed the sin of sodomy."[25]

Male cross-dressing and the accusation of unnatural effeminacy that attended it was further complicated by the rules determining what constituted the act itself. A woman had only to put on breeches. For a man nothing so extreme was necessary. He had to do no more than indulge in wearing excess ornament or simply display obvious affectation. Several decades after Castiglione's gathering of courtiers censured men who "curl their hair ... pluck their eyebrows" and otherwise affect the manners of females as "common whores," the papal nuncio to Venice Giovanni della Casa weighed in on the subject. In his *Galateo* of 1558, he warns members of his sex against embellishing themselves "like a woman, for his adornments will then contradict his being." Ultimately, he will be reduced to a status beneath that of even a lowly prostitute, for men who indulge in "extremely ornate" dress, "put curls in their hair and beards," and apply an amount of "make-up to their faces, necks, and hands" that "even a harlot" would shun put on the "hose of Ganymede." Della Casa's reference to Ganymede, the pretty-boy adolescent abducted by Jove in search of sexual pleasure, seems to say it all.[26] Shakespeare used the reference to a particularly witty end in *As You Like It*. Playing with the destabilization of the English stage and the sexual dynamics afforded by having young male actors play female roles, he cast Rosalind as Ganymede, thereby making "the equation between women and boys not only explicit, but explicitly sexual."[27] Between the clothing and the name, the latter was perhaps the greater signifier, made all the more so by "a moment unique in Shakespeare," the moment Ganymede turns to the audience and "undoes her gender: 'If I were a woman, I would kiss as many of you as had beards that pleased me.'"[28] As Stephen Orgel reminds us, "Boys were, like women—but unlike men—acknowledged objects of sexual attraction for men." Moreover, the boy player was no less of an eroticized attraction for women.[29] Rosalind/Ganymede thus provides tantalizing possibilities and delightful satisfaction to all.

Offstage and beyond enabling prostitutes to charge higher fees for their services, cross-dressing had practical advantages for women. It provided them with access to otherwise forbidden places. One of those places was the monastery. No less of a canonical text than Jacopus de Voragine's *Golden Legend*, written around 1260 and printed in Europe more than any other text between 1470 and 1530, recounts the lives of two female saints, Marina (Marinus) and Eugenia (Eugenius), who dressed as men in order to retire to a hermetic life.[30] Their examples, as well as that of Pelagia, whose life was detailed by Lucillo Martinenghi in 1590, must have been compelling, or so suggest the actions of Suor Gratiosa Raspi and Suor Eugenia di Tommasso da Treviso. In 1618 Suor Gratiosa attempted to flee the Franciscan convent of San Sepolcro in Venice not to escape the stringency and depravation of the order, but to place herself in the even more religiously rigorous environment of the Camaldoese hermitage at Monte di Rua. When questioned by authorities, she explained, "This thought [dressing as a man] came to me having read that Saint Marina and Saint Eufrosina had each led a life in a monastery of friars."[31] Suor Eugenia had another motive. Victimized sexually in the 1450s by a priest affiliated with the Benedictine convent of Santa Maria Annunziata Le Murate in Florence and realizing that as a woman she was at a disadvantage to press her case against him, Suor Eugenia dressed as a man, ran away from the convent, and lived in two male observant Franciscan houses before finally undertaking a pilgrimage to Jerusalem.[32]

PLAYING THE PART

The question raised by these incidences and texts is whether clothes were used merely as a disguise or functioned as constitutive signs in the sense of the aphorism "clothes make the man" (or woman). An answer is not easily determined since the circumstances in which cross-dressing was enacted, including theatrical performance, varied significantly. Citing Stephen Gosson's reference to the Deuteronomic code in *Playes Confuted* of 1582, Laura Levine answers the question in the context of the polemics of antitheatricality with a query of her own. Referencing Gosson as well as Stubbes, who in 1583 argued that garments "are set downe for signes distinctive between sexe and sexe, to take unto us those garments that are manifest signes of another sexe, is to falsify, forge and adulterate, contrarie to the expresse rule of the words of God," Levine asks, "What is it that the man who puts on women's clothing 'falsifies, forges and adulterates'? Is it the 'signes' or the gender which the sign stands for?" Although Gosson betrays anxiety about female impersonation, he "never explicitly makes a claim which would challenge the notion of a definite gender beneath the sign." His anxiety establishes male cross-dressing as a lie with the potential to become truth, "an idea which implies that there is nothing fixed underneath."[33]

In *Th' Overthrow of Stage-Playes* of 1599, the English scholar of theology and admitted performer of a transvestite role in his youth John Rainoldes suggests a variant anxiety of that expressed by Gosson. It was not so much the possibility of a fiction morphing into a reality that was the problem, but rather the provocation of erotic thoughts aroused in the audience and/or female-attired actor through "remembrance and imagination." Citing Dionysius Carthusianus, he warns his reader that even when worn by a male "the apparell of wemen ... is a great provocation of men to lust and lecherie." For him garments are mneomonic, prompting the mind of the spectator to imagine "a thing desirable."[34] The general inquisitor and bishop of Evora, Portugal, Manuel do Valle de Moura seems to have concurred. In *De ensalmis* of 1620, a text that focuses on countering the satanic, de Moura expresses concerns about the effects of theater on the audience. Specifically, he worries about the "phantasmatic" cues of vulgar language and effeminate gestures that can induce the viewer to imagine what is not represented.[35] As Ann Rosalind Jones and Peter Stallybrass note, Rainoldes's translation of Dionysius Carthusianus tends to raise more questions than provide answers. Is the female body somehow "imprinted upon or within the clothes? ... Will the desire be homo- or hetero-erotic and will it be directed toward another or toward the self?"[36] These queries raise another. What exactly is it that arouses "phantasmatic" desire and provokes anxiety: the clothes, the body beneath the clothes, or the indeterminacy that oscillates wildly between the two? It is hard to know especially since voyeuristically suggestive and performed moments of onstage revelation typically rupture gender fantasizing by interrupting the imagination. As Susan Zimmerman explains, there was no shortage of "strategies for interrupting and displacing dramatic fictions, including 'send-ups' of the transvestite convention itself."[37] Dispelling confusion could also be achieved by authorial direction. Before the plot of *La venexiana* begins to unfold, the play's anonymous author delivers an instructive warning to the audience. "Don't imagine that you are seeing women, although they are dressed as such, because, with those clothes taken off them, they aren't just creatures to be loved, but lovers, as you are men."[38] Of course, "conversations" between players and audiences could also work the other way around, perpetuating the masquerade, as does Shakespeare's Rosalind, by reminding us that in the eyes of the Renaissance beholder, "Boys and women are for the most part cattle of this [same] color" (*As You Like It*, 1.2.388–89).

The type of double cross-dressing that takes place in works like Thomas Middleton's *No Wit, No Help Like a Woman's* of ca. 1611 plays to the instability feared by Gosson and others. In Middleton's comedy the character of Kate Low-water, played by a male dressed as a female, sheds his/her woman's garments and dons those of a man in order to seduce and thereby humiliate the widowed Lady Goldenfleece. Coupled with situational humor, such costume changes "focus audience attention on ... [the] body as erotic object." While this might render the body a "playground for comic [and erotic] deception," it also makes members of the audience privy to the secrets of masked intrigue.[39] Sexual identity is not in dispute even as gender identity is in disguise. The humiliation of Lady Goldenfleece in *No Wit* is unfounded, for in truth Kate, no less than Shakespeare's Rosalind, is what she pretends to be, a male. Discussing Shakespearean allusions by female characters to their lack of male anatomy, Janet Alderman concurs. "The joke, of course, is that the 'women' do not in fact lack anything: the transvestite comedies repair the 'lack' in women at least in part by calling attention to the body of the boy actor who underwrites the representation of women on stage."[40] This "interplay between clothing and undressing," say Jones and Stallybrass, "organized gender around a process of fetishizing, which is conceived both as a process of fixation and as indeterminable. If the Renaissance stage demands that we 'see' particular body parts [in bedroom scenes and situations of undressing] ... it also reveals that sexual fixations are not the product of any categorical fixity of gender."[41] Theatrical scenarios such as these make abundantly clear what is also true offstage: gender is performative.

Neither ludic play nor the instability of gender was restricted to the stage. It was very much a part of festive misrule. In his autobiography the sculptor and well-known self-promoter Benvenuto Cellini recounts an artists' banquet staged in Rome to which the best artists of the day, including Michelangelo and Giulio Romano, invited their favorite courtesans. Finding himself at the last moment without a companion, Cellini invited his sixteen-year-old neighbor Diego to be his companion. As the evening wore on general good cheer took hold, prompting the assembled to devise additional diversions. A beauty contest was arranged. Diego, appropriately disguised and renamed Pomona, entered the competition and won. All went well until "Pomona," tired and bored, attempted to escape the revelry by claiming to be indisposed—a "month or so with child." Seeking to verify Pomona's announcement, the women seated on either side of her/him reached beneath the mass of skirts only to discover by touch what was hidden to sight.[42] Such antics were common, especially at festive gatherings during carnival. Annibale Caro's *La statua della Foia ovvero di*

Santa Nafissa, which was presented to Michelangelo, Sebastiano del Piombo, and other members of Rome's Accademia della Virtù in 1538, for example, blends obscenity with sexual ambiguity in a discussion about a fictive statuette representing a hermaphroditic Santa Nafissa, identified by Caro as the patron of prostitutes.[43]

If Caro's *Diceria di Santa Nafissa* participated in the festivities of pre-Lenten misrule, it did so without the potent ramifications for civil unrest that inhered in times of sanctioned license. During popular festive periods—carnival, the Feast of Fools, merriment of May, and Fastnacht—the hegemonic gender ideology imaged in pedagogical prints was turned upside down.[44] Safeguarded by the license of the comic and excused by the indulgence of the festive, women in trousers and men in skirts chastised both sexes, villainizing the former for overstepping boundaries while mocking the latter for allowing the transgression. According to Natalie Zemon Davis, permissible gender inversion proved an effective model for undermining as well as reinforcing societal norms by "widen[ing] behavioral options … sanction[ing] riot," and allowing "political disobedience for both men and women in a society that allowed the lower orders few formal means of protest."[45] Changing clothes and social change went hand in hand.

The interrelationship of festive misrule and peasant rebellion has been established.[46] The degree to which gender inversions facilitated class rebellion cannot be evaluated here. It can be said however, that the sex-reversal disguise seems to have been a persistent feature of revolt, enabling a "Lady Skimmington" or "Captain Dorothy" to lead the charge.[47] What *is* relevant to the present discussion is the recognition of garments as "signes distinctive between sexe and sexe" and the possibilities afforded by their misuse. Not only did they disguise the shrouded body, but in the context of festive misrule they could efficaciously mask the temperament of a masquerading male intent upon challenging established order.

Essentialist presumptions concerning gender and the distribution of the four humors contributed to the success of the disguise. At moments of misrule and with the identity of the obstreperous virago of ritual (Mad Meg and Mère Folle, for example) in question, the masquerading male could and did behave badly.[48] Moreover he/she did so with impunity: "In Normandy and Brittany, the husband might have to answer for [his wife's] crimes in court, and everywhere the *sexus imbecillus* might be punished less severely. The full weight of the law fell only on the ruling male."[49] Weak of will, women could not be held wholly responsible for their actions. Neither could a man who impersonated a woman so long as his masquerade remained intact. To be female, whether in truth or through the signification of clothes, was to possess a degree of license not accorded the male. Cognizant of the liberties granted to the *sexus imbecillus*, men dressed as women to push for social change. When rebellious infractions took place during the topsy-turvy times of carnival and other seasonal festivities, as seems often to have been the case, both the disguise and the defense were all the more effective.

THE DOUBLE TROUBLE OF TWINS

If festive license allowed gender and social codes to be violated without serious consequence, then staging plays in which cross-dressing was a critical plot element was particularly appropriate during carnival when the audience no less than the performers masked their identity.[50] In fact, the carnival humor of the *commedia erudita* of early sixteenth-century Italy was often staged when social order was inverted by absurdities, tricks, and deceptions. Niccolo Machiavelli's *La mandragola* and Ludovico Ariosto's *I suppositi, Il negromante*, and *La Lena* were all represented during carnival week.[51] So too were early performances of Bernardo Dovizi da Bibbiena's *La calandra*, a play in which "women and men [as well as] masters and servants repeatedly disguise themselves across gender and class lines" to the point where "gender demarcations are hard to come by." The first performance of *La calandra* was staged in Urbino on February 6, 1513, that is, on the Sunday before Lent. The second staging in Rome two years later occurred during carnival. Moreover, the play's debut was immediately followed by performances on Monday and Tuesday when the noble audience came, according to an anonymous chronicler, *in abito dissimulato*.[52] Audience disguise was not, however, restricted to pre-Lenten performances. Among the attractions Thomas Coryat chronicled on his trip to Venice in 1608 was a theatrical performance where he "observed certaine things that I never saw before … I saw women act" and "Cortezans came to this Comedy, but so disguised that a man cannot perceive them, for they wore double-maskes upon their faces" and donned black capes. They were not alone. "I saw some men also in the Play house, disguised in the same manner with double visards." In light of the extent of the full disguise Coryat details—faces hidden behind double masks and visors—it is surprising that he could distinguish the masked courtesans from the masked men "said to be their favorites."[53] The practice of attending the theater in disguise is a curious one. At the very least it must have enhanced plots of complex gender doubling and class inversion, affording the audience the same degree of license accorded the actors, which in light of Coryat's travel diary must have been a confounding delight to all.

Within the genre of *commedia erudite*, Bibbiena's *La calandra* clearly enjoyed preeminent popularity. The irresistibility of this "anarchic fantasy of sex
and one-upmanship" must surely be the result of the author's ingenuity in
recasting a classical source.[54] As many have noted, *La calandra* owes a debt to
Plautus's *Menaechmi* or *The Twin Brothers*. Yet Bibbiena's retelling of the tale of
the sons of the merchant Moschus separated at the age of seven and thereafter
entangled in a web of humorous confusion until they are once again united at
the play's conclusion departs from its classical model in a significant way. The
twin sons have become twins of different sexes, Lidio and Santilla, who also
goes by a feminization of her brother's name, Lidio femina. Moreover, each
one assumes the identity of the other and, as only comedic fate can have it, they
do so in a time and place that not only and inevitably allows their paths to repeatedly cross but demands that each masquerade as their twin. Contributing
to the intrigues of amorous pursuits that are the essence of *commedia erudita*
are the interventions of a magician, the bungling ineptitude of a cuckold husband, and the supporting roles played by each twin's servant. Near the end of
the play Santilla changes clothes with her servant, who also dresses as a man,
in order to hide the philandering escapades of Calandro's wife with her twin
brother. As Valeria Finucci states, "Almost every character, male or female,
changes attire and gender with such frequency that Bibbiena himself, apparently los[es] control of his own play."[55]

The same sort of antics take place in Ludovico Ariosto's *Orlando furioso*,
published first in 1516 and then in its definitive form in 1532. Here the twins
are Bradamante and Ricciardetto. Bradamante, who roams the woods dressed
in armor, falls asleep only to be seen by the daughter of the Spanish king.
Falling immediately in love, the princess advances toward the "knight" only
to discover that he is a she. Disappointed but ever hopeful that a miraculous
transformation will occur, the princess brings Bradamante to the castle for the
night. In the morning Bradamante flees and once home relates the adventure.
Her twin brother hears the tale, and with his curiosity piqued and libido raised
he goes to the castle to take his sister's place. In Ariosto's epic as in Bibbiena's
La calandra magic or rather presumed magic has its place. That night Ricciardetto tells the princess that the miracle she hoped for has indeed happened. A
nymph has changed her from a woman into a man. Moreover, in both Bibbiena's comedy and Ariosto's saga *vestirsi un altra persona* has an emphasis on
seeming rather than being that can be resolved only by admitting the fallacy of
sight and appealing to the unassailable truth disclosed by the sense of touch.
Ricciardetto encourages the happy but incredulous princess to touch as well
as look at the changes in his body while Calandro's equally disbelieving wife

laments the loss of what she can no longer feel. Lidio, who at this point is really his twin sister Lidio femina, is missing precisely what Bradamante/Ricciardetto has acquired. "I have touched him and felt him all over ... I feel he has lost that which is most prized."[56]

This appeal to touch, something endemic to many works of the period both within and beyond the borders of the Italian peninsula, must be considered in light of the overall play of ambiguity pervading an age Rosalie Colie characterized as one gripped by a *paradoxia epidemica*. In *Libro di natura d'amore,* first published in 1525 then followed by at least eleven sixteenth-century editions, Mario Equicola privileges touch over the remaining four senses. It is touch, not sight, that provides us with the most "varied, multiple, and continuous pleasure."[57] If this is the case, then in the context of plays like *La calandra* and epic romances such as *Orlando furioso*, clothes understood as visual "signes distinctive between sexe and sexe" are revealed as fallible when subjected to tactile inspection. Coupled with the appeal to the sense of touch, scenes of cross-dressing and re-cross-dressing whether on the stage or in the pages of a romance "constitute moments of high gender consciousness."[58] How were such moments of awareness processed? The answer to this query resides in remembering that in the end the player is unmasked, truth is always revealed, gender identity is reassumed, and order is restored. Yet it is worth remembering that if, as Butler and others have argued, identity is performative, then staged performance no less than dialogues that presented idealized portraits of courtiers and ladies could be utilized in different ways. Carnival masquerading could provide an effective model for social transgressions.

ONE *AND* THE OTHER: HERMAPHRODITES

When Aretino tells the courtesan La Zufolina that he knows there are those who wish to sleep with her for no other reason than to discover if she is in fact an *ermafrodito* or merely one in jest, he does so taking obvious delight in the *inganno*, or deception.[59] Aretino's letter stands in sharp contrast to Stubbes's *Anatomie of Abuses*. When Stubbes labels those who wear the apparel of the other "Hermaphroditi, that is, Monsters of both kindes, half women, half men," he does so with dismay and disdain for the "unnatural."[60] So which was it: a titillating jest or an unnatural horror? An answer is perhaps as elusive as determining the sex of this female/male. Depending on the texts referenced, the hermaphrodite represents prelapsarian harmony and human totality, an aesthetic ideal, or an example of nature gone awry.

A consideration of medical texts aside, two principal classical texts provide the bases for Renaissance opinions: Plato's *Symposium* (189e–190) and
Ovid's *Metamorphoses* (8. 285–388). In the first of these Aristophanes seeks
to explain "the real nature of human kind, and the change which it has undergone." Long, long ago, "There really was a man-woman ... a being which
was half male and half female." When these dual-sexed beings threatened to
revolt against the gods, they were bisected. Ever since the now distinct male
and female have sought to reunify their halves to resume their state of conjoined perfection. Ovid's account of the origins of the dual-sexed being is quite
different. The naiad Salmacis is overcome by love for the handsome youth
Hermaphroditus. Her feelings are not shared and Hermaphroditus spurns her
amorous overtures. Salmacis therefore devises a plan to secure his affections.
She hides by a spring waiting for the youth to stop and bathe. When he does,
she dives into the water, embraces him, and prays to the gods that she might
forever be united with him. Those dwelling on Mount Olympus answered her
heartfelt invocations.

The stories differ from one another in both chronology and tone. In the
Ovidian myth sexual distinction precedes sexual union. In the Aristophanic
tale it is the reverse. Moreover the conjoining of the handsome Hermaphroditus with the infatuated Salmacis is deformative as opposed to constitutive
of the complete flawlessness of the androgyne.[61] Over time both accounts of
the origins of the hermaphrodite were filtered through moralizing and biblical
texts. Marsilio Ficino, for example, synthesized Plato's *Symposium* with Paul's
first epistle to the Corinthians to formulate the Neoplatonic concept of love
as the mediator for agape.[62] In his *Dialoghi d'amore* of 1535, Leone Ebreo
opted to read the story from *Symposium* in light of Genesis. God's creation of
human kind in his own image, he contends, should be understood as Adam
embodying both sexes. He "combined in himself male and female without
division."[63] By contrast and in keeping with the medieval *Ovid moralisé*, Dante
has Guido Guinizelli declare in *Il Purgatorio* (24: 82–88), "Our sin was hermaphrodite ... because we ... follow[ed] [our carnal] appetites like beasts." As
Ann Rosalind Jones and Peter Stallybrass have observed, two dominant trends
have emerged in the analysis of the dual-sexed figure. "In the first, the hermaphrodite is read as the problem which a binary logic attempts to erase ... In
the second, the hermaphrodite is understood as the vanishing point of all binary logics, a figure which embodies the dissolution of male and female as
absolute categories."[64] They argue against both contentions. Identifying the
hermaphrodite as "the *production* of gender in Renaissance Europe," they see
"*either* the fixity of a binary logic *or* its dissolution" as problematic since "all

attempts to fix gender are ... revealed as *prosthetic*" and thus fetishistic.[65] The sixteenth-century French surgeon Ambroise Paré lends support to their view. In *Des monsters et prodiges* of 1573, Paré identifies four categories of hermaphroditic beings: 1) the male hermaphrodite in whom only the male sexual organs function, 2) the female hermaphrodite with only functional female organs, 3) the hermaphrodite with neither male nor female functional organs, and 4) the hermaphrodite in whom both male and female organs do function.[66] The social and legal implications of the last category were particularly problematic since it allowed for sex as well as gender identity to exist *in potentia*. On the one hand, the truly dual-sexed hermaphrodite, who, says Paré, has the reproductive capacity to perform *either* as a male *or* as a female, dissolves normative distinctions by the act of individual choice. On the other hand, this type of hermaphrodite reasserts constructed gender norms through the very act of making that choice, then acting upon it. Having decided which sex she/he will be, he/she puts on the clothes, or prosthetic props, proper to that choice. thereby allowing garments to function as "signes betwixt sexe and sexe" while effacing the notion of an essential sex beneath the clothes. Clearly this was the case with the dual-sexed "man ... who dressed as a woman" Jacques Du Clercq mentions in his *Mémoires*.[67] It was also true of Marie/Marin le Marcis.

Jacques Duval, whose *Des Hermaphrodits* contains the most complete listing of references to hermaphrodites up to its date of publication in 1614, reviewed the case. "We had been told about a girl who, having been baptized, named, nourished, raised, and always clothed like the other girls of her lot ... was finally recognized to be a man, and as such had carnal knowledge of a woman," not unlike the sodomizing, cross-dressed, and dual-sexed "man" reported in Du Clercq's *Mémoires*.[68] For this, the "poor woman-man" was to be paraded naked through the streets before being hanged, strangled, and finally burned. Duval was among the physicians called on by the court to review the evidence, namely Marie/Marin's body. Physical examination revealed a *"member viril"* that could discharge semen as well as urine. More relevant to the court proceedings was the fact that this "virile member" could contract, concealing itself within the body where it remained invisible to the eye but, significantly, vulnerable to the touch.[69] Although Duval was unable to identify definitively whether Marie/Marin was a man or a hermaphrodite, his discovery satisfied the judges enough for the court to rescind the death sentence. Curiously, however, Duval's detection of a semen-producing penis was not factored into the new judgment. Despite the presence of a penis Marie/Marin was ordered to dress as a woman for four years or until one gender declared itself over the other. Within ten years the issue was settled. According to Duval, "This womanly man is now restored to an even better manly state than he had before ... [He] undertakes, performs, and completes all duties pertaining to a man, he has a beard on his chin, and that which is necessary to content a woman, and to beget children with her." Jusepe de Ribera's portrait of Maddalena Ventura is a visual pendant to Duval's Marin-Marie. Pictured with her husband by her side and her child nursing at her engorged breast, the heavily bearded and hairy-chested Maddalena unabashedly meets the inspecting gaze of the viewer. Following a visit to the painter's studio in February 1631, the Venetian ambassador, who took note of Maddalena's beard and chest hair, declared her and, one can assume by extension, Ribera's painting to be a "marvelous thing."[70]

During the Renaissance period the hermaphroditic body was a multivalent site. As Kathleen Long, Ann Rosalind Jones, Peter Stallybrass, Patricia Parker, Lorraine Datson, Katharine Park, Julia Epstein, Ruth Gilbert, myself, and others have demonstrated, it was viewed as the embodiment of spiritual wholeness as well as a personified place of violence and possession. It was at once a monstrous thing and wondrous marvel, a being that both threatens and delights.[71] It provided satirists with a vehicle to criticize the court culture of Henri III of France. It also

FIGURE 4.2: *Sleeping Hermaphrodite* (detail), second century A.D. Paris, Musée du Louvre. Photo by the author.

supplied perplexed Europeans with a logical explanation for the behavior of the Native American "two-spirit," tribesmen who performed duties they gendered feminine. Additionally it proffered by way of the famed *Sleeping Hermaphrodite,* an aesthetic based upon the principle of conjoined contrarieties captured by the chiastic twist of the classical figure (figs. 4.2 and 4.3).[72] The varied readings imposed on the hermaphroditic body during the Renaissance are perhaps a product of its resistance to the prevailing system of identifying one thing against its opposite. In contrast to male and female, the hermaphrodite refuses to align itself with the associative values that comprise contrariety (male, right, one, good, or female, left, multiple, evil). Instead it occupies the space between polarities and in doing so offers possibilities of being that go beyond binary limits.

By the end of the seventeenth century, the hermaphrodite had essentially become a medical anomaly, a person rather than a vehicle to convey an ideology. In 1686, one physician wrote to another describing one of the patients in the women's ward at the hospital of St. Jacques in Toulouse. "The visage is feminine and also agreeable. The throat is lovely and also the breasts are well

FIGURE 4.3: *Sleeping Hermaphrodite,* second century A.D. Paris, Musée du Louvre. Photo by the author.

formed ... [but] at the center of th[e] fente, hangs a virile member of considerable thickness and strength." This member is "well formed" and capable of a
"strong erection."[73] There is no mention of illicit sexual activity as was the case
with Marie/Marin, the dual-sexed "man" mentioned by Du Clercq, or Marie
Germain, who is cited in Paré's *Des monsters et prodiges*, and then again in
Michel de Montaigne's travel journal.[74] The physician's letter records an observation of anatomical fact. It does not pass moral judgment.

Pythagorean contrariety would become Cartesian dualism. Reductionism
is the principle of incompatibility that underlies the assumptions of both philosophical systems, establishing the body as a site of signification and a vehicle
for expression. Reductionism, of course, denies interactions between two distinct, mutually exclusive concepts, such as masculinity/femininity or mind/
body, suggesting that the gap between them cannot be bridged, yet during
the Renaissance that divide was crossed, often with impunity. If gender is, as
Judith Butler argues, "the *appearance of substance* ... a constructed identity, a
performative accomplishment" in which the "mundane social audience" participates and hence "comes to believe," then clothing can be understood as a
constituting, cultural convention rife with possibility.[75] However, in contrast
to the body, clothing was far less stable. Whether or not audience and actors
alike came to believe in the illusion did not affect their engagement with it as a
strategy to act or act up as the other. Indeed, given the popularity of incidences
of cross-dressing on the stage, in the pages of chivalric romances, and during
carnival and times of sanctioned misrule, on city streets and country lanes, it
is both useful and appropriate to think about cross-dressing—indeed any form
of dressing and self-fashioning—as a performative act.

Butler is surely correct in viewing gender identity and performance, both
ritualized and theatrical, as coming together through repetition, which "is
at once a reenactment and reexperiencing of a set of meanings already socially established." In this way "social laws" are rendered "explicit."[76] During
the Renaissance, as in other periods, the day-to-day performance of gender
identity—the putting on of clothes in one's wardrobe—made manifest these
laws and thereby reinscribed the binary frame. However, at other times and in
situations that were not routine, performance embraced inversions and played
with ambivalences. While it is true that on occasion the inversions enacted during extraordinary times provided a model for transgressions aimed at initiating
a process of social change through acts of civil disobedience, by and large such
actions were carried out at times and in situations and places that left no doubt
who was who. This pervasive capacity to see beneath a veil of clothes and behind the pretense of a mask underscores the importance of not underestimating

either the savvy of an audience or the entrenched depth of a social system. Reflecting on the question posed at the beginning of this chapter—was gender inversion during the Renaissance a transgression or was it instead as normative as the very norms it opposed?—I would suggest that more often than not it is the latter. In fact, "transgression," at least with respect to dress, was coded by the same conception of social performance and ritualized behavior that determined adherence to societal norms. Ultimately, the curtain fell on the players, juridical review passed judgment, the short-lived license of carnival and misrule came to an end, and the status quo remained firmly in place.

CHAPTER FIVE

Sex, Religion, and the Law: Disciplining Desire

N. S. DAVIDSON

The word *taboo* was introduced to the English language by Capt. James Cook. In his *Voyage to the Pacific Ocean*, Cook reported that "when any particular thing is prohibited to be eaten or made use of, [the people of Tonga] say it is *taboo*." The book provides examples of people, places, objects, and actions that were set apart in this way: as James King—who accompanied Cook on his final voyage and subsequently brought his narrative to publication—explained, the word is "used to express any thing sacred, or eminent, or devoted."[1] Cook's *Voyage* was hugely popular in the 1780s and 1790s, and in the following century or so, the term he had adopted from the south Pacific was extended both geographically to other cultures and conceptually to a wide range of restrictions.[2] Its most celebrated appearance is probably in the title of Sigmund Freud's *Totem und Tabu*,[3] where the notion is applied in particular to the prohibition on incest. Sexual relations with, and marriage to, members of the same clan was, Freud thought, forbidden in all cultures and societies. Violation of that taboo was everywhere punished forcibly, and even by death, in order to avert the greater danger to the whole community that it was believed would follow automatically without a suitable act of atonement and purification.[4] Freud insisted that the prohibition had no rational base;[5] it could not even spring from concern for the health of any children born of an incestuous relationship, since it applied to couples who were related only by marriage and affinity.[6] He traced the taboo instead to the universal infantile desire of boys for their mothers and sisters, a desire from which most males free themselves as they grow up, but that survives, unconsciously, in them all: the desire and the prohibition thus coexist.[7] In more recent times, Freud believed, the taboo had been reinforced by religious and legal restrictions, but its origins lay deep in the human psyche.[8]

The anthropologist Claude Lévi-Strauss, writing in the 1940s, also believed in the universality of the incest taboo.[9] Indeed, he argued that the prohibition on incest was "*the* prohibition in the most general form, the one perhaps to which all others ... are related as particular cases."[10] In his view, though, its origins should be sought not in the unconscious, but in the social context of human societies, and in particular in the use of women by men as objects of exchange. If sex and marriage were confined within a single family, that family would be cut off from the wider community. The continuous and reciprocal circulation of women, on the other hand, serves to create alliances between families.[11] The incest taboo is not therefore simply a ban on undesirable forms of sexual behavior; it serves a positive purpose, integrating smaller units into the larger group and so guaranteeing cohesion and solidarity within society as a whole.[12]

The incest taboo has of course been discussed and explained many times, especially by scholars in anthropology and sociology.[13] Not everyone, though, has shared the conviction that incest is the central element in prohibitions on sexual activity. Judith Butler, for instance, has argued that the prohibition on homosexual practices must precede the prohibition on incest, since the incest taboo presupposes the generality of heterosexual desire.[14] Mary Douglas prefers, in her hugely influential *Purity and Danger*, first published in 1966, to set the incest taboo within a broader awareness of society's need to protect its understanding of "the distinctive categories of the universe."[15] Taboos control any actions that seem to challenge the accepted classifications, such as the distinctions between human and animal, family and nonfamily, or married and nonmarried; each one therefore "reduces intellectual and social disorder" and protects "a vision of a good community."[16] Douglas holds, however, to the idea that taboos are effective because it is believed that any breach of the prohibitions will be punished automatically, and will thus invite danger onto either the offender or the whole community. Taboos are thus seen as a function of the natural working of the universe.[17]

A belief in the universality of taboos is nonetheless a commonplace among many modern scholars. Maureen Quilligan has argued recently, for example, that "the interdiction against incest is a constant in all human societies, pivotal at all periods and in all places."[18] But that belief has also been challenged. Toward the end of his life, Michel Foucault suggested that incest was not seen as a major problem before the nineteenth century, and that the assumption that its prohibition was universal in earlier times was no more than a reflection back on the past of modern preoccupations.[19] That is not to insist that there were no laws against incest or other "taboo" sexual activities in the past, but merely that such rules may not be innate in either individuals or communities. In fact, it is hard to see how the universal explanations for the incest taboo can account for the extended detail of premodern laws against the marriage of family members or for the widespread approval of celibacy in Western societies before the Reformation, let alone the many other legislative attempts to police sexual behavior that did not involve incest. What is at issue is whether taboos are—as Mary Douglas has said—"spontaneous devices" supported by a "community-wide complicity";[20] or whether we are dealing simply with a set of rules drawn up by those in power. Douglas herself has suggested, for example, that "the taboo-maintaining rules will be as repressive as the leading members of society want them to be ... when the controllers of opinion want a different way of life, the taboos will lose credibility."[21] This latter view certainly helps to explain the diversity of both rules and behavior in late-medieval and early-modern Western Europe, a diversity that talk of "taboos" tends to conflate.

Even at the end of the Middle Ages, in fact, the universality of contemporary rules about sexual behavior was questioned. In the late fourteenth century, for instance, John Gower observed that the world must have been populated in the earliest times by the incestuous unions of the children of Adam and Eve; similarly, the children of Noah's three sons must have been responsible for repeopling the earth after the Flood. Indeed, at the time of Christ, he claimed, marriage between cousins was common; only later was marriage within the second and third degree (that is, of individuals who shared grandparents or great-grandparents) prohibited.[22] Nonetheless, by the beginning of the fifteenth century, a familiar list of sexual offenses had been developed in Catholic Europe, based in part on Biblical injunctions, though reinforced also by the provisions of ancient Roman law. The key text was Leviticus chapter 18, part of the Jewish Holiness Code, which warns the Children of Israel against a series of immoral acts said to be commonly practiced by the peoples who had occupied the land before them, thought at the time to include incest, sex with a menstruating woman, adultery, male homosexual behavior, and bestiality: "Defile not ye yourselves in any of these things: for in all these the nations are defiled which I cast out before you: And the land is defiled: therefore I do visit the iniquity thereof upon it, and the land itself vomiteth out her inhabitants."[23] But the list of offenses inherited by the Christian West was often extended. At the end of the fourth century, for example, Jerome urged widows not to remarry, despite Paul's explicit statement that remarriage was acceptable.[24] Similarly, whereas the rules in Leviticus 18 seem to prohibit marriage to couples only within the first degree, the Fourth Lateran Council in 1215 confirmed the ban on marriages up to the fourth degree—that is, of individuals who shared a common great-great-grandparent.[25]

So although there was no explicit concept of "taboo" in the fifteenth, sixteenth, and seventeenth centuries, there was a widely acknowledged consensus about the need to restrict some forms of sexual behavior. A typical list of these sexual sins was provided by Thomas Gainsford in his *Rich Cabinet* of 1616:

> Lechery is a filthinesse of such beastly varietie, that men may sinne with men, women with women: man may sinne by himselfe, by or with his owne wife, with beasts in abhominable prostitutions: with their own blouds and kinred in incestuous maner: with other mens wives in adulterous copulation: with all sorts in filthy licentiousnesse: and in all, both abuse GOD, and confound themselves in body and soule.[26]

Gainsford's list conveniently gathers these offenses into two groups. First, forbidden behavior: sexual acts that could not lead to reproduction, such as same-sex activities and bestiality that defied the established boundaries of gender and species; masturbation; and heterosexual acts thought likely to impede or avoid conception, such as anal sex, sex beyond the age of fertility, or sex while the woman was menstruating or pregnant.[27] At the same time, Gainsford lists behavior that could lead to reproduction but involved partners whose relationship was improper: sex with family members, whether related by blood or marriage. Leviticus 18 had condemned sexual relations with the wife or husband of a blood relative; in line with Genesis 2, however, where husband and wife are said to become "one flesh," both consanguinity and affinity were routinely seen as impediments to lawful marriage.[28] Adultery—the only sexual offense listed in the Ten Commandments—was unacceptable, too.[29] Within the Catholic tradition, sex with male or female religious (monks, friars, nuns) was also outlawed, for members of the monastic and regular orders were believed to be betrothed spiritually to Christ. If they had sex with a layperson, therefore, they were guilty of adultery; if they had sex with each other, they were guilty of incest.[30]

Sexual offenses of this kind were often characterized in the medieval and early-modern periods as crimes not only against God, who had legislated clearly against them in the Bible, but also against nature. Nature was regularly seen as God's representative and agent on earth: in the fifteenth century, for instance, the celebrated canonist Niccolò de' Tudeschi, known as Panormitanus, explained, "Whenever humans sin against nature whether in sexual intercourse, worshipping idols, or any other unnatural act, the church may always exercise its jurisdiction ... For by such sins God Himself is offended, since He is the author of nature."[31] Clearly, sins against nature included more than just sexual offenses (Panormitanus later mentions usury as well as idolatry), but all such offenses were prohibited by God and nature alike. And since God's law and nature's law were in turn seen as consistent with reason—as Thomas Aquinas had argued in the fourteenth century, "the first rule of reason is natural law"[32]—they were accessible to all and must be obeyed by all. The Spanish Dominican Juan Ginés de Sepúlveda therefore insisted in his *Democrates primus* of 1535, "The laws of nature apply to all men and every time": not even God himself can abrogate them.[33]

There was some disagreement about the scope of natural law. Some argued that even animals observed its provisions. John Bishop, for example, repeated the story told by Aristotle of the camel that was tricked by its owner into intercourse with its own mother, hidden for the purpose under a blanket: "But after he had served her, knowing by the falling off of the clothe, that it was his damme, for just anger killed his keeper with his teethe."[34] It was usually claimed, though, that it was the recognition and observance of divine and natural law that distinguished humans from animals. In the 1480s, Pico della Mirandola used both classical and Islamic precedents as support for the insistence that "they who have deviated from divine law become beasts";[35] a century later, Barthélemy Batt urged young men to consider "how foule, how filthie, and also how unseemely for man this lust and pleasure is, which maketh us (being the workmanship of the divine God) not only like to beastes, but also to swine, goates dogges, and the most savage and bruitish beastes in the worlde."[36]

Whether natural law applied to all creatures or only to humans, however, it was regularly asserted that nature provided the best guide to right living. As Bartolomeo Scala maintained in his *Ducendane sit uxor sapienti*, written at the end of the 1450s, "He who follows nature as the best guide to living never errs."[37] But here was a paradox: for it was God, and nature, that were responsible for sexual desire. God had clearly ordered humans—even before the Fall—to "be fruitful, and multiply, and replenish the earth,"[38] and God and

nature had therefore provided them with the ability to reproduce: as Aquinas
explained, "The female ... is according to the tendency of nature ... directed
to the work of procreation. Now the tendency of the nature of a species as a
whole derives from God, who is the general author of nature."[39] And sex was
made pleasurable precisely to encourage that reproduction.[40] Luther made the
same point in the sixteenth century:

> To conceive children is as deeply implanted in nature as eating and drink-
> ing are. That is why God gave us and implanted into our body genitals,
> blood vessels, fluids, and everything else necessary to accomplish it. The
> person who wants to prevent this and keep nature from doing what it
> wants to do and must do is simply preventing nature from being na-
> ture.[41]

What made sexual acts sinful was engaging in them purely for pleasure, or
in ways that made conception impossible. That was why marriage had been
ordained by God: to tame and control the sexual desires implanted by nature.
The celebrated humanist Poggio Bracciolini, who married in his mid-sixties,
made this clear: "In what way can one who abstains from marriage avoid
being an adulterer or a fornicator or becoming more attached to another more
detestable vice? ... One should embrace the married state, since it is a more
virtuous life."[42] What was permitted, therefore, was intercourse within marriage for the purpose of procreation. But this did not mean that every form of
reproductive sexual activity within marriage was acceptable. There remained
a strong sense that—despite nature's dispositions—sexual activity was invariably touched with some element of sinfulness. Erasmus, for example, argued
that marriage was designed for those too weak to remain chaste; and even
in marriage, he said, intercourse should be infrequent, a matter of necessity
rather than of joy. "Indeed, even the sort of physical contact that is unavoid-
able should be as chaste as possible. In the begetting of children, infrequent
rather than regular intercourse is more successful, and the remedy is intended
for our inescapable natural weakness, not for perverted lust."[43] Of course,
not all "natural" intercourse in marriage did result in pregnancy; what mattered was that the couple should be open to that possibility. Francis de Sales
put the point clearly in 1609: "The marriage debt should always be paid and
performed as faithfully and frankly, as if it were with the hope and desire of
children, although on some occasions there might be no such expectation."[44]
Sexual activities outside marriage, or for any other reason even within
marriage, were thus "unnatural," especially if they were designed solely for

pleasure or to avoid reproduction. Masturbation, sex with the woman on top, anal intercourse, same-sex activities, and bestiality were all therefore condemned;[45] "those lusts," in fact, claimed Samuel Pufendorf, "which have no other end but obscene titillation are inconsistent with natural law."[46] All such activities were, furthermore, likely to be punished by God and nature alike. In some cases, the punishment would fall directly on the individual or individuals concerned, perhaps as some sort of serious illness. At other times, it might fall on the child born of the sinful union. In 1600, for instance, an anonymous pamphlet suggested that in the previous January, a female servant had given birth to a "monstrous, deformed infant" in her uncle's household in Colwall, Herefordshire, after she had had sex with two of her uncle's sons, her cousins. The author describes this monstrous birth as an example of the sort of "punishment" due for all such "fleshly lusts and desires," naming not just incest but also "Onanisme, Whoredome, Adulterie and Fornication, with other Sodomitical sinnes of uncleannesse and pollutions" as likely attractors of such retribution.[47] On occasion, though, when sexual offenses of this kind had been tolerated for any length of time, it was expected that the punishment would fall on the community as a whole rather than on the individual offenders, in the form of epidemics, earthquakes, or some other environmental or communal disaster. In 1535, Gonzalo Fernández de Oviedo y Valdés thus explained the defeat of the peoples of America by the Spanish as God's reaction to their "abominable sins": sodomy, cannibalism, and human sacrifice.[48] Pius V similarly explained the wars that had afflicted Italy in the sixteenth century as a punishment for the sexual sins of the Italian people.[49] As God had punished the sinners of Sodom and Gomorrah and their neighbors in the time of Abraham, so he would punish their successors in the present.

The intellectual structure of this approach to sexual behavior provided the framework within which the secular authorities of late-medieval and early-modern Europe acted against sexual crimes. When we examine the legislative and judicial records of the time, we find that the language used echoes that of the theologians and lawyers we have already encountered. The Portuguese law against sodomy, for instance, promulgated by Afonso V in the mid-fifteenth century is characteristic:

> The sin of Sodomy appears, above all sins, the most vile, unclean and impure; no other can be found that is so abhorrent to God and the earth. Not only does it cause offence to the Creator of nature, who is God, but

one can also say that the whole creation, both heavenly and human, is offended by it. So dreadful indeed is this sin, that when men speak of it, even if they do not act on it, the air itself is unable to tolerate it, but is naturally corrupted and loses its natural virtue. For this sin, God brought the Flood upon the earth; for this sin, he destroyed the cities of Sodom and Gomorrah; for this sin, he destroyed the Knights Templar in one day.[50]

Such expressions are typical,[51] and the fear of divine punishment, and of the social disruption that could be caused by such sins, prompted many governments to prescribe the death penalty for crimes "against nature." In 1650, for instance, the republican government in England insisted that both incest and adultery be punished by execution.[52] And even where the death penalty was not imposed by the state, the punishments laid down by law were severe. The *Ordonnantie van de polityen* enacted by the States of Holland in 1580 prescribed fifty years' exile for any married person, male or female, who committed adultery, whether the other party was married or unmarried,[53] while in sixteenth-century Spain, a husband who believed that his wife had committed adultery was legally entitled to murder both her and her lover.[54]

Unlike the law in Holland, however, the Spanish legislation made no reference to adultery committed by a married man with an unmarried woman. This obvious double standard was motivated, in part at least, by a desire to discourage behavior that might cast doubt on the legitimacy of any children born to an adulterous wife. This question was of particular urgency in Spain because of the local preoccupation with *limpieza de sangre*, purity of blood. The insistence on knowing for certain the father and mother of any individual had sprung from a belief that an infamous act committed by one person created a stain (*macula* in Latin) that would be passed on indelibly to future descendants, making them also liable to commit the same crimes.[55] Such thinking was enshrined in a series of statutes that banned converted Jews and their descendants from public office, universities, guilds, cathedral chapters, and religious orders, and also from employment by Inquisition tribunals.[56] Similar restrictions applied to descendants of other non-Catholics—Muslims and heretics[57]—and of anyone with ancestors who had not been noble. The military confraternity of Molina de Aragón, northeast of Guadalajara, for example, refused admittance in the sixteenth century to applicants descended from anyone employed in manual or servile labor as well as from non-Catholics.[58] In France, too, we find an insistence that "true" nobility was defined by purity of descent: Christophe Bonours's *Eugéniarétilogie ou Discours de la vraie noblesse*, published in 1616, defined nobility as an "ancient and immemorial purity of free blood, not mixed with the servile and the vile."[59] In the European colonies in the New World, descent from members of the defeated American peoples or from enslaved Africans was often viewed in the same way, so that any sexual relations between Europeans and natives or Africans was considered an offense, one that was at times treated as almost more serious than any other. In the mid-seventeenth century, for example, a Jesuit missionary in Chiloé, an island off the southern coast of Chile, wrote to Rome for permission to marry Spanish men and women within the prohibited degrees in order to avoid the need for them otherwise to marry non-Europeans: incest was obviously considered the less shocking option.[60]

In much of this thinking, the focus was the act itself rather than the intention of the actors: an act of incest committed by two people ignorant of their relationship was still incest. And frequently, legislation was issued by government even when there was no obvious moral panic to justify it. The republic of Dubrovnik issued its first law on sodomy in 1494, prescribing decapitation for those found guilty, but the local records contain no suggestion that same-sex activity was widespread in the city at the time.[61] Sexual offenses were seen as a threat to the safety of the community at all times, even when they were not prevalent. And the coincidence of secular and ecclesiastical concerns about sexual crimes was further illustrated by the involvement of both state and church tribunals in their prosecution. The allocation of responsibility for prosecuting sodomy is instructive here. In the kingdom of Aragón, sodomy was a matter for the Inquisition; in the kingdom of Castile, for secular courts. Venice, Florence, Lucca, and Dubrovnik established lay magistracies in the fifteenth century to deal with sodomy; in Rome, Pope Paul IV entrusted the offense to the Inquisition in 1557, a decision reversed by his successor, Pius IV, in 1560. Two years later, however, Pius confirmed the decision of King João III to entrust sodomy to the Inquisition in Portugal. In England, sodomy was a matter for ecclesiastical jurisdiction until 1533–1534, when it was made a felony and transferred to the lay courts; legislation under the Catholic Queen Mary reversed that policy in 1553, but her Protestant sister Elizabeth I confirmed it again in 1563. Such changes of jurisdiction did not, however, affect the consensus of both church and state that such a heinous sin required both prosecution and punishment.

The appearance of unanimity can nonetheless mask significant differences in both attitude and policy even at the highest levels, for the precise details of what was sinful varied from place to place and could change over time. Such differences were sometimes the product of significant disagreements about matters of basic principle. The Spanish Jesuit Tomás Sánchez, for example, writing at the turn of the sixteenth and seventeenth centuries, insisted that the only "natural" position for intercourse, even for a married couple, was the so-called missionary position, with the woman on her back and the man above and facing her. All other positions, Sánchez insisted, were to some degree sinful.[62] The French physician Nicolas Venette, writing later in the seventeenth century, agreed that marital sex with the woman on top was to be condemned. He argued, however, that marital sex with the man behind the woman was "natural and anatomical"; it was in fact preferable, he said, because it was "the most natural and the least voluptuous" position possible.[63]

At other times, differences of opinion arose from debates about the precise meaning and interpretation of the accepted Biblical injunctions on sexual behavior. Early Protestant reformers were all deeply critical of the Roman church's gradual extension in the Middle Ages of the incest prohibitions set out in Leviticus 18; they were equally dismissive of the papacy's claim that it had the authority necessary to issues dispensations from those restrictions, as exemplified most famously, perhaps, in Julius II's permission issued in December 1503 for Prince Henry of England to marry his brother Arthur's widow, Catherine of Aragon, in defiance of the wording of Leviticus 18.16.[64] Luther himself argued, in his *Babylonian Captivity* of 1520, that incest laws should be based on the prescriptions of Leviticus 18 alone.[65] He seems not to have noticed at that point that the text of Leviticus 18 omits any explicit reference to sexual relations between a man and his daughter; and it was only in 1522 that Luther quietly added that relationship, without further explanation, to his own list of "the persons related by consanguinity and affinity who are forbidden to marry according to the Scriptures, Leviticus 18."[66] Other reformers in time did acknowledge openly that scriptural guidance on incest was insufficient, and that the church had as a result to devise its own list of prohibitions.[67] But different Protestant denominations then produced variant lists. One disagreement centered on the marriage of cousins. Melanchthon, in Germany, believed that first cousins should not be permitted to marry;[68] but the *Table of Kindred and Affinity*, which lists the unions considered incestuous by the Church of England, made no mention of cousins at all.[69]

Definitions of sodomy varied as well. In Lucca, the secular magistracy known as the *Offizio sopra l'onestà*, established in 1448, focused its attention on cases of anal penetration, whether of females or of males.[70] In Portugal, by contrast, the Inquisition claimed jurisdiction only over cases where anal penetration was accompanied by ejaculation, at least until the middle of the seventeenth century.[71] Swiss tribunals seem to have made little or no distinction when deciding how to punish two men found guilty of anal intercourse;

in Florence, however, the *Ufficiali di notte*, created in 1442, routinely punished adult men who allowed others to sodomize them with harsher penalties than men who had not taken that role, a policy that was subsequently formalized in law in 1542.[72] And attitudes to sexual relations between women remained even more uncertain. The Apostle Paul seems to condemn such acts in the same passage in which he condemns acts between men.[73] Since the focus of medieval and early-modern thinking was the misuse of potentially procreative sex, however, activities involving two women were not always viewed so seriously in those periods. The Criminal Code issued in 1532 by the Emperor Charles V did indeed make sex between women an offense punishable by death;[74] but the English buggery statute issued in the following year made no mention of women at all, even though it did prescribe the death penalty for sex between men.[75]

There were significant differences in the type and frequency of punishments issued for sodomy, too. In fifteenth-century Zurich, only about 1 percent of the death sentences handed down by the Council were for same-sex acts, while in Bruges, over 21 percent of executions were for sodomy.[76] Attitudes could also vary over time within a single jurisdiction. In several Italian cities, rates of prosecution for sodomy declined across the fifteenth, sixteenth, and seventeenth centuries, and the death penalty was applied less frequently despite the unchanged requirements of the law.[77] In Portugal, however, the number of prosecutions for sodomy increased significantly in the seventeenth century: Portuguese Inquisition tribunals in fact dealt with more cases between 1620 and 1644 than in the whole of the sixteenth century.[78]

In cases of rape, however, we find that the courts' response was often rather lenient. Successful convictions were in fact rare except when the victim was young and a virgin. When she was sexually experienced, her attacker frequently escaped without any serious punishment at all, and if she was married, the act of rape was frequently seen as more an offense against her husband than against her.[79] Some states failed even to register rape as a crime. Holland, for example, had no explicit law on rape, and the rape of a married woman was often viewed as nothing more than a case of adultery, even when the offender was a close blood relative.[80] In France, it was sometimes claimed that the rape of a prostitute was no crime at all unless she was married.[81]

In the seventeenth century, a more fundamental intellectual prompt for changing attitudes to sexual crimes resulted from a significant evolution in the understanding of nature. As we have seen, throughout the medieval and early-modern periods, divine and natural law were generally taken to be identical. By the middle of the seventeenth century, though, this easy assimilation was coming under question. In his first major work, written between 1604 and 1606, Hugo Grotius had stated confidently that "just as the will of God—constituting the norm of justice ... is revealed to us through nature, so also is it revealed through the Scriptures."[82] Twenty years later, however, in his *De jure belli et pacis*, Grotius seems to remove the priority of the will of God over nature, arguing instead that "the Law of Nature is so unalterable, that God himself cannot change it. For tho' the Power of God be infinite, yet we may say, that there are some Things to which this infinite Power does not extend."[83] God cannot will, for instance, that the sum of two and two should be anything other than four, or that what is intrinsically evil should not be evil. Natural law is therefore independent of the will of God. Indeed, in the preliminary discourse of the book, Grotius insists that *"the Mother of Natural Law is human Nature itself."*[84]

This sort of thinking had important implications for sexual behavior. Grotius himself acknowledged that seeking for natural reasons to prohibit the marriage of persons related by blood or affinity was "a Task not only difficult but impracticable."[85] The prohibitions of Leviticus 18 are therefore "not derived from the mere Law of Nature," even though they are an expression of God's will.[86] Similar arguments were put forward later in the century by both Samuel Pufendorf and Christian Thomasius: the former suggested that even the marriage of a parent and his or her child might not be contrary to the law of nature, while the latter claimed explicitly that no marriage restrictions could be justified on that basis.[87] Thomasius similarly cast doubt on the view that natural law prohibited bigamy.[88]

These scholars were not, of course, arguing that incest and bigamy should be legalized—only that they were not contrary to the law of nature. But in so doing, they were making a clear distinction between the law of God and the law of nature. And increasingly we find that the notion of nature was separated off from questions of theology, and so also from questions of ethics. That distinction was already apparent toward the end of the sixteenth century in Jean Jacques Boissard's *Emblematum liber*: "Nature grants that man can live; virtue that he can live well."[89] In this way, nature was identified with the material world rather than with the world created by human culture, and the natural world was thus gradually divested of obvious moral intentions. As early as 1559, for instance, the Dutch physician Levinus Lemnius, while not openly denying that monstrous births should be interpreted as punishments for sin, had explained such births in purely natural and nonjudgmental terms: as a result of a faulty womb, or corrupt seed, or sex during the woman's period.[90]

And once "nature" had broken free from theology, it could become an independent source of authority for human behavior. Such thinking was not in fact unprecedented. In the early fourteenth century, Pietro d'Abano, a physician and philosopher who taught in both Paris and Padua, made use of a purely naturalistic explanation for the desire felt by some men for anal intercourse. In these men, Pietro claimed, the passage that conveyed semen to the penis was blocked, so that it could only be released into the anus. They therefore needed stimulus by vigorous friction in that area to provoke an ejaculation. Sodomy was therefore for them (though not for all men) a natural solution to an innate physical problem that was not curable, and for which they could not be held morally accountable.[91] By the early sixteenth century, an even more subversive argument in favor of anal intercourse had been developed by Antonio Vignali, one of the founders of the Sienese Accademia degli Intronati, in his *La cazzaria*, first published in the 1530s. One of the participants in this dialogue, Arsiccio, insists that the belief that anal intercourse is "against Nature" is "a thing beyond all the imagination of Nature. And if Nature had not wanted men to bugger each other, she would not have made it such a pleasant thing." Indeed, "the opposite is true," he continues, for the anus receives the penis as easily as does the vagina.[92] About one hundred years later, a similar argument was deployed by Antonio Rocco, a Franciscan in Venice, in his *L'Alcibiade fanciullo a scola*, one of whose characters insists that "actions are natural when nature inclines us to them." That sodomy therefore "should not be called 'against nature'—and indeed is not 'against nature'—is clearly demonstrated by the law of nature itself."[93]

A fascinating parallel to this type of thinking can be found in Isaac de Benserade's almost contemporaneous play, *Iphis et Iante*, first produced in Paris during the carnival season of 1634. The play is based on a fable in Ovid's *Metamorphoses*, which tells the story of Iphis, a girl who had been brought up as a boy by her mother because her father had vowed to kill the child if his wife gave birth to a daughter. In Ovid's version, Iphis is then betrothed by her father to a neighbor's daughter, named Iante. As the wedding approaches, her mother (who of course knows the truth about her) and Iphis pray in desperation to Isis, who saves the day by transforming Iphis into a man. What is interesting in Benserade's telling of the story is that, in contrast to Ovid's version, it is only after the wedding that the miraculous transformation of Iphis takes place. This allows the author to dwell on the reciprocal love of the two women before the wedding, and, still more startlingly, on their continuing passion for each other even after Iante has discovered that Iphis is a woman. Iphis insists after her true identity is revealed that her love as a woman for Iante is natural: "I showed you my heart, you saw how it burned … Your eyes saw a heart that was reduced to cinders, a heart that your glance had already consumed … a heart that nature had made unlike the hearts of others."[94] Iante agrees: "Our hearts were injured by the same wound; not to have loved each other would have been to force nature."[95] The fable of Iphis and Iante of course made a very appropriate story for a carnival play, given its origin in the world turned upside down of same-sex desire. But its argument that the love the two women had for each other was natural clearly implied that they could not be held responsible morally for their emotional and nuptial preference.

An insistence on the naturalness of sexual desire appears also in some thinking about relations between men and women. Far from insisting that sexual activities were licit only when they led to (or could potentially lead to) procreation, some writers openly rejected the notion that intercourse for any other purpose should always be condemned. In the early sixteenth century, for example, the Scottish philosopher John Major claimed that it was no more a sin to have sex for pleasure than to eat a beautiful apple for the pleasure of it.[96] Major would never, of course, have applied the same reasoning to sexual activity outside marriage, or to same-sex activities between men or women. But the idea that sexual pleasure was its own justification, irrespective of whether it might lead to procreation, was potentially applicable to all sexual activities, and thus subversive of traditional views.

It is clear, too, that the official views espoused by the authorities of church and state were not always shared by their subjects. In some cases, we find that expectations within society were stricter than those set out in theology or the law. Luther, for example, had argued that marriage was a purely civil matter, which should not be dissolved because of religious differences. As far as he was concerned, therefore, a marriage between a man and a woman of different faiths remained valid.[97] In the Lutheran city of Augsburg, however, we find that cross-confessional marriages of the kind that Luther had refused to condemn became increasingly uncommon in the later sixteenth century and were rare after 1648, even though they remained completely legal under the city's laws.[98] German guilds, too, frequently required a higher standard of sexual morality of their members than the authorities of either church or state: guild masters whose wives gave birth less than nine months after their marriage were regularly expelled, for instance.[99]

On the other hand, we can also point to cases where behavior that was clearly condemned by the law was nonetheless tolerated within society. This was particularly true among populations that were mobile, or that were resident in territories far from the centers of government, where the established rules of sexual behavior were almost impossible to enforce effectively. Concerned by reports of settlers who had entered bigamous marriages in the New World, for instance, the Spanish Crown ordered local bishops in the Americas in 1544 to investigate the life history of any males who appeared to be living apart from their first wives. The fact that this legislation had to be reissued in 1565, 1569, and 1579 suggests that the bishops' enquiries did little to reduce the problem.[100] In South America, too, despite the official disapproval of sexual relations between Europeans and native Americans, marriages between Spaniards and native women were common. After the defeat of the final Inca ruler in Peru, Tupac Amaru, by the Spanish in 1572, for example, his niece, known as Beatriz, was married to a Spanish soldier named Martín de Loyola, a nephew of Ignatius Loyola, the founder of the Jesuits. Their daughter Lorenza was later to marry a son of Francisco Borja, the Jesuits' third general.[101]

But evidence of popular toleration can be found in Europe, too. Even though the Catholic Church prohibited the marriage of couples related within the fourth degree[102]—meaning that the wedding even of third cousins should not have been countenanced—such marriages were familiar in the village of Saint-André-les-Alpes in southeastern France. Similarly, records survive there of cases where two, or even three, siblings from one family married two, or even three, siblings from another family. Some families would extend these arrangements over time and agree on a series of such marriages for two or three generations. Even though these relationships were considered incestuous by the Church, they were acceptable within the community because they helped to consolidate local alliances. They also served to reduce the cost of the marriage when a brother and sister from one family married a sister and brother from another, since the dowries exchanged between the two families were usually of equal value.[103] Elsewhere, tolerance of same-sex activities was common.[104] And comments reported in the records of Inquisition tribunals in Spain indicate a relatively relaxed view of extramarital heterosexual relationships. Bartolomé Donat, for instance, a tinworker tried in Granada in 1605, was reported to have said that "having carnal relations with a woman, even if she is married, is no mortal sin ... if you pay for it."[105]

Late-medieval and early-modern thinking about sexual offenses continued, broadly speaking, to be based on Scripture. God's instruction to humans to multiply was recorded in Genesis, and in order to enable and encourage that reproduction, he had also implanted in them a natural sexual desire. But the prohibitions recorded in Leviticus—against incest, sex with a menstruating woman, adultery, same-sex activities, and bestiality—set limits to the occasions on which they could satisfy that desire. These prohibitions were held to be an expression not only of God's law but also of the law of nature, a law that was accessible to and binding on all humans, including those who were neither Jews nor Christians. Human sexual activity should thus be confined to hetero-sexual marriage only, and even within marriage to activities that resulted in procreation. The use of sex for any other purpose, or with any other partner, was forbidden, and liable to punishment by both God and nature.

This theoretical foundation served in turn as the basis for the legislation on sexual behavior issued by ecclesiastical and secular authorities. But the transi-tion from theory to practice—from Scripture through legislation to the admin-istration of justice—was characterized by intellectual and practical variation, both geographically and chronologically. Lawmakers varied in the detail of their understanding of what counted as a sexual offense, and courts and tribu-nals followed differing prosecuting practices. This was true even for offenses such as incest and sodomy that were universally condemned in principle.

So can we view the sexual prohibitions of late-medieval and early-modern Europe as taboos? In the sense intended by Freud and Lévi-Strauss, who be-lieved that taboos were innate, universal, and unchanging, probably not. The debates among theologians and lawyers, and the variant practices of the courts, suggest that there was rather less common ground on sexual questions than might at first appear. And the frequency with which the prohibitions were ignored, as well as the tolerance of infractions so often displayed by the offend-ers' neighbors, indicate that communal expectations of sexual behavior were frequently at odds with the demands of church and state.

We might therefore be inclined to conclude that sexual norms were cul-turally defined, constructed rather differently by different societies at differ-ent times. This was certainly the view of Michel de Montaigne, whose essay on custom suggests that "human reason is a dye spread more or less equally through all the opinions and all the manners of us humans, which are infinite in matter and infinite in variety." He records societies where, he claims,

> men can marry each other ... where ten or a dozen men and their wives share the same bed ... where, in return for money, fathers let guests have sexual enjoyment of their children, and husbands of their wives; where it is honourable to have children by one's mother, for fathers to have sexual intercourse with their daughters and with their sons, and where, when they gather for a festival, all can lie with each other's children ... else-where again there is no sin in having wives in common ... To sum up then, the impression I have is that there is nothing that custom may not do

and cannot do ... it is as much by custom as by Nature that males lie with males. The laws of conscience which we say are born of Nature are born of custom; since man inwardly venerates the opinions and the manners approved and received about him, he cannot without remorse free himself from them nor apply himself to them without self-approbation.[106]

But as the evidence from this period indicates, it was possible, despite what Montaigne suggests, for individuals to break away from "custom"—from the restraints and prohibitions accepted publicly by society and internalized in such a way that they seem at first sight natural and universal. Montaigne himself recalls, in the diary of his journey to Italy in 1580–1581, a ceremony at the church of San Giovanni a Porta Latina in Rome a couple of years before in which "certain Portuguese ... had entered into a strange brotherhood. They married one another, male to male, at the mass, with the same ceremonies that we observe in our marriages, ... read the same wedding gospel, and then went to bed and cohabited."[107] And, as we have seen, some contemporaries were prepared to challenge the inherited customs intellectually too, arguing, for example, that same-sex relations and incest—even the sexual pairing of a parent with his or her child—could be judged legitimate, at least in terms of natural law. These infractions and challenges to inherited views indicate a lack of communal compliance with the expected behavioral norms and cast doubt on the extent to which custom reflected innate beliefs. The reality was richer, and more complex.

CHAPTER SIX

Sex, Medicine, and Disease: Welcoming Wombs and Vernacular Anatomies

CYNTHIA KLESTINEC

Questions of anatomical difference play a central role in debates about early modern and modern sexuality. Indeed, they tend to organize those debates. In his account of sexuality as a modern phenomenon, for example, Arnold Davidson insists on the distinction between a psychiatric style of reasoning and an anatomical one that preceded it: in the second half of the nineteenth century, sexual identity was "no longer exclusively linked to the anatomical structure of the internal and external genital organs" but rather was linked to "impulses, tastes, aptitudes, satisfactions and psychic traits"; these new concepts made "it possible to detach questions of sexual identity from facts about anatomy."[1] The argument—that sexuality derives from psychic traits rather than anatomical parts—rests on the conclusion that prior to the mid-nineteenth century, questions of sexual identity were inseparable from facts about anatomy. It has been repeatedly suggested that this was a product of the Enlightenment: male and female anatomical bodies were not only incommensurate to one another,

radically different rather than stronger or weaker versions of one another; they
were also the core foundation for assessments of normal or normative sexual
identities.[2]

New methodologies rather than contested chronologies have underscored
the shifting terms and meanings of sexuality. Just as Davidson triangulates
psychiatry, sexuality and identity, historians of the Enlightenment have
queried the legal, scientific, and medical discourses that constitute sexuality in
the Age of Reason.[3] Only recently, however, have inquiries into the relationship between anatomy, medicine, and sexuality in the Renaissance adopted
a similarly interdisciplinary approach. Earlier studies focused almost exclusively on the learned traditions of anatomy, medicine, and natural philosophy.[4]
While this focus illuminated the relationship between humanism and medicine,
it tended to overestimate the cultural power of these medical traditions and
obscure the rich, vernacular context that provided shape and definition to both
medical ideas and sexual identity.[5] As many of the essays in this volume demonstrate, scholars have begun to explore the intersections between anatomy,
medicine, religion, kinship, politics, and the law. In particular, they have turned
to vernacular traditions, to the material practices of geographically specific, lay
cultures in order to explore the interaction between medicine on the one hand,
and health and healing, family and kinship, and religion and devotion on the
other.[6]

In the sixteenth century, anatomy began to consolidate itself into a recognizable discipline; it became an important part of the curriculum for medical
education, an area of academic research, and a supportive environment for
early empirical practices. It continued, however, to derive its explanatory and
cultural power from a wide range of sources. These included ancient and
contemporary works of philosophy, medicine, and anatomy and academic
practices of dissection and vivisection. But they also included devotional
practices, domestic habits, and literary traditions. From this rich cultural
substrate (which could be extended), the links between anatomy, sex, and
identity became less fleeting, more substantial, and more meaningful in the
period, ca. 1450–1650. To determine how and where these links formed,
more attention has been given to the vernacular traditions associated with
anatomy and the body. The vernacular reception of learned anatomy, for example, suggests that anatomized bodies reflected and responded to spiritual
and secular beliefs and that together, these illuminate the subject of identity,
including sexual identity.

In the Renaissance, vernacular writers worked with the learned medical
tradition, particularly with Aristotle and Galen's ideas about conception,

generation, and reproductive anatomy.[7] They also assimilated this material with Hippocratic and Galenic ideas about the humoral body and with treatments and other features of daily practice.[8] In the context of an increasingly competitive and diversified marketplace, these writers created a medical vernacular that helped to construct (in addition to their own authority) the ideas, practices, and discourses of sex and sexuality in the Renaissance.[9] The medical vernacular appears in texts and treatises on medical and surgical procedures, on midwifery, on household "physick" and a number of other topics that respond to what Margaret Pelling has called the general and pervasive concern for healthy living in the sixteenth century.[10] In these texts, discussions of anatomical difference tell us something about the way sex—its parts, procedures, and products— became partially responsible for the shape of one's identity and the nature of her and his experience in the world.

Vernacular discussions of anatomical difference include information on anatomical parts and processes, as we would expect, but they also attach emotive, affective characters to anatomy. It was not enough for writers to describe the structural features of the uterus, for example; they also had to describe it as "joyous," happy to be the meeting place for male and female sperm.[11] The emotive character of anatomy is often elided in studies of Renaissance anatomy because these tend to focus solely on the learned, academic tradition and often on its proto-scientific merits.[12] The Renaissance anatomical body has served as an emblem of early modern science, a body that reflects nascent practices of empirical inquiry, detached observations, scientific authority, and cold clinical analysis.[13] This "body" seems to be almost exclusively the product of visual apprehension despite the fact that the learned traditions of anatomy depended on touch and hearing as well as sight. In the late sixteenth century, for example, medical students, professors, and bystanders went to the anatomical theater in Padua to hear rhetorically refined orations on anatomy; only later did the theater lend itself to touching and inspecting the dissected parts.[14] Beyond the pedagogical culture of the university, vernacular anatomies coupled the sensory and the sensitive. Anatomical parts were described as warm and welcoming; opened bodies were the occasion for intimate exchange rather than cool detachment.

This was due in part to how anatomical information connected to a set of familiar ideas and beliefs. Anatomy was used alongside, not in place of, a wider lexicon of the body. Writers connected anatomy to the traditions of affective piety, to sacred bodies that revealed physical signs of sanctity and to complex processes of identification; women, for example, were encouraged to identify with the physical pain of the Virgin Mary, Christ, and eventually Eve.[15]

In the medical vernacular, writers also developed secular connections between anatomy, domesticity, and hospitality.[16] The "joyous" uterus and female anatomy in general became broadly appealing to male readers who associated women with hearth and home and to a new category of female readers who wished to see their management of domestic space celebrated. These super- and subrational features allow us to resurrect the "impulses, tastes, aptitudes, and satisfactions" that were produced and promoted in discussions of anatomy and anatomical difference, desires that do not fit nineteenth-century under-standings of sexuality but that nevertheless constitute Renaissance linkages between the body, identity, and sex.

ANATOMICAL NORMS

Renaissance medical writers discussed anatomical norms and alternatives to them.[17] This section provides a series of examples from medical and literary sources that help to situate questions of anatomical difference in relation to questions of identity. Learned men at the universities and courts across the Continent and in England were familiar with normative anatomical structures or those that regularly appeared in animal and human bodies (and in classi-cal and contemporary texts that described them). These men, though, were also and increasingly intrigued by sex variations that they classified as preter-natural, cases where Nature acted extraordinarily and demonstrated virtuos-ity: these included hermaphrodites and bearded women.[18] These preternatural enticements could be described as marvels and wonders or as monsters. In his *De hermaphroditorum monstrosorumque partum natura* (1614), Caspar Bauhinus doubled the wonder, featuring not just a hermaphrodite but a set of hermaphroditic twins (fig. 6.1). This was not imaginative excess, for as he explained, the illustration depicted the twins, joined at the back, who were born at Rorbach, near Heidelberg, in 1486. Bearded women were also seen as both wonders and monsters. As Will Fisher has explained, they might be called monsters (rather than masculine women) to underscore the question-able nature of their humanity rather than their gender; or in contrast, they could be called wonders and celebrated as exceptional cases of their kind.[19] For example, on José de Ribera's portrait of the bearded woman, Magdelena Ven-tura, commentators emphasized her great ability to fulfill the roles of mother and wife.[20] These marvelous variations placed a special charge on the study of human anatomy; they also underscored, by way of contrast, the construction of anatomical norms.

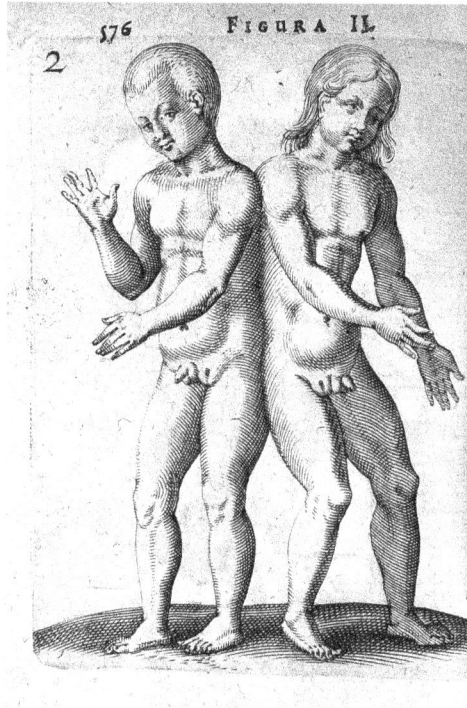

FIGURE 6.1: Hermaphrodite twins joined at the back, born at Rorbach near Heidelberg, 1486. From Caspar Bauhinus, *De Hermaphroditorum Monstrosorumque Partuum Natura* (Oppenheim: H. Galler, 1614), plate II. [Engraving 1614 By: Theodor de Bry] Wellcome Library, London.

Renaissance professors and medical practitioners derived anatomical norms from several classical sources. Aristotle's texts provided philosophical, theoretical terms and frameworks while Galen's texts supplied the details of structural anatomy as well as explanations of processes that were theoretical and therapeutic in orientation; and finally, Hippocratic writings tended to emphasize aspects related to medical practice and the running and regulation of bodies. As they confronted these ideas in newly published editions and in the filtered versions offered by Avicenna and others, Renaissance scholars explored their differences, teasing out their variations. For example, Gianna Pomata has shown that Renaissance medical practitioners treated cases of menstruation in men, and they understood the condition according to Hippocratic and Galenic ideas about humoral excess and balance: a man menstruated (presumably from the anus) because his body contained a pathological excess, a plethora, of blood, and purging it was a necessary means to restoring a balance of the humors.[21] Menstruating men were not stigmatized or seen as effeminate because menstruation was necessary to the healthy body. While the male body was often the standard for explanations of anatomy, physiology, and health, this example shows that sometimes, the female body could be the archetype, the norm, for understanding a bodily function or malfunction.

In other cases, Renaissance writers endorsed Aristotle's writings on sex difference and their normative characteristics. According to Aristotle, sex difference depends first on a categorical definition: male is that which generates in another; and female is that which generates in herself.[22] For Aristotle, anatomical differences serve this principle: the uterus is internal because it guards, shelters, and matures the conception.[23] When Aristotle turns to the processes of conception, he develops his argument that only the male supplies sperm and that the testes produce the sperm; the female does not emit sperm despite the fact that "the uterus is double just as the testes are."[24] Governing these ideas is an understanding of sex difference as the result of a heat differential: males have more natural heat than females, and for this reason, Aristotle says, male genitalia are pushed outside the body while female genitalia remain inside; the innate heat of the male body meant that it, rather than the female body, was perfect and complete; it had reached a developmental state of perfection.[25] Based on heat, the male body supplied the norm for anatomical differences related to sex.

Renaissance writers also looked to Galen's works and especially his arguments for the existence of female sperm, which was weaker and less hot than its male counterpart (it was also tightly connected to female orgasm). Debates on the existence of female sperm and female orgasm tended to produce alternatives to Aristotle's theory of sex difference. Like Pomata's case of the menstruating man, these debates indicate that ideas about sex difference were case specific: writers marshaled different material for practical treatments, vernacular discussions, learned demonstrations, and debates. They adjudicated these discrepancies in both learned and vernacular medical writing. In his *Della contemplatione anatomica* (1564), Prospero Borgarucci, a medical professor in Padua, explained, "I remember having seen with my own eyes a woman, who was cut in the lower parts, having yet been full in her vessels with a certain material ... genital semen [*seme genitale*]." He concludes his discussion of the existence of female sperm, noting that between Aristotle, Galen, and Hippocrates, there is "the greatest discord."[26] Points of tension also appeared in the vernacular tradition. Boccaccio, for example, included a story of male pregnancy in the *Decameron* that used Aristotle's ideas as a point of departure.[27]

CALANDRINO'S PREGNANCY

Not naming Aristotle specifically, Boccaccio begins his story with Calandrino, a simpleton whose aunt has recently died and left him 200 lire. Hoping to swindle Calandrino, Bruno and Buffalmacco, Florentine tricksters, design a practical joke—to convince Calandrino that he is pregnant so that he will pay for treatment, to the tune of 200 lire. The story combines several aspects of early medicine—the procedures of diagnosis and treatment, the contractual agreement between patient and practitioner, medical theories of conception, and vernacular understandings of the body and parturition.[28] It also distorts Aristotelian notions of anatomical difference in order to explore non-normative sexual practices and the relationship between anatomy and identity. Learning from the doctor that he is pregnant, Calandrino exclaims: "Oh Tessa, you did this to me, you're the one that always wanted to be on top, I told you this would happen … How will I give birth to this child? Where will it come out?"[29] Agreeing to pay for the doctor's treatment, he cries: "Just so long as I don't have to give birth, because I don't know how to do it! When women are about to give birth, I've heard them make such a racket [*gran romore*], even though they have a large thing [*buon cotal grande*] to do it with; I'm sure that with that pain, I would die before I gave birth." Calandrino understands his pregnancy as a basic obstruction. The logic participates in widespread beliefs about illness resulting from internal impediments (the body's inability to purge itself). Calandrino's explanation, however, also figures the male body as inadequate to the task. Calandrino has no "large thing." His pregnancy becomes the occasion to lament the anatomical imperfections of the male body.

This is funny for a number of reasons, not least of which is the fact that Boccaccio has managed to tell a story that inverts the most basic assumptions we have about reproduction and anatomy, namely that men inseminate and women get pregnant and grow fetuses. In terms of early Renaissance theories of conception, the story is critical of several aspects of Aristotelian sex difference. First, counter to Aristotle, the story treats the male body as an imperfect version of the female body. Second, also counter to Aristotle, Calandrino's logic allows for the existence of female sperm—quite powerful sperm, too, for the story emphasizes Tessa's sexual desire and by extension, her internal heat. Together, these form the basis for Calandrino's identity crisis. Masculine identity, as Michael Rocke has explained, was dictated in part by the convention of taking a dominant role in sex: "The association of virility with dominance was one source of the religious ban against couples engaging in intercourse with the woman on top, an 'unnatural' position considered emblematic of woman's usurpation—or man's abdication—of males' superior status."[30] Indeed, when Calandrino imagines punishing Tessa for her "lust," he contemplates first beating her and then withholding sexual pleasure: "But if I get out of this mess, she'll die from frustration … before I let her have it again!" Rather than take the dominant role in intercourse and in punishment, Calandrino responds by withholding sexual favors, entering an economy of sexual exchange that was characteristically reserved for women rather than men.[31]

Although these medical conceits are taken to comic extremes, they provide one way of imagining the relationship between anatomy and identity. The story elaborates Calandrino's identity crisis, shifting back and forth from questions of anatomy and reproduction to questions of sexual norms and masculine/feminine identity. Calandrino understands his pregnancy as a physical obstruction and as a punishment for his and his wife's failure to fulfill their normative sexual roles. Because his pregnancy transforms his male body into an imperfect female one, it causes him to consider his sexual and social roles as female and his identity as problematically feminine. Mixing Aristotelian theory with the rustic ignorance of Calandrino, the story indicates the wide variation between learned and lay conceptions of bodies, anatomies, and identities. In more formal writings on anatomy as well, vernacular writers and readers productively adapted the learned traditions of anatomy and medicine, transforming Aristotelian and Galenic explanations as well as structural descriptions and illustrations into material that could ground and intensify their "impulses," "satisfactions," and "anxieties."

WELCOMING WOMBS

Depictions of the uterus in the sixteenth century provide an informative example of how vernacular traditions reacted to and shaped learned discussions of anatomy and sex difference. With the more frequent and widespread practice of human and animal dissection in the sixteenth century, the study of anatomy flourished. Under the guidance of such luminaries as Berengario da Carpi (ca. 1460–1530), a Bolognese surgeon, the study of anatomy helped to secure observations as a new form of evidence.[32] Andreas Vesalius (1514–1564), the Flemish anatomist who taught at the medical schools in Padua and Bologna, conducted many dissections and criticized his colleagues for the blind faith in texts, their unwillingness to trust their own eyes; his successor, Gabriele

Falloppio (1523–1562) published his major work, *Observationes anatomicae* (1551), a work that attests to the interest in observation by participating in the new genre of medical writing, called *observationes* or *historia*.[33] The emphasis on observation resulted in the "discovery" of morphological structures such as the fallopian tubes and the clitoris. These structures provided alternatives to the idea of sexual isomorphism—was the clitoris or the vaginal canal the homologue to the penis?—and were used in legal and medical debates about sex difference.[34] Though novel, investigations of morphological structure, as well as the commentary tradition of medical humanists, were joined by more traditional aspects of lay culture. Not only did affective traditions of piety help constitute late medieval and Renaissance anatomy, as recent studies have shown, but emerging accounts of the self and traditions of hospitality helped vernacular writers to construe the meaning of anatomical difference and in particular, the anatomy of the uterus.[35]

In his introductory work (*Isagogae breves*, 1522), Berengario da Carpi turned to the subject of sex difference. He described not only the anatomy of the uterus but also its relationship to male reproductive organs:

> The entire uterus with its testicles [or ovaries] and seminal vessels is similar to the members of generation in men, but the male members are completed outside, since they are thrust out on account of their heat. The members of women are diminished and retained within the body because of their lesser heat. The uterus is, as it were, a converse [analogous] instrument. For the neck of the uterus is like a penis, and its receptacle with testicles and vessels is like the scrotum.[36]

This description of sex difference follows Aristotle's account: based on sufficient heat, the male body is complete, and the female is a derivative, incomplete version of it. Berengario cast the uterus as a passive receptacle, a container of menstrual blood and male seed. This sexual isomorphism did not appear at the beginning of his description, where it would imply an overriding structural or conceptual framework—the kind that would dictate the meaning of particular details. Instead, it appeared at the end. Perhaps it was an afterthought or a useful mnemonic device for remembering the parallels between male and female anatomy (without denying the existence of structures with no parallel in the male body).[37]

In Berengario's text, the description of sexual isomorphism accompanies an illustration of two uteruses (fig. 1.19): the first uterus (on the bottom) features the organ, viewed from the front after a dissection, with its connective

structures, the second (on the top) is a uterus, viewed from the back before extended dissection; its dots signify cotyledons, the orifices or termination points
of blood vessels in the uterine wall.[38] The necks of the uteruses or vaginal canals
conform to the textual description, for the similarities between them and the penis
hardly need Berengario's commentary to become evident. Unlike the textual description, however, the illustration also emphasizes the connective structures of
the uterus. These are Galenic in origin, for Galen was quite taken by the number
and kinds of connections between the uterus and the other parts of the body: "It
may be said, the uterus is fused with [structures], attached to others, suspended
from others; some entwine it, some support it."[39] Berengario highlighted Aristotle's theory of sex difference as well as Galen's attention to the particulars of the
uterus, to what Galen called "exact" rather than "general" matters.[40]

But the illustration contains an element that has no classical origin or
empirical correlation, for the receptacle of the uterus is drawn or outlined in
the shape of a heart. The format of the heart-shaped uterus appears again in
one of Berengario's illustrations of the uterus *in situ* (fig. 6.2).[41] The icon of the
heart was well known and would have been layered with a variety of symbolic
meanings during this period. But while Berengario comments on the image's
similarity to the penis, its similarity to a heart is never mentioned. Following
Berengario, Vesalius published *De humani corporis fabrica* (1543), which included among several illustrations of reproductive anatomy, one of the uterus
and vaginal canal (fig. 6.3).[42] The textual description emphasized sexual isomorphism, and this well-known illustration seems intentionally designed to
reinforce the idea: the reproductive anatomy of the female was the very same
as that of the male, only inverted. Here, however, the uterus is again indented.
With a cleft in the middle of its upper region, the uterus is shaped like a heart.
On the significance of this visual parallel, anatomists remained silent. When
Vesalius's illustrations migrated to England and emerged in vernacular English
treatises, however, the analogy between the heart and uterus took legible form.
English writers embedded this illustration in a context rich with medieval and
Renaissance notions about spirituality, physiology, and domesticity. Not only
did this context solidify a relationship between the uterus and the heart, rather
than the penis, but it also transformed the unique organ into a conveyer of
ideas about anatomy and identity.

Although learned practitioners—anatomists, physicians, and scholars—
imposed rhetorical as well as professional barriers between themselves and their
vernacular counterparts—surgeons, midwives, empirics, apothecaries, and magical healers—the stories, texts, and images that traveled between these groups
reveal considerable exchange and mutual dependence.[43] In England, Vesalius's

ideas and images first emerged in the publications of Thomas Gemini.[44] Gemini's anatomical compendia contained the illustrations of the *Fabrica* and parts of the descriptive text of Vesalius's works. Through his acquaintance or business partnership with Gemini, Thomas Raynalde published the *Birth of Mankind* (1545; (fig. 6.4)), an English midwifery manual that augmented an earlier midwifery text (*Birth*, Richard Jonas, 1540) with a full chapter or "first book" on anatomy.[45] By the third edition in 1560, Raynalde's book included the anatomical illustrations of the reproductive organs, all of which are Vesalian in origin. Taken together, Gemini's compendia and Raynalde's *Birth* represent the earliest reception of Vesalius's work on English soil.

Both works attest to a complicated process of transmission and assimilation.[46] Gemini included the Vesalian material, both illustration and explanatory text, alongside a much older anatomical treatise, taken from a fourteenth-century

FIGURE 6.2: Female, standing. Jacobus Berengarius Carpensis, *Carpi commentaria cum amplissimis additionibus super Anatomia Mundini* (Bologna: H. de Benedictis, 1521), plate CCXXVI (bis). Wellcome Library, London.

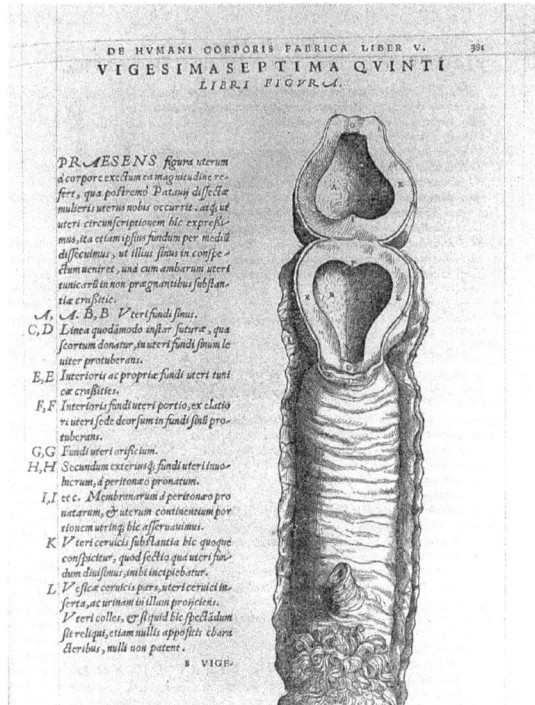

FIGURE 6.3: Female anatomy, uterus resembling a penis. Andreas Vesalius, *De humani corporis fabrica* (Basel: Oporinus, 1543), liber V, page 381, figure 27. Wellcome Library, London.

manuscript (that was also the basis for Thomas Vicary's work on surgery).[47] As vernacular medical publications of the first half of the sixteenth century demonstrate, surgeons' needs were practical both in terms of content (how-to manuals) and in terms of form (vernacular as opposed to Latin). The *Judgement of Urines* or the *Judicial of Urine* or the *Seeing of Urines* was reprinted no less than seven times between the 1540s and the 1570s. Thomas Vicary's *English Man's Treasure* or the *Treasure of Poor Men* received ten printings between 1539 and 1552. Translated works, though fewer in number, were also frequently reprinted. For example, Thomas Berthelet printed the English translation of Ulrich von Hutton's work on syphilis and the magical cure of guacum four times between 1533 and 1540. The English translation of the *Regimen sanitatis salerni* was printed by Thomas Berthelet as early as 1528 and enjoyed at least five printings by 1557. As this brief survey suggests, the principle

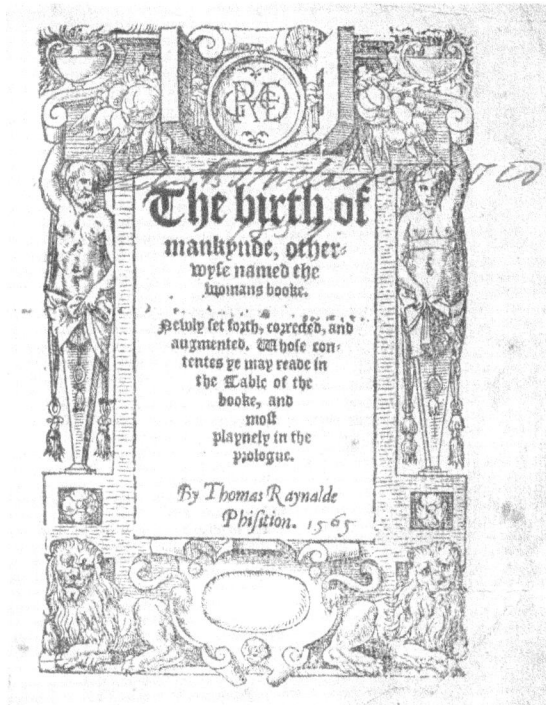

FIGURE 6.4: Thomas Raynalde, *The byrth of mankynde, otherwyse named the womans booke* (London: n.p., 1565), title page. Wellcome Library, London.

behind publishing medical material in the vernacular was based in part on its practicality. Although new, original material was available, innovation was defined very broadly. Gemini could proclaim the newness of his project despite the fact that it partially derived from a fourteenth-century manuscript that had likely been circulating for decades, if not centuries. Indeed, the reader's familiarity with the older material may explain the continued success of his vernacular edition.

Similarly, Raynalde set the strikingly new section on anatomy against both ancient and medieval material on childbirthing procedure, the care of infants, and the diseases of women.[48] Books on midwifery were part of a larger print culture in the period that included technical writing on such diverse topics as how to read urine, how to treat insomnia and cramps to the salutary effects of mineral baths and separate herbals for boils, fistulas, and bad breath. Female readers, in particular, were familiar with domestic technologies such as cooking and silkworm propagation, and household "physick" as well as midwifery; between 1475 and 1575, the eighty-five practical guides directed to women generated 290 editions.[49] The numerous editions reinforce the claim that the expansion of the book trade reveals a thirst for practical, not just literary or historical, works.

This tradition of technical writing not only emphasized practical problems and solutions, but it also made learned knowledge accessible.[50] Anatomical illustrations became a paragon for this kind of accessibility. In contrast to learned (Latin) anatomy texts, Gemini wrote that the illustration could be read repeatedly by "unlatined" surgeons.[51] Surgeons, unable to attend university lectures on anatomy, could use the illustration as a pedagogical tool: it provided a mediated experience of an actual dissection and it explained the text. Raynalde also linked the anatomical illustration to dissection. He describes the illustrations "as lively and express[ive] figures ... [in which you can] exactly and clearly perceive [female anatomy] as though you were present at the cutting open or anatomy of a dead woman."[52] Just as quickly, however, Raynalde changed his course, dismantling that link by insisting that the illustration reflected the living, female body. He writes: Do not think that the "utility and profit of this first book" or the knowledge it contains "to be of little ... value"; "take it as the foundation" which will "illuminate" and enlighten "your wits and understanding," for both the text and the images show "how everything comes to pass within your body in time of conception, of bearing, and of birth."[53] The text describes the anatomical structures associated with the maternal, living body. And the illustrations serve the text. Like the text, the illustrations were meant to be revelatory, and Raynalde thematized illumination with a series of metaphors: light indicated knowledge and understanding rather than exposure; darkness pointed to ignorance and shame.

As Mary Fissell has explained, Raynalde was mindful of his female readers. He emphasized the role of woman in conception and generation: he acknowledges man "as principal mover and cause of generation," but he also says that "(no displeasure to men) the woman doth confer and contribute much more, what to the increase of the child in her womb and what to the nourishment thereof after birth."[54] He also emphasized the importance of anatomical knowledge for his female readers: "To be short, all the wittiness and artificial, crafty invention and diverse manners of ministrations in the noble science of physick proceed and spring [from] the profound knowledge of anatomy. Therefore my advice and utter counsel is that all women in whose hands this little book shall chance to come, with all diligence do force themselves perfectly to the understanding of this first book."[55] This context helps to explain why Raynalde diverged from Gemini when it came to the uterus. Gemini combines sexual isomorphism with Galenic details of the uterus, its shape, texture, and connections to other organs. Following Galen, he explained that the uterus was "full of sinews" and in its humoral complexion, "cold and dry"; following Aristotle, the uterus was the "house or receptacle" where generation takes place and "the seed of man" is "nourished"; returning to Galen, he situates the uterus "between the bladder and straight entrails [intestines]"; and he explains the form of the uterus as "a man's yard turned inward" and describes the "two arms coming from the spring top of the testicles."[56] For Raynalde, however, the uterus looked different.

Raynalde praised the wondrous nature of the uterus. Alongside Vesalius's illustration, he explained that the uterus was endowed with a special magnetic quality: an attracting power "which is inset and given to the womb to attract and draw towards itself the seed parted from the man."[57] The wonder of the uterus extended beyond its ability to nourish seed into conception, to attract sperm, and to expand and contract itself. Despite contractions, the organ remains "very smooth, moist, glistering, and reddish, as it were a little red tempered with a great deal of white; the inside also … is smooth."[58] Here, Raynalde generated the wonder of the uterus out of the contrast between the organ's form and its function: the uterus remained smooth while it contracted and expanded. "Glistering" highlights the theme of illumination, for the word was reserved for glittering, illuminated objects such as silver and gold swords, white raiments, red jewels, shiny leeches, and glowworms.

Raynalde's attention to the shape of the uterus is also noteworthy. The bottom of the uterus (which is featured at the top, in apposition to the vaginal canal), he writes, "is not perfectly round bowlwise [sic], but rather like the form of a man's heart, as it is painted, saving that the partition or cleft in the uterus between both corners, the right and the left, is not so profoundly dented inwards as the cleft in the heart."[59] Explicating and extending the Vesalian image, Raynalde draws an analogy between the uterus and a man's heart rather than his penis. He sees a uterus shaped like a painted heart, where "painted" signals properties of similitude as well as color and artifice, in the sense of manmade. These properties derive from medieval and early Renaissance artifactual rather than anatomical traditions. The image of the uterus looks like a painting of a heart rather than a heart seen in a dissection.

The iconographic representation of the heart has a long history. Eric Jager has identified several medieval traditions that used heart-shaped books and helped to make the heart shape into an iconic symbol (fig. 6.5). These books, which were used and also represented in paintings of spiritual practice, focused on devotional practices; they might include prayers and images that together operated as inspirational sources for the practices of affective piety (all of which reveal a special concern for women and female readers).[60] Second, these books could serve more personal ends, providing a cumulative record of an individual's life, thoughts, and deeds; these books were to be opened at the Last Judgment; this use reflected the inwardness of penitential practices after the Fourth Lateran Council as well as the visual media (stained glass, sculpture, painting) depicting the metaphorical books of the Last Judgment.[61] As material culture flourished in the fifteenth and sixteenth centuries, the iconic representation of the heart "acquired a more individual content and a more popular presence, it also assumed ever more concrete forms, from the saint's inscribed heart to the heart-shaped manuscript book," both of which helped to perfect its visual image and encourage the association between the heart

FIGURE 6.5: Master of the View of Sainte-Gudule: *Young Man Holding a Book*. New York: The Metropolitan Museum of Art.

and identity.[62] As Jager explains, this image reflects both, for the book is a personal testament to the sitter's faith or an account of his worldly achievements, and it is featured in the portrait, the genre that articulated a dominant strand of Renaissance individualism.

Raynalde's heart-shaped uterus referred to an anatomical structure, but it acquired special significance in a midwifery manual as the organ central to the processes of conception, generation, and parturition. Raynalde cast the uterus as an intact, illuminated, glittering object, an object that inspired wonder and awe. The emphasis on the heart as a spiritual symbol may also have mediated potential concerns about dissection.[63] It also valorized the spiritual practices associated with affective piety.[64] Women localized their piety in the heart, and readily identified with Mary's Immaculate Conception. The practices of affective piety brought conceptions of the heart and the womb into radical proximity with one another.

Raynalde also added a secular dimension to his chapter on anatomy, one that derived from the discourse of hospitality.[65] In the prologue, he says he will follow the example of those who "bid any guests to dinner or supper, [and] are wont first to declare, what shall be their cheer: what fare, and how many dishes they shall have: praying them to take it in good worth, and to look for neither better nor worse than hath been mentioned of"; and he then expects the reader to act like a dinner guest, "entering into the reading of this little treatise" but staying "diligent and attentive" to its contents, and the "utility and profit that may ensue."[66] Recommending the first book on anatomy as a kind of first course, Raynalde hopes to prepare the reader for the subsequent books. When Raynalde subsequently suggests that his book will enable a woman to understand her physician's recommendations, it is especially significant that this hypothetical encounter is located within a scene of hospitality. Although the discourse of hospitality would be aligned with pastoral settings and recreations by the mid-seventeenth century, it tended to mute issues of prestige and class configurations in the sixteenth century. Felicity Heal explains: "Both status differentiation and social distance between donor and recipient were diminished (or perhaps even temporarily effaced) when hospitality became more widely practiced throughout the social order."[67] In Robert Pricket's *Times Anotomie* (1606), hospitality is opposed to pride—"Prides painted prodigalitie,/Hath cut the throat, of wonted hospitality"[68]—and thus a virtue suitable to all, a commonality among social groups. Raynalde spoke of midwives in both positive and negative contexts, and his mention of a physician was not necessarily intended to undercut the authority of the midwife. Rather, it was redescribed as a social interaction, akin to a dinner party, where status differentiation and social distance between host, hostess, and guest were momentarily effaced.[69]

The theme of hospitality made the access of private spaces available. In Thomas Storer's poem on the life and death of Thomas Wolsey (1599), for example, the servants of the king are told, "Let not your stately palace walls decline/No desolation may confusion bring/To those fair monuments, but them shine,/Old famous Hospitality t'enshrine."[70] Controlled and managed by servants, the king's home is both opened and kept from a state of decline, an aspect signaled by its continually fair monuments. Overlaid with the language of hospitality, Raynalde's uterus could be similarly controlled and managed, opened at appropriate times, and its wondrous quality could be reflected in its anatomical description as glimmering and illuminated. Raynalde's rhetoric and his explication of anatomical images suggests that traditions of devotion and piety were combined with new ideas about domesticity and the hospitable home; together, these helped make the uterus and female anatomy familiar. Set within the discourse of hospitality, the womb would be welcoming, accepting of male sperm, giving of its own material; its activities and contributions would both forestall decline and exemplify the virtue of hospitality.

The welcoming womb may also have encouraged an alternative understanding of conception, one that drew more fully on Galenic rather than Aristotelian origins. At the end of the period, in *The Practice of Physick* (1658), Lazarus Riverius (Lazare Rivière, 1589–1665), imagined the womb or uterus to be actively engaged in the process of conception: "skip[p]ing as it were for joy, [so that it] may meet her Husband's Sperm, graciously and freely receive [it], and draw it into its innermost Cavity or Closet, and bedew and sprinkle it with her own Sperm, and powered forth in that pang of Pleasure, [so that] by the commixture of both, Conception may arise."[71] The uterus retained its attracting abilities. For Riverius, however, its performance was linked to the existence of female sperm and female pleasure. Riverius offered both, in stark contrast to Aristotelian ideas about sex difference and female passivity. The context was normative or heteronormative, but the female played a more active role. And the residue of the heart-uterus relationship is still evident, for it is the uterus rather than the heart that "skips" joyously as (married) lovers unite and conceive.

The associations between the heart and the uterus persisted in both vernacular and Latin medical works. In his translation of Lanfranco's work on surgery, John Halle wrote in 1565 that the ovaries (or testicles) were shaped like almonds and that the uterus was outwardly like a bladder but inwardly "like a painted heart."[72] The association emphasizes the difference between surface and interior, perhaps extending the fascination with interiorized conceptions of the self.[73] Learned anatomical illustrations did not depart from but rather shared in these traditions. Felix Platter (1536–1614) maintained the connection between the heart and the uterus. Platter, professor of anatomy at Basel University, undertook an intensive study of skeletal structure from both male and female specimens. His illustration of the sternum bone, however, appears to be modeled on Vesalius's illustration of female reproductive anatomy (compare figure 6.6 with figure 6.8): Platter has inverted the image of the reproductive organs, placing the heart-shaped hole at the base of the sternum.[74] As Michael Stolberg explains, Helkiah Crooke used the illustration to show that the second bone of the sternum in women was occasionally perforated with a "broad hole much like a heart."[75] Crooke reinterpreted the image so as to emphasize the accuracy of anatomical illustration, transforming the metaphorical relationship between the heart and the uterus into an empirical one. For both Platter

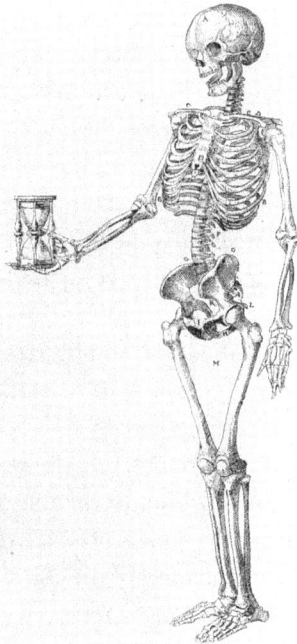

FIGURE 6.6: Skeleton with hourglass. Felix Platter, *De corporis humani structura et usu* (Basel: 1583), plate II. Wellcome Library, London.

and Raynalde, however, the relationship between the heart and the uterus was based not on empirical evidence but rather on other systems of meaning, which included ideas of sanctity, devotional practices, and the language of domesticity. These connected the heart and the uterus; and these were being tapped by vernacular and learned writers as resources for constructing and understanding late medieval and Renaissance bodies.

CONCLUSION

In the 1560s, in an English midwifery manual, the heart-shaped uterus began to generate commentary. The uterus was associated with iconic, sympathetic, and generative or fertile hearts. The English reception of learned, anatomical illustrations not only highlights the relationship between the heart and the uterus; it also extends it with secular and current ideas about hospitality. Raynalde's text made the uterus and female anatomy at once awesome and homely.

Catalyzed by the vernacular tradition, the analogy between the heart and the uterus began to shape the learned traditions of anatomy and medicine. In the seventeenth century, learned medicine became institutionalized and more authoritative, and the variation and debate between anatomical norms diminished. Nevertheless, the relationship between the heart and the uterus persisted. In his treatise on the motions of the heart and the circulation of blood (*Exercitatio anatomica de motu cordis et sanguinis in animalibus*, 1628), William Harvey (1578–1657) began by describing the heart as "the foundation of life" and the "Sun of the Microcosm." He then compared the heart to the King, who is "the foundation of his Kingdoms, and the sun of his microcosm." The suggestion that Kings multiply Kingdoms emphasizes the fertile, productive capacity of the heart.[76] The heart, according to Aristotle, was the most important, vital organ in the body; and while Harvey depended heavily on Aristotle and ancient anatomy, his intellectual framework also drew from contemporary traditions that made the heart, in addition to the uterus, an organ of fertility. Set within an anatomical treatise, the King's productive heart seems to be not an alternative to but another manifestation of the chiastic relationship between the heart and the uterus.[77] Other traditions reflected the microcosm and the womb rather than the heart (fig. 6.7). As the learned traditions of anatomy and medicine continued to evolve, the heart and the uterus continued to respond to each other, to mirror each other, a reflection that originates in the vernacular reception of Vesalius's works and the iconographic representation of the heart-shaped uterus.

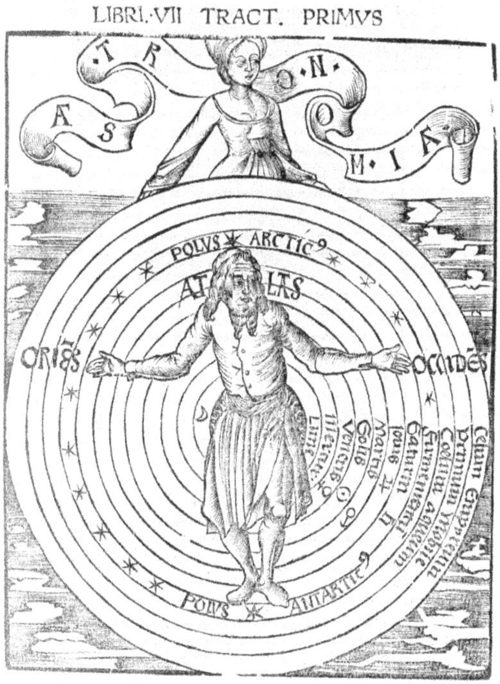

LIBRI·VII TRACT. PRIMVS

FIGURE 6.7: Geocentric diagram of the universe, with the figure of Atlas in the centre. From Gregor Reisch, *Margarita philosophica* (Freiburg: Schott, 1503), libri VII, tract. Primus folio m2 verso. Wellcome Library, London.

As this case and the foregoing discussion have indicated, Renaissance anatomy and medicine did not develop in isolation or solely among learned men and their students. Rather in the vernacular spheres of writing, publishing and reading, the anatomy of sex difference circulated as a variety of concepts, practices, and norms. These helped to shape the way people understood their bodies, and in this sense, anatomy came to inform sexual identity and Renaissance sexuality. It helped to ground desires and anxieties about masculine identity, in the case of Calandrino, and about open, visible wombs, in the case of Raynalde's midwifery text.

At the end of the period, as anatomy and identity became more tightly linked, female anatomy shed much of its spiritual dimension and became increasingly objectified. While several factors enabled this development, it is worth highlighting two that depended on the book. As Wendy Wall has shown,

Renaissance authors used literary and rhetorical strategies that repeatedly constructed and displayed a private sphere and "cast the reader into the role of voyeur, one who partakes of forbidden discourse and is complicitous in stealing a glance at clandestine worlds."[78] Her analysis begins with a discussion of the frontispiece of Vesalius's *Fabrica,* which depicts the dissection of a female cadaver, her womb, in front of a large, boisterous and male audience (fig. 6.8). She suggests it as a visual counterpart to the voyeuristic prefaces of early modern English texts. Apart from the erotic and the voyeuristic, however, another strategy was also at work. Renaissance writers connected female anatomy to the private, domestic sphere by way of the concerns for hospitality. Authors like Raynalde adopted the language of hospitality, placing the female body in its anatomized, reproductive, and parturient states at home, where it could be accessed, viewed, and stabilized. Perhaps the docile and domesticated female body helped male practitioners to gain a stronger foothold in the domain of women's health as the subsequent debates between midwives, man-midwives,

FIGURE 6.8: Anatomical demonstration. Andreas Vesalius, *De humani corporis fabrica* (Basel: Oporinus, 1543), title page. Wellcome Library, London.

accoucheurs, and surgeons would suggest.[79] It also provided a new way of imagining the private life and the private self.

Finally, with all the overt attention placed on the female body, one must ask about the male body and male reproductive anatomy. How did male anatomical parts reflect or help constitute ideas of masculinity and male sexual identity? If the womb was welcoming, was the penis a proper guest? There is some evidence to suggest that the penis, for much of the Renaissance, was a source of modesty. When Baldasar Heseler attended the lectures of Matteo Corti (1475–1572) and the counterpart dissections of Andreas Vesalius in Bologna in 1540, he seemed not a little squeamish when Corti turned to the topic of the penis.[80] Why would the public discussion of the male sexual organ elicit such a response (when the public discussion of female sex organs elicited eagerness and excitement)? Perhaps it was his northern upbringing; perhaps it was a moment of self-reflection or self-identification (his penis was being discussed); or perhaps it was linked to social-sexual practices of pederasty. The complexities of sexual identity in the Renaissance depended in part on the traditions and practices of anatomy. Anatomy was one place where norms were constructed, queried, and criticized; and in the hands of lay writers and readers, anatomy provided a limited but nevertheless powerful set of sensory and sensitive ideas about the sexual dimensions of the human body.

CHAPTER SEVEN

Sex, Popular Beliefs, and Culture: "In the Waie of Lecherie"

WALTER STEPHENS

The study of early modern European magic and witchcraft through treatises and trial records has revealed abundant information about the probable sexual practices and beliefs of common, mostly illiterate people between 1450 and 1650, and indeed, for at least a half century on either side of these dates. In the fifteenth century, the arts and sciences underwent a radical renewal due to the reevaluation and rediscovery of classical Roman and Greek written culture, through texts and inscriptions. Concurrently, literate elites of western Europe noticed afresh and reevaluated ideas and practices among their own contemporaries, including the illiterate masses of common people. Directly or indirectly, most of these beliefs concerned what would be known by about 1500 as witchcraft. Research since 1970 demonstrates that early modern witchcraft, whether understood as popular culture or as elite interpretations of it, was profoundly influenced by notions of gender, and often explicitly concerned issues of sexuality.[1]

THE SOURCES

Peter Burke observes that "the popular culture of early modern Europe is elusive." Much of it was orally transmitted, and "words fly away."[2] The rest was expressed in equally impermanent fashion, through festivals and performances. Like their words, common peoples' activities were documented only when literate, socially dominant contemporaries took interest in them. Any acknowledgment or record of beliefs and practices of the folk was contingent upon either condescension or condemnation by literate observers, their authoritative approval or authoritarian correction: literate people had to find illiterates' words and activities strange, amusing, or threatening. However, this alterity does not force oral culture into strict polarization between popular and elite characteristics or elements; instead, it creates a hybrid discourse. Authors like Villon, Pulci, and Rabelais and preachers like Savonarola or St. Bernardino of Siena spoke from within or between two cultures, as Aron Gurevich insists: the *clericus* usually bore a residue of the *idiota* or *simplex,* while the latter had an injection of the *clericus*.[3] Thus, literate insider-outsiders might be too familiar with a culture's folkways to consider many of them worthy of record, while the records left by complete outsiders, lacking such mundane familiarity, could misconstrue social and symbolic contexts.

Moreover, when they took note of folk customs, literate locals were often hostile witnesses: "Other popular activities are documented simply because the authorities in church or state were trying to suppress them."[4] Trial records, public sermons, handbooks for confessors, and various legal documents therefore constitute an indispensable but biased resource for investigating popular beliefs. Thus, as Burke warns, written evidence of popular culture is always indirect at best; Gurevich waits for such texts to "blurt out" information which their authors "probably did not intend to say at all, and what is more, could not consciously have disclosed."[5] Texts can only suggest performances or conversations, even if observers attempt to transcribe immediately and respectfully, and texts are still less perspicuous when interpreted centuries later. When documented at all, popular culture is a palimpsest, to be deciphered warily.

Even since the advent of electronic audio and video recording, transmission of unsophisticated people's thoughts and beliefs remains an elusive goal. Reliable testimony depends on asking the proper questions, which neither local knowledge nor an anthropological—that is, external—perspective can guarantee. In the early modern period, investigation turned the cultural divide into a hostile frontier, and judicial interrogators, acting for civic or ecclesiastical courts, often asked unsympathetic questions drawn from formularies (standardized lists). Confessor-priests also might begin from written lists of questions, but confessional secrecy normally prohibited recording answers. Carlo Ginzburg maintains that modern historians are condemned to resemble inquisitors, since they depend on the hostile questions investigators asked and the evasive answers they received.[6] However, Ginzburg, Burke, Gurevich, and others have shown that indirect evidence for what the folk believed can be sifted both from the questions asked and from answers given.

Burke pointed to the work of Ginzburg, Keith Thomas, and Alan Macfarlane[7] as particularly fruitful examples of oblique approaches to popular culture, and the intervening decades have vindicated his choices. All three historians have performed and inspired valuable demonstrations that witchcraft records and confessors' manuals provide rich sources for understanding common people, including their sexuality, from the fifteenth through the seventeenth centuries.

MAGIC, WITCHCRAFT, AND POPULAR CULTURE

Although based on an asymmetry of power, the interaction of literate and illiterate people was ultimately dialogic. As Ginzburg asserts, "the lack of communication on a cultural level" in trial records can permit "rather paradoxically, the emergence of a real dialogue—in the Bakhtinian sense of a clash of unresolved voices."[8] Understanding the importance of magical thinking to popular sexuality requires comprehending the total dialogic process, and thus inquiring how "witchcraft" became such a murderous obsession of literate Europeans. The answer is complex, involving first, the singular definition of witchcraft developed by Christian writers between 1400 and 1700; second, the concomitant misrepresentation of illiterate beliefs about the connection between magic and sexuality; and third, the degree of continuity between early modern popular culture and pre-Renaissance or even pre-Christian beliefs and mores. These questions allow us to envision the extent to which European witchcraft, in the form most familiar to modern readers, might reflect oral, traditional culture.

The concept of witchcraft in early modern Europe resulted from a gradual process of accretion that occupied much of the fifteenth century. When fully formed, the "cumulative concept"[9] identified all popular magic as witchcraft: that is, a form of communication and cooperation between maleficent humans and evil spirits. This characteristic distinguishes the early modern witchcraft construct both from concepts of magic, sorcery, and witchcraft in other known cultures and, more importantly, from the concepts that held sway among literate Europeans before 1400. The peculiar character of this cumulative concept resulted from the dialogue between literate and illiterate cultures.

The date 1450 marks a crucial moment in the dialogue and is documented in one of the seminal texts of early modern writing about magic, Jean Vinet's *Treatise Against Those Who Invoke Devils (Tractatus contra demonum invocatores)*. Vinet, a Dominican inquisitor active at Carcassonne in southern France, composed his tract before the Latin and vernacular vocabularies had found stable terminology for "witches" and "witchcraft." Like other writers of the period, he railed against a supposed new breed of heretics, who, far from being ignorant dupes of demons (or Satan himself), knowingly worshiped them and made agreements binding the evil spirits to wreak harm on good Christians.

Just as important as crimes against third parties were the personal interactions that literate men imagined taking place between these "invokers" and demons (fig. 7.1). Before agreeing to harm the invokers' victims, demons allegedly demanded a formal agreement (or pact) that bound the invokers to reciprocity. Writers like Vinet described several forms of reciprocation, but Vinet placed particular emphasis on "the depositions and confessions of some women, who confess that they have coupled with demons."[10] The shockingly transgressive sexuality imputed to witches supposedly reflected obstinate religious devi-

FIGURE 7.1: Illustration from Ulrich Molitor, *On Witches (Von den Unholden und Hexen)*, woodcut, 1489.

ance, and demonic copulation allegedly formalized the wrongful worship. The conflation of harmful magic, sex, and demonolatry differentiates the European construct after 1400 from magical beliefs in other cultures and, to a large extent, from earlier notions on European territory. Early modern intellectuals quite literally demonized sexuality: except in England, female witches were regularly forced to confess having sexual intercourse with demons.[11] Likewise, the demons' attacks on victims designated by the witches supposedly weakened, subverted, or corrupted the legitimate sexuality of non-witches.

The formal pact or covenant between witches and demons reflected the literate notion that in themselves witches were powerless, and relied on demons for just this reason. After 1400, literate observers assumed that European witches could perform few types of harm unaided, and then only against absolutely helpless individuals. Even in cases of alleged infanticide, witches needed demons' assistance to circumvent the vigilance of parents and pass unnoticed.[12] By contrast, illiterate Europeans, like people in other cultures, thought the witch controlled the power to do harm; although magic might involve spirits, they were not the sole or primary source of harmful power.[13]

A unique feature is the overwhelming predominance of women among persons accused or convicted of witchcraft in early modern Europe: of 35,000 to 50,000 executions between circa 1400 and 1700, about 80 percent were women.[14] However, although Vinet was already placing major emphasis on the sexuality of female witches, women only gradually came to predominate among accused witches; even some late witch hunts largely targeted males. Nonetheless, the stereotypical witch became female, making witchcraft literature largely a discourse on female sexuality, reflecting the presupposition that, since women *should* be powerless, "any disordering manifestation of women's power, influence, or behavior must be understood in terms of sexual perversity."[15]

After 1400 these features—demonolatry, sexuality, the witch's powerlessness without a demonic co-conspirator, and the progressive gendering of witchcraft as female—mark European witchcraft as a concept of magic that was not dependent on timeless oral tradition.[16] Rather, "witchcraft" was the cumulative product of a new interaction between the popular culture of illiterate village people, in which magical beliefs were central to sexuality, and the culture of literate elites, especially churchmen and lawyers, obsessed by the need to uncover and extirpate religious and political subversion. The attention of learned men was newly drawn to accusations of magical harm that simple people traditionally made against each other, because literate conceptions of evil spirits had undergone radical changes. Since about 1200, demonology had developed into a systematic, "scientific" discussion of ontology and causality, under the aegis of Scholastic philosophy and theology. Folk magic seemed to offer confirmation of demonic activity.[17]

Thus "witchcraft" developed from demonological theories devised and spread by literate men who were, on the whole, suspicious and hostile toward the magical culture of illiterate country and village people. Literate demonology profoundly misconstrued illiterate conceptions of the nature and functioning of magical harm, inserting demons as a third element in a relation where they had previously figured little, if at all.[18] Nonetheless, when carefully evaluated, written records of accusations, and the explanations of them distilled by literate demonologists, can offer the oblique insight into popular sexuality that Peter Burke described.

POPULAR MAGIC AND SEXUALITY

In the restrictive and often precarious environment of agricultural communities, jealousies and hostilities, sometimes nourished over long periods, could break out into accusations of murder, destruction of livestock or crops, theft of property, and attacks on sexuality (barrenness, impotence, or alienation of affection).[19] When the enmity was strong and the evidence of guilt (by judicial standards) was not, magical explanations, many of them traditional, came easily to the uneducated. At the village level, magical harm was to a great extent already gendered as female, even before being misconstrued as demonic witchcraft. Practices of magic and sorcery, and fears of falling victim to witchcraft perpetrated by elusive malefactors, were already often "female" by definition, since women were less physically (i.e., obviously) powerful, and since their traditional work involved childbirth, care of children and the ill, preparation of the dead for burial, food preparation, and aspects of agriculture and animal care. In village society, the most vulnerable were vulnerable to women.

Early medieval secular law codes had sometimes punished magical crimes, but until the late fourteenth century, belief in the efficacy of magic was largely discountenanced by the Church, and considered evidence of one's ignorance or weak faith. Penitentials (manuals for confessors) and various forms of Church decree advised parish priests and confessors to refute accusations and confessions of crimes committed by magical means, and to prescribe penance or excommunication to individuals who persisted in making them.[20] But during the decades around 1400, some influential churchmen and lay judges began opposing the literate consensus on the illusoriness of magic. Increasingly, they took seriously accusations of magical harm and harshly prosecuted and punished the alleged perpetrators.[21] The energy that, in previous centuries, had been expended explaining that magical crimes could not take place was now refocused toward explaining *how* they took place, and more importantly, *that* they took place in reality, rather than in the deluded imaginations of ignorant people. Jean Vinet was one of the pivotal figures in this monumental change of attitude. By 1484, Pope Innocent VIII could declare as an established fact, in the bull *Summis desiderantes affectibus,* that numerous apostate Christians of both sexes denied their baptism and defected to the forces of Satan, copulated eagerly with devils, and wrought extreme harm on children, livestock, crops, and human fertility, by means of "incantations, charms and conjurings, and by other abominable superstitions and sortileges, offenses, crimes, and misdeeds."[22] The *Hammer of Witches (Malleus maleficarum,* 1486/7), which habitually carried this bull as its preface, declared that all witchcraft originated in carnal lust, and that witchcraft *(maleficium)* should be called the crime of *maleficae* rather than of *malefici,* since the great majority of its practitioners were women.[23]

There is no single trigger for this rapid change in literate attitudes toward magical crime. Developments in social, economic, epidemiological, and political realities had been causing major discouragement for over a century: the Great Famine of 1315–1317, the Black Death of 1347 and following years, the Hundred Years War (1337–1453), the exile of the Papacy to Avignon (1309–1377), the Great Schism (1378–1417) with its competing popes, the dissension between popes and church councils, and many other negative developments had made the fourteenth century one of the most "calamitous" in European history, so much so that Europe seemed to be "on the brink of the apocalypse."[24] In addition to these developments, heresy had become a major influence on Europeans since the late twelfth century, provoking the institutionalization of the Inquisition (1230s–1370s), the "Crusade" against the Cathars of Southern France (1208–1229), and the establishment of the preaching orders (Dominicans in 1216 and Franciscans in 1223) to combat the unlicensed preaching and other activities of groups who contested doctrines and practices of the Roman Church (Waldensians, Cathars, Hussites, and others).

HERESY AND THE LITERATE DISTRUST
OF COMMON FOLK

Definitions of heresy were devised by the self-perpetuating guardians of orthodoxy, the ecclesiastical hierarchy of popes, cardinals, bishops, priests, and (after 1258) inquisitors like Vinet. These were men educated in the fine distinctions of logical, textual, and legal analysis at universities and in the *studia* or theological seminaries of religious orders such as the Dominicans and Franciscans. They distrusted the capacity and willingness of common people to understand and abide by the rules of worship and conduct established by the Roman Church, yet to enforce these norms they depended upon informants drawn from the same classes, some of whom were interviewed under torture. After 1400, even secular courts, where witchcraft was treated as a civil crime, were penetrated by the religious condemnation of it as sin and heresy.

The cross-fertilization of antiheretical and antimagical thinking produced the stereotypical activities of witchcraft—mass movements of anti-Christian conspirators, nocturnal orgies, demonolatry, infanticide, cannibalism—accusations leveled against people identified only as heretics between the late twelfth and early fifteenth centuries. The sexualization of magic and sorcery as "witchcraft" after 1400 could also be termed the "bewitching" of sexual deviance, since heretics had long been imagined by their ecclesiastical enemies as shamelessly perverted.[25] In the early 1400s, clerical descriptions of supposed Waldensians, "Vaudois," and "Gazarii" (Cathars) are indistinguishable from later portrayals of witches: sexually licentious, cannibalistic demon worshippers, inimical to the health and reproduction of good Christians, their crops and animals. The Council of Basel (1431–1437) helped create the literate stereotype of witchcraft, for it brought together several articulate churchmen for long periods, enabling them to confabulate and compare notes about heretical movements (especially the Hussites) and common people's supposed diabolical practices. Their treatises soon propagated these ideas, inspiring further developments in the stereotype.[26]

POPULAR BELIEFS ABOUT DEMONS AND SEXUALITY

Before 1400, written descriptions of ordinary people's sexual beliefs and practices—given by recorders of secular law codes and Church documents—appear to be less radically skewed by literate preoccupations. The role of demons in common people's sexuality is smaller the further back in time one travels. Although demons might offer sexual temptation, sexual relations between humans and demons were not considered widespread or evidence of apostasy. Rather than mass movements of avid paramours of demons, records before 1400 (and some later ones) portray individual humans as sexual victims of demons. The *Malleus maleficarum* actually declared that until about 1400, women had not voluntarily coupled with demons (an opinion that eerily corroborates historical evidence about the date at which literate witchcraft stereotypes began consolidating).[27] St. Bernard of Clairvaux (d. 1153) is the protagonist of a famous story about an incubus, that is, a demon who had sexual intercourse with a woman. The monk was approached by a woman who complained that, for six years, she had been sexually molested by a demon. According to thirteenth-century sources, Bernard heard her confession sympathetically and prescribed penance. He also excommunicated the demon through a formal exorcism, driving it from the town. In the version told two centuries later by the *Malleus,* the saint also directed that the woman place his own staff in her bed to block the demon's access.[28]

Males could also be victimized: the succubus preyed on them just as the incubus oppressed women. Vincent of Beauvais (d. 1264) told of a statue of Venus onto whose finger a bridegroom placed his wedding ring while playing ball. The statue (evidently animated by a demon) confiscated the ring, and thenceforth, whenever the man attempted to have sex with his wife, "Something cloudy and dense rolled between his body and his wife's." Eventually, owing to the intervention of a necromancer and another demon, "Venus" relinquished the ring.[29] Although the physician Johann Weyer (d. 1588) attributed most witchcraft confessions to mental illness, he collected both written and oral stories about human-demon interactions and quoted the confession of a handsome youth "that for many months he had been beset by a *succuba* (as they say) with the fairest form that he had ever seen." The being would enter his bedroom at night through closed walls and doors, overcome his resistance, and have relations with him until dawn, when she departed "almost noiselessly." Like the woman cured by St. Bernard, the young man had tried numerous expedients for ridding himself of this being, but none had worked. The bishop to whom he confessed advised him to move to another locality and undertake rigorous fasting and prayer; after a few days, he was completely cured.[30]

In Europe and elsewhere, such beliefs in demonic sexual predators had an extremely ancient history. The story of the "sons of God" taking wives among the "daughters of men" (Gen. 6:4) had been interpreted until late antiquity to mean that fallen angels mixed with women. Even a few early modern witchcraft theorists invoked the story as proof of incubi, despite their knowledge that medieval biblical exegetes had roundly condemned this interpretation since St Augustine (d. 430).[31] The biblical Book of Tobit related that the demon Asmodeus killed the first seven husbands of Sarah, until the angel Raphael taught her eighth fiancé how to defeat the demon; Asmodeus often figured in writings on incubi. St. Augustine himself heard other stories of demons' attempts to perform "filthiness" with women. The terms he used, *silvani, fauni,* and *dusii,* imply that his sources were varied. Augustine remained neutral on the question, declining to deny the possibility outright, but clearly remaining troubled by some of its implications about the nature of demons and their relations with humans.[32] Stories of succubi also predate the Hebrew Bible: ancient Mesopotamian mythologies describe a voluptuous womanlike demon, Lilitu, who seduced men and then killed them; Lilitu survived in Rabbinic traditions about Lilith.[33]

While European illiterates would not have known about Lilith or the "daughters of men" on their own, the antiquity of such mythology corroborates the hypothesis that medieval stories of demonically abused men and women seeking help from churchmen reflect actual experiences of common people. The shame and dread they expressed over these episodes, like the horrific feats of Lilitu and Asmodeus, reflect deep ambivalence about sexuality.

POPULAR SEXUALITY AND THE UNCANNY

But the symptomatology was physiological as well as psychological and probably reflects an origin that was somatic as well as cultural. Demonic sexual attacks are supposed to have usually happened at night, and very frequently in bed. The sufferers characteristically related the episodes as if they had been awake at the time, but the evidence suggests that the "attacks" took place during particularly vivid dreams: incubi and succubi appeared "from nowhere," perhaps coming through walls, barred doors, or shuttered windows. This uncanny feature probably reinforced the idea that the molesters were supernatural. Many sufferers complained of difficulty breathing and of feeling crushed, particularly in the chest; they often felt paralyzed and unable to move. "Incubus" had been a medical term for these symptoms since ancient times, for which natural explanations were available outside the context of witchcraft. As Reginald Scot proclaimed in 1584, "In truth this *Incubus* is a bodilie disease ... although it extend unto the trouble of the mind: which of some is called the Mare [nightmare] ... ingendred of a thicke vapor proceeding from the cruditie and rawnesse in the stomach." Under the influence of personal animosities, these symptoms were sometimes attributed to "hagriding," a variant wherein a specific witch was alleged to "ride" her sleeping victim, causing bad dreams and physical exhaustion.[34]

Symptoms suggest a very particular phase of sleep, the hypnopompic or in-between state preceding full wakefulness (*demi-sommeil*, *dormiveglia*, or *Halbschlaf*), a gradual transition from sleep to waking. There is a striking similarity between the symptomatology of these premodern sufferers and that of "alien abductees," who, since the 1960s, complain of being sexually abused by extraterrestrial beings. Some "abductees" affirm being taken bodily through the walls of their bedrooms; rather than being raped or sexually importuned in their beds, they report being whisked onto futuristic spaceships, where aliens subject them to humiliating and often painful physical examinations and surgical interventions, sometimes purloining their eggs or sperm for artificial reproduction, or inserting microchips and other invisible devices into their bodies. The most dramatic difference from the incubus paradigm is the modern victims' report that alien kidnappers seem well-intentioned, despite their cruelty.[35]

The physiological constants from ancient to postmodern times suggest that, in this hypnopompic dream state, sensations of paralysis and awareness of vulnerability to attack or humiliation are consistently sexualized, but that emotions of vulnerability have changed idiom: in the incubus stories reported to ecclesiastics, the threat was typically represented by the opposite sex. The modern "alien abduction" variant elides the element of gender: the sexless aliens reflect the impersonal demeanor of modern physicians and the depersonalizing procedures to which, with the best intentions, they subject patients. Yet vulnerability remains sexualized despite the lack of overt sexual aggression. Likewise, the oxymoronic, uncanny stereotype of the "hag" or elderly woman portrayed someone who was physiologically desexualized but endowed with long experience and traditional knowledge about sex, fertility, and death.[36] So it may be that some of the animosity toward older women in early modern accusations of witchcraft, particularly "hag-riding," encoded similar fears of humiliation and victimization by bearers of specialized medical and sexual knowledge.

WOMEN'S DREAMS, SEXUALITY, AND THE SUPERNATURAL

In this period as in others, sexuality and the involuntary exercise of imagination in dreams seem to have been mutually reinforcing, but particularly in the phenomena that became identified with witchcraft. Indeed, it seems likely that the combination of women's specialized knowledge and a culturewide experience of stereotyped uncanny dreams was one of the oldest folkloric elements recorded by medieval clerics. Documentation reveals that the change in attitude toward folkloric culture that launched the witchcraft stereotype around 1400 correlates to a radical reversal of literate attitudes toward a centuries-old description of European women's putative beliefs. At the beginning of the tenth century, a canon law collection included reports that certain women espoused pagan superstitions. One document, known as Canon *Episcopi,* warned bishops to have their clergy seek out women who averred that, on certain nights, "Diana, the goddess of pagans," summoned them to attend on her, and that, in her company "an innumerable multitude" of women rode great distances during "the silence of the night" on the backs of beasts. The Canon did not specify the precise nature of this night ride or its accompanying activities, though the reference to Diana might imply some relation to cults of the moon, and perhaps of fertility. Yet this could be an erroneous conclusion: the Canon apparently distorts the evidence, naming the nocturnal pagan goddess most familiar to literate clerics rather than the indigenous northern European cultic goddess.[37]

The Canon grants no validity whatever to this belief, dismissing the entire experience as an illusion caused by the "dreams and nocturnal visions" of women. By their idolatrous belief in the divine nature of "Diana" and the reality of the dream, the women enslave themselves to the Devil. Satan "transfigures himself into an angel of light" by posing as a beneficent divinity, and somehow projects various experiences onto the mind of the sleeping woman, involving people both known and unknown to her. The Canon does not display a sophisticated psychological theory: it merely distinguishes between experiences that happen "in the body" and those that happen only "in the spirit," that is, in the mind alone. The literate filter through which this stereotypical, gender-specific dream passes in the text appears to be relatively thin, and the Canon probably echoes the ritual or cultic components of one or more pre-Christian beliefs.[38]

Later writers encrusted the testimony with Christian ideology even as they added some authentically folkloric-sounding details. At the beginning of the eleventh century, another compiler implied that some women said they performed the night ride at the command of Satan, and he specified that the "other women" seen in any woman's dream were actually demons. He also called the nocturnal divinity "Diana," but in another passage referred to her parenthetically as "she whom common folly calls the witch Hulda," a more plausible nomenclature.[39]

In the mid-twelfth century, the Canon *Episcopi* was incorporated into the collection that became the definitive standard for canon law, Gratian's *Decretum*. Its inclusion put the text within reach of an even larger audience than before. Around the same time, in 1154, John of Salisbury added further details, some of which may be genuine. Rather than "Diana," he mentions the women's divinity as "a *noctiluca* [night-shiner, i.e., the moon] or Herodias or a witch-ruler of the night," apparently confusing the Germanic Hulda or Holda with the nemesis of John the Baptist. Rather than a ride, he describes the dream experience as "nocturnal assemblies at which they feast and riot and carry out other rites," and implies strongly that "simpleminded" men as well as "poor old women" have this belief. He also mentions activities at the "assemblies" that resemble later descriptions of the witches' sabbat: rewards and punishments of those attending, the killing and eating of infants, and the miraculous, safe return of the infants to their own cradles. John condemned all these beliefs as illusions foisted on ignorant, credulous simpletons by "sporting demons."[40]

Afterward, as Edward Peters remarks, these accusations received "remarkably little attention" until the mid-fourteenth century, when Jacopo Passavanti, a Florentine Dominican, mentioned the dream in a vernacular Italian text for preachers, saying that both "Diana, the ancient goddess of the Greeks" and "Herodias, who had John the Baptist killed" were the leaders of the night ride. He referred to the whole company as female witches (*streghe*) and recorded a variant version, which he called the *tregenda,* a word that would later indicate the witches' sabbath. In Passavanti's variant, demons impersonated particular men and women in order to be witnessed by third parties passing by, who would spread scandal by reporting the "dishonorable" activities of the demons, thereby defaming the people who had been impersonated. This variant could be a literate interpretation of visionary experiences of common people unnerved by the necessity of traveling at night, who thought they witnessed their own neighbors performing murderous or sexual atrocities. (Hawthorne's "Young Goodman Brown" vividly evokes this uncanny state of mind, though in a later context, when Puritan layfolk fully subscribed to demonic causality.[41])

Like the incubus-complex of dreams, the night-traveling complex indicates that the popular experience of sexuality had a considerable element of the uncanny, even before being reimagined in a thoroughly demonic vein by suspicious literate witnesses. Other stories, involving demonic-seeming ghosts or even "animate" statues, carry the same message (fig. 7.2).[42]

FIGURE 7.2: Hans Baldung Grien, *Witches* (*Hexen*), woodcut, 1508.

FEMALE PHARMACOLOGY

Less than a century after Passavanti, around 1440, evidence emerged that, at least in some instances, the stereotypical night-traveling dream may have been caused by hallucinogenic drugs. Two churchmen, Alonso Tostado and Johannes Nider, independently transmitted anecdotes that apparently refract experiences of actual women, rather than repeating literary commonplaces. In both instances, a woman insisted that her night traveling happened in reality rather than in dreams but challenged skeptics to disprove her experience. In his *Formicarius* or *Anthill* (1437/8), Nider recounted that, about 1380, a woman tried to convince a Dominican friar that he was wrong to dismiss her claim to travel with Diana. If Nider's story was genuine, (1) its reference to Diana suggests that the friar was citing Canon *Episcopi* as his authority for skepticism; (2) this woman's contention was more extreme than those of earlier women: she believed she actually flew through the air rather than galloped across the earth's surface. She arranged for the Dominican and his chosen witnesses to observe her next experience. Rather than a bed, she had prepared a tub as vehicle for her "flight" and fell asleep after rubbing an ointment on herself and speaking some magic words. Not only did the woman not fly away, but she injured herself when her tub fell off the bench where she had perched it, owing to her excited movements in her sleep.[43]

Tostado relates a similar incident, in which a woman offered to demonstrate her flight to skeptical neighbors (no clergyman is mentioned). Like the other woman, she used an ointment and ritualistic words and fell into a deep sleep. Reviving after several hours, she recounted a detailed experience involving "various pleasures" and claimed to have seen several people known to herself and her neighbors. But her neighbors, who had expected something of the sort, had taken advantage of her anesthesia and had beaten her and burned her in several places during her dream. Only gradually, as the effects of the drug wore off, did she become aware of her injuries; once she did, she had to admit that her happy experience had been a dream.[44]

Paradoxically, Nider was arguing for a certain amount of demonic reality in the experience, for he concentrated on the woman's magical formula— "demonic words"—rather than her ointment. Similarly, Tostado averred that, although the woman in his story was deluded, there were women who performed the flying for real, in the flesh, and in the company of demons. Yet Tostado argued strongly that the anesthetic properties of the drug, as well as its hallucinogenic qualities, were entirely natural (i.e., not supernatural), maintaining that it belonged to a class of "substances that by their very nature take away the sense of pain."[45] As with earlier versions, these experiences seem to reflect something that common people probably did or believed. The ulterior motives of the clerical authors account for a certain amount of ideological distortion, but the core of the dream experience seems folkloric.

Nider and Tostado represent a transitional point, somewhere between the centuries-old view that women were deluded by dream experiences and the triumph of a fully demonized witchcraft stereotype a few years later. In that stereotype, prejudices about women's sexuality soon overwhelmed the core of probable folk belief, as literate men tried ever harder to prove that night flight was a real, waking bodily experience of transportation by demons, and that it involved deliberate sexual transgressions. Even when describing the deluded woman, Tostado asserted that witches (*maleficae*) claimed that the night traveling had as its goal orgiastic gatherings where "men and women … enjoy every sort of pleasures, both in food and in sexual intercourse."[46] The sexualization of such stories may reflect a core of popular reality as well as literate prejudice: a writer of the 1520s tells of a man who promised a witch that he would attend a sabbat if she worked love magic to procure him the girl he desired. After enjoying the girl sexually, the man flew to the sabbat with both witch and girl, on the back of a seeming horse, after all three used the witch's unguent.[47] It does seem, after stripping away as much literate prejudice as possible from these and related stories, that certain women, as far-scattered as Spain and Switzerland, were familiar with drugs that could produce pleasurable dreams, which may have had an element of sexual symbolism (e.g., flight) and wish fulfillment. The drugs required partial or complete nudity, being absorbed through the skin, and some might have stimulated sexual pleasure. It is possible that slightly later accounts, telling of naked women anointing their pudenda and/or the sticks that they straddled in order to fly, have an element of fidelity to actual practice, both in their sexual, phallic symbolism and in the means of delivering the drug (perhaps through the membranes of the vagina).[48] Some drugs may have been derived from the toxic secretions of certain toads, and it has been suggested that toads are linked both to words for witches and to certain representations of the uterus in the form of a toad, both of which suggest very old symbolism.[49] However, recent researchers speculate that similar practices were associated with shamanistic rituals, involving travel to other dimensions or worlds, in search of supernatural counsel or magical objects for the benefit of entire communities rather than for individual hedonism. Once again, the exact nature and chronology of such practices is uncertain, as the records are written, external to the folk cultures involved, and largely hostile.[50]

LOVE MAGIC

Such knowledge of herbal and animal derivatives was common among women (and many men) in traditional European societies, and both preparation and use of these substances were frequently accompanied by ritual incantations.[51] Indeed, much folk magic involves ritual knowledge and practice; furthermore, its aims were often sexual in nature or intent. Love magic attempted to control the emotions of others (and incidentally granted mastery over one's own emotions). Love magic could be attempted at any stage of a relationship or infatuation: to gain the love of the desired person, to ensure his or her fidelity, to punish infidelity or abandonment. Since needing love magic implied a position of powerlessness or vulnerability, women and ecclesiastics may have practiced it more commonly than males of the laity.[52] But "manly" men were its beneficiaries as often as they were its targets. When Benvenuto Cellini fell in love with a beautiful Sicilian girl jealously guarded by her mother, a Sicilian priest performed elaborate necromantic rituals on his behalf in the Coliseum during two successive nights.[53] Love magic could also be divinatory, seeking to ascertain one's prospects, either generally, in the marriage market, or with regard to a desired individual. (The girls at Salem, Massachusetts, who unleashed the witch panic of 1692 had apparently experimented with divination that sought to identify future husbands' professions by mixing raw egg and water.)[54] Alternatively, divination might be employed to discover the whereabouts of a lover or spouse who had disappeared.

Techniques for forcing love included the use of bodily detritus, including excrement: the *Malleus maleficarum* tells of a woman who gained the love of men by mixing her feces in their food, while Johann Weyer recounts hearing that breaking a man's love for a woman required placing her feces in his shoes.[55] Menstrual blood was supposedly effective in binding love, as were certain herbs, picked at propitious times to the accompaniment of ritual chants. Sacramental elements, such as holy water and chrism oil, and even the Eucharistic elements could constrain love: mixing the wine or host with the victim's food or drink was powerful compulsion. Witches supposedly caused husbands to hate their wives by burying the heads or skins of snakes under the thresholds of their houses.[56]

Among the most dreaded spells were those intended to render married men impotent: without producing legitimate offspring a man was sexually shamed as well as economically handicapped. "Tying the points," or creating complicated knots in string or laces, especially during a man's wedding ceremony, was particularly dreaded: unless the string was found and untied carefully and thoroughly, the man would remain impotent. Knots tied in bands and cords of men's clothing were especially favored for this purpose; knotting a wolf's penis was also effective, as was breaking off the tip of a knife in the door of the victimized couple's bedchamber.[57] Weyer relates that one remedy "to be free from the evil eye and from sexual impotence" required the bridegroom to urinate through the wedding ring.[58] The evil eye was an extremely ancient superstition: one glance from an angry or envious person could cause numerous harms to adults, including impotence and infertility. One uncanny sexual malady that apparently occasioned considerable dread was the "theft" of the penis or testicles, caused by bewitchment. In all likelihood, the syndrome expressed a vicious cycle wherein panicky fear of impotence led to further shrinking of the genitalia and finally to a psychotic conviction of their disappearance. Although witchcraft texts like the *Malleus maleficarum* converted these cases into bizarre narratives of stolen penises (including colonies of them living in treetop nests and behaving like birds), the basic fear seems plausibly folkloric, given the constant dread of impotence in medieval and early modern society. In fact, witch panics caused by epidemics of stolen penises have surfaced as recently as 2008 in some African societies.[59]

UNCANNY INFANTICIDES

Determining the degree to which sexual practices and fears associated with magic were actually folkloric is tricky, since the literate men who discussed them in writing and print often drew parallels with practices and personages mentioned in Classical and Biblical texts, as the Canon *Episcopi* had done with "Diana." Nonetheless, it is likely that, when ancient practices were the term of comparison, they corroborated the genuinely folkloric character of their modern equivalents (always assuming the latter were described with some accuracy). This is the case with infanticide.

Fear of witchcraft in sexual matters extended to the birth and welfare of small children, who were thought to be stealthily menaced in manifold ways. The evil eye could actually kill small children.[60] Since ancient Roman times, tales had been told of the *strix,* a nocturnal birdlike creature who menaced and killed infants in their cradles, sucking their blood or otherwise consuming them. *Strix* was the word for a screech owl as well as this creature, and the *lamia,* an uncanny womanlike creature, was also vampiric and cannibalistic.[61] Both names became common designators for ordinary mortal witches before 1500. Several early texts describe female witches who

allegedly changed themselves into cats to facilitate attacking and killing ba-
bies in their cradles. Stories told by Saint Bernardino of Siena (d. 1444),
the *Malleus* (1486/7), Bartolomeo Spina (d. 1546), and other authors between the 1420s and the 1530s seem to reflect genuine folk distrust of both
cats and elderly women: the stealthiness of cats and the alleged perversity of
older women shine strongly through such anecdotes, as does the fragility of
infant life.[62] Literate demonologists seem to have transcribed these stories
straightforwardly, limiting their interference to insisting that women could
not turn into cats, as common people believed; rather, demons created the il-
lusory metamorphoses to disguise witches' infanticides.[63] Along with stories
of night traveling, these stories suggest that common people found sexual
experience of all sorts uncanny.

POSSESSION

The phenomena of demonic possession featured strongly in literate culture
thanks to the New Testament and to medieval miracle stories; both were widely
disseminated among the folk by preaching and the visual arts. Thus it is difficult
to know how common beliefs concerning possession were before ecclesiastical
demonology brought it to prominence. At any rate, the sexual aspects of possession phenomena became ever more strongly evident in this period. Possession oppressed the sufferer's body as well as her mind, and female demonic
possession was often an even more highly somatic experience than female
mysticism. Written accounts of female possession often show a disquietingly
voyeuristic tendency: since the sufferings of the victim must be observed and
"read" through the contortions of her body, there was sometimes a considerable sexualization in descriptions of the phenomena, and even in the words of
the possessed. Some victims seemed to take pride in their affliction, and some
complicity between victim and demon is often implied or stated. Exorcisms
became increasingly widespread and public during the period of witchcraft
persecution, particularly at the turn of the seventeenth century, when veritable
epidemics of female possession occurred. Possession could be turned into a
highly theatrical public performance of these disturbing aspects, as happened
to the nuns of Loudun in the 1630s.[64]

PICTORIAL REPRESENTATION

The graphic arts of the fifteenth through the early nineteenth centuries explicitly
displayed witchcraft phenomena as sexual. From the crude woodcuts adorning

FIGURE 7.3: Hans Baldung
Grien, *Three Witches* (*Hexen*),
woodcut, 1514.

the works of Ulrich Molitor (ca. 1489) to the exquisite compositions of
seventeenth-century painters, the subject of witchcraft was a pretext—and
sometimes little more—for displays of the naked female body, whether young,
old, or in-between. The anatomy of male witches was never displayed in witchcraft iconography with anything approaching the explicitness of female witch
nudes, even during periods when male nudity was aesthetically acceptable.
The drawings and engravings of Hans Baldung Grien (d. 1545) in particular
explored an uncommonly thorough range of feminine body types, postures,
and symbolic sexual accoutrements during the first quarter of the sixteenth
century (fig. 7.3).[65]

In summary, early modern popular culture, to the extent that it can be
disentangled from the written sources, associated sexuality and gender with
far more than sex in the modern sense. The web of social relations, fears,
aspirations, and attempts to control the behavior of relatives and neighbors
meant that corporeality, fertility, and social status were mutually implicated.
For these reasons, witchcraft and magic, with their uncanny overtones of
mysterious causality, remain rich sources for studying popular beliefs. In witchcraft documents, the *vox populi* can often be heard above the hostile crosstalk
of literate culture that distorted the assumptions of the record keepers.

CHAPTER EIGHT

Prostitution: Looking for Love

GUIDO RUGGIERO

Paradoxically across the long sixteenth century the perception of prostitution appeared to be moving in two virtually opposite directions at once. On the one hand, it was viewed with increasing insistence as reprehensible morally, socially, and economically. But at the same time it flourished and was celebrated as never before, provided a wide range of services that were perceived as needed, fit relatively comfortably into the social and marital order of society, and even played a role in widely shared desires to more strictly define social distinctions. And significantly, to a great extent this paradox in conflicting perceptions turned on the apparently simple question of love: I would like to argue that to a surprising degree prostitution in the Renaissance was as much about buying love and falling in love as about sex. Thus to simplify greatly, when prostitution was viewed in terms of love (and love and sex) it tended to be viewed positively, and when it was viewed in terms of sex (and sex and money) it tended more and more to be viewed negatively.

We are so conditioned by a modern vision of prostitution as an economic and exploitative relationship that it is difficult to imagine that love could be an important part of its Renaissance reality. Certainly at the time prostitution was exploitative and economics played a major part in that exploitation, but significantly Renaissance prostitution was just that—Renaissance, not modern—and much more was involved. To set the stage and perhaps break a bit of our stereotypical vision of prostitution, let me take you to a house rented by two women who were labeled by their neighbors as prostitutes (*puttane*), pimps (*ruffiane*), and magicians (*herberie*). It was a late summer night in 1581 when the maid of a gold worker named Pietro called him to the window to look into the home of Margarita and Barbara. He recalled:

> She said, "Come over here if you want to see something interesting." I went immediately to my window from which you can see into the house of Margarita who I saw totally nude ... and there was a table set with small loaves of bread and a jug of red wine and another of water. At the head of the table there was a lit candle. Margarita had turned her back to the table and was leaning against it ... she was masturbating as Barbara stood before her with a smoking oil lamp.

He then related how Margarita climbed onto the table and rubbed her body with the bread and wine—perhaps in some echo of the Last Supper—as Barbara read from a book. Finally she climbed down from the table, undressed Barbara, and they began casting beans.[1]

The accounts of Pietro's maid and Pietro's brother, who also watched, were if anything more lurid, and they leave us wondering what those two women were doing that late-summer evening. Yet for their voyeuristic watchers and the Venetian Holy Office, which heard their testimony, the answer was obvious: they were prostitutes using heretical love magic to attract lovers. Margarita and Barbara eventually freely admitted a wide range of love magic designed to measure, attract, and hold the love of men. And although they admitted that these men paid for their services, they referred to them as lovers, not clients, and it is clear that love and its magic were an important part of their emotional relationships with them. In fact, in this they were not unusual, because, where the information exists, prostitution and love magic regularly went hand in hand, and prostitutes were widely assumed to be experts in such magic whether they were or not. That in turn leads to the suggestive question that if prostitution was merely an economic relationship where men paid for sex, why were prostitutes using love magic? There were many other types of magic that could be used to make others do what one wanted (and presumably pay for sex): magic that from time to time prostitutes used, although more often to harm rivals than to gain clients. A much more likely answer is that prostitutes expected or at least hoped that their clients were looking for love as well as sex and that both clients and prostitutes saw love as an important part of prostitution. To make that point, however, we have to look more closely at Renaissance prostitution.

In a perhaps justly little-known, untitled one-act comedy embedded in the "Seventh Night" of *Le piacevoli e amorose notti dei novizi* written around 1550 by Pietro Fortini, the servant of a young Sienese nobleman describes how his master, Oresto, was making a name for himself in Rome: "[Recently] Messer Oresto, gentleman of Siena, came to Rome. For his retainers he had made an impressive livery. He invited to dinner those [important men] who happened to visit him. He dressed nobly. *He wished to play with that special courtesan*. And [he did] other impressive deeds."[2] Suggestively in this short list of "impressive" deeds that were helping his master catch the eye of the people who mattered in Rome, Oresto includes playing with "that special courtesan" (*la tal cortigiana*), in other words, a courtesan of enough note in the city that she would add to his reputation. Clearly this ideal courtesan was not a simple sex worker. She was much more, and tellingly, polite and refined love was one of the things that made her and her art special.

Written in Siena apparently in the context of an ongoing rivalry between local literary societies, *Le piacevoli e amorosi notti* was one of the more transgressive texts, both erotically and in terms of genre, of a rather playfully transgressive group of works produced there across the century. As was the case for prostitution in general, most literary accounts of Renaissance courtesans tended to present them as either evil, grasping, hard-hearted sirens ever ready to empty the purses of those who unwarily fell into their clutches, or as desirable objects of love who were highly appreciated adornments of gentlemen.[3] Fortini presented the courtesan protagonist of this comedy, Doralice, following the second model as the epitome of the "honest" courtesan—polite, well mannered, full of grace and understanding. She entered the comedy in the fifth scene of the first and only act, observing with admiration the manners and the figure cut by Oresto from a distance: "Certainly he has the grace of a nobleman, gentle and mannerly."[4] Informed by one of his servants that he was "young, handsome, rich, open-handed and moreover his wife was the most beautiful daughter of Siena,"[5] she responds with measured words, noting that a good wife was the capstone to his other impressive qualities—a noble and honest sentiment from a noble and honest prostitute.

Significantly, although she also refers to his wealth, it is merely one of his many positive attributes, and the closest she comes to expressing any more self-serving interest in that wealth is this courtly sentiment: "Such people one desires to please and keep their friendship, because they are capable of recognizing such benefits."[6] In fact, the relationship that she initiates with Oresto is one rich in courtly graces and manners, where money plays a minor role. When, for example, shortly thereafter in scene eight, she and Oresto begin to plan a night of pleasure together, he asks a supportive pedant—there are two pedants in this comedy, one honest and helpful, the other stereotypically self-serving, domineering, and corrupt—to pay ten scudi to have a meal prepared for them. She objects: "Your lordship is too kind and gentle; do you think the provisions [for a meal at my house] are lacking?"[7] When he replies that that is much less than "your ladyship deserves," she continues the courtly dance of compliments: "All the gentleness, all the courtesy, all the handsomeness that there is in the world is to be found in your lordship."[8]

Of course, all this banter might have served to cover more grasping realities, but significantly they are virtually absent in the comedy. Only the negative character, the second and evil pedant, Flavonio, attempting to demean Doralice, alludes slyly in the midst of apparent compliments to the negative attributes of the stereotypical money-hungry whore: "Messer Oresto, today you can brag about something that not many men in Rome can claim, if you go to play with this lady, for she is the most beautiful, delicate, desired and rich courtesan that today one can find in this city *common to all men*."[9] This draws a quick and revealing rebuke from Doralice: "There are quite a few more beautiful, richer and *more common* than me."[10] Modesty about beauty and wealth aside, she objects to Flavonio's claim that she is common to all men, for that implies she is a common whore who is willing to sell her body to any buyer to make money.

Behind this give-and-take lay a crucial reality: the Renaissance courtesan was perched atop a social hierarchy of prostitution, and that position in many ways turned on the fact that she was not available to all, not common and money grubbing; rather, she honestly selected the best men as lovers and rejected the unworthy. Moving from the imaginative world of literary characters such as Doralice and Oresto to the urban world where prostitution flourished, as social stratifications became increasingly significant and carefully drawn across the Renaissance, it is not surprising to find that social distinctions were also being more careful drawn among prostitutes.

A brief review of those distinctions provides a clearer view of the complexity of high Renaissance prostitution. In larger Italian cities like Rome, Venice, Florence, and Naples and a few cities of northern Europe, several levels of prostitution flourished. At the bottom were the numerous women who worked from time to time as prostitutes to survive in the tough urban environment of the day. Some were married and attempting to help their families survive economically; some were unmarried (from the countryside or poor families) and also pressed by circumstances to occasionally prostitute themselves. Archival documents occasionally refer to these women in passing, especially criminal documents, and it is interesting to note that they were often seen by their neighbors as good and honorable, their prostitution notwithstanding. In fact, it appears that their willingness to sacrifice their bodies for their families often added to their positive reputation as long as they were perceived as doing so out of necessity, occasionally and quietly. A woman who flaunted her practice or earnings, however, was another matter and quickly garnered the condemnation of neighbors and complaints to authorities, especially when her practice disrupted the neighborhood. These irregular prostitutes avoided the registration that was required for taxation (and occasionally for health purposes) and thus were formally illegal. But their practice was at a level well below the disciplining potential of most policing and judicial bureaucracies and thus was largely ignored by authorities.

In archival documents registered prostitutes who worked in larger brothels, usually publicly run or sublet to important local families, were more visible. Such brothels in the late Middle Ages and early Renaissance were usually at the center of cities, although there was a trend as the sixteenth century progressed to move them to lesser-trafficked areas of the city or outside the walls in a move to protect decorum and sustain at least the image of a more moral city. This trend culminated in many cities in the official closing of brothels in the later sixteenth century. In the north of Europe this was associated with the Reformation and the ideal of creating a more morally pure society, and in the south it was often associated with Catholic reform and aggressive preachers who stressed the immorality and dangers of prostitution. But earlier, the public brothel at the center of Renaissance cities was seen as a positive accoutrement of the urban environment, as the well-known fifteenth-century paean to Florence by Panormita dedicated to Cosimo de' Medici reveals:

> At the heart of the city there is a place full of joy ... Seek the grandeur of the high dome of Santa Reparata [the cathedral] or ask for the magnificent church of God that shows the Lamb [the Bapistry]. Once there bear to the right a few paces ... and ask for the Mercato Vecchio. There halfway down the street stands a happy whorehouse which you will know by the very smell of the place. Enter and give my greetings to the whores and madams ... The blond Helena and the sweet Matilda will greet you ... You will see Giannetta and ... the naked and painted breasts of Claudia ... Here you can find anything that is illicit.[11]

Although it may at first seem strange, as Jacques Rossiaud pointed out for France, many of these houses were organized much like convents, with an "abbess" responsible for the discipline of "sisters" and a form of isolation that often required prostitutes to live in the house and observe curfew. Convents, however, were one of the few models for organizing the life of women living outside of the normative family structure of Renaissance society, and in both types of houses women were pursuing goals that made their placement problematic and their sexual separation from regular society seem necessary. Rossiaud notes that in French cities prostitutes used the brothel as a base but often went out into the streets, taverns, and baths of the city to recruit clients.[12] In Florence, however, and other Italian cities they were usually required to work from the brothel itself and in theory, although probably not in fact, their time outside the brothel was carefully limited and disciplined both by those in charge of the brothel and municipal authorities.[13]

A third group of prostitutes to be found in most sixteenth-century cities were registered women (where legally required) who worked independently, often managed by a procurer or procuress. *Ruffiani* (male pimps) or *ruffiane* (female), as they were often called in Italy, arranged contacts, protected prostitutes, and were in turn supported by them. It appears that before the sixteenth century males dominated this business, but women played a more and more important role across the century, frequently mothers or ex-prostitutes, perhaps reflecting a somewhat less violent tenor of business, especially at the higher levels. In Italy, there also appears to have been a certain association of the matchmakers who arranged marriages, *sensale di matrimonio*, especially at lower social levels, with *ruffiani*, perhaps because at lower social levels it was relatively easy to slide from one to the other. In fact, there existed several gradations of matchmakers, moving from those who arranged marriages at the most positive level from the point of view of licit society, through to those who helped arrange nonmarital matches and affairs (go-betweens or *mediani* as they were sometimes called) based on love, on down to those who actually pimped for prostitutes.

Whether a woman was managed by a procurer or not was often contingent upon her age and the price she could command. Younger women were frequently recruited and controlled by their *ruffiani* and were at their mercy unless they could find some way to escape their clutches. At times criminal records reveal that in the case of more mature women, these relationships were stabilized to a degree by a concubinal liaison or even marriage. Unfortunately, we have little information on how such relationships worked. Clearly, many were exploitative, as criminal prosecutions tend to reveal, but there are also suggestive examples of more supportive relationships where it appears a lower-class couple was working to survive together aided by the earnings of prostitution, and again love was often invoked in these relationships by both members of the pairing when they became visible in the criminal records.

A literary example is provided by Ludovico Ariosto's well-known comedy *La Lena*. Set in early sixteenth-century Ferrara, the aptly named protagonist Lena (*lena* was a synonym for *ruffiana*) had been prostituted by her husband, Pacifico, for years. No longer young, she had begun to move on to setting up love affairs. She also was employed as a servant in the home of her longtime, aged lover Fazio, with the support of her husband. In this, in a way, she seems to sum up in one character the probable career path of a *ruffiana*, and one that was presented with some sympathy by Ariosto. Although she plays the hard bargainer in helping to set up the young lover Flavio with the woman he desires, Livinia, who just happens to be Fazio's daughter, her traitorous deed is partially excused by Fazio's mistreatment of her in their own relationship, which is portrayed as more than economic. In fact, their quarrels have the flavor of lovers' quarrels, a perspective confirmed by the conclusion of the comedy: in the end, after the young lovers marry, Lena and Fazio make up and plan to spend the night happily together in celebration, with her husband's blessing.

What is most interesting, however, for this ménage à trois is the way their relationship is portrayed. Pacifico accepts his wife's affair with Fazio as long as it supports them but becomes intensely jealous and threatens violence when he assumes, erroneously, that she has made love to the young Flavio merely for pleasure. Their confrontation over this is particularly revealing. Pacifico reproves her: "Now look, Lena, what your evil and whorish ways have led you to!" When she replies aggressively, "Who made me a whore?" he tries to duck the issue, claiming that her sexual desire is the cause of all the problems. But she parries, "Actually it was your insatiable greed that reduced us to poverty; and if I had not come to your rescue giving myself up to a hundred jerks you would have starved to death. Now for the sacrifices that I made for you, you criticize me, calling me a whore." Tacitly admitting her case, Pacifico tries to regain the upper hand, reproving her for not being more reserved. But she rejects even that, claiming that if she had accepted every person whom he had brought her, she would have been no better off than the whores in the public brothel and would also have had to allow herself to be sodomized. Once again selectiveness is a crucial marker for Lena (and Ariosto's portrayal of her), and working in a brothel is seen as toward the bottom of the hierarchy of prostitution. Continuing to back down and trying to reestablish some sort of a peace,

Pacifico finally claims that he will accept everything that she has done but insists that she not "pimp (*ruffianar*) the daughters of honorable men," referring to her bringing together Fazio's daughter with Flavio. But once again Ariosto gives Lena winning lines:

> If I were to remain young forever, it would be easy enough for me to maintain the two of us as I have up to now [via prostitution]. But like the ants that prepare for the winter it is only right that poor women like me prepare for our old age and while we are still capable learn a new trade (*arte*) ... And what trade could I do which I would be better prepared for and more capable of than this [pimping]?[14]

In a nutshell Lena makes her case that the move from prostitution to pimping is a logical progression, and the archival records suggest it was one that was often followed. More telling yet is the way that Ariosto presents Lena's situation sympathetically, even with her aggressive behavior and her betrayal of her master and lover Fazio. Both her prostitution to aid her husband and her new career as a *ruffiana* are portrayed as understandable. She is even given the winning lines in her argument with her husband, and lest anyone think that this is one of those reversals that is put right at the end of the play as in so many comedies, it should be noted that this one ends with a promise that after the marriage of the young lovers, Flavio and Licinia, things will return to "normal" for Lena, Pacifico, and Fazio—their illicit ménage à trois will continue, a thoroughly Renaissance "happy" ending.

As the sixteenth century progressed, however, *ruffiani* and *ruffiane* became more frequently the targets of moral reformers and governments anxious to curtail more flagrant and open forms of prostitution. To a great extent such attacks paralleled initiatives to first move brothels from the center of the city to the periphery and then in many cities to close them down altogether. Highly visible pimps in the streets propositioning clients also gave the lie to the more moral urban center that was being urged on society in Italy and other areas influenced by the Catholic Reformation, while, of course, in many ways in Reformation Europe, Protestant cities led the way in attacking pimps. But the attack on *ruffiani* also had an economic dimension, for governments, as they outlawed them, often referred to the way *ruffiani* preyed upon the poor women they prostituted. Laws were passed in many cities that attempted to break the hold of pimps on prostitutes via debt slavery and also attempted to limit their ability to recruit prostitutes using various scams based on false promises of marriage adopted to lure girls from the countryside. Yet even in this, economics played a secondary role to morality, as pimps were seen as not earning with their labor the money they collected from the women they prostituted, and in this they were perceived as sinners much like bankers and usurers.

Prostitutes, who worked for pimps or on their own, usually frequented particular establishments or areas of the city. Especially important in most cities were baths, taverns, and inns. In Venice, the baths, or *stue*, as they were called, most associated with prostitution were originally clustered around the public brothel, the Castelletto, at the heart of the city near the Rialto bridge. In fact, the buildings that housed them can still be seen today if one wanders in the back streets to the southeast of the Rialto just off the beaten path that leads to the large square of San Polo. In Florence the crowded warren of streets just north of the Arno, east of the Mercato Vecchio and southeast of main cathedral church, the Duomo, again pretty much at the heart of the city, was well furnished with baths and taverns that offered a full range of sins including drinking, gambling, and prostitution. As I have discussed in more detail else-where, this area "contained a host of taverns including the Bertuccie, Chias-solino, Fico, Malvagia, Panico, and Porco, names that in themselves virtually promised the whole program of the illicit world (respectively: the Monkey/Pussy/Ugly Whore; the Little Whore House/Little Confusion/Little Outhouse; The Fig/Cunt; the Wicked Woman; the Panic; and Pig/Depraved)."[15] It is im-portant to note that in Florence, and it seems more generally in Italy, it was not just women who worked as prostitutes from taverns, inns, and baths; young men also plied the trade. Some places even featured male prostitution. For ex-ample, in Florence the main cathedral, the Duomo, the Ponte Vecchio, and the warren of streets around the Via dei Pellicciai and two taverns, the Buco (near the Ponte Vecchio in an alley that still bears its name) and the Del Lino (not far from the Mercato Vecchio and just east of the Via dei Pellicciai), apparently offered virtually only male prostitutes.[16]

Along with part-time workers moving in and out of the profession as their needs pressed them, brothel and bordello workers and independent prostitutes, registered or unregistered, working for a procurer or on their own, from the late fifteenth century courtesans emerged as the elite of the trade—as Fortini's Doralice reveals well. Her response to Flavonio's not so subtle put-down that she is a woman common to all men quoted earlier in that context takes on deeper meaning. In fact, that she is not common to all men is the key to the plot of the play, for the evil pedant Flavonio, for all his negative comments about her, has also fallen in love with her and plans to trick his master into paying for his own night with her—a plan destined to founder in large part because as a base pedant he does not have enough social standing to be accepted by a courtesan like Doralice as her lover. But that is getting ahead of the story. As if to leave no doubt on the issue, Doralice tells Flavonio: "I am for all those people who most please me, especially those who have a magnanimous heart and are noble and well mannered, like messer Oresto here, and not everyone visits my house."[17] The point is clear: what Doralice claims sets her apart and makes her a courtesan is her ability to select the best, most noble, and well mannered men as her partners; the rest cannot even visit her house.

And she has selected the young Oresto as a worthy lover; thus, as noted earlier, the young couple plan an evening of pleasure Renaissance style. First, they will go to the baths together—Doralice suggests a bath run by a friend of hers that is of the higher tone that she requires—then they will return to her house for a sumptuous dinner followed by a night of love and pleasure. Flavonio tries to derail these plans immediately, warning his master that the streets of Rome are not safe at night, but Doralice reassures him that they are perfectly safe. Oresto, already the willing lover, readily accepts her word over his tutor's and warns the latter, "I am not a child [anymore]."[18] The deeper implication of that apparently simple comment is that as long as Oresto had accepted an inferior position to his pedant/tutor he was in a passive childlike position, but now that he is in love and making decisions on his own, their relationship has changed. Correctly reading the situation Flavonio worries about the new independence of his master and what a beautiful young courtesan like Doralice will mean for his own rapidly evaporating authority. A grumbling soliloquy makes the point:

> If she takes him with her to the bath and he sees such a beautiful creature naked there is the danger that he will not leave her ... It is all well and good that she is young and pretty ... but there is a real danger that if he does he will do something unwise. Young men are young ... If he falls for her and does not return from her what will happen to me?

Although Flavonio's fears are self-serving and presented in a negative way, they nonetheless were well attuned to one of the dangers of Renaissance prostitution relating to love that has been often overlooked. For while prostitutes served men of all ages, in most cities the clients that theoretically were their most important were young men (*giovani*) like Oresto.

In most societies young men and their sexual desires are viewed as problematic, but in sixteenth-century Europe young men were seen as especially troublesome, and there is every indication that they lived down to their reputation. What made this situation specific to the day, however, requires a brief discussion. First, youth (or adolescence, as it was also called in the period) was a longer period for males than it is today. It began in the early teens with the onset of puberty, when males were seen as passive and feminine both socially and sexually. As youths grew older and developed the bodily characteristics that the Renaissance associated with a more active manhood, such as facial hair and a heavier, more muscular body, it was assumed that males would become more active and aggressive. This transition was expected to occur in the late teens or early twenties at the latest. At social levels and in areas of Europe where youths of this age could be economically independent, marriage and a more settled family life ideally followed quickly. But in Italy and much of Europe, especially for the upper classes, things were not so easy. Wherever marriage and economic and social empowerment were delayed, youths found themselves in a rather difficult situation. Expected to be active and aggressive, they were largely still economically and socially passive, and even sexually they found little opportunity to express the active sexuality expected of them.

One result of this situation was the culture of sodomy that recent studies have identified as being an important part of the life of youths in Renaissance cities like Venice and Florence. There older youths, at least in theory, played the role of the active, aggressive partner in sexual relations with younger, passive partners in a way that almost perfectly followed the vision of the sexual and social development of youth. But young men expressed their new aggression and active roles in other ways as well, often violently. Scholars have discussed how important that violence was both in the cities and countryside of France, especially among youth groups, and similar groups appear to have played a role in the charivari, *mattinate,* and *baie* that scholars are beginning to investigate in Italy. Premarital sex or adultery with married women were also responses to this problem. Both are ubiquitous in literature, and premarital sex was seen as fairly normal at lower social levels, where ideally pregnancy was followed by marriage. Yet at higher social levels, where marriage was usually arranged and a matter of family alliances rather than personal choice, young men finding lovers among their social peers was rarely seen as positive. Down-class sex was easier to accept, but the social and economic costs of pregnant servants and concubines could be significant as well. In sum, the problems associated with falling in love, and actively expressing it, were great for male youths, and it seems likely they became greater over the period as society ideally became more aristocratic, mannerly, and peaceful.

Eventually, of course, it was assumed that this stage would pass and males would reach a full adulthood. But marriage and true economic and social power for upper-class males—the prerequisites for full adult status—often had to wait until well into a man's thirties. Inexpensive, public prostitution provided an opportunity for virtually all male youths to demonstrate an active role in sex. The fact that a prostitute who was bought ideally played the passive role to the youthful male's new active one may have actually helped make the transition from passive to active seem less threatening than it might otherwise have been. Certainly there were literary accounts and warnings in prescriptive texts about aggressive and domineering prostitutes who took advantage of youthful inexperience. Moreover many cities actually passed laws to protect youthful customers from being exploited economically. But read against the grain, these may reflect a concern to make sure that money bought what it was supposed to buy for a youthful customer, a securely passive partner to his now active sexual desires.

Another theoretical plus of the prostitute was that as a professional—not so much a sex worker as a sex artisan—she could be presumed to know how to *play* the passive loving role required and also how to help teach young men their active role. Forming young men sexually ideally (probably very ideally) could be seen as their true art. Be that as it may, one of the problems with this whole range of services prostitutes offered was that for upper-class males, common prostitutes were just that—common. And as society across the Renaissance became progressively more aristocratic, male youths in that transition from passive to active were under increasing pressure to move beyond common prostitutes to seek a higher class, more refined partner worthy of love. Thus it is hardly surprising that courtesans began to appear in Italy in the late fifteenth century as more courtly and aristocratic societies were winning out virtually everywhere. Much like Doralice, they offered much more than sex or even love for money. They offered both, of course, but they also offered refined courtly manners, educated conversation, and fine lodgings plus food, games, often music and play, and, as noted, they selected only the best to be their lovers. Thus they were labeled "honest," and upper-class youths in the great cities sought out their company as yet another marker of their social status and their new active role in society.

Significantly, however, "courtesan" was merely a label, and a contested one at that. Many prostitutes could claim such status and try to live up to it if they could win the support of a notable lover or two. In fact, in cities like Rome, Florence, and Venice, it appears such claims were made well down the social ladder of prostitution. This, almost certainly, played a major role in Doralice's apparently innocent remark to a servant in front of Oresto when organizing the night she planned to spend with him: "But if by chance Monsignor Farnese or his brother should wish to come visit me [this evening], someone [in my house] can tell them that I am not in."[19] Ottavio Farnese (1524–1586) and his brother, the cardinal Alessandro (1520–1589), were the sons of Pier Luigi Farnese, himself the son of the powerful pope Paul III (1468–1549; 1534–49). Clearly young Oresto, still labeled a *giovane* and just beginning to break free from his domineering pedant-tutor, had arrived when Doralice was ready to turn away cardinals and nephews of popes to enjoy an evening with him! And in turn, given her potential visitors she was far from a common whore.

Turning from literature to testimony before the Holy Office in Venice, when the Venetian courtesan Andriana Savorgnan was investigated for the love magic she supposedly used to win the love and the hand of the noble Marco Dandolo in marriage in the 1580s, her mother, Laura, was asked by that office: "Could you clear up for us whether your daughter has been a courtesan or a public prostitute here in Venice?" Her answer echoed Doralice's. "She has been a courtesan given her clients." Under further questioning she named the names that confirmed that those clients were from the topmost ranks of Venetian society: "They were Santo Contarini, Piso Pisani, Fillipo da Canal, the Count Scipio Avrogado, Paolo Robazzo ... and then there was the Celsi called Lorenzo and Messer Nicolo Corner, son of Messer Zorzi and Marco Dandolo."[20] That answer demolished her adversaries' claim that Andriana was a common whore, and the Holy Office left that issue behind to consider the more damning accusation that she had used love magic to win the hand of young Marco Dandolo. But once again here, outside of literature we find male youths finding pleasure, status, and love as the active sexual partners of courtesans. And lesser men with similar desires who could not quite move in the circles of cardinals or even the elite of the Venetian nobility, if they were willing to pay the price, could find prostitutes who claimed courtesan status or at the least appeared to be less common and more refined.

But the claim that Andriana Savorgnan used love magic to win Marco Dandolo's love brings us back to the issue of the association of such magic with prostitution that opened this essay. In fact, when one looks at the archival documentation generated by prostitution, three areas stand out: first, the economic, where the exploitation of customers and that of prostitutes was disciplined by government; second, the repression of violence, often youthful, associated with prostitution; and third, the sorting out of love, love magic, and the passions that prostitution elicited. Perhaps most significantly, prostitutes in Italy practiced a wide range of love magic to gain and hold the love of clients that would have made little sense if there was no expectation on their part that love was involved in their trade. In the sixteenth century we find prostitutes in Venice, for example, who had a regular diagnostics and program of love magic that they used for their art. First, there were several forms of measuring magic to evaluate how "close" a lover was in the sense of how deeply emotionally attached he was to her. The most common of these was the casting of beans, referred to in the case that opened this essay, where a prostitute or a cunning woman in her pay would throw a specific number of beans either marked or with markers that identified the prostitute and her lover as well as other competitors for his favor. A reading of how the beans fell allowed the prostitute to calculate what level of magic was necessary to hold or win a lover. Similar types of magic made use of the links of hearth chains and spanning distances with one's hand.

Gaining or retaining love involved several types of magic. Relatively simple prayers could come quite close to being mere prayers asking for a lover's love or return; but many of these prayerlike spells went well beyond asking for the aid of God, the Virgin, or specific saints to attempt to force their help in gaining love. And some, of course, called on the darker forces of the devil and his minions. Words were also used in written form, most notably as *carte di voler bene*, written-out spells often with symbols that were used to touch a lover and that then bound his love to the person who had touched him. More material magic used parts of the human body or animals and the metaphorical connections that seemed powerful at the time between these things and love. Magnets with their powers of attraction were popular, as were the hearts of animals and the bodily fluids associated with love and reproduction. Finally, of course, anti–love magic was also ubiquitous. Punishing magic that "hammered" an ex-lover or a competitor involved again all of the preceding, usually in a magic that reversed the positive binding force of the spell or objects; their destructive effect was occasionally reported with gory detail in criminal records.

In sum, prostitutes were deeply involved with love magic, and that involvement strongly suggests that they and many others assumed that love was a significant part of their trade. One key to this turned on the fact that love in the Renaissance was seen as a considerably different passion from the rather mild and mellow passion we celebrate today. It is not that modern love is all hearts and flowers. In fact, we are surrounded by disturbing crimes of passion that we carefully disassociate from love and a somewhat less disturbing range of "strange" deeds associated with love gone astray where negative passions are seen as overwhelming, more "normal" responses to love. In the Renaissance, however, at least some forms of love were viewed as much stronger and more violent. To simplify greatly, it might be suggested that there were at least four broad categories of love in early modern Europe: spiritual love, family love, friendship love, and passionate love. Spiritual love in its purest sense was the highest and most powerful. Aimed first at God, the Virgin Mary, and the pantheon of saints, for the mystic it could actually obliterate all the rest of life, while for more normal people it was a point of reference and source of spiritual power—and for many it provided a rationale for the violent and bloody religious wars that rocked Europe. More mundane was family love, but the ties that bound a family together, especially across generations, ideally were cemented by a deep and powerful emotional attachment. Of course, that was the ideal, and the reality could fall far short of that, with bitter battles within and between families at all social levels. But in a way the very violence of such battles attests to the power of the emotions involved. Less recognized by scholars until recently were the emotional ties associated with friendship, but the deep emotional relationships with friends that both men and women desired were the basis of extremely powerful attachments that were often the most important emotional bonds in people's lives.

Passionate love, however, between a man and a woman, while idealized in literature, was even as an ideal a dangerously powerful emotion. Thus Flavonio, in Fortini's comedy, moved by this virtually mad passion for the courtesan Doralice, goes against all his stereotypic pedantic sexual interests in young boys, puts at risk his own situation as tutor to Oresto, and tries to substitute himself for his master in her bed even as he realizes that she is unlikely to accept him. In a soliloquy, he explains his betrayal of his master: "In sum I want to see if at his expense I can satisfy my desire and enjoy her [Doralice] ... For her beautiful face surpasses everything and if I cannot find a way to have her, I would burn all my books and not want to study or be a pedant anymore."[21] Such sudden passion might be disregarded as merely a literary convention that assumed people fell suddenly and madly in love, a victim of this violent emotion, if not for the fact that again we have a great deal of documentary evidence that real people outside of literature not only felt the same sudden onset of passionate love but accepted and feared that this was normal. Clearly this was a dangerous passion. Moreover, imaginative and prescriptive literature stressed that it could disappear with the same alacrity and unnerving whimsy with which it appeared.

Interestingly, even that theoretically most Machiavellian of males, Niccolò Machiavelli himself, opined that he could not live without this mad passion that swept him up and left him powerless before its force. In a letter of 1515 to his good friend Francesco Vettori that was typical of much of his extensive correspondence on the subject, Machiavelli wrote about his love for his current courtesan mistress, La Riccia: "Those chains with which he [the God of Love] has bound me are so strong that I have given up completely on being free ... They weave a sort of web that forces me to conclude that I cannot live happily without that quality of life."[22]

This was not an emotion to base a marriage upon in the eyes of most people; it was simply too strong, too violent, too unstable. Thus parents and families insisted upon negotiating marriages for their children and attempted at all costs—but not always with success—to block love matches made between youths themselves. Tellingly, as a result, there was little association of passionate love and sex in marriage; at best there was a hope that the "marital debt," as it was called at the time, would be fulfilled with pleasure—limited in the eyes of religious moralists—and an ongoing warm affection that might grow up between well-matched couples. Although there is much more that could be said, the point is simply that in sixteenth-century Europe, matrimony and the marital bed were not likely places to seek passionate love. And while comedies, *novella,* and other forms of literature suggested that young men might enjoy love with young unmarried women as well as occasionally with married women and widows, society and law frowned on such activities, and a stern code of honor also made such love difficult to pursue. Court records reveal nonetheless that it was pursued and that for many there was a definite price to pay for having done so, suggesting how strong was the desire for loving relationships.[23] In the end, however, prostitution was a much better alternative for young men (and not-so-young ones also, like Machiavelli) seeking love along with sex. Society expected young men to seek love, and prostitution, especially at higher levels, offered it relatively safely, for ideally when the strong passion passed, a young man simply stopped paying for the relationship and moved on to new passions or settled down to marry and theoretically embark upon a more stable and controlled life.

In this context the presentation of the young Oresto seeking the love of a mannered and cultured Roman courtesan, Doralice, in Fortini's comedy takes on a deeper meaning. Oresto was already married, as one of his servants makes clear to Doralice early in the comedy. As noted earlier, she has nothing but praise for the youth and his marriage, even seeing it as making him more attractive, noting that although many claimed that a man needs only three happinesses, he actually has four: "The first: that he is young, handsome and healthy ... the second: rich, open handed and well mannered; the third: he has a young pretty wife to live with; the fourth: he rides a handsome horse, is well dressed and *can fulfill his desires as he does,*" implicitly with a courtesan.[24] In sum, Oresto's pretty young wife is just another sign of his desirability. In fact, the comedy makes clear from the onset that his Roman visit is to gain experience to round him out as his youthful years are coming to a close. And the experience that virtually all the characters agree he should enjoy is not just the body of Doralice, but her love as well.

Flavonio, given his own mad love for Doralice, of course, is the only one who does not agree, and he plots to derail their love. First, he takes Oresto aside and warns him in lurid terms that Doralice is riddled with syphilis. When Oresto replies that he has seen no signs of the disease on her skin and that he will certainly note any that evening in the baths when they are naked together, Flavonio counters that the baths of Rome are notoriously dark. He then attacks those who have encouraged the affair, concluding, "Your wife awaits you with faith her dear, sweet spouse! Your mother awaits you, her praiseworthy son, and you will return home a pretty son without hair, without a nose, without teeth, full of open sores, overwhelmed by pain, blind, deaf, and stinking." One can add little to Oresto's response: "My heavens, Flavonio, you have virtually killed me with the fear your terrible words have evoked."[25]

Although prostitution was associated with disease before syphilis struck Europe at the end of the fifteenth century, the apparently new disease quickly was closely linked to prostitution and helped add to the growing negative vision of the practice, a fact underlined by Doralice's anxiety to disprove Flavonio's claim when she learns of it. In the meantime, however, Oresto, overwhelmed with fear of the disease, accepts Flavonio's suggestion that he cancel his planned evening with Doralice with the excuse that he has been called unexpectedly to the home of a powerful noble. But true to his high-minded ways and good manners, he insists that he pay for the evening not enjoyed with fifty scudi and adds a gold chain for good measure, which he instructs Flavonio to give to Doralice with his apologies. Flavonio, however, gives her only the gold chain and his master's apologies, then offers her the fifty scudi as if they were his to pay for an evening of his own with her.

Her suspicions aroused (and nothing else), she agrees to meet him at her house later and immediately goes in search of Oresto to find out the truth.[26] Encountering the loyal pedant first, she learns of Flavonio's syphilis slander. Outraged and anxious to disprove his claim in order to not lose face, status, and other potential lovers, she and the good pedant set out separately to find Oresto. Arriving just after the latter has explained to his master how he has been duped, there follows a sort of recognition scene where she reveals to Oresto, apparently by accident, her body unblemished by syphilitic sores. Oresto begs her forgiveness for his lack of faith in her with passionate words of love: "Dear lady, patron, life of my life, I stand before you a sinner. My lack of courtesy has been returned by your great courtesy to me and thus I deserve to be deserted, thrown out, hated and derided thanks to that criminal." Doralice replies tellingly, "You deserve to be *loved*, served, and honored, because in a gentle heart (*cor gentile*) evil ways never reside."[27] Thus with passion and gentle mannered ways between fine courtesans and young gentleman, the mad passion of love finds a safe and ordered place in society, at least in the imaginative world of the happy endings required in comedies. Love triumphs even over the call for harsh punishment that the other characters argue Flavonio's treachery richly deserves—for the young lovers nobly decide to merely see him shamed for his betrayal.

And in a way, just as their love makes Doralice and Oresto more noble, love, as far as it reached down in the social scale of prostitution, helped to sustain a more noble and positive vision of the art in contrast to a more prescriptive and negative one that was gaining ground at the same time. Simply put, looking for love made Renaissance prostitution, for all its harsh economic and social realities, an ideally rich, positive, and definitely much more complex activity than modern commercial metaphors would suggest.

CHAPTER NINE

Erotica: The Sexualized Body in Renaissance Art

BETTE TALVACCHIA

In the course of the period stretching from the fifteenth to the seventeenth centuries the strongest impulse manifest in the visual arts was the urge toward increased naturalism, mediated by a pronounced commitment to idealization. The stylistic results could differ, but the impetus was impressively uniform. This approach developed above all in the major cultural centers of the Italian peninsula but was diffused by the travel of artists north and south of the Alps, by the increasing circulation of prints during this period, and by the traditionally international nature of courts and their long reach in matters of patronage. Idealized naturalistic expression in images developed with, responded to, and sustained a dialogue with other significant cultural currents throughout Europe, such as humanistic education, religious thought, and political ideologies.

The particular category of the eroticized body—and the use of the sexually eloquent figure to convey symbolic meaning—found a forceful place within stylistic systems that privileged the absolute beauty of the human form. The description of human, physical beauty is inseparable from its component of sexual valence, and thus the issue of the erotic holds tremendous import for the art of this period. Since the eroticized body is complicit in the expression of gender, that is, in a culture's construction of what it means to be female or male, erotic imagery is an eloquent conveyor of the sexual values of the society that creates it.

FIGURE 9.1: Paolo Veronese, *Mars and Venus United by Love*. Metropolitan Museum of Art, New York.

One of the crucial sites for the development of the physically perfected, eroticized body was in the corpus of mythological narratives.[1] The impact on the Renaissance artist of classical texts, both visual and verbal, cannot be overvalued (fig. 9.1). The rich vein of erotica in Greek and Roman culture was a lodestone for artists seeking mainstream expression for a genre that had been consigned to the margins during the intervening centuries. The most fecund visual strategies for the incorporation of erotic motifs in Renaissance art came from the classical tradition, and the practice received societal sanction from the high intellectual status and the respect accorded to ancient culture. As will become clear, one of the chief ways in which acceptable erotica could be transformed into unconventional or transgressive imagery was to strip it of classical references.

CLASSICAL SOURCES OF EROTIC IMAGERY

The realm of mythological narrative was a safe site for the display of erotic imagery, and treatments of the "loves of the gods" were particularly fertile subject matter. The stories were easily available in Ovid's *Metamorphoses*, and their origins in a symbolic system of explication for natural phenomena provided a necessary layer of interpretive possibilities to justify the content when it verged too enthusiastically toward the lascivious. The sophisticated cultural reference acted as a respectable cover for exuberantly exposed flesh, as in the case of Giulio Romano's portrayal of an aroused Jupiter approaching a reclining Olympia, who will shortly conceive their son, Alexander the Great. The implicit reference to dynastic concerns and the generation of heroes implicit in the fresco, painted in the Palazzo del Te, the private villa of Federico Gonzaga in Mantua, was appropriate to the imagery of a powerful ruler allied to the emperor; its explicitness well suited its luxurious setting and the personal taste of its patron.[2] Federico's enjoyment of these scenes where the puissance of a deity is expressed through his sexuality is underscored by the fact that he also commissioned Correggio, another artist valued for his classicizing and very sensuous style, to paint a series of Jupiter's amorous escapades and partners. The resulting canvases can be read on several levels as interpretations of classical symbolism where generation equals power, and where the patron is equated with Jupiter.[3] The series also displays sensuous figures in sexual situations, whose enjoyment is authorized by recourse to symbolic value, an automatic validation in the view of contemporary cultural consensus.

This interpretive operation functioned for the representations of mythological narratives in all media whether (in our terms) fine art or decorative art. And, of course, Renaissance culture was particularly fond of evaluating the success of artists who insisted on rivalry with past achievements by enveloping the classical stories in classicizing forms. This rivalry became a motif of connoisseurship, another interpretive layer that justified a high quotient of permissiveness in the art in question. This was serious conceptual business, and the artist strove to outdo ancient predecessors according to their terms and standards.

From within the mythological narratives individual personages emerged to become favored iconic subjects. Their isolation from the narrative context did not diminish their ability to function as vehicles that transmitted erotic impulses. These mythological figures remained well within the boundaries of the acceptable by the distancing effect of their association with an older, venerated tradition. Even in instances where the remnants of the linkage were arguably tenuous, their valorizing authority was upheld and if necessary insisted upon in the cultural discourse created around the images. The repertoire of goddesses, especially Venus, was featured in countless paintings and sculptures. These figures were displayed before the viewer for visual pleasure, a pleasure derived from the contemplation of beauty. Since physical beauty could be understood as a reflection of metaphysical splendor, this process of apprehension further connected to Renaissance belief in the nobility of sight with its honored function as a window to higher knowledge.

This nexus of conditions and interests created a complex approach to the construction of idealized representations of beauty and sexuality, perhaps merging nowhere as interestingly as in a particularized category of portraiture. Representations of individuals in the guise of mythological or legendary figures borrowed easily readable iconography to gain license (along with expanded possibilities) for the creation of highly sexualized (and gendered) images that retained the necessary level of propriety.

Striking examples in this category were painted by Agnolo Bronzino for powerful patrons, where he presented Cosimo de' Medici as Orpheus and configured Andrea Doria as Neptune (fig. 9.2).[4] Exploiting the license bequeathed by the mythological role-playing, in both cases these leaders appear in heroic

FIGURE 9.2: Agnolo Bronzino, *Portrait of Andrea Doria as Neptune*, 1550–1555. Pinacoteca di Brera, Milan (Reproduction British Library).

nudity with no lack of decorum but a large dose of sexual brio. This type of portrait is so divergent from our own conventions for portraying world leaders that full interpretations remain elusive. The issue is even more contested when it devolves around portraits that allow women to assume mythological roles, due in large part to our inability to name the sitter. The fact that we have lost the identity of the sitters has dimmed our awareness of the portrait nature of these images of sensuous female beauty, as opposed to our recognition of its function in the examples of Duke Cosimo and Admiral Doria, as just mentioned.

Titian's representation of a favored and very recognizable model as Flora, a minor deity of the woodlands, is a case in point (fig. 9.3). Just as we must evaluate the lurking presence of dark roots at the base of Flora's "golden" hair—surely a visual key to the specificity of the model—we must insist on the evidence of what we see along with what we can imagine. Portrait conventions are used in the painting's format, an indication of the genre to which the painting belongs, including the single figure shown in half-length, placed in midground, with the figure itself creating the space it occupies, in an otherwise

FIGURE 9.3: Titian, *Flora,* ca. 1515–17. Galleria degli Uffizi, Florence.

empty space. The morphology of the portrait type has been employed, yet "Flora" has been named by the flower placed in the woman's extended hand. The *camicia* (white linen undergarment) worn by the subject reinforces the dual identity: it is an article of contemporary clothing, but because of its free-flowing, diaphanous qualities, it was also used in theatrical productions as costuming for ancient personages.[5] The viewer is thus invited to accept the image as that of a contemporary beauty who is posing as a goddess, and the charge (in all senses) of her alluring sexuality can be transferred to her alter ego, whose role she is enacting. This is most likely the same strategy that Titian employed for the notorious *Venus of Urbino,* where the subject is both a representation of the goddess of love in all of her sensual splendor and a portrait of a recognizable woman, whose sexualized presentation is covered by the decorum of her mythological guise.[6]

GENDER AND SEXUALITY IN PORTRAITURE

Portraits without the benefit of mythological cover-ups could certainly present the sitter's beauty with an emphasis on sexual attraction, but these often substitute what might be called a poetic approach, which endowed the attraction with a more ethereal quality. This may be appreciated in Raphael's decidedly glamorous rendering of the wealthy Florentine Bindo Altoviti (fig. 9.4), in several of Lorenzo Lotto's male portraits (e.g., *Man with Rose Petals*), and in most of Titian's oeuvre. An egregious symbol of seduction is present in his *Man with a Glove* (ca. 1520, Musée du Louvre), displaying the bared hand as an erotic element, whose significance as a sign for the allure of uncovered flesh was popularized in the Petrarchan tradition. Another instance of the motif can be seen in Titian's slightly earlier *Portrait of a Man* in the Metropolitan Museum's collection (fig. 9.5). All of these sitters have been willfully constructed as beautiful, ornamental, and sensual; in sum as objects of desire, a classification that would not have been seen as trivial or pejorative, given the nobility the period bequeathed to such desires transmitted by beauty.

The sensuous portrait, which constructed both females and males as objects of desire, had a prominent place in sixteenth-century developments. It replaced earlier approaches that tended toward two divergent strategies: either to underscore the rank and status of the sitter at the expense of individualization, or to closely observe the subject's physiognomy, with less departure from nature. In the first category, profile portraits held sway in Italy in the late fifteenth century. Especially popular for the representation of women in connection with their betrothal and marriage, the profile format emphasizes a

FIGURE 9.4: Raphael, *Portrait of Bindo Altoviti*, 1512–1515. National Gallery of Art, Washington, DC.

strong, elegant contour of the face, with stylized features and little modeling. Lavish brocade clothing, splendid jewels and elaborate coiffures are standard elements, portrayed with more telling detail than the subject's face. The ensemble constructs the woman's identity through her raiment and bequeaths status by turning her into a precious object of beauty.[7]

By the end of the fifteenth century, Leonardo da Vinci initiated a move toward increased naturalism in the portraits of women, notably in the highly influential portraits of Mona Lisa, and Ginevra de' Benci in the National Gallery in Washington. Leonardo's intense studies of nature and his familiarity with human anatomy combined to provide a model in Italian art for portraiture infused with naturalism. In particular, his placement of female subjects within natural settings arguably conveys a view of woman as symbolic of the workings of nature.[8] The move toward an idealized naturalism then dominated the Italian tradition, taken up notably by Raphael, with the consequences that have been mentioned for increasing the visual seduction of portraits across gender lines.

FIGURE 9.5: Titian, *Portrait of a Man,* ca. 1515. Metropolitan Museum of Art, New York.

SEXUALITY IN SACRED NARRATIVES

Given the premium placed on physical beauty, including its attendant sexual charge, protagonists of sacred narratives also were often depicted in a manner that communicated cultural values of gender and sexuality. This is especially true when the mise-en-scène is imbued with carnality, such as in the dramas of Susanna and the Elders, Joseph and Potiphar's Wife, or Judith and Holofernes. While sometimes representations of these stories are understood as excuses for the creation of provocative images, the opposite is true. The narratives were significant for their moralizing function, dealing explicitly with issues of sexual temptations and sins, and the artists were called upon to present them with the force and attraction adequate to their subject. The viewer was made to comprehend viscerally the danger of undisciplined sexual attraction, as in the case of the Elders' ruinous conspiracy against the chaste and principled Susanna, or to marvel at triumphant sexuality used as a weapon against an enemy, as in Judith's fearless and successful plot against the ferocious Holofernes. Warning about that same power and drive of female sexuality when turned toward ignoble ends dominates the tale of Joseph, characterized as an innocent victim, temporarily defeated by the slander of Potiphar's wife (otherwise unnamed), whose rampant and illicit sexual desire was heroically spurned by the young man.

In all of the cases in which the issue of sexuality lies at the heart of the narrative, it is straightforwardly featured in the visual representation. If the sexual situations and nudity were presented in a compelling and attractive style by the master so that they articulated cultural values concerning corporeal beauty, so much the better for the impact of the lesson to be learned. There was a belief with regard to visual experience that a progression of awareness should take place in the intellectual process, beginning with attention gained on the most basic plane of human reaction, and then moving upward toward a more exalted sphere of intellection that transcended earthly concerns. There was a wide zone of comfort in the interim, which helps to account for the broader acceptance of combinations of spiritual and carnal imagery in Renaissance visual culture.

It is of striking importance that as a small number of women began to be recognized as professional artists in the sixteenth and seventeenth centuries, they were often called upon to sculpt or paint the stories centering on female protagonists. This mechanism is still little understood, since the subjects were generally popular and also treated by male artists. However, we can hypothesize that there was a compelling novelty in commissioning or viewing such subjects as expressed by women, with the implication that new interest would come from the female artist's self-identification with the subject. Thus we read Giorgio Vasari commenting in 1568 that the sculpted relief of *Joseph and Potiphar's Wife* by Properzia de' Rossi expressed the artist's personal anguish at her rejection by a lover.[9] In contemporary scholarship, debates continue about the amount of biographical information that should enter into the interpretation of the numerous paintings of biblical heroines by Artemisia Gentileschi, whose career began in Rome in the second decade of the seventeenth century with the new, dramatic style of Caravaggio as a major point of reference.[10]

Just as we have seen with regard to mythological characters, both the male and female protagonists of biblical stories could also be excerpted from the narrative context to operate in isolation for symbolic ends. The figures of Judith and of Salome, whose stories are as titillating as they are cautionary, became especially popular for iconic treatment. This is most delightfully attested by the many examples of noble ladies from the Saxon court who took on the raiment of Judith under Lucas Cranach's amused transformations, where opulent and self-conscious beauties pose for their role as the virtuous heroine (fig. 9.6). No less popular was the staging of the other side of the coin, when women

FIGURE 9.6: Lucas Cranach, *Judith with the Head of Holofernes,* ca. 1530. Metropolitan Museum of Art, New York.

portrayed as Salome acted as seductive admonition and visual alarms to the destructive force of unbridled sexuality.[11] The prized quality of these paintings for their patrons and privileged viewers was that they willfully conjure the very reactions they admonish against, a strategy that increased their worth as works of art while introducing an element of lasciviousness authorized by the moral referent upon which the imagery is based.

When the element of portraiture is not present, iconic representations could test the boundaries of the permissible in conveying disturbing content. Hans Baldung's *Judith* is provocatively displayed in total nudity, with legs crossed, darting a sly look down toward the decapitated head dangling from her hand, with a most unfeminine sword held triumphantly in the other.[12] The Renaissance artist's accepted function as a visualizer of biblical messages about sexuality and its role in sacred history is jeopardized by Baldung's sophisticated manipulation of traditional details, so that his interpretations almost constitute a questioning of the heroine's motives and virtues.

Other cultural attitudes, such as misogyny and fear of female sexuality, reinforced negative readings of certain elements within the representation of biblical heroines, with undertones sometimes strong enough to cloud the overt subject and displace its conventional, positive interpretation. A comment recorded about Donatello's sculpture of *Judith Slaying Holofernes* provides an instructive example. It comes from the record of a meeting in 1504, whose purpose it was to decide upon the placement of Michelangelo's *David*. The first speaker proposed that it replace the *Judith* on the *ringhiera* in front of the Palazzo Signoria because it was "an emblem of death ... and it is not fitting that the woman should kill the man."[13] This assessment ignores the heroic iconography connected to Judith's valorous feat and downgrades it to the simple fact of a woman overpowering a man, a gender reversal unacceptable to the speaker; in his eyes it constitutes a baleful image, unfit to represent his city.

SEXUAL METAPHORS IN RELIGIOUS ART

Competing agendas for the messages conveyed, with their complex layering of the symbols employed, endowed religious scenarios with multivalent interpretive possibilities. Most strikingly, deeply eroticized characterizations of Adam and Eve had a notable occurrence in the period under discussion (fig. 9.7). The Tree of Knowledge became in this tradition the font of sexual awareness, the site at which the first couple failed the original test of sexual continence. The development of this theme in northern Europe was especially rich in this interpretation of the fall of mankind, where the original sin was explicitly described as sexual in nature.

Hans Baldung Grien's 1511 woodcut is one of the most explicit presentations of the carnal explanation of the fall. In the print Adam fondles Eve's breast as the entwined couple stands beneath an inscription unequivocally declaring "Lapsus Humani Generis," or "The Fall of Mankind," to be the subject, as the serpent looks on (figure 9.8).

On a much more positive note, human carnality was re-ennobled by the fundamental tenet of Christian salvation history, in which the deity assumes human form. Visual language found a ready means of communicating the Incarnation, with its affirmation of human corporeality, in images of Christ, whose nudity proclaims his full human nature. The most unambiguous, yet still permissible, avowal appeared in the exhibition of the Holy Child's genitalia, marking his transformation into a male human being. The *ostentatio* of the Infant Christ employs the sexualized body as a metaphor for the process of redemption; it is the paradigm from which all of the incidences of

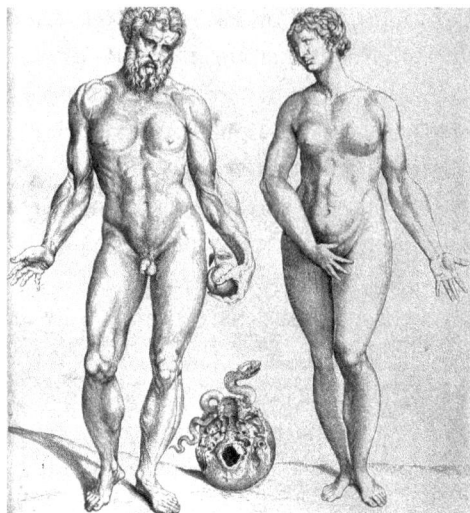

FIGURE 9.7: *Thomas Geminus, Adam and Eve,*
from *Compendia totius anatomae delineatio,*
1545. Wellcome Library, London.

idealized nudity in the transmission of sacred subjects take their authority
and meaning.[14]

The opulent physicality of saints such as Mary Magdalene, Agatha, John
the Baptist, and Sebastian, consistent in the conventions that developed in
their representation, had its roots first of all in the glorification of the human
body through the doctrine of Christ's Incarnation. It was then further emphasized and developed in visual terms through the stylistic values of the
Renaissance, where art aspired to the construction of perfection. The saints
who received the most pronounced dose of sexuality were those whose bi-
ographies yield the most fertile terrain for explication through sensuous imagery.

Mary Magdalene's legendary youthful life as a prostitute conjured her
depiction with a panoply of physical charms, which might be enticingly
glimpsed through thick cascades of abundant hair. With attention well captured, the viewer is instructed by other details and attributes to move on to
a consideration of the saint's repentance of her formerly worldly life and
sexual sins.[15] Saint Sebastian's origins as a soldier in the elite personal sentry
of Diocletian (the emperor connected to mass persecution of Christians) led
to the assimilation of his arrows to those of the plague-disseminating Apollo,
whose beautiful features he also eventually assumed. The bodies of these
saints, and Sebastian in particular, became a privileged locus for the artist's

FIGURE 9.8: Hans Baldung Grien, *Adam and Eve,* 1511, chiaroscuro woodcut, Rosenwald Collection, 1943.3907. National Gallery of Art, Washington, DC.

display of virtuosity with the human form, a physique in which sexual allure was insisted upon as part of its nature.[16]

The expression of sexuality as an inherent part of nature, whose representation had a comfortable place in religious imagery, extended to even its most exalted human protagonist, Mary, the Mother of Christ. According to the beliefs propagated by her cult within the Catholic Church, she achieved perfection of body and spirit; her imagery as developed by artists reveals this ideal state through the expression of flawless loveliness. The canons of beauty and the artistic means to realize them necessarily changed through the decades and from one region to another. In all cases, however, delineations of the Virgin Mary were endowed with the local concepts of beauty as indicators of her perfection and impeccability.

In certain instances, especially in the cases of courtly styles with elaborate codes of beauty, the resultant images can ostensibly cross the boundaries of the decorous or seemly, and history is replete with documentation to that effect from the fifteenth century to our own time. This brings up the crucial point of the relative and subjective nature of the discourses that construct the rules of decorum. Particularly with regard to works of art, acceptability or censurability has always been determined locally, with attitudes changing even over relatively brief stretches of time. No generalization can be offered about the censorship of works of art that will be valid for the entire period of the Renaissance, or which functions for northern as well as southern Europe—the variations must be explored for each cultural area, and indeed decade by decade.

In this essay focus is placed on consideration of the images that reveal and construct attitudes toward sexuality and body imagery as a principal strategy of representation. During the centuries from 1400 to 1600 there was a broad consensus about the efficacy of the symbolic use of the human form in art, a form that incorporated the expression of beauty and sexuality. This majority view, however, was consistently opposed by a vocal minority, and indeed the balance changed appreciably over time, especially after the mid-1500s, and particularly in response to the battles of religious ideology in northern Europe.

Throughout the Renaissance and before the increased polemic of the Reformation, the preponderance of images of the Madonna emanates a worldly beauty and human sexuality that were developed as metaphors for the highest spheres of spiritual attainment. The reality of Mary's motherhood, the vehicle of her participation in the history of redemption, was insisted upon in numberless devotional images of the Madonna and Child. By far the largest group defines her motherhood simply by placing the child in her lap or within her embrace, visual statements that do not disturb the concept of the virgin birth of Christ, that is, the doctrine declaring Mary to have conceived her child miraculously rather than through human sexual contact. A relatively small number of images in the fifteenth and sixteenth centuries demonstrate Mary's motherhood in more physical terms by showing her as the *Madonna Lactans*, or Nursing Madonna. This iconography was never dominant, but it was tenacious and diffused throughout the Renaissance, as attested from the earliest Trecento examples, such as Ambrogio Lorenzetti's painting of ca. 1325 in the museum of Siena's Cathedral; the version by Lorenzo di Credi from ca. 1490 in the National Gallery, London; and Andrea Solario's early sixteenth-century example in the Louvre. Examples from major Flemish artists of the fifteenth century were particularly influential, notably Jan van Eyck's treatment of the subject and Rogier van der Weyden's *Medici Madonna*, both now in the Städel Museum in Frankfurt (fig. 9.9).

FIGURE 9.9: Rogier van der Weyden, *Virgin and Child with Four Saints (Medici Madonna)*. Städel Museum, Frankfurt.

When the subject of the nursing divinity is delineated with the elegance and worldly sophistication of courtly style, it moves to the borders of acceptability. Such is the case of the version by Jean Fouquet from the mid-fifteenth century, in which the Madonna appears in the guise of a contemporary beauty, and her exposed breast becomes an eroticized motif (fig. 9.10). However, so far from being intentionally blasphemous, it is simply a presentation of the theme in one particular artist's individual manner, a style of painting that was acclaimed in and conditioned by its ambiance, the French court of Charles VII. Moreover the panel, now in Antwerp, originally formed part of a diptych, facing images portraying Etienne Chevalier, the court treasurer, and his patron, Saint Steven; it was produced within the context of traditional devotional imagery.

The bare breast of the Madonna, then, takes its place in that category of the admirably erotic, where carnality retains its nobility by virtue of the "proper" ends for which it is employed. That the Madonna's breast could be exposed to

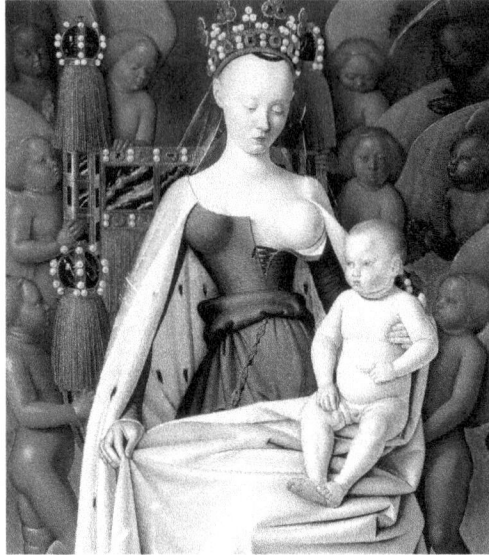

FIGURE 9.10: Jean Fouquet, *Virgin and Child Surrounded by Angels,* ca. 1450. Koninklijk Museum voor Schone Kunsten, Antwerp (The Yorck Project).

glorify her motherhood, and thus her womanhood, should be kept in mind as a possible interpretive value for other subject matter. Fundamentally, uncovering a breast is a visual statement of femaleness, without the expectation of merely or exclusively erotic associations. It was not limited to a performance of obscene or even lascivious sexuality. Most often the breast signified more neutrally "biologically female," a statement of fact that could be made in many cases without thoughts of impropriety attached.[17]

SEXUAL IMAGERY IN SECULAR ART

Sexual imagery in secular art can be seen in the iconography formulated by women who ruled during the sixteenth and into the seventeenth centuries. The Medici princesses who became queens of France made impressive use of paintings to declare the legitimacy and authority of their reigns.

The most monumental was Marie de' Medici's commission to Peter Paul Rubens to paint in the Palais du Luxembourg an extensive cycle of frescoes in the early 1620s, treating the significant events of her life. In the scene of *The Felicity of the Regency of Marie de' Medici,* the queen is enthroned, wearing royal regalia, but with one breast revealed (fig. 9.11). Sanctioned by the allegorical nature of the message, no lack of decorum attends the exposure of the queen's breast. The artist wrote a gloss for the scene, specifying that it depicts

> the flowing of the Kingdom of France, with the revival of the sciences and the arts through the splendour and the liberality of Her Majesty, who sits upon a shining throne and holds a scale in her hands, keeping the world in equilibrium through her prudence and equity.[18]

The exposed breast asserts that the ruler is biologically female while the rest of the attributes describe her authority and power. The insistence is necessary, since the right to rule was generally not attributed to women; the biological symbol defines femininity at the same time that it denies the traditional limitations imposed on the gender. This early seventeenth-century example shows a strong woman taking in hand the tool of propagandistic expression to

FIGURE 9.11: Peter Paul Rubens, *The Felicity of the Regency of Marie de' Medici*, 1622–1625. Musée du Louvre, Paris (Reproduction British Library).

construct an image of her place in the arena of power, with the artist adeptly gendering the imagery for his exalted female client.

In these instances of self-representation a point must be made about the direct intervention of these powerful women in establishing images that assert both their femaleness and their rule. Women participated more than has been acknowledged in foregrounding their sexual identity as a strategy of representation, and not only in the rarefied cases of queenship. For example, recent scholarship discloses that Hélène Fourment was the owner of the portrait known as *Het Pelsken*, painted by her husband, Peter Paul Rubens, in the 1630s (fig. 9.12).[19] Since it displays Hélène's near nudity caressed by a sumptuous fur, the image has been discussed exclusively in terms of male spectatorship. Instead, close collaboration can be posited between the artist and his subject—his partner in marriage—who was an energetic and accomplished woman from a socially prominent family. The couple's joint will assigns *Het Pelsken* to Hélène's ownership. This action determined her control of an image that forcefully reveals her sexuality as visibly, compellingly attractive.

The portrait, however, should not be imagined as unmediated; rather, it imposes Rubens' idealization of female beauty on Hélène's features, as it poses her in the gestures of the *Venus Pudica*. The components of the portrait are further complicated by the very garment that alluringly drapes and discloses her physicality. The fur wrap is a domestic garment but one that was worn at home by men. The subtle cross-dressing, according to taste, might add an erotic charge or a comment on the decidedly female subject's command of a male mantel, in other words, her ability to take on a man's role. The fact that "Pels" signifies "skirt," with application in slang for "female," enriches its interpretive potential. The importance of the attribute is emphasized in Rubens' testament by the painting consistently being referred to as *Het Pelsken*, or the Little Fur. The art-historical pedigree of the painting makes a claim to exalted lineage, since it visually refers to Titian's *Woman with a Fur Wrap*, in its turn exploiting the conventions of Venus imagery extrapolated from the mythological corpus. Hélène's active collaboration and proud ownership of the painting suggest the complex issues that attend to the concept of agency with regard to portraiture in the Renaissance and Early Modern periods.

MOCKING THE HEROIC TRADITION

Hélène Fourment's participation in the creation and disposition of a richly erotic image also indicates the caution that should accompany our readings of the eroticized portrayal of the female body. However, there did exist, especially

FIGURE 9.12: Peter Paul Rubens, *The Fur (Het Pelsken)*, 1630s. Kunsthistorisches Museum, Vienna (Reproduction British Library).

in northern Europe, a strong tradition of cautionary images that pivoted on dangerous encounters with the allure of female sexuality. At times the warning took a humorous turn, as in the theme of the topsy-turvy world, where wives ruled over husbands and women "unnaturally" dominated men. This last point was made with unmitigated glee and maliciousness in renderings of *Phyllis Riding Aristotle*, where the mistress of Alexander literally mounts the elderly sage, reducing him to the comical—and grossly undignified—position of a prancing pony, responding to her commands. Two amusing renditions of the couple are preserved in the collections of the Metropolitan Museum. Both originated in the Southern Netherlands and, curiously, are incorporated into luxury objects used at table. One takes the form of an *aquamanile*, a small metal pitcher employed to wash hands. The other presents the scene on the bottom of a plate showing Phyllis merrily pulling back the philosopher's clothes to spank his exposed buttocks (fig. 9.13).

One of the earliest drawings of Hans Baldung Grien depicts the subject, which he reconsiders in a woodcut version that is even more strongly sexualized, with Phyllis fully nude astride the philosopher, who is bridled with a bit in his mouth, while her whip stabs at his rump. Although not many examples of this theme survive in Italian art, a spirited drawing by Leonardo

FIGURE 9.13: Plate with *Phyllis and Aristotle*, Anonymous, Southern Netherlands, ca. 1480. Metropolitan Museum of Art, New York.

da Vinci in the collection of the Kunsthalle in Hamburg adds the lascivious detail of a bedroom interior, with a frenzied Phyllis astride her vanquished mount.[20]

The vein of ribald humor situated within a moralizing intention is a component that clearly enjoyed success with contemporary audiences. By the sixteenth century Aristotle was replaced by Achilles as the favorite cautionary hero who fell to female wiles and manipulation, apparently with physical prowess supplanting intellect as the proof of virility in cultural imagination. Hiding from his manly duty to join the warring Greeks against the Trojans, Achilles ceded to Omphale's suggestion that they exchange clothing. The switch of highly gendered garments reifies the transposition of the couple's respective status, with the Homeric hero taking second place to an alluring woman. The contrast of male muscles bulging within supple fabrics intended for a female form is strongly drawn in most representations of the subject, especially pronounced in Annibale Carracci's rendition in the Palazzo Farnese.[21]

Sharing the mock-heroic spin on the mythological world, the story of Venus predominating over Mars unequivocally upsets the gender equation desired by society. When the goddess of love subdues the god of war, resoundingly establishing a reign of "women on top," the planets can only fall out of alignment, and chaos disrupts the earth. Botticelli conveys this frightening thought in a typically lyrical manner in a painting from the 1480s, whose alert and diaphanously draped Venus indulgently presides over a nearly naked, spent Mars.[22] In the next century Rosso Fiorentino, in an expertly sardonic attitude, configures a tiny, timid Mars being pushed and pulled toward the bed of a towering, complacent Venus, who will clearly win any sexual competition. These images, calculated to garner a reassuring laugh in view of absurd situations that run counter to reality, might be interpreted to disclose a certain level of anxiety.

The daughters of this complacently powerful Venus populate scenes of "ill assorted lovers," highly amusing narratives in their representations of withered, craggy old men who lecherously approach seductive young women. The flirting, of course, is a prelude to the girls having the better of their antiquated suitors, generally and suggestively indicated by inflated purses that hang at the man's waist, which will soon be emptied. But if these rollicking scenes add mirth to their preaching, other subjects show sinful sexuality to be no laughing matter.[23]

More macabre in symbolism and effect, the combination of gruesome embrace and desirable female flesh takes on sinister tones in representations of Death and the Maiden. Another subject that received widespread development in northern Europe, it makes explicit the perceived connection of sexuality to sin and death. The view that unsanctioned erotic activity was potentially pestilential as well as sinful took new force as European societies suffered the brutal manifestation of particularly virulent strains of syphilis, which spread with rapidity from the end of the fifteenth century throughout the continent.

THE MEDIUM AND THE TRANSGRESSIVE MESSAGE

It will be noted that many of these subjects were made specifically as prints, a medium that allowed for relatively wide diffusion (and profit) from a modest financial investment in production. These factors, along with the increased anonymity for both artist and customer, explain why prints became by far the favored medium for erotic subject matter that crossed the boundaries of the socially acceptable into the category of the transgressive. The low cost allowed for an expanded clientele, a much larger and diversified group of purchasers than the traditional commissioning patrons. When patrons did enter into the equation with regard to erotic images that tested the limits of propriety, they at times might still have commissioned large-format panel paintings or frescoes. However, in these instances access to the images was strictly limited, with the location and viewing completely controlled by the owner.

Another medium that held appeal for the elite connoisseur was the bronze statuette, which could be placed discreetly or viewed in private circumstances. While made of a costly material, its restricted dimensions required only a limited amount. The small-scale bronze obviated the commitment of time and workforce necessary to a sculpture for life-size or monumental productions. The tactile pleasure of holding the exquisitely finished, cool, and smooth statuettes of erotic subject produced in large quantity by the sculptor Andrea Riccio in Padua, for example, must have been a compelling aspect of their desirability. The subjects treated in this genre were in large part tied to the erotica of the classical world, portraying ithyphallic satyrs, nude deities, nymphs, and heroes. The identification of these small-scale, highly finished sculptures with ancient tradition was so complete that another acclaimed master of bronze statuettes, Pier Jacopo Bonacolsi, was universally referred to as "L'Antico." Connected to the Gonzaga court in Mantua, Bonacolsi was valued for both his contemporary production of classicizing statuettes and his connoisseurship of antique pieces.[24]

Woodcuts and engravings, however, were the mediums that came closest to a Renaissance equivalent of mass production (in terms of both quantity and quality), with engravings representing the higher end of the product range in both aspects. The majority of images that portray erotic subjects construed as transgressive by Renaissance culture survive in drawings and prints. The former medium was suitable given its personal nature; the latter was pertinent for its ease of production and profit-making potential. The largest category produced topics of transgressive sexuality, whose protagonists were overwhelmingly female in gender; but the art itself was socially sanctioned by its negative attitude toward the subject, or relegation of the scene to the safely distanced world of ancient culture.

In northern Europe the favored subject expressive of outlawed female sexuality was that of witches engaged in their demonic activity. Although scholars have interpreted this corpus in relation to the historical persecution of women as witches, a recent and thoroughly documented analysis points out the discrepancy of dates, with much of the imagery produced in the late fifteenth and early sixteenth centuries, while the intense persecution of "witches" took place in the late sixteenth and into the early seventeenth centuries.[25] This study further demonstrates the wealth of references to witches in classical literature and compellingly argues that the images from the early Renaissance are "more plausible as poetic constructions motivated by artistic goals and a fascination with the underside of the ancient world."[26] The more ignoble aspects of the classical corpus were largely employed for satire in their original settings, and this potential was fully exploited in Renaissance appropriations. The demonizing imagery associated with witches was a channel for the misogyny that informed parts of Renaissance culture and a vehicle for expression of transgressive sexual impulses.

Although not as diffuse in the Italian tradition, the representation of *streghe* did have a cultural impact. A truly startling instance is found in Parmigianino's bizarre etching from the 1530s of a *Witch Riding a Phallus*. The most convincing explication of the image comes from Charles Zika (2003), who has explored the ways in which representations of witchcraft in the sixteenth century related to discourses of sexuality. In particular, female witches were seen as seeking to appropriate male sexuality and power for themselves, inverting the social order. Since power was often linked to the sexual and gendered as a male attribute, this woman's symbolic harnessing of the penis and mastering it by mounting is a strong visual statement of threatening, castrating female sexuality.

From another body of literature found in their classical models, however, Italian artists in the main preferred to feature the Amazon as the embodiment of threatening female power. The legendary culture of the Amazons proscribed the presence of males, privileged war as a primary occupation, and canceled the very essence of their femaleness by the mutilation of their right breast. While occasionally the heroism of Amazons was represented, more often their subversion of the proper social order was a prime cautionary message of the visual narration.

Within the constructs of contemporary culture, the Renaissance heralded the "honest courtesan" as the approved agent of transgressive female sexuality. She was morally culpable, but, in the higher economic ranges of society where she dwelt, socially accepted within elite male circles. Although a category of courtesan portraits has often been posited, especially with regard to sixteenth-century Venetian art, the existence of such a subgenre is open to debate, and its defining aspects are far from clear. The fact that professional models did not exist in this period made courtesans and prostitutes the most procurable women for the job, which complicates our understanding of the putative genre. In the famous case of Titian's *Flora*, the model is recognizable from other of the master's paintings, and so presumably is a woman with whom he had easy and intimate access. Her role in the painting of a semi-deity from the ancient world who had been taken up as the protector of prostitutes in some traditions, but as the custodian of virtuous, wifely characteristics in others, leaves the reading open to diametrically opposed interpretations.

Whether images of erotic content were intended to be received as symbolic or purely provocative is far from clear in certain cases. In these instances sexuality has been used as a conveyor of significance, but we have lost the key to understanding whether the message was calculated to transcend the flesh or to reside in its titillation. Perhaps the most notorious and puzzling work in this category survives in a painting dated to the last quarter of the sixteenth century from the School of Fontainebleau, *Women in the Bath*, now in the collection of the Uffizi Gallery. The nudity of the two women—one seated on the rim of the tub, exposing buttocks and back, one immersed to the waist in the water, revealing her breasts—is emphasized by the sumptuous fabric that encircles the tub and the filmy sheet that drapes it. Although looking in divergent directions, the two women are linked by the exchange of a ring, which one places on the extended third finger of her companion with an emphatic gesture. The painting's enigmatic action indicates a symbolic intent, while its color scheme, a concentration of white, gold, and red, may refer to contemporary poetic devices that praise the harmony of a beloved's skin, hair, and lips in terms of these hues.[27]

Whether freighted with emblematic meaning or not, the piquant voyeurism of these paintings, and their explicitly sexual situations, contrast strongly with the more widespread genre of double portraits of males. In particularly eloquent versions by Raphael (one of which shows him affectionately embracing an unknown friend, another with two friends in poses that are mirror images), an air of comfortable homosociality reigns. While charged with affection and familiarity, the images do not convey sexual congress as the prevailing message.

CROSSING THE BOUNDARY

In contrast, an explicit sexual situation is portrayed by Francesco Salviati in his drawing of three nude men grouped together. Two older men flank a youth; the figure on the right turns his head to make contact with the shoulder of the young man, while from the left a man with a flowing beard clutches the central figure's genitalia.[28] The pen and ink drawing is elaborated with areas of wash, but no printed or painted version of this grouping is known to exist. It is not surprising that this transgressive subject remained in the more intimate medium of drawing. However, another instance of a similar scene rather startlingly appears in the stucco decorative border created by Giovanni da Udine in the arches of the Vatican Loggia. The prestige of the project and its patron—with Raphael's workshop responsible for the execution of the request by Pope Leo X—makes the appearance of the motif all the more startling. However puzzling to our understanding, the classicizing style of the figures, their placement high on an arch, and the tradition of allowing frivolous details to border the fields of major subjects allow for the possibility of such inclusions in the cultural atmosphere of Rome in the first quarter of the sixteenth century.

If such decorative details rest on the periphery of the acceptable, other usages slip over the limits of propriety into the realm of the obscene, as constructed by Renaissance conventions. These images constitute what we would define as "pornographic," or what in Italian discourses is denoted by the word *disonesto*. Obscene imagery was circulated almost exclusively through print media, first in single sheets and eventually incorporated with texts in printed books.

The most notorious example of obscene images in the Renaissance were the engravings known as *I modi*, originally a series of sixteen drawings by Giulio Romano in the early 1520s, showing heterosexual couples engaging in sexual relations, material that was decidedly *disonesto* in Renaissance cultural discourse.[29] MarcAntonio Raimondi, a printmaker associated with Raphael's workshop, engraved the set. This ignited a succession of unprecedented events, including confiscation of the plates, imprisonment of the engraver, and composition of sonnets by the notorious writer, Pietro Aretino, to accompany the images. The combination of the prints and sonnets in bound editions created a paradigm for printed erotica that flourished over the next several centuries.

The most significant Italian artist to emulate Giulio Romano's transgressive model was Agostino Carracci, with a group of prints from the late years of the sixteenth century collectively referred to as the *Lascivie*. Recent studies have clarified the occasional nature of the prints, with subjects taken variously from the Old Testament, mythology (typically with a twist in conventional iconography), and scenes of satyrs. One of the most significant aspects of Carracci's prints is that they contravene the directives that abounded in recent treatises for artists to cease their emphasis on erotic subjects and nude figures. This is especially striking for works created in the cultural sphere of Bologna, whose powerful archbishop, Cardinal Gabriele Paleotti, published his extremely influential discourse *On Sacred and Profane Images* in 1582.[30] The fact that the artist executed these works in the shadow of the committed reformer, who had been a zealous participant in the council of Trent, attests to the limited reach of the reforms—an issue that still demands clarification in the history of art.

Finally, a point should be made (which deserves volumes of study) that during the Renaissance obscenity was used for satirical ends, and purposely to provoke outrage from proper society. The previously mentioned Pietro Aretino was a master in this field. Along with his production of obscene texts that satirized cultural conventions and political institutions, he created an obscene personal device contained on a medallion, whose "head" was a face composed of phalluses, with the motto "The Scourge of Princes." This emblem is eloquent of Renaissance culture's employment of the obscene as a conveyor of invective, delegating disruptive sexuality to flagellate its chosen enemies.

The construction and exploration of sexuality in the visual arts proved to be an exceptionally vigorous and varied component of contemporary cultural production throughout the Renaissance. Since the majority of the most modern artists of the period privileged the human form as a vehicle of expression, human sexuality necessarily became a focus within a range of genres, especially portraiture and narrative, as well as a protagonist in the visualization of symbolic systems. Engaging with developments in other areas, the art of this period looked to ancient culture for approaches to the expression of sexuality, especially with regard to explicit and transgressive erotica. Given the high cultural status of ancient texts, both visual and verbal, references to this corpus became a veil of propriety that often functioned as a cover for imagery that pushed at the boundaries of acceptability during this time.

As technical skill and ideological commitment to various styles based on naturalism, the rendition of nature observed, and the idealization of forms proliferated, a pronounced element of carnality came to imbue much religious imagery. The result was received with attitudes that changed dramatically throughout the period, ranging from strong consensus to adamant criticism. Reception was further fragmented by the increased distribution of images with the introduction of print media, which helped to usher in an expansion of possibilities for both visual and verbal texts, and indeed their combination.

At the beginning of the seventeenth century, developing an erotically charged realism as a fundamental basis for his style, Caravaggio introduced a confrontational body, aggressive in its dialogue with the viewer, whose startling element of surprise elicited powerfully emotional responses. The serene and dazzling seduction of Renaissance perfection appears open and innocent by comparison, even in its most brazen moments. It was a dazzling carnality, easily recognizable as belonging to an ideal realm beyond the earthly sphere, well suited to aesthetic mediation. The pronounced earthliness of Caravaggio's strand of sexuality provided a forceful option in the ensuing period, which countered Renaissance practice to the point of renewing the force of the erotic in visual expression.

NOTES

Chapter 1

1. Luca and Francesco Cavalli-Sforza, *Perché la scienza? L'avventura di un ricercatore* (Milan: Mondadori, 2005), 252: Il patrimonio genetico determina le caratteristiche strutturali del nostro organismo, fisico e psicologico. Il patrimonio culturale viene appreso durante la vita sin dalla più tenera infanzia e condiziona la nostra esistenza, le nostre scelte e molti aspetti della nostra vita di relazione, ed è a volte inevitabilmente in contrasto con quanto ci viene trasmesso per via genetica (translation by the author). For the discussion that follows see especially chapter 13, "L'evoluzione culturale," 252–78. See also Linda Stone and Paul F. Lurquin, *A Genetic and Cultural Odyssey: The Life and Work of L. Luca Cavalli-Sforza* (New York: Columbia University Press, 2005).

2. Cavalli-Sforza, *Perché la scienza,* 258: Nel caso della biologia ciò che evolve è il Dna, mentre nel caso della cultura ciò che evolve sono le idee, o possiamo dire le conoscenze, nel senso che le nostre conoscenze sono composte di idee che affiorano alla coscienza e che ci scambiamo l'un l'altro. Entrambi—Dna e idee—vengono trasmessi, cioè riprodotti nei nostri discendenti.

3. Summarized by Stone and Lurquin, *A Genetic and Cultural Odyssey,* 99.

4. For a highly influential discussion of a one-sex model of sexuality and the importance of degrees of heat in determining sexuality, see Thomas Laqueur, *Making Sex: Body and Gender from the Greeks to Freud* (Cambridge, MA: Harvard University Press, 1990).

5. See the chapter by Ann Rosalind Jones in this volume.

6. Giorgio Vasari, *The Lives of the Painters, Sculptors and Architects,* trans. Gaston du C. de Vere (New York: Knopf, 1996), 2:651.

7. For this illuminating insight as applied to the field of medicine, see the chapter by Cynthia Klestinec in this volume.

8. Roberto Zapperi, *The Pregnant Man* (Chur: Harwood Academic, 1991). Also see the example discussed by Klestinec in chapter 6 of this volume.

9. Katharine Park, *Secrets of Women: Gender, Generation, and the Origins of Human Dissection* (Zone Books, 2006).

10. Peter Stallybrass, "Worn Worlds: Clothes and Identity on the Renaissance Stage," in *Subject and Object in Renaissance Culture*, ed. Margreta de Grazia, Maureen Quilligan, and Peter Stallybrass (Cambridge: Cambridge University Press, 1996), 302.

11. Ibid., 304.

12. Carole Collier Frick, *Dressing Renaissance Florence* (Baltimore: Johns Hopkins University Press, 2002), 149.

13. Ibid., 154.

14. The work of Diane Owen Hughes is fundamental to cultural studies of the sumptuary laws. See her essay, "Sumptuary Law and Social Relations in Renaissance Italy," in *The Italian Renaissance: The Essential Readings*, ed. Paula Findlen (Oxford: Blackwell, 2002), 124–50.

15. William Shakespeare, *Hamlet, Prince of Denmark*, I, iii, 68–74. *William Shakespeare: The Complete Works*, ed. Alfred Harbage (Baltimore: Penguin, 1971). References are to act, scene, and lines.

16. Peter Burke, "The Courtier Abroad: Or the Uses of Italy," in *The Book of the Courtier by Baldesar Castiglione*, ed. Daniel Javitch (Norton, 2002), 390.

17. Javitch, *Book of the Courtier,* 89.

18. Michel Pastoureau, *The Devil's Cloth: A History of Stripes* (New York: Washington Square Press, 1991), 13–14.

19. Ibid., 16–19.

20. Javitch, *Book of the Courtier,* 89.

21. Rembrandt Duits, "Figured Riches," *Journal of the Warburg and Courtauld Institutes* 33 (1970): 84.

22. This outfit also featured the crucially important *sacra cintura*, a belt of symbolic religious significance. See Louise Bourdura and Anne Dunlop, *Art and the Augustinian Order in Early Renaissance Italy* (Aldershot: Ashgate, 2007), 179, n. 43.

23. Mary D. Garrard, "Here's Looking at Me: Sofonsiba Anguissola and the Problem of the Woman Artist," *Renaissance Quarterly* 47 (1994): 583.

24. See the chapter by Fredrika Jacobs in this volume.

25. Giovanni Della Casa, *Galateo: A Renaissance Treatise on Manners,* ed. Konrad Eisenbichler and Kenneth R. Bartlett (Toronto: Centre for Reformation and Renaissance Studies, 1994), 41.

26. Duke Cosimo de' Medici attempted to revive the practice of prostitutes wearing yellow veils or ribbons in mid-sixteenth-century Florence. For this information see Doretta Davanzo Poli, "Le cortigiane e la moda," in *Le cortigiane di Venezia dal trecento al settecento* (Milan: Berenice Art Books, 1990), 99.

27. Pastoureau, *The Devil's Cloth,* 13.

28. See the chapter by Fredrika Jacobs in this volume.

29. Olwen Hufton, "Istruzione, Lavoro e Povertà," in *Monaca, Moglie, Serva, Cortigiana: Vita e immagine delle donne tra Rinascimento e Controriforma,* ed. Sara F.

Matthews-Grieco (Florence: Morgana Edizioni, 2001), 90. For examples of the prints, see illustrations 61a, 61b, 73a, and 73b.

30. Guido Ruggiero, *The Boundaries of Eros* (New York: Oxford University Press, 1985), 119.

31. Desiderio Erasmus, *On Good Manners for Boys,* in *Collected Works,* trans. Brian McGregor (Toronto: University of Toronto Press, 1985), vol. 25, 278.

32. Gordon Williams, *A Dictionary of Sexual Language and Imagery in Shakespearean and Stuart Literature* (London: Athlone Press, 1994), 268. If the author's contention that "pins" can indicate "penis" is correct, then the possibilities for puns and double meanings proliferate. See the entries s.v. *cod, codpiece, pins.*

33. Shakespeare, *Complete Works, The Two Gentlemen of Verona,* II, vii, 55–56.

34. Anne Hollander, *Sex and Suits: The Evolution of Modern Dress* (New York: Kodansha International, 1994), 43.

35. For the symbolic use of bared breasts as the supreme signifier of female sexuality, see my further thoughts in chapter 9 of this volume.

36. Leah L. Otis, *Prostitution in Medieval Society: The History of an Urban Institution in Languedoc* (University of Chicago Press, 1985), 75.

37. For the situation in Florence see John K. Brackett, "The Florentine *Onestà* and the Control of Prostitution, 1403–1680," *The Sixteenth Century Journal* 29 (1993): 273–300.

38. See the chapter by Guido Ruggiero in this volume.

39. See the chapter by Nicholas Davidson in this volume.

40. The remarks in the following paragraph on canon law and fornication are based in large part on the discussion found in James A. Brundage, "Carnal Delight: Canonistic Theories of Sexuality," *Proceedings of the Fifth International Congress of Medieval Canon Law,* ed. Stephan Kuttner and Kenneth Pennington (Vatican City: Biblioteca Apostolica Vaticana, 1980), 361–85.

41. Michael Rocke, *Forbidden Friendships: Homosexuality and Male Culture in Renaissance Florence* (Oxford: Oxford University Press, 1996), 146.

42. Ibid., especially 10–16 for introductory remarks to the issue.

43. For example, the chapter by Helmut Puff in this volume focuses on the city of Nuremberg but provides a methodological basis for approaching the European situation.

44. Margaret A. Sullivan, "The Witches of Dürer and Hans Baldung Grien," *Renaissance Quarterly* 53 (2000): 334.

45. Bodo Brinkmann, *Hexenlust und Sündenfall. Die seltsamen Phantasien des Hans Baldung Grien* (Petersberg: Michael Imhof Verlag, 2007), 35.

46. See the chapter by Walter Stephens in this volume.

47. See my discussion about the use of the categories *onesto/disonesto* during the Renaissance in *Taking Positions: On the Erotic in Renaissance Culture* (Princeton, NJ: Princeton University Press, 1999), 101–24.

48. Elizabeth S. Cohen, "Honor and Gender in the Streets of Early Modern Rome," *Journal of Interdisciplinary History* 22 (1992): 597.

49. Ibid., 618.

50. See the edition edited by Amedeo Quondam, Modena, Panini, 1993.
51. Pliny, *Natural History,* ed. H. Rackman (Cambridge, MA: Harvard University Press, 1952), 5.
52. See Bette Talvacchia, "The Art of Courting Women's Laughter," in *New Perspectives on Women and Comedy,* ed. Regina Barreca (Philadelphia: Gordon and Breach, 1992), 213–22.
53. Beth L. Holman, ed., *Disegno: Italian Renaissance Designs for the Decorative Arts* (Dubuque, IA: Kendall, 1997), 66–67.

Chapter 2

1. Galen's theory was laid out in a now classic essay by Thomas Laqueur, "Orgasm, Generation and the Politics of Reproductive Biology," in *The Making of the Modern Body: Sexuality and Society in the Nineteenth Century,* ed. Catherine Gallagher and Thomas Laqueur (Berkeley: University of California Press, 1987), 1–41; see also Katharine Park, "Medicine and Magic: The Healing Arts," in *Gender and Society in Renaissance Italy*, ed. Judith C. Brown and Robert C. Davis (New York, Longman, 1998), 129.
2. Baldasar Heseler, Andreas Vesalius's *First Public Anatomy at Bologna, 1540: An Eyewitness Report* (Uppsala: Almquist and Wiksells, 1959), 181, cited in Merry Wiesner, *Women and Gender in Early Modern Europe,* 2nd ed. (Cambridge: Cambridge University Press, 2000), 141.
3. In Cissie Fairchilds, *Women in Early Modern Europe, 1500–1700* (London: Pearson/Longman, 2007), 121.
4. Benjamin Roberts and Leendert Groenendijk, "'Wearing Out a Pair of Fool's Shoes': Sexual Advice for Youth in Holland's Golden Age," *Journal of the History of Sexuality* 13, no. 2 (2004): 147.
5. Kevin P. Siena, "Pollution, Promiscuity, and the Pox: English Venereology and the Early Modern Medical Discourse on Social and Sexual Danger," *Journal of the History of Sexuality* 8 (1998): 559.
6. Thomas Heywood (?), *A Pleasant Conceited Comedie, Wherein Is Shewed How a Man May Chuse a Good Wife from a Bad* (London, 1620), sig. B3-v.
7. John Milton, *Eikonoklastes* (London, 1650), 64.
8. Matteo Palmieri, *Della Vita civile,* written 1429, published Florence, 1529; ed. F. Battaglia (Bologna: Zanichelli, 1944), English translation in Michael Rocke, "Gender and Sexual Culture in Renaissance Italy," in *Gender and Society in Renaissance Italy,* ed. Judith C. Brown and Robert C. Davis (Longman, 1998), 145.
9. Juan Luis Vives, *De institutione foeminae Christianae* (1529), English version in *The Education of a Christian Woman,* ed. and trans. Charles Fantazzi (Chicago: University of Chicago Press, 2000), 181–82.
10. Fairchilds, *Women,* 142.
11. James Farr, *Authority and Sexuality in Early Modern Burgundy, 1550–1730* (Oxford: Oxford University Press, 1995), 137.
12. David Cressy, *Birth, Marriage and Death: Ritual, Religion and the Life-Cycle in Tudor and Stuart England* (Oxford: Oxford University Press, 1997), 147–50.

13. Laqueur, "Orgasm, Generation," 103.
14. Farr, *Authority and Sexuality*, 150.
15. Fairchilds, *Women*, 55.
16. Leon Battista Alberti, *I Libri della Famiglia*, ed. Guido Ruggiero and Alberto Tenenti (Turin: Einaudi, 1972), English version in *The Albertis of Florence*, ed. and trans. Guido Guarino (Lewsburg, PA: Bucknell University Press, 1971), 122.
17. Moderata Fonte, *Il Merito delle Donne*, Venice, 1600, English version in Virginia Cox, ed. and trans., *The Worth of Women* (Chicago: University of Chicago Press, 1997), 210.
18. Ann Crabb, *The Strozzi of Florence: Widowhood and Family Solidarity in the Renaissance* (Ann Arbor: University of Michigan Press, 2000), 247.
19. Christiane Klapisch-Zuber, *Women, Family and Ritual in Renaissance Italy* (Chicago: University of Chicago Press, 1985), 226.
20. Cristelle Baskins, *Cassone Painting, Humanism and Gender in Early Modern Italy* (Cambridge: Cambridge University Press, 1998), 116–17.
21. Laqueur, "Orgasm, Generation," 110.
22. Giovanni Marinelli, *Le medicine partinenti alle infermità delle donne* (1563, 1574), cited in Joanne Ferraro, *Marriage Wars in Late Renaissance Venice* (Oxford: Oxford University Press, 2001), 88.
23. Park, "Medicine and Magic," 129.
24. Rocke, "Gender and Sexual Culture," 156.
25. Ferraro, *Marriage Wars*, 88.
26. Ibid., 94.
27. Farr, *Authority and Sexuality*, 178.
28. Fonte, *Il Merito*, 77.
29. Francesco Petrarca, *Canzoniere*, 159, in *Petrarch: Selected Poems*, trans. Anthony Mortimer (Tuscaloosa: University of Alabama Press), 69.
30. My translation, following Robert M. Durling, ed. and trans., *Petrarch's Lyric Poems: The Rime Sparse and Other Lyrics* (Cambridge, MA: Harvard University Press, 1976), 628.
31. Maffeo Venier, cited and translated by Margaret F. Rosenthal, *The Honest Courtesan: Veronica Franco as Citizen and Poet in Sixteenth-Century Venice* (Chicago: University of Chicago Press, 1992), 188–89.
32. Elizabeth S. Cohen and Thomas V. Cohen, *Daily Life in Renaissance Italy* (Westport, CT: Greenwood Press, 2001), 93.
33. Laura Battiferra degli Ammannati, in Victoria Kirkham, ed. and trans., *Laura Battiferra and Her Literary Circle: An Anthology* (Chicago: University of Chicago Press, 2006), 380, n. 59.
34. Chiara Matraini, *Rime e prose*, Lucca: Busdraghi, 1555, English version in Elaine Maclachlan, ed. and trans., *Chiara Matraini: Selected Poetry and Prose* (Chicago: University of Chicago Press, 2007), 5.
35. Daniela Hacke, *Women, Sex and Marriage in Early Modern Venice* (Burlington, VT: Ashgate, 2004), 117.
36. Ferraro, *Marriage Wars*, 98.
37. Alexander Cowan, *Marriage, Manners and Mobility in Early Modern Venice* (Burlington, VT: Ashgate, 2007), chapter 6.

38. Martha Feldman, "The Courtesan's Voice: Petrarchan Lovers, Pop Philosophy and Oral Traditions," in *The Courtesan's Arts: Cross-Cultural Perspectives,* ed. Martha Feldman and Bonnie Gordon (Oxford: Oxford University Press, 2006), 105–23.

39. For such portraits, see Allison Levy, *Re-Membering Masculinity in Early Modern Florence: Widowed Bodies, Mourning and Portraiture* (Burlington, VT: Ashgate, 2006), figs. 3.9–3.13, 3.22.

40. Cowan, *Marriage, Manners,* 140–42.

41. Geoffrey Robert Quaife, *Wanton Wenches and Wayward Wives: Peasants and Illicit Sex in Early Seventeenth Century England* (New Brunswick, NJ: Rutgers University Press, 1979), 145.

42. Crabb, *The Strozzi,* 28.

43. For a biography of the Countess of Shrewsbury, see Santina Levy, *Elizabethan Treasures: The Hardwick Hall Textiles* (London: National Trust/Harry Abrams, 1998), 9–14.

44. Lauro Martines, "Poetry as Politics and Memory in Renaissance Florence and Italy," in *Art, Memory and Family in Renaissance Florence,* ed. Giovanni Ciapelli and Patricia Lee Rubin (Cambridge: Cambridge University Press, 2000), 49.

45. Marguerite de Navarre, *L'Heptaméron,* Nouvelle 48, English version in *The Heptameron,* tr. Paul A. Chilton (Penguin, 1987), 417–21.

46. Fonte, *Il Merito,* 29.

47. Ibid., 51–52.

48. Lucrezia Marinella, *La Nobiltà e excellenza delle donne coi' difetti e mancamenti degli huomeni,* Venice: Ciotti, 1600, 1601, 1621, English version in *The Nobility and Excellence of Women and the Defects and Vices of Men,* edited and translated by Letizia Panizzi and Anne Dunhill (Chicago: University of Chicago Press, 1999), 135–36.

49. Marinella, *Nobility,* 138.

50. Henry Abelove, "Some Speculations on the History of Sexual Intercourse during the Long Eighteenth Century in England," *Genders* 6 (1989): 128.

51. Samuel Pepys, *The Diary of Samuel Pepys: A New and Complete Transcription,* vol. 9 (1668), ed. Robert Latham and William Matthews (London: Bell, 1976), 337.

Chapter 3

1. A. Röver-Kann, *Albrecht Dürer: Das Frauenbad von 1496* (Bremen: Kunstverein, 2001), 28–32; J. Chipps Smith, *Nuremberg: A Renaissance City, 1500–1618* (Austin: University of Texas Press, 1983), 98. My gratitude goes to Patricia Simons, who responded with formidable feedback to an earlier version of this chapter.

2. E. Wind, 'Dürer's "Männerbad": A Dionysian Mystery', *Journal of the Warburg and Courtauld Institutes* 2 (1938), 269–71.

3. Röver-Kann, *Frauenbad,* 28. Cf. M. Sonnabend, "Das Männerbad," in *Albrecht Dürer: Die Druckgraphiken im Städel Museum* (Frankfurt am Main: Städel Museum, 2007), 52–53; J. L. Koerner, *The Moment of Self-Portraiture in German Renaissance Art* (Chicago: University of Chicago Press, 1993), 435. The seated man

to the right looks like the aged Pirckheimer; at the time this woodcut was made, he would have been in his mid-twenties, however. The figure resembles the central reveler in Andrea Mantegna's *Bacchanal with Silen,* a print copied by Dürer ca. 1494 (cf. Sonnabend, "Das Männerbad," 52).

4. See, for instance, Yvonne Ivory, *The Homosexual Revival of Renaissance Style, 1850–1930* (New York: Palgrave Macmillan, 2009).

5. M. Rocke, *Forbidden Friendships: Homosexuality and Male Culture in Renaissance Florence* (Oxford: Oxford University Press, 1996), 149.

6. Georg Wickram's collection of facetiae, *Das Rollwagenbüchlin* (1555/1556), explicitly mentions bathhouses as a venue for the retelling of the "fabliaux and stories" (*schwenck und Historien*) included in the collection. See Georg Wickram, *Das Rollwagenbüchlin*, ed. J. Bolte (Stuttgart: Reclam, 1968), 5.

7. L. Roper, "Was There a Crisis in Gender Relations in Sixteenth-Century Germany?" and "Drinking, Whoring, and Gorging: Brutish Indiscipline and the Formation of a Protestant Identity," in L. Roper, *Oedipus and the Devil: Witchcraft, Sexuality, and Religion in Early Modern Europe* (London: Routledge, 1994), 37–52, 145–67.

8. L. Roper, "Tokens of Affection: The Meanings of Love in Sixteenth-Century Germany," in *Dürer and His Culture*, ed. Dagmar Eichberger and Charles Zika (Cambridge: Cambridge University Press, 1998), 152.

9. Most notably in the drawing *The Rape of Europa,* see K.-A. Schröder and M. L. Sternath (eds.), *Albrecht Dürer* (Vienna: Albertina, 2003), 168–69, or the engravings *The Ravisher or a Young Woman Attacked by Death* of ca. 1495, see G. Barnum, *Albrecht Dürer and His Legacy*, London: British Museum, 2002, 110; *The Lovers and Death* of ca. 1498, see Sonnabend, *Albrecht Dürer*, 82–83; and *Coat of Arms with a Skull* of ca. 1503, see Barnum, *Albrecht Dürer,* 148. By contrast, see the drawing *The Lovers* of ca. 1492/94; see Schröder and Sternath, *Albrecht Dürer*, 138–39.

10. A. G. Stewart, *Before Bruegel: Sebald Beham and the Origins of Peasant Festival Imagery* (Aldershot: Ashgate, 2008).

11. A. Bray, *The Friend* (Chicago: University of Chicago Press, 2003), especially 307–23. While there is an extensive literature on male bonding, the line of research relevant here was inspired by scholars who integrate homoeroticism into their accounts; see K. Theweleit, *Male Fantasies*, trans. Stephen Conway (Minneapolis: University of Minnesota Press, 1987); E. Kosofsky Sedgwick, *Between Men: English Literature and Male Homosocial Desire* (New York: Columbia University Press, 1985). See also D. Kent, *Friendship, Love, and Trust in Renaissance Florence* (Cambridge, MA: Harvard University Press, 2009).

12. The Etzlaub map has been reprinted numerous times; see, for instance, Smith, *Nuremberg*, 91; Barnum, *Albrecht Dürer*, 103–4; Th. Eser and A. Grebe, *Heilige und Hasen: Bücherschätze der Dürerzeit* (Nuremberg: Germanisches Nationalmuseum, 2008), 124–25.

13. On Nuremberg, see G. Strauss, *Nuremberg in the Sixteenth Century: City Politics and Life between Middle Ages and Modern Times* (Bloomington: Indiana University Press, 1976), 247–48; Smith, *Nuremberg*, 39–44; D. Hotchkiss Price,

Albrecht Dürer's Renaissance: Humanism, Reformation, and the Art of Faith (Ann Arbor: University of Michigan Press, 2003). On homoeroticism and humanism, see G. Dall'Orto, "'Socratic Love' as a Disguise for Same-Sex Love in the Italian Renaissance," in *Male Homosexuality in Renaissance and Enlightenment Europe*, ed. K. Gerard and G. Hekma (New York: Harrington Park Press, 1989), 33–65.

14. B. Brinkmann, *Witches' Lust and the Fall of Man: The Strange Fantasies of Hans Baldung Grien* (Frankfurt am Main: Michael Imhof, 2007), 103. Importantly, silverpoint drawings could not be corrected. Dürer's earliest self-portrait was executed in this manner; see Koerner, *The Moment*, 36.

15. Different translations are offered by Brinkmann, *Witches' Lust*, 104 ("with the erect member of the man in the anus") and Stephen Orgel, who is currently preparing a new version of his essay "Ganymede Agonistes" (originally published in *GLQ: A Journal of Lesbian and Gay Studies* 10 [2004]: 485–501): "with a man's prick up your asshole."

16. Brinkmann, *Witches' Lust*, 104; I. Reiche et al., "Spatially Resolved Synchrotron-Induced X-Ray Fluorescence Analyses of Metal Point Drawings and Their Mysterious Inscriptions," *Spectrochimica Acta Part B: Atomic Spectroscopy* 59 (2004): 1657–62. Thanks to Stephen Orgel for this reference.

17. Brinkmann, *Witches' Lust*, 104.

18. Brinkmann, *Witches' Lust*, 102; Smith, *Nuremberg*, 125.

19. Given the content of the superscript, which could be described as vernacular in tone, one might consider the possibility of Dürer providing the text (in mockery?) and Pirckheimer translating it on the spot, turning the making of the portrait sketch into a playfully collaborative effort.

20. Ca. 1502, Dürer designed an ex libris for Pirckheimer featuring the coat of arms of Pirckheimer and his wife, Crescentia Rieter, as well as a trilingual superscript in Hebrew, Greek, and Latin (Ecclesiasticus 1.16) and the designation or motto "for him [i.e. Pirckheimer] and [his] friends" (*sibi et amicis*). See Eser and Grebe, *Heilige und Hasen*, 70–71.

21. H. Puff, *Sodomy in Reformation Germany and Switzerland 1400–1600* (Chicago: University of Chicago Press, 2003). Cases of heterosexual anal intercourse came to court only rarely.

22. Since no systematic study of sodomy or other persecutions exists for the city, this assessment is based on a review of general historiography on early modern Nuremberg. For other cities, see the studies by M. Boone, "State Power and Illicit Sexuality: The Persecution of Sodomy in Late Medieval Bruges," *Journal of Medieval History* 22 (1996): 135–53; and Rocke, *Forbidden Friendships*; G. Ruggiero, *The Boundaries of Eros: Sex, Crime, and Sexuality in Renaissance Venice* (New York: Oxford University Press, 1985). See also A. Bray, *Homosexuality in Renaissance England* (London: Gay Men's Press, 1982).

23. Georg Steinhausen, ed., *Briefwechsel Balthasar Paumgartners des Jüngeren mit seiner Gattin Magdalena, geb. Behaim (1592–1598)* (Tübingen: Litterarischer Verein, 1895), 238 (August 15, 1594). Cf. Steven Ozment, *Magdalena and Balthasar: An Intimate Portrait of Life in Sixteenth-Century Europe Revealed in the Letters of a Nuremberg Husband and Wife* (New Haven: Yale University Press, 1986), 78.

24. K. Löcher, "Madonna und Kind (Haller-Madonna)," in *Nürnberg 1300–1550: Kunst der Gotik und der Renaissance* (Munich: Prestel, 1986), 276–78; A. Scherbaum, "Madonna mit Kind (Haller-Madonna)," in *Albrecht Dürer*, ed. K.-A. Schröder and M. L. Sternath (Vienna: Albertina, 2003), 178–81.

25. N. Holzberg, *Willibald Pirckheimer: Griechischer Humanismus in Deutschland* (Munich: Wilhelm Fink, 1981). See also the title page Dürer designed for Pirckheimer's 1515 Latin translation of Lucian, *De ratione conscribendi historiae*, in Eser and Grebe, *Heilige und Hasen*, 68–69.

26. Pseudo-Lucian, "Affairs of the Heart," in *Lucian*, vol. 8, trans. M. D. Macleod (Cambridge, MA: Harvard University Press, 1979), 150–235. While Macleod wrote, "It is obvious from the style of this dialogue that the author is not Lucian but an imitator" (147), this *communis opinio* has recently been challenged by James Jope ("The Authenticity of the Lucianic *Erotes,*" forthcoming); see http://jjope. blogspot.com/2009/05/authenticity-of-lucianic-erotes.html (accessed July 3, 2009). On Pirckheimer's interest in the Lucianic opus, see Holzberg, *Willibald Pirckheimer,* 120–29, 155–58, 221–26, 248–62, 298–301; and Brinkmann, *Witches' Lust,* 97–102.

27. Ovid, *Metamorphoses IX–XII*, ed. D. E. Hill (Warminster: Aris and Phillips, 1999), 47.

28. H. Puff, "The Death of Orpheus (according to Albrecht Dürer)," in *Dead Lovers: Erotic Bonds and the Study of Premodern Europe*, ed. Basil Dufallo and Peggy McCracken (Ann Arbor: University of Michigan Press, 2006), 71–95.

29. See, for instance, I. Rowland, "Revenge of the Regensburg Humanists, 1493," *Sixteenth Century Journal* 25 (1994): 307–22.

30. For Dürer, see H. Sahm, *Dürers kleinere Texte: Konventionen als Spielraum für Individualität* (Tübingen: Niemeyer, 2002).

31. D. Knox, *Ironia: Medieval and Renaissance Ideas on Irony* (Leiden: Brill, 1989).

32. H. Rupprich, ed., *Dürer: Schriftlicher Nachlass*, vol. 1, *Autobiographische Schriften/ Briefwechsel/Dichtungen* (Berlin: Deutscher Verein für Kunstwissenschaft, 1956), 39–60; M. Conway, *The Writings of Albrecht Dürer* (London: Peter Owen, 1958), 45–60.

33. L. Grote, *Albrecht Dürer: Reisen nach Venedig* (Munich: Prestel, 1998).

34. M. Miller, *Material Friendship: Service and Amity in Early Modern French Literature* (Ph.D. diss., University of Michigan, 2008).

35. There are multiple discourses at play—discourses of mentorship, fatherhood, friendship, servitude, and so forth. Dürer's Venice trip was made possible by a loan from Pirckheimer; see Rupprich, *Schriftlicher Nachlass*, 42 (January 6, 1506).

36. In a letter of February 28, 1506, Dürer says that he read a letter by Pirckheimer addressed to another Nuremberger (ibid., 46). The surviving correspondence is replete with references to messenger friends and a dense web of communications between Nuremberg and Venice.

37. Rupprich, *Schriftlicher Nachlass*, 41–42 (January 6, 1506), 46 (February 28, 1506), 47–48 (March 8, 1506), 48–49 (April 2, 1506), 50–51 (April 25, 1506), 52–53 (August 18, 1506), 57 (September 23, 1506), 58–59 (October 13, 1506).

38. Ibid., 42 (January 6, 1506), 49 (April 2, 1506), 52 (August 18, 1506).

39. Ibid., 52 (August 18, 1506).

40. Ibid., 55 (September 8, 1506). See also 43 (February 7, 1506) or 46 (February 28, 1506), when Dürer writes that he wishes Pirckheimer were in Venice as well.

41. Ibid., 55 (September 8, 1506).

42. Ibid., 57 (September 23, 1506).

43. Ibid., 44 (February 7, 1506).

44. Ibid., 55 (September 8, 1506). Having participated in military campaigns, Pirckheimer had a great interest in soldiery, weaponry, and military science. In the same passage, Dürer announces playfully his desire to become an "Italian mercenary" (*welscher lanczknecht*) himself, men who in a previous letter were ridiculed for their foppery (52, August 18, 1506). *Hüpsch,* with its wide-ranging meanings, clearly denotes good looks in Dürer's letters of September 23, 1506, and October 13, 1506 (57–58).

45. Ibid., 59: "Vnd als jr schreibt, jch soll pald kumen oder jr wolt mirs weib kristieren, jst ewch vnerlawbt, jr prawt sy den zw thott" (October 13, 1506). An enigmatic passage at the letter's end seems to call on Pirckheimer to report on his having had intercourse with his wife.

46. Ibid., 47 (March 8, 1506).

47. Holzberg, *Willibald Pirckheimer*, 67–68. The answer to this question is made more difficult by the fact that many letters and documents were burnt after Pirckheimer's death, "ne public elegant multi quod vni dumtaxat priuatim doctorum hominum scripsit amicitia," so Thomas Venatorius to Erasmus (September 6, 1531, 2537 Allen; Holzberg, *Willibald Pirckheimer*, 14). To my knowledge, the issue of Dürer's sexual predilections was first raised, or rather silenced, by Heinrich Wölfflin in 1905: "We shall not discuss whether Dürer had any personal interest in the subject [of the drawing]" with regard to the aforementioned *Death of Orpheus*: H. Wölfflin, *The Art of Albrecht Dürer*, trans. Alastair and Heide Grieve (London: Phaidon, 1971), 52. The theme of Dürer's sexual orientation does not go away. More recently, M. Mende has taken it up in a nonchalant fashion; see his "Wer war Dürers Kuschelhase?" in *Die Welt*, February 26, 2003, www.welt.de/printwelt/article420380/Wer_war_Duerers_Kuschelhase.html.

48. D. Halperin, *How to Do the History of Male Homosexuality* (Chicago: University of Chicago Press, 2002), 115–17; Rocke, *Forbidden Friendships*, 87–147; Puff, *Sodomy*, 91–92. See also R. Mazo Karras, *Sexuality in Medieval Europe: Doing Unto Others* (London: Routledge, 2005), 23.

49. Lorenz Beheim to Willibald Pirckheimer, March 19, 1507: "Sed sua barba bechina impeditur, quam sine dubio torquendo crispat quottidie, ut dentes aprinos extantes assimilando repraesentet. Ma il gerzone suo abhorret, scio, la barba sua." Rupprich, *Schriftlicher Nachlass*, 254.

50. Cf. Rocke, *Forbidden Friendships*, 158.

51. See C. Walker Bynum, "The Body of Christ in the Later Middle Ages: A Reply to Leo Steinberg," in *Fragmentation and Redemption: Essays on Gender and the Human Body in Medieval Religion* (New York: Zone Books, 1991), 79–117.

52. F. Anzelewsky and S. Morét, "Drei Kriegsleute, 1489," in *Dürer Holbein Grünewald: Meisterzeichnungen der deutschen Renaissance aus Berlin und Basel* (Ostfildern-Ruit: Gerd Hatje, 1997), 94–95.

53. F. Anzelewsky, *Dürer: Werk und Wirkung* (Erlangen: Karl Müller, 1988), 116–17.

54. J. K. Eberlien, *Albrecht Dürer* (Reinbek: Rowohlt, 2003), 60–61.

55. R. Scribner, "Vom Sakralbild zur sinnlichen Schau: Sinnliche Wahrnehmung und das Visuelle bei der Objektivierung des Frauenkörpers in Deutschland im 16. Jahrhundert," in K. Schreiner and N. Schnitzler (eds.), *Gepeinigt, begehrt vergessen* (Munich: W. Fink, 1992), 309–36.

56. B. Hinz, "Nackt/Akt: Dürer und der Prozess der Zivilisation," *Städel Jahrbuch N.F.* 14 (1993): 199–230. Characteristic in this regard is the woodcut of a draftsman drawing a reclining female nude by means of a geometrical device. This illustration was a supplement to the second edition of the *Underweysung der messung* (Instruction of Measurement), whose first edition Dürer oversaw in 1525. When Agnes Dürer and the woodcutter Hieronymus Andreae prepared the second edition (1538), they made use of Dürer's corrections and additions that survive in manuscript form (Eser and Grebe, *Heilige und Hasen*, 56–57). While Dürer had replaced the original lute with a reclining male nude, the 1538 edition placed the lying female figure in front of the device, charging the operation erotically.

57. Patricia Simons contends persuasively that bathing scenes did not originate with an Orientalizing mode, as has been argued, but rather offered a cultural interface in which the sexuality of women came into view; see her "Images of Bathing Women in Early Modern Europe and Turkey," in *Crossing Cultures: Conflict, Migration and Convergence,* ed. Jaynie Anderson (Melbourne: Miegunyah Press, 2009), 321–27.

58. Röver-Kann, *Frauenbad*.

59. Pseudo-Lucian, "Affairs of the Heart," 194–95.

60. M. E. Wiesner, "Women's Defence of Their Public Role," in *Gender, Church and State in Early Modern Germany* (London: Longman, 1998), 6–29; Wiesner, *Women and Gender in Early Modern Europe*, 2nd ed. (Cambridge: Cambridge University Press, 2000), 143–210; H. Andreadis, "The Sapphic-Platonics of Katherine Philips, 1632–1664," *Signs* 15 (1989): 34–60; V. Traub, *The Renaissance of Lesbianism in Early Modern England* (Cambridge: Cambridge University Press, 2002), 341–42.

61. Erasmus, "Coniugium," *Opera Omnia Desiderii Erasmi Roterodami*, vol. 1, *Colloquia*, ed. L.-E. Halkin, F. Bierlaire, and R. Hoven (Amsterdam: North Holland, 1972), 301–13; Erasmus, "Marriage," *The Colloquies of Erasmus*, trans. Craig R. Thompson (Chicago: University of Chicago Press, 1965), 114–27. See also Barbara Correll, "Malleable Material, Models of Power: Woman in Erasmus's 'Marriage Group' and 'Civility in Boys,'" *English Literary History* 57 (1990): 241–62.

62. Erasmus of Rotterdam, "Virgo misogamos" and "Virgo poenitens," *Colloquia*, 289–97; "The Girl with No Interest in Marriage" and "The Repentant Girl," *The Colloquies of Erasmus*, 99–111 and 111–14.

63. M. Luther, "Vom ehelichen leben," *Martin Luthers Werke: Kritische Gesamtausgabe*, vol. 10:2 (Weimar: Böhlau, 1907), 275–304; here, 289.

64. G. Sercambi, "De libidine," in *Novelle*, vol. 1, ed. G. Sinicropi (Bari: G. Laterza, 1972), 144–47.

65. Bourdeille, Seigneur de Brantôme, *La vie des dames galantes*, ed. Pascal Pia and Paul Morand (Paris: Gallimard, 1981). See the discussion in Guy Poirier, *L'homosexualité dans l'imaginaire de la Renaissance* (Paris: Champion, 1996), 119–28.

66. Röver-Kann, *Frauenbad*, 33–40; Smith, *Nuremberg*, 183, 193.

67. J. L. Levy, "The Erotic Engraving of Sebald and Barthel Beham: A German Interpretation of a Renaissance Subject," in *The World in Miniature Engravings by the German Little Masters 1500–1550*, ed. St. H. Goddard (Lawrence, KS: The Spencer Museum of Art, 1988), 40–53. See especially *Death and the Three Nude Women* by Barthel Beham (1525–1527), a plate later reworked by his brother Sebald: a reworking of Dürer's *The Four Witches* (cat. no. 49a and 49b, 182–83).

68. Goddard, *The World in Miniature Engravings*, 180–81; Röver-Kann, *Frauenbad*, 36 (dated as 1548 and with Hans Sebald Beham's monogram). K. Löcher, *Barthel Beham: Ein Maler aus dem Dürerkreis* (Munich: Deutscher Kunstverlag, 1999), 39 (laterally reversed, without monogram, presented as Barthel Beham's work). See also J. Muller, *Barthel Beham: Kritischer Katalog* (Baden-Baden: Heitz, 1958), 53. According to *The World in Miniature* the print measures 81 × 56 mm.

69. J. Saslow, *Ganymede in the Renaissance: Homosexuality in Art and Society* (New Haven, CT: Yale University Press, 1986); L. Barkan, *Transuming Passion: Ganymede and the Erotics of Humanism* (Stanford, CA: Stanford University Press, 1991); Traub, *Renaissance*, 158–275.

70. The oven itself is reminiscent not only of Dürer's *Women's Bath* but also of another erotic scene by the same artist, the so-called *Dream of the Doctor* or *The Temptation of the Idler* (ca. 1498); see Barnum, *Albrecht Dürer*, 123–24.

71. U. Rublack, "Sexual Difference, Law and Subjectivity in Early Modern Germany," in *After the History of Sexuality: German Interventions*, ed. D. Herzog, H. Puff and S. Spector (New York: Berghahn, forthcoming).

72. Judith M. Bennett and Amy M. Froide, eds., *Singlewomen in the European Past* (Philadelphia: University of Pennsylvania, 1999).

73. M. Schilling, *Bildpublizistik der frühen Neuzeit: Aufgaben und Leistungen des illustrierten Flugblatts in Deutschland bis um 1700* (Tübingen: Niemeyer, 1990), 208–14, 382–84, 429–33. The print, previously held at the Stadtarchiv Augsburg, is lost.

74. B. Brinkmann sees in Baldung the *gerzne* mentioned in Beheim's 1507 letter discussed earlier, the supposed origin of visual punning, if not backstabbing, in Baldung's painting of witches now in Frankfurt. The rejection scenario Brinkmann outlines is not unlikely, though the notion of Dürer's or Baldung's art as something of a confessional for the insider, even if professed as speculative, strikes me as in need of further exploration.

75. S. Schade, "Zur Genese des voeyuristischen Blicks: Das Erotische in den Hexenbildern Hans Baldung Griens," in *Frauen, Kunst, Geschichte: Zur Korrektur des herrschenden Blicks*, ed. C. Bischoff (Marburg: Anabas, 1984), 98–110.

76. A. Schnyder, ed., *Malleus Maleficarum von Heinrich Institoris (alias Kramer) unter Mithilfe Jakob Sprengers aufgrund der dämonologischen Tradition zusammenge-*

stellt: Wiedergabe des Erstdrucks von 1487 (Hain 9238) (Göppingen: Kümmerle, 1991), 28–29, 56, 110. An English translation has recently appeared in print: *The Hammer of Witches: A Complete Translation of the Malleus Maleficarum,* trans. Christopher S. Mackay (Cambridge: Cambridge University Press, 2009).

77. One example is found in R. von Dülmen, "Imaginationen des Teuflischen," in *Gesellschaft der Frühen Neuzeit: Kulturelles Handeln und sozialer Prozeß* (Vienna: Böhlau, 1993), 91, 96. In the case of Appolonia Mayr (Augsburg 1686), the sexual practice in question was anal intercourse between the devil and the accused woman, whereas in the second example cited by the author, the precise practice is not made explicit. The connection between sodomy/bestiality and witchcraft also surfaced in the well-researched *Zauberer Jackl* trials in Salzburg when witchmaster Jackl was said to have introduced a coterie of young men into sexual relations with animals; see H. Nagl, "Der Zauberer-Jackl-Prozeß: Hexenprozesse im Erzstift Salzburg 1675–1690," *Mitteilungen der Gesellschaft für Salzburger Landeskunde* 112/113 (1972/73): 385–540, and 114 (1974): 79–21; G. Mülleder, "Unterschiedliche Deliktvorstellungen bei Ober- und Unterbehörden am Beispiel der Salzburger Zauberer-Jackl-Prozesse (1675–1679)," in H. Eiden and R. Volmer (eds.), *Hexenprozesse und Gerichtspraxis* (Trier: Spee, 2002), 349–94.

78. Among the visual elements that signal inversion are the postures and gazes of women, especially in the 1514 drawing, now in Vienna, with the woman-witch in the foreground gazing through her limbs, head bent down.

79. C. Zika, "She-Man: Visual Representations of Witchcraft and Sexuality," in *Exorcizing Our Demons: Magic, Witchcraft and Visual Culture in Early Modern Europe* (Leiden: Brill, 2003), 269–304; here, 281.

80. Koerner, *The Moment,* 317–62.

81. L. Weigert, "Autonomy as Deviance: Sixteenth-Century Images of Witches and Prostitutes," in *Solitary Pleasures: The Historical, Literary, and Artistic Discourses of Autoeroticism,* ed. Paula Bennett and Vernon A. Rosario II (New York: Routledge, 1995), 19–47. The dedication and themes represented are less definitive than Weigert suggests. Theoretically, the dedicatory superscript could even be taken to address a female cleric, though this seems a stretch of the evidence.

82. P. Simons, "Lesbian (In)Visibility in Italian Renaissance Culture: Diana and Other Cases of *donna con donna,*" in *Gay and Lesbian Studies in Art History,* ed. W. Davis (New York: Harrington Park Press, 1994), 81–122.

83. Zika, "She-Man," 292.

84. H. Decker-Hauff and R. Seigl, *Die Chronik der Grafen von Zimmern: Handschriften 580 und 581 der Fürstlich Fürstenbergischen Hofbibliothek Donaueschingen,* vol. 2 (Constance: Jan Thorbecke, 1967). This section is taken from my forthcoming essay, "Towards a Philology of the Premodern Lesbian," in *The Lesbian Premodern,* ed. Noreen Giffney, Michelle Sauer, and Diane Watt (New York: Palgrave). See that article for recent literature on this chronicle.

85. Decker-Hauff, *Die Chronik,* 212.

86. H. Lemay, "The Stars and Human Sexuality: Some Medieval Scientific Views," *Isis* 71 (1980): 127–35.

87. Decker-Hauff, *Die Chronik,* 212.

88. Cf. K. J. Dover, *Greek Homosexuality* (New York: Vintage, 1978), 172–84; B. J. Brooten, *Love Between Women: Early Christian Responses to Female Homoeroticism* (Chicago: University of Chicago Press, 1996), 29–60.

89. Plato, *The Symposium*, trans. Christopher Gill (London: Penguin, 1999), 22–23 (189d–190d).

90. R. Gilbert, *Early Modern Hermaphrodites* (New York: Palgrave, 2002).

91. J. Cadden, *Meanings of Sex Difference in the Middle Ages: Medicine, Science, and Culture* (Cambridge: Cambridge University Press, 1993), 224.

92. Decker-Hauff, *Die Chronik*, 212.

93. H. Puff, "Female Sodomy: The Trial of Katherina Hetzeldorfer (1477)," *Journal of Medieval and Early Modern Studies* 30 (2000): 41–61.

94. K. Simon-Muscheid, "Frauen in Männerrollen," in *Arbeit—Liebe—Streit: Texte zur Geschichte des Geschlechterverhältnisses und des Alltags*, ed. Dorothee Rippmann et al. (Liestal: Verlag des Kantons Basel-Landschaft, 1996), 102–21.

95. She is described as a "little girl" (*Meitlin*), potentially a rhetorical-judicial strategy by the documents' authors to release her from jail as a minor, which seemed the desired outcome.

96. Staatsarchiv Basel-Stadt, Criminalia 4 12, Elisabeth Hertner (1647). My gratitude to Susanna Burghartz for having called my attention to this document.

97. Sodomy is indeed the legal term and context brought to bear on this case.

98. Since there are no formal trial records, the council seems to have followed this course of action.

99. Stewart, *Before Brueghel*.

100. Röver-Kann, *Frauenbad*, 38; Smith, *Nuremberg*, 266.

101. H. Puff, "Sodomie und Herrschaft: Eine Problemskizze," in *Liebe und Widerstand: Ambivalenzen historischer Geschlechterbeziehungen*, ed. I. Bauer, C. Ehrmann-Hämmerle, and G. Hauch (Vienna: Böhlau, 2005), 139–57.

102. Antoninus of Florence, *Summa* (Basel: J. Amerbach, P. Froben, n.d.), P5r.

103. B. Cellini, *My Life*, trans. Julia Conaway Bondanella and Peter Bondanella (Oxford: Oxford University Press, 2002), 321. See also M. A. Gallucci, *Benvenuto Cellini: Sexuality, Masculinity, and Artistic Identity in Renaissance Italy* (New York: Palgrave, 2003).

Chapter 4

This chapter's epigraphs are taken from Ambroise Paré as cited in A. R. Jones and P. Stallybrass, "Fetishizing Gender: Constructing the Hermaphrodite in Renaissance Europe," in *Body Guards: The Cultural Politics of Gender Ambiguity*, ed. J. Epstein and K. Straub (New York: Routledge, 1991), 83; Phillip Stubbes, *The Anatomie of Abuses in Ailgna: Containing a Discoverie or Briefe Summarie of Such Notable Vices and Corruptons, as now raigne in many Christian Countreyes of the World* (London: Richard Jones, 1585), 38v; and Baldassare Castiglione, *Il Cortegiano* (Florence: Felice Le Monnier, 1854), bk. 3, chap. 4, 172.

1. Castiglione, *Il Cortegiano*, bk. 2, chap. 2, 76: "[N]iuno contrario è senza l'altro suo contrario." Castiglione cites a number of these: health is understood in

relationship to sickness, truth is recognized when correlated with falsehoods, and "pleasure can never be enjoyed if something unpleasant has not preceded it."

2. R. W. Hanning and D. Rosand, eds., *Castiglione: The Ideal and the Real in Renaissance Culture* (New Haven, CT: Yale University Press, 1983), ix.

3. The definition of gender adopted in this paper reflects that of J. Butler, *Gender Trouble: Feminism and the Subversion of Identity* (New York: Routledge, 1990), 112.

4. Aristotle, *Physics*, 188a19–30; *Metaphysics*, 1004b.29–1005a, 1075a.28, 107a29–1087b. Also see G.E.R. Lloyd, *Two Types of Argumentation in Early Greek Thought* (Cambridge: Cambridge University Press, 1971), 11–13.

5. Castiglione, *Il Cortegiano*, bk.1, chap. 47, 62.

6. Ibid., bk. 1, chap. 19, 29.

7. Ibid., bk. 1, chap. 4, 172–77.

8. William of Worcester, *Boke of Noblesse: Addressed to King Edward IV on his Invasion of France* (London: J. B. Nichols, 1860), 9.

9. Butler, *Gender Trouble,* 112, 33.

10. Ibid. Clearly Butler's vision for the future cannot be imposed on the past.

11. Stubbes, *Anatomie of Abuses*, 38v, paraphrases Deuteronomy 22:5: "What man who soever weareth womans apparel is accursed, and what woman weareth mans apparel is accursed also. Now whether they be within the limits and bandes of that curse, let them take heede.'

12. V. L. Bullough, "Transvestites in the Middle Ages," *American Journal of Sociology* 79 (1974): 1381–94; and N. Z. Davis, *Society and Culture in Early Modern France: Eight Essays* (Stanford, CA: Stanford University Press, 1975), 129.

13. J. E. Howard, "Crossdressing, the Theatre, and Gender Struggle in Early Modern England," *Shakespeare Quarterly* 39 (1988): 418.

14. *Letters of John Chamberlain* as cited in S. Orgel, *Impersonations: The Performance of Gender in Shakespeare's England* (Cambridge: Cambridge University Press, 1996), 83–84.

15. Stubbes, *Anatomie of Abuses*, 39v. Also see J. E. Howard, *The Stage and Social Struggle in Early Modern England* (London: Routledge, 1994); A. R. Jones and P. Stallybrass, *Renaissance Clothing and the Materials of Memory* (Cambridge: Cambridge University Press, (2000); and S. Vincent, *Dressing the Elite: Clothes in Early Modern England* (Oxford: Berg, 2003).

16. Harrison as cited in Howard, *Stage and Social Struggle, 95.*

17. Stubbes, *Anatomie of Abuses, 38v.*

18. Howard, *Stage and Social Struggle*, 95–96.

19. P. F. Brown, *Private Lives in Renaissance Venice* (New Haven, CT: Yale University Press, 2004), 183.

20. T. Coryat, *Coryat's Crudities,* facsimile of the 1611 edition (London: Scolar Press, 1978), 264, 266.

21. C. Vecellio, *Costumes Anciens et Modernes/Habiti antichi e moderni di tutto il mondo* (Paris: Didot Frères Fils, 1980), 121.

22. P. Aretino, *Lettere*, ed. P. Procaccioli (Rome: Salerno, 1992), 4: 234–36, n. 374.

23. Stubbes, *Anatomie of Abuses*, 38v.

24. M. Rocke, *Forbidden Friendships: Homosexuality and Male Culture in Renaissance Florence* (Oxford: Oxford University Press, 1996), 153–54, 107–9, notes that while there are documents identifying some participants as *travestito,* these individuals were not necessarily the passive partner. Indeed, the term *travestito* "likely meant not a man dressed as a woman but a man masqueraded." Also see Jonathan Goldberg, *Sodomites: Renaissance Texts, Modern Sexualities* (Stanford, CA: Stanford University Press, 1992). Androgynous dress was nonetheless problematic. The polemical *Hic Mulier: Or, The Man-Woman: Being a Medicine to cure the Coltish Disease of the Staggers in the Masculine-Feminines of our Times* and *Haec-Vir: Or The Womanish-Man: Being an Answere to a late Booke intituled Hic-Mulier* (1620) speak to the issue.

25. F. Reiffenberg, ed., *Mémoires de Jacques Du Clercq,* in *Collection des chroniques nationals francaises* (Paris: Dondey-Dupre, 1826–27), 39: 13. I am indebted to Jessica Roussanov for bringing this reference to my attention.

26. G. Della Casa, *Galateo,* trans. Konrad Eisenbichler and Kenneth R. Bartlett (Toronto: Center for Renaissance and Reformation Studies, 1986), 53–54. For a discussion of Ganymede as a sign of homosexuality, see J. M. Saslow, *Ganymede in the Renaissance: Homosexuality in Art and Society* (New Haven, CT: Yale University Press, 1986); and L. Barkan, *Transuming Passion: Ganymede and the Erotics of Humanism* (Stanford, CA: Stanford University Press, 1991).

27. Orgel, *Impersonations,* 57. Although the commedia dell'arte began to employ women in the 1560s, actresses were not admitted onto the English stage until 1660. See M. Shapiro, "The Introduction of Actresses in England: Delay or Defensiveness?," in *Enacting Gender on the English Renaissance Stage,* ed. V. Comensoli and A. Russell (Urbana: University of Illinois Press, 1999), 178.

28. Orgel, *Impersonations,* 63.

29. Ibid, 70–71.

30. V. L. Bullough and B. Bullough, *Cross Dressing, Sex, and Gender* (Philadelphia: University of Pennsylvania Press, 1993), 51–52.

31. M. Laven, *Virgins of Venice: Broken Vows and Cloistered Lives in the Renaissance Convent* (New York: Viking, 2002), 16–17.

32. K.J.P. Lowe, *Nuns' Chronicles and Convent Culture in Renaissance and Counter-Reformation Italy* (Cambridge: Cambridge University Press, 2003), 165–66.

33. L. Levine, *Men in Women's Clothing: Anti-Theatricality and Effeminization 1579–1642* (Cambridge: Cambridge University Press, 1994), 20–21.

34. Rianoldes as cited in Jones and Stallybrass, *Renaissance Clothing,* 216.

35. A. Maggi, *The Rhetoric of Satan* (Chicago: University of Chicago Press, 2000), 91.

36. Jones and Stallybrass, *Renaissance Clothing,* 216.

37. Zimmerman, S., "Disruptive Desire, Artifice and Indeterminacy in Jacobean Comedy," in *Erotic Politics: Desire on the Renaissance Stage,* ed. S. Zimmerman (New York: Routledge, 1992), 44. Also see Jones and Stallybrass, *Renaissance Clothing,* 207–19.

38. *La venexiana* as cited in V. Finucci, *The Manly Masquerade: Masculinity, Paternity, and Castration in the Italian Renaissance* (Durham, NC: Duke University Press, 2003), 203.

39. Zimmerman, "Disruptive Desire," 46, 50.

40. J. Adelman, "Making Defect Perfection: Shakespeare and the One-Sex Model," in *Enacting Gender on the English Renaissance Stage*, ed. V. Cosmensoli and A. Russell (Urbana: University of Illinois Press, 1999), 24.

41. Jones and Stallybrass, *Renaissance Clothing*, 217.

42. B. Cellini, *La vita*, in *Opere*, ed. B. Maier (Milan: Rizzoli, 1968), 114–19.

43. For a discussion of Caro's text, see P. Simons and M. Kornell, "Annibal Caro's After-Dinner Speech (1536) and the Question of Titian as Vesalius's Illustrator," *Renaissance Quarterly* 61 (2008): 1073–74.

44. Davis, *Society and Culture*, 124–51. Also see Bullough and Bullough, *Cross Dressing*, 74–77; P. Burke, *Popular Culture in Early Modern Europe* (Aldershot: Ashgate, 1994), 16–65, 184–85. S.F.M. Grieco, "Pedagogical Prints: Moralizing Broadsheets and Wayward Women in Counter Reformation Italy," in *Picturing Women in Renaissance and Baroque Italy*, ed. G. A. Johnson and S.F.M. Grieco (Cambridge: Cambridge University Press, 1997), 61–87, has illustrated how moralizing broadsheets, which reached their height of popularity between 1560 and 1620, "represented gender relations in a kind of stereotyped iconographic shorthand, where each group of figures was easily recognizable and would automatically trigger a number of associations in the viewer's mind."

45. Davis, *Society and Culture*, 131.

46. See for example, T. Pettitt, " 'Here Comes I, Jack Straw': English Folk Drama and Social Revolt," *Folklore* 95 (1984): 3–20; B. Smith, *Homosexual Desire in Shakespeare's England* (Chicago: University of Chicago Press, 1991); and Y.-M. Bercé, *Fête et révolte: Des mentalités populaires du XVIe au XVIIe siècle* (Paris: Hachette, 1976).

47. Pettitt, "Jack Straw," 13–15; and Davis, *Society and Culture*, 147–50.

48. J. Cadden, *Meanings of Sex Difference in the Middle Ages: Medicine, Science, and Culture* (Cambridge: Cambridge University Press, 1993), 183–95; and I. Maclean, *The Renaissance Notion of Woman: A Study in the Fortunes of Scholasticism and Medical Science in European Intellectual Life* (Cambridge: Cambridge University Press, 1980), 41–44.

49. Davis, *Society and Culture*, 146.

50. This is not to say that cross-dressing was restricted to the comedic. In Shakespeare's tragic *Merchant of Venice* Shylock's daughter dresses as a man to escape her father and run away with her beloved while Portia and her maid dress as men to plead the merchant's case in court.

51. Finucci, *Manly Masquerade*, 200. Finucci devotes an informative chapter to androgynous doubling, 189–223.

52. Ibid., 200. *Calandra* was known as *Calandria* in many of its later editions. For plot summary, see Finucci, *Manly Masquerade*, 192–93; and D. Radcliff-Umstead, *The Birth of Modern Comedy in Renaissance Italy* (Chicago: University of Chicago Press, 1969), 268–69. Also see P. D. Steward, "A Play on Doubles: The 'Calandria,'" *Modern Language Studies* 14 (1984): 22–32.

53. Coryat, *Crudities*, 247–48.

54. "The play was revived and reprinted more than any other in the genre—twenty-six separate editions between 1521 and 1600." See R. Andrews, *Scripts and Scenarios:*

The Performance of Comedy in Renaissance Italy (Cambridge: Cambridge University Press, 1993), 48.

55. Finucci, *Manly Masquerade*, 191.

56. V. Finucci, *The Lady Vanishes: Subjectivity and Representation in Castiglione and Ariosto* (Stanford, CA: Stanford University Press, 1992), 201–2; and Finucci, *Manly Masquerade*, 204.

57. M. Equicola, *Libro di natura d'amore: Di nuovo ricorretto, e con soma diligenza riformato* (Venice: G. B. Bonfadino, 1583), 124.

58. W. Schleiner, "Cross-Dressing, Gender Errors, and Sexual Taboos in Renaissance Literature," in *Gender Reversals and Gender Cultures: Anthropological and Historical Perspectives*, ed. S. P. Ramet (London: Routledge, 1996), 99.

59. Aretino, *Lettere*, 235. Similarly, Bibbiena has Lidio's befuddled lover ask the magician whether her lover is a hermaphrodite.

60. Stubbes, *Anatomie of Abuses*, 38v.

61. A difference in terms, androgyne versus hermaphrodite, is discussed by M. Rothstein, "Mutations of the Androgyne: Its Function in Early Modern French Literature," *Sixteenth Century Journal* 34 (2003): 409–37.

62. See 1 Corinthians 13:12 (authorized King James version). S. R. Jayne, *Marsilio Ficino's Commentary on Plato's Symposium* (Columbia: University of Missouri Press, 1944), 155.

63. K. P. Long, *Hermaphrodites in Renaissance Europe* (Aldershot: Ashgate, 2006), 8–9.

64. Jones and Stallybrass, "Fetishizing Gender," 80.

65. Ibid, 80, 105–6.

66. Long, *Hermaphrodites*, 44.

67. See note 25.

68. Long, *Hermaphrodites*, 80–108, provides an in-depth and thoroughly footnoted analysis of the case. Also see L. Daston and K. Park, "The Hermaphrodite and the Orders of Nature: Sexual Ambiguity in Early Modern France," *Gay and Lesbian Quarterly* 1 (1995): 419–38.

69. According to Paré, Marie came to a ditch while running through a field. When she landed after having jumped over it, male genitals hidden within her—now his—body descended. Michel de Montaigne repeated the story in his travel journal dated September 1580. See P. Parker, "Gender Ideology, Gender Change: The Case of Marie Germain," *Critical Inquiry* 19 (1993): 337–64.

70. The painting is now in the Palacio Lerma, Toledo. For the ambassador's text, see A. E. Pérez Sánchez and N. Spinosa, *Ribera 1591–1652* (Madrid: Museo del Prado, 1992), cat. no. 32. Had the ambassador chosen the term *tavola*, which is feminine, rather than *ritratto*, which is masculine, the subject being described as a "*cosa maravigliosa*" would have been explicitly ambiguous.

71. In addition to the previously cited sources, see L. Daston and K. Park, "Hermaphrodites in Renaissance France," *Critical Matrix* 1 (1985): 1–19; and R. Gilbert, *Early Modern Hermaphrodites* (New York: Palgrave, 2002).

72. For a discussion of the use of the hermaphroditic figure to critique the French court in general and Henri III specifically, see Long, *Hermaphrodites*, 189–213.

For a postulation of an ideal anarchical state inhabited by hermaphrodites, see
J. M. Patrick, "A Consideration of La Terre Australe Connue by Gabriele de Figny,"
PMLA 61 (1964): 739–51; for the hermaphrodite as an aesthetic, see F. H. Jacobs,
"Aretino and Michelangelo, Dolce and Titian, *Femmina, Masculo, Grazia,*" Art
Bulletin 82 (2000): 51–67.

73. "An extract of a letter [December 4, 1686] written by Mr. Veay, Physician at Toulouse to Mr. de St. Ussans, concerning a very extraordinary Hermaphrodite in the
city," communicated by Dr. Aglionby. Reg. Soc. S., *Philosophical Transactions of
the Royal Society of London (1686)* (London: C. and R. Baldwin, 1809), vol. 16,
356–57.

74. Parker, "Gender Ideology," 337–39.

75. J. Butler, "Performative Acts and Gender Constitution: An Essay in Phenomenology and Feminist Theory," *Theater Journal* 40 (1988): 520.

76. Ibid., 526.

Chapter 5

1. The word appears frequently in all editions of this text: see J. Cook, *A Voyage to
the Pacific Ocean undertaken by Command of His Majesty for making Discoveries
in the Northern Hemisphere* (R. Morison and Son, 1785), 1: 319; Cook, *A Voyage
to the Pacific Ocean, undertaken, by the Command of His Majesty, for making
Discoveries in the Northern Hemisphere* (G. Nicol and T. Cadell, 1784), 3: 164.

2. See, for example, F. B. Jevons, *An Introduction to the History of Religion* (Methuen, 1902), chaps. 6–8.

3. Freud first published this work as four separate essays in *Imago* 1 (1912) and 2
(1913). The first English translation was published in 1918.

4. S. Freud, *Totem and Taboo: Some Points of Agreement between the Mental Lives
of Savages and Neurotics* (Routledge and Kegan Paul, 1950), 4–7, 10–11, 23–24,
82–83.

5. Ibid., 36.

6. Ibid., 6, 144; cf. also 61–63.

7. Ibid., 19, 37–38, 42, 78, 142–44.

8. Ibid., 23–24, 37, 41–42, 145.

9. C. Lévi-Strauss, *The Elementary Structures of Kinship* (Eyre and Spottiswoode,
1969), 8–9. The book was first published in French in 1949.

10. Ibid., 493.

11. Ibid., 51, 61–62, 129–30, 454, 478–80. For his views on Freud, see 490–92.

12. Ibid., xxviii–xxix, 291, 480–81, 490, 493.

13. See, for example, E. Durkheim, "La prohibition de l'inceste et ses origines,"
L'Année sociologique 1 (1897): 1–70; B. Malinowski, *The Sexual Life of Savages
in North-Western Melanesia: An Ethnographic Account of Courtship, Marriage
and Family Life among the Natives of the Trobriand Islands, British New Guinea*
(G. Routledge and Sons, 1929), especially chaps. 13–14; T. Parsons, "The Incest
Taboo in Relation to Social Structure and the Socialisation of the Child," *British
Journal of Sociology* 5 (1954): 101–17.

14. J. Butler, *Gender Trouble: Feminism and the Subversion of Identity* (New York: Routledge, 1990), 63–64, 76–67.

15. M. Douglas, *Purity and Danger: An Analysis of Concepts of Pollution and Taboo* (Routledge, 2002), xi.

16. Ibid., xi–xii, xx, 5, 66–67, 163.

17. Ibid., xii–xiii, 3–4, 164–66.

18. M. Quilligan, *Incest and Agency in Elizabethan England* (University of Pennsylvania Press, 2005), 9.

19. M. Foucault, *Politics, Philosophy, Culture: Interviews and Other Writings 1977–1984* (Routledge, 1988), 262–63, 302; and his earlier *History of Sexuality*, vol. 1, *The Will to Knowledge* (London: Penguin, 1978), 109–10. Cf. also J. Goody, "A Comparative Approach to Incest and Adultery," *British Journal of Sociology* 7 (1956): 286–305.

20. Douglas, *Purity and Danger*, xi–xii; cf. xiii: "Taboo is a spontaneous coding practice which sets up a vocabulary of spatial limits and physical and verbal signals to hedge around vulnerable relations."

21. Ibid., xiii; cf. also xvii–xviii, 4–5, 149–51, 161–62.

22. J. Gower, *Confessio amantis*, 8.59–147. The whole of book 8 is devoted to the sin of incest.

23. Leviticus 18.24–25 (King James authorized version). Genesis 19.1–25—the destruction of Sodom and Gomorrah—and Romans 1.26–27 were also used as the basis for the condemnation of same-sex activities. For Roman law, see O. F. Robinson, *Criminal Law of Ancient Rome* (Duckworth, 1995), chap. 5.

24. Jerome, *Against Jovinian* 1.14–16; cf. Paul's statement in 1 Corinthians 7.39. Hostility to second marriages survived in the Russian Orthodox Church: D. H. Kaiser, "'Whose Wife Will She Be at the Resurrection?' Marriage and Remarriage in Early Modern Russia," *Slavic Review* 62 (2003): 304–14.

25. N. P. Tanner (ed.), *Decrees of the Ecumenical Councils* (Sheed and Ward, 1990), 1: 256–59; cf. also the earlier decrees of the First and Second Lateran Councils of 1123 and 1199, 190–91 and 200–201.

26. T. Gainsford, *The rich cabinet furnished with varietie of excellent discriptions* (R. Iackson, 1616), 82v–3r.

27. Cf., for example, J. A. Brundage, *Law, Sex and Christian Society in Medieval Europe* (Chicago: University of Chicago Press, 1987), 91–92, 155–56, 451–52.

28. Genesis 2.24; Leviticus 18.8, 14–16.

29. Exodus 20.14; cf. Deuteronomy 5.18 and Leviticus 18.20.

30. A. Friedberg (ed.), *Corpus juris canonici* (Tauchnitz, 1879), vol. 1, col. 100. Cf. Thomas More's condemnation in 1529 of Martin Luther's marriage to the former nun Katharina von Bora as "open incestuous lechery without care or shame": T. Lawler, G. Marc'hadour, and R. C. Marius (eds.), *A Dialogue Concerning Heresies* (New Haven, CT: Yale University Press, 1981), 375.

31. Quoted by J. Boswell, *Christianity, Social Tolerance, and Homosexuality: Gay People in Western Europe from the Beginning of the Christian Era to the Fourteenth Century* (Chicago: University of Chicago Press, 1980), 331. Cf. also the reference of Alain of Lille in the twelfth century to nature as "the vicar of God, the

author': N. M. Häring, "Alain of Lille, 'De planctu naturae,'" *Studi Medievali* 19 (1978): 825.

32. Thomas Aquinas, *Summa Theologiae*, ed. T. Gilby (Blackfriars in conjunction with Eyre and Spottiswoode, 1966), 28: 104–5.

33. J. G. de Sepúlveda, *Opera* (Ex typographia regia de la gazeta, 1780), 4: 234–35. Cf. the very similar view of the Protestant Philipp Melanchthon in his *Enerratio Symboli Niceni* of 1550: P. Melanchthon, *Opera quae supersunt omnia*, ed. H. E. Bindseil (C.A. Schwetschke, 1855), vol. 23, col. 295: "Such laws are truly natural, and bind all peoples in all times."

34. J. Bishop, *Beautiful blossomes* (H. Cockyn, 1577), 51r. Bishop's Aristotelian source was *Historia animalium* 9.47. Cf. also T. Beard, *The theatre of God's iudgements* (Adam Islip, 1597), 359, using an example of incest.

35. G. F. Pico della Mirandola, "Oration on the Dignity of Man," in *The Renaissance Philosophy of Man: Selections in Translation,* ed. E. Cassirer, P. O. Kristeller, and J. H. Randall (Chicago: University of Chicago Press, 1948), 226. Cf. also G. Boccaccio, *Famous Women*, ed. V. Brown (Cambridge, MA: Harvard University Press, 2001), 22–23, on a case of incest between a mother and her son—"something more beastly than human."

36. B. Batt, *The Christian mans closet*, tr. W. Lowth (Thomas Dawson, and Gregorie Seton, 1581), 95v.

37. A. Brown (ed.), *Bartolomeo Scala: Humanistic and Political Writings* (Medieval and Renaissance Texts and Studies, 1997), 269.

38. Genesis 1.28.

39. Aquinas, *Summa Theologiae*, 13: 36–37.

40. See, for example, Peter of Spain (later Pope John XXI), "Questions on the Viaticum," in M. F. Wack, *Lovesickness in the Middle Ages: The Viaticum and its Commentaries* (University of Pennsylvania Press, 1990), 246–47.

41. Martin Luther, "Against the Spiritual Estate of the Pope and the Bishops falsely so called," in *Luther's Works,* ed. H. T. Lehmann (Fortress Press, 1970), 39: 297.

42. P. Bracciolini, "An seni sit uxor ducenda dialogus," written in 1437, the year after his marriage, in R. Fubini (ed.), *Poggius Bracciolini: Opera omnia* (Bottega d'Erasmo, 1966), 2: 692. Luther again took a very similar line in the sixteenth century: see his "The Estate of Marriage," *Luther's Works*, 45: 18–19, 45.

43. D. Erasmus, "The Institution of Christian Matrimony," in *Collected Works of Erasmus: Spiritualia,* ed J. W. O'Malley and L. A. Perraud (Toronto: University of Toronto Press, 1993), 69: 387.

44. Francis de Sales, "Introduction a la vie dévote," in *Œuvres*, ed. A. Ravier and R. Devos (Gallimard, 1969), 241. The book was first published in 1609. De Sales subsequently mentions sterility and an existing pregnancy as reasons why there might legitimately be no expectation that sex would lead to conception (242).

45. See, for example, A. Gomez, *Opus præclarum … super legibus Tauri* (Andreas à Portonarijs, 1575), 309r–11r; B. de Medina, *Breve instruction de como se ha de administrar el sacramento de la penitencia* (Herederos de Mathias Gast, 1579), 119v–20r; E. Coke, *The third part of the Institutes of the laws of England* (W. Lee and D. Pakeman, 1644), 58; and cf. Aquinas, *Summa Theologiae*, vol. 43, 244–45.

46. S. Pufendorf, *De jure naturae et gentium* (Sumtibus Adami Junghans, 1672), 752.

47. *A most straunge, and true discourse, of the wonderful judgement of God: Of a monstrous, deformed infant, begotten by incestuous copulation, betweene the brothers sonne and the sisters daughter, being both vnmarried persons* (Richard Iones, 1600), 1–4; cf. P. Boaistuau, *Histoires prodigeuses les plus mémorables* (Iean Longis & Robert Le Mangnier, 1560), 12v: "These monstrous creatures are the result most often of the judgement, justice, punishment and curse of God, who permits fathers and mothers to produce such abominations in horror at their sin." Boaistuau was also known as Pierre Launay.

48. G. Fernández de Oviedo y Valdés, *Historia general y natural de las Indias, islas y tierrafirme del mar océano* (Real academia de la historia, 1851–1855), 1: 124; cf. J. de Damhouder, *Praxis rerum criminalium* (Ioannem Bellerum, 1562), 284.

49. Pius V, "Cum primum," dated April 1, 1566, in *Bullarum privilegiorum ac diplomatum Romanorum Pontificum amplissima collection,* ed. C. Cocquelines (Sumptibus Hieronymi Mainardi, 1745), vol. 4, part 2, 284–85.

50. Afonso V, *Ordenaçoens do Senhor Rey D. Affonso V* (Real Imprensa da Universidade, 1792), 5: 53–54; similar legislation was issued by Dom Afonso's successors in 1521 and 1606.

51. Cf., for example, the *pragmática* of Ferdinand and Isabella of Spain dated July 22, 1497, *Recopilacion de las leyes destos reynos, hecha por mandado ... del rey ... Philippe Segundo* (Iuan Iniguez de Lequerica, 1592), 2: 197v–8r. This drew on earlier legislation from the thirteenth century: R. I. Burns (ed.), *Las siete partidas* (University of Pennsylvania Press, 2001), 5: 1427.

52. "An Act for suppressing the detestable sins of Incest, Adultery and Fornication," in *Acts and Ordinances of the Interregnum, 1642–1660,* ed. C. H. Firth and R. S. Rait (His Majesty's Stationery Office, 1911), 2: 387–89.

53. *Ordonnantie van de polityen binnen Hollandt* (Aelbert Heyndricsz, 1586), 11–12.

54. *Recopilacion de las leyes,* 2 : 196v–7r. This reversed the thirteenth-century law that had prohibited wife-murder: Burns, *Las siete partidas,* 5: 1417.

55. For a clear statement of this belief, see J. Escobar del Corro, *Tractatus bipartitus de puritate et nobilitate probanda* (Sumptibus Laurentij Durand, 1637), 8, 10–12.

56. For the earliest statute, issued in 1449 by the municipal authorities of Toledo, see E. Benito Ruano, *Los orígenes del problema converso* (Real Academia de la Historia, 2001), 83–92.

57. See, for example, the questions used by the Inquisitors in Mexico when considering candidates for employment in the seventeenth century: E. Frutta, "Limpieza de sangre y nobleza en el México colonial: la formación de un saber nobiliario (1571–1700)," *Jahrbuch für Geschichte Lateinamerikas* 39 (2002): 221–22. In the Low Countries, Joos de Damhouder categorized sex with a Muslim or a Jew as sodomy and a crime against nature: *Praxis,* 285.

58. A. Domínguez Ortiz, *Las clases privilegiadas en la España del antiguo régimen* (Istmo, 1973), 46–47.

59. Quoted by J. P. Zuñiga, "La voix du sang: Du métis á l'idée de métisage en Amérique espagnole," *Annales: Histoire, Sciences Sociales* 54 (1999): 432.

60. Zuñiga, "La voix du sang," 443–44; cf. S. B. Schwartz, "Brazilian Ethnogenesis: *Mestiços, mamelucos,* and *pardos*," in *Le Nouveau Monde, Mondes nouveaux: L'expérience américaine,* ed. S. Gruzinski and N. Wachtel (Éditions de l'École des hautes études en sciences sociales, 1996), 14–16, 21–22. Edmund Spenser was equally concerned at marriage between the English and the Irish: "A View of the Present State of Ireland," in *The Works of Edmund Spenser,* ed. E. Greenlaw, C. G. Osgood, F. M. Padelford, and R. Heffner (Johns Hopkins University Press, 1932–1957), lines 2125–30.

61. B. Krekić, "'Abominandum crimen': Punishment of Homosexuals in Renaissance Dubrovnik," *Viator: Medieval and Renaissance Studies* 18 (1987): 339–42.

62. T. Sánchez, *Disputationum de sancto matrimonii sacramento* (Apud Martinum Nutium, 1607), 2 : 672–73.

63. N. Venette, *De la generation de l'homme, ou tableau de l'amour conjugale* (Claude Joly, 1716), 236–39. This was the eighth edition; the text was first published in 1696.

64. For the text of Julius II's bull, see G. Burnet, *The History of the Reformation of the Church of England,* ed. N. Pocock (Clarendon Press, 1865), 4: 15–16.

65. *Luther's Works,* 36: 99.

66. *Luther's Works,* 45: 7. On Scriptural grounds, Luther continued to believe, however, that it was legitimate for a man to marry his niece or a woman her nephew.

67. See, for example, Andreas Osiander's *Von den verbotenen Heiraten* of 1537, in his *Gesamtausgabe,* ed. G. Müller and G. Seebaß (Gütersloher Verlagshaus Mohn, 1985), 6: 411–33.

68. See, for example, Melanchthon, *Opera,* vol. 16, cols. 518–20, or vol. 23, col. 295.

69. The *Table* has since 1681 been printed at the end of the Anglican *Book of Common Prayer.* It is based on the list drawn up by Archbishop Matthew Parker in 1560 and published in 1571: *An admonition. To all suche as shall intende hereafter to enter the state of matrimony godly, and agreably to lawes* (R. Wolfe, 1571).

70. *Decreti penali fatti in diversi tempi, dall'illlustrissimo et eccelentissimo Consiglio dell'illustrissima, et eccelentissima Repubblica di Lucca* (Baldassar del Giudice, 1640), 123.

71. L. Mott, "Meu menino lindo: Cartas de amor de um frade sodomita, Lisboa (1690)," *Luso-Brazilian Review* 38 (2001): 98–100, 108. According to Sir Edward Coke, *emissio seminis* was not necessary in England for a successful prosecution of buggery: "there must be *penetratio,* that is, *res in re* ... the least penetration maketh it carnal knowledge": Coke, *The third part,* 59. Damhouder had made use of the same argument in the sixteenth century: *Praxis,* 283.

72. H. Puff, *Sodomy in Reformation Germany and Switzerland, 1400–1600* (Chicago: University of Chicago Press, 2003), 29, 69, 91; M. Rocke, *Forbidden Friendships: Homosexuality and Male Culture in Renaissance Florence* (Oxford: Oxford University Press, 1998), 100–105.

73. Romans, 1.26–7.

74. G. Radbruch (ed.), *Die Peinliche Gerichtsordnung Kaiser Karls V. von 1532 (Carolina)* (Reclam, 1962), 78.

75. Henry VIII's *Acte for the punyshment of the Vice of Buggery*, in *The Statutes of the Realm*, vol. 3 (The Record Commission, 1817), 441. Sir Edward Coke seems to have believed that the only way a woman could commit buggery or sodomy was "with a beast": Coke, *The third part*, 59.

76. For Zurich, see Puff, *Sodomy*, 25; for Bruges, M. Boone, "State Power and Illicit Sexuality: The Persecution of Sodomy in Late Medieval Bruges," *Journal of Medieval History* 22 (1996): 143, 145: the figure of 21 percent is for the shorter period of 1490–1515.

77. N. Davidson, "Theology, Nature and the Law: Sexual Sin and Sexual Crime in Italy from the Fourteenth to the Seventeenth Century," in *Crime, Society and the Law in Renaissance Italy*, ed. T. Dean and K.J.P. Lowe (Cambridge: Cambridge University Press, 1993), 89–90, 94–96; Davidson, "Sodomy in Early-Modern Venice," in *Sodomy and Deviant Sex in Early Modern Europe*, ed. T. Betteridge (Manchester University Press, 2002), 75; M. Hewlett, "The French Connection: Syphilis and Sodomy in Late-Renaissance Lucca," in *Sins of the Flesh: Responding to Sexual Disease in Early Modern Europe*, ed. K. Siena (Toronto, Centre for Reformation and Renaissance Studies, 2005), 243–44.

78. Mott, "Meu menino lindo," 99.

79. Similarly, the rape of an unmarried woman was frequently treated as a crime against her father and next of kin. See L. Roper, *The Holy Household: Women and Morals in Reformation Augsburg* (Clarendon Press, 1989), 83–86; M. Chaytor, "Husband(ry): Narratives of Rape in the Seventeenth Century," *Gender and History* 7 (1995): 395–97.

80. M. van der Heijden, "Women as Victims of Sexual and Domestic Violence in Seventeenth-Century Holland: Criminal Cases of Rape, Incest, and Maltreatment in Rotterdam and Delft," *Journal of Social History* 33 (2000): 626, 628–32, 635.

81. I. Papon, *Recueil d'arrests notables des cours souveraines de France* (Nicolas Buon, 1601), 513v.

82. H. Grotius, *De iure praedae commentarius: Commentary on the Law of Prize and Booty*, ed. M. J. van Ittersum (Liberty Fund, 2006), 56–57.

83. H. Grotius, *The Rights of War and Peace*, ed. R. Tuck (Liberty Fund, 2005), 1: 155.

84. Grotius, *Rights of War*, 1: 93.

85. Ibid., 2: 526–27. Grotius exempted the marriage of a parent with his or her own child: 528–31.

86. Ibid., 2: 531.

87. Pufendorf, *De jure naturae*, 805, 808, 812–13; C. Thomasius, *Institutionum jurisprudentiæ divinæ* (Sumptibus et Typis Viduae Christophori Salfeldii, 1717), 478–83: the first edition of this work was published in 1688.

88. C. Thomasius, *Dissertationem juridicam de crimine bigamiæ* (Georgius Beyer, 1685), caps. 4–5.

89. J. J. Boissard, *Emblematum liber* (Theodorus de Bry, 1593), 19.

90. L. Lemnius, *De occultis naturae miraculis* (Apud Ioannem Birckmanum, 1573), 37–39. Cf. also Fortunio Liceti's *De monstrorum causis, natura, et differentiis* (Apud Paulum Frambottum, 1616).

91. P. de Abano, *Expositio problematum Aristotelis* (Paulus de Butzbach, 1475), part 4, prob. 26. There is a useful translation of this passage in K. Borris (ed.), *Same-Sex Desire in the English Renaissance: A Sourcebook of Sixteenth and Seventeenth-Century Texts* (Routledge, 2003), 134–40.

92. A. Vignali, *La cazzaria: The Book of the Prick*, ed. I. F. Moulton (Routledge, 2003), 99–100; Vignali's text was written in the 1520s. Cf. also Davidson, "Sodomy," 73–74.

93. L. Coci, *Antonio Rocco: L'Alcibiade fanciullo a scola* (Salerno, 1988), 51. This text was written in Venice about 1631, and published there, anonymously and probably without Rocco's knowledge, in or just before 1651. See also Davidson, "Sodomy," 71–73.

94. I. de Benserade, *Iphis et Iante: comédie*, ed. A. Verdier (Lampsaque, 2000), 91–92.

95. Ibid., 68. The text of this play was first published in 1637. Ovid's version of the fable can be found in his *Metamorphoses*, book 9. For an analogous use of the notion of nature as applied to individual desires, see the trial of pastor Johannes Blass in Zurich in 1695 reported by H. Puff, "Nature on Trial: Acts 'Against Nature' in the Law Courts of Early Modern Germany and Switzerland," in *The Moral Authority of Nature*, ed. L. Daston and F. Vidal (Chicago: University of Chicago Press, 2004), 242–43.

96. J. Major, *In quartum Sententiarum quæstiones vtilissimæ* (In officina Iodoci Badii, 1519), 278r. This commentary on Peter Lombard's *Sentences* was first published a decade earlier, when Major was teaching in Paris. Cf. also M. de Magistris, *Questiones morales … de fortitudine* (Johan Petit, 1511), 95r–6v.

97. *Luther's Works*, 54: 315; M. Luther, *Werke: Kritische Gesammtausgabe. Tischreden* (Weimar: Böhlau, 1912–1921), 5: 607.

98. E. François, *Protestants et catholiques en Allemagne: Identités et pluralisme, Augsbourg, 1648–1806* (A. Michel, 1993), 128, 204–7.

99. I. V. Hull, *Sexuality, State and Civil Society in Germany, 1700–1815* (Ithaca, NY: Cornell University Press, 1996), 43.

100. *Recopilacion de leyes de los Reynos de las Indias* (Consejo de las Indias, 1681), 1: 33v.

101. Zuñiga, "La voix du sang," 444. The Jesuit church in Cusco, Peru, contains group portraits that celebrate these two marriages. For criticism of the *limpieza de sangre* laws, see A. de Córdoba, *Quæstionarium theologicum, siue, Sylua amplissima decisionum, et variarum resolutionum casuum conscientiae* (Sumptibus Baretij Baretij, 1604), 432–47.

102. See canon 50 of the Fourth Lateran Council, cited in note 25.

103. A. Collomp, *La maison du père: Famille et village en Haute-Provence aux XVIIe et XVIIIe siècles* (Presses universitaires de France, 1983), 113–24.

104. Puff, *Sodomy*, 84–87; Davidson, "Sodomy," 74–77; Hewlett, "French Connection," 251–52. Mexican confessors' manuals show surprisingly little interest in either same-sex activities or heterosexual sodomy: see, for example, J. Bautista, *Confessionario en lengua mexicana y castellana* (Melchior Ocharte, 1599), 48v–51r.

105. M. H. Sánchez Ortega, *La mujer y la sexualidad en el antiguo régimen: La perspectiva inquisitorial* (Akal, 1992), 202.

106. M. de Montaigne, *The Complete Essays*, trans. and ed. M. A. Screech (Penguin, 2004), 126–30. Montaigne's sources for these statements included Herodotus and other ancient authors, as well as Francisco López de Gómara's *Historia general delas Indias*, first published in 1552–1553; he probably used the French translation by Martin Fumée, *Histoire generalle des Indes occidentales et terres neuues*, published in 1568.

107. *The Diary of Montaigne's Journey to Italy in 1580 and 1581*, trans. and ed. E. J. Treichmann (Harcourt, Brace, 1929), 151. The Venetian ambassador in Rome had reported this event in a letter of August 1578: quoted by Borris, *Same-Sex Desire*, 90. A number of the men involved were subsequently executed.

Chapter 6

1. Arnold Davidson, "Sex and the Emergence of Sexuality," *Critical Inquiry* 14 (1987): 22.

2. The point is made by Thomas Laqueur, *Making Sex: Body and Gender from the Greeks to Freud* (Cambridge, MA: Harvard University Press, 1990). In *Making Sex*, Laqueur argued that premodern sexuality (pre-1700) was based on a set of relative differences between male and female (such as differences in heat) and that, in contrast, modern sexuality (post-1700) bases sexual difference in the biology of two sexes, specifically on the notion that male and female bodies are incommensurate to each other. Male and female bodies represent not degrees of difference but differences of kind. For the Renaissance and based largely on Aristotelian theories of conception and Galenic descriptions of anatomy, Laqueur emphasizes isomorphism: the one sex is male, and the female is a lesser, derivative version of it. The one-sex model was also studied by Londa Schiebinger, "Skeletons in the Closet: The First Illustrations of the Female Skeleton in Eighteenth-Century Anatomy," in *The Making of the Modern Body: Sexuality and Society in the Nineteenth Century*, ed. C. Gallagher and T. Laqueur (California: University of California Press, 1987), 42–82. For alternative assessments of premodern sexuality and implicit and explicit critiques of Laqueur's work, see the studies by the following authors: Ian Maclean, *The Renaissance Notion of Woman: A Study in the Fortunes of Scholasticism and Medical Science in European Intellectual Life* (Cambridge: Cambridge University Press, 1980); Joan Cadden, *Meanings of Sex Difference in the Middle Ages: Medicine, Science, and Culture* (Cambridge: Cambridge University Press, 1993); Katharine Park and Robert A. Nye, "Destiny Is Anatomy," *The New Republic* (February 18, 1991), 53–57; Patricia Parker, "Gender Ideology, Gender Change: The Case of Marie Germain," *Critical Inquiry* 19 (1993): 337–64; Gianna Pomata, "Menstruating Men: Similarity and Difference of the Sexes in Early Modern Medicine," in *Generation and Degeneration: Tropes of Reproduction in Literature and History from Antiquity through Early Modern Europe*, ed. V. Finucci and K. Brownlee, 109–52 (Durham, NC: Duke University Press, 2001); and Valerie Traub, "The Psychomorphology of the Clitoris, or, the Reemergence of the *Tribade* in English Culture," in Finucci

and Brownlee, *Generation and Degeneration* (both reprints of earlier publications: Pomata, "Uomini mestruanti. Somiglianza e differenza fra i sessi in Europa in età moderna," *Quaderni storici* 79 (1992): 51–103; and Traub, "The Psychomorphology of the Clitoris," in *GLQ: A Journal of Lesbian and Gay Studies* 2, no. 2 [April 1995]: 81–113); Michael Stolberg, "A Woman Down to the Bones: The Anatomy of Sexual Difference in the Sixteenth and Early Seventeenth Centuries," *Isis* 94 (2003): 274–99; and Helen King, "The Mathematics of Sex: One to Two, or Two to One?" In *Studies in Medieval and Renaissance History: Sexuality and Culture in Medieval and Renaissance Europe*, ser. 3, vol. 2, ed. P. Soergel, 47–58 (New York: AMS Press, 2005).

3. Michel Foucault's work is the basis for the methodological and topical emphasis: *The Birth of the Clinic*; and to a lesser extent, *Discipline and Punish*.

4. For example, Charles Singer, *A Short History of Medicine* (New York: Oxford University Press, 1928).

5. As Katharine Park ("Was There a Renaissance Body?" in *The Italian Renaissance in the Twentieth Century*, ed. A. Grieco, M. Rocke, and F. G. Superbi [Florence: Olschki, 1999], 325), has explained, "Recent historians of the body, imbued (despite themselves) with modern ideas of the body as in the first instance a medical and scientific object, have, if anything, tended to pay too much attention to the history of science and medicine, ascribing to medieval and early modern scientific and medical discourse a cultural authority and a foundational status that dates only from the middle of the nineteenth century." On medical humanism, see the following: A. Wear, R. K. French, and I. M. Lonie, eds., *The Medical Renaissance* (Cambridge: Cambridge University Press, 1985); Jerome Bylebyl, "Medicine, Philosophy, and Humanism in Renaissance Italy," in *Science and the Arts in the Renaissance*, ed. J. Shirley and F. D. Hoeniger, 27–49 (Washington, DC: Folger Library, 1985); Andrew Cunningham, *The Anatomical Renaissance* (Brookfield, VT: Scolar Press, 1997); and Andrea Carlino, *Books of the Body: Anatomical Ritual and Renaissance Learning* (Chicago: University of Chicago Press, 1999).

6. On health and healing, see David Gentilcore, *Healers and Healing* (1998) and G. Pomata, *Contracting a Cure: Patients, Healers, and the Law in Early Modern Bologna* (Baltimore: Johns Hopkins University Press, 1998), originally published as *La promessa di guarigione: Malati e curatori in antico regime* (Gius. Laterza & Figli, 1994). On kinship and religion, see K. Park, *Secrets of Women: Gender, Generation, and the Origins of Human Dissection* (New York: Zone Books, 2006); and Mary Fissell, *Vernacular Bodies: The Politics of Reproduction in Early Modern England* (Oxford: Oxford University Press, 2004).

7. For an extensive analysis of the transmission of ancient ideas and medieval adaptations, see Joan Cadden, *Meanings of Sex Difference*, 11–53. For an analysis of the rhetoric of learned anatomical texts, see Eve Keller, *Generating Bodies and Gendered Selves: The Rhetoric of Reproduction in Early Modern England* (Seattle: University of Washington Press, 2007).

8. On the Hippocratic tradition, see Cadden, *Meanings of Sex Difference*, 15–21; D. Cantor, ed., *Reinventing Hippocrates* (Brookfield, VT: Ashgate, 2002); and Wesley D. Smith, *The Hippocratic Tradition* (Ithaca, NY: Cornell University Press,

1979). For questions related to the female body, in addition to Cadden, see King, *Hippocrates' Women: Reading the Female Body in Ancient Greece* (London: Routledge, 1998).

9. On the medical marketplace, see K. Park, *Doctors and Medicine in Early Renaissance Florence* (Princeton, NJ: Princeton University Press, 1985); and D. Gentilcore, *Medical Charlatanism in Early Modern Italy* (Oxford: Oxford University Press, 2007). On vernacular anatomies, see A. Carlino, *Paper Bodies: A Catalogue of Anatomical Fugitive Sheets, 1538–1687* (London: Wellcome Institute for the History of Medicine, 1999); and Bette Talvacchia, *Taking Positions: On the Erotic in Renaissance Culture* (Princeton, NJ: Princeton University Press, 1999).

10. Margaret Pelling, "Trade or Profession? Medical Practice in Early Modern England," in *The Common Lot: Sickness, Medical Occupations and the Urban Poor in Early Modern England,* 230–58 (London: Longman, 1998).

11. The description comes from Lazarus Riverius. See note 71.

12. Several studies have cautioned against the assimilation of sex and sexuality. In addition to Davidson, see Caroline Walker Bynum, "The Body of Christ in the Later Middle Ages: A Reply to Leo Steinberg," *Renaissance Quarterly* 39 (1986): 399–410.

13. Park, "Renaissance Body," 330, suggests that the oversight is a result of the choice to pursue Foucault's ideas about the clinical gaze rather than his ideas about discipline. The importance of the anatomical body in the history of sexuality parallels its importance in the history of science, which is curious and deserving of more inquiry. On the parallel, see Richard Sugg, *Murder After Death: Literature and Anatomy in Early Modern England* (Ithaca, NY: Cornell University Press, 2007), esp. "Vivisection, Violence, and Identity."

14. I develop this idea in "Civility, Comportment, and the Anatomy Theater: Girolamo Fabrici and His Medical Students in Renaissance Padua," *Renaissance Quarterly* 60 (2007): 434–63.

15. In addition to the work of Bynum, see Park, *Secrets of Women,* chaps. 1–2; Fissell, *Vernacular Bodies,* chaps. 1–2; and Nancy Caciola, *Discerning Spirits: Divine and Demonic Possession in the Middle Ages* (Ithaca, NY: Cornell University Press, 2003), chap. 4.

16. On domesticity and various forms of affective attachment, see Roger Chartier, ed., *A History of Private Life: Passions of the Renaissance* (Cambridge, MA: Belknap Press, 1989), 3: 447–91.

17. As contemporary studies of intersex variations and sexual polymorphism have shown, the anatomy of sex difference has many possible outcomes. See the work of Steven Epstein, *Inclusion: The Politics of Difference in Medical Research* (Chicago: University of Chicago Press, 2007); and Mary Bloodsworth-Lugo, *In-Between Bodies: Sexual Difference, Race, and Sexuality* (Albany: State University of New York, 2007).

18. Lorraine Daston, "Marvelous Facts and Miraculous Evidence in Early Modern Europe," *Critical Inquiry* 18 (1991): 93–124; elaborated in L. Daston and K. Park, *Wonders and the Order of Nature, 1150–1750* (New York: Zone Books, 1998), chap. 6.

19. W. Fisher, "The Renaissance Beard: Masculinity in Early Modern England," *Renaissance Quarterly* 54 (2001): 155–87.

20. Fisher, "Renaissance Beard," 170–71, is careful to explain that with the portrait of Magdelena Ventura, writers emphasized her breast, her breast-feeding, and her role as wife and mother; much cultural work, that is, was done to reinscribe this bearded woman within gender-social norms.

21. Pomata, "Menstruating Men."

22. Aristotle *Generation of Animals* 1.2. See also 2.1–3.

23. Ibid., 1.12.

24. Ibid., 1.17 for the male, and 1.3 for the female.

25. See note 22.

26. Prospero Borgarucci, *Della contemplatione anatomica* (Venice: Vincenzo Valgrisi, 1564), 152.

27. For the Italian, Giovanni Boccaccio, *Decameron*, ed. Vittore Branca (Turin: Einaudi, 1992), 2: 1047–53; and in English, Boccaccio, *The Decameron*, trans. M. Musa and P. Bondanella (New York: Penguin, 1982), 662–67.

28. For example, convinced that he's sick, Calandrino sends for the doctor while complaining, "I feel I don't know what's inside me." The line foreshadows the diagnosis of pregnancy, but it also illustrates the way people understood disease as a basic obstruction, an impediment that inhibited the body's natural ability to purge itself. See Pomata, *Contracting a Cure*, 130–32. On male pregnancy, see Roberto Zapperi, *The Pregnant Man*, trans. B. Williams (Chur: Harwood Academic, 1991), first published as *L'uomo incinto: La donna, l'uomo e il potere* (Cosenza: Lerici, 1979); Katharine Eisaman Maus, "A Womb of His Own: Male Renaissance Poets in the Female Body," in *Sexuality and Gender in Early Modern Europe: Institutions, Texts, and Images*, ed. J. Turner, 266–88 (Cambridge: Cambridge University Press, 1993); and Sherry Velasco, *Male Delivery: Reproduction, Effeminacy, and Pregnant Men in Early Modern Spain* (Nashville, TN: Vanderbilt University Press, 2006). For studies of anatomy in literature and the relationship between anatomy and the self, see Janet Adelman, *Suffocating Mothers: Fantasies of Maternal Origin in Shakespeare's Plays, Hamlet to The Tempest* (New York: Routledge, 1992); Jonathan Sawday, *The Body Emblazoned: Dissection and the Human Body in Renaissance Culture* (London: Routledge, 1995); *The Body in Parts* (1997); and Sugg, *Murder After Death*.

29. Boccaccio, *Decameron*, 1047–53; *The Decameron*, 662–67.

30. Michael Rocke, "Gender and Sexual Culture in Renaissance Italy," in *Gender and Society in Renaissance Italy*, ed. J. Brown and R. Davis (London: Longman, 1998), 153. Rocke further explains that "in this regard, males' sexual and gendered norms were as rigid as those imposing chastity on females. Potency figured among the constitutive features of masculinity, such that a man's failure to achieve erection was grounds for annulment of his marriage or divorce." See also Natalie Zermon Davis, "Women on Top," in *Society and Culture in Early Modern France: Eight Essays*, 124–51 (Stanford, CA: Stanford University Press, 1975).

31. This story, like many others in the *Decameron,* celebrates that instability in the social realm, where men are made to serve women and husbands become handmaids

to their wives' lustful desires. While women were routinely called out for their tendency to commit lustful acts, the story insistently casts Mona Tessa as a good wife, an honest woman: she blushes when Calandrino exposes their passions, and as an intelligent woman, she quietly grumbles about her husband's ignorance when she discovers, at the end of the story, the practical joke and its instigators. If Boccaccio used the tale to celebrate Florentine wit, embodied in the figures of Bruno and Buffalmacco, then Tessa's ability to discover the practical joke sets her above Calandrino and equal to those Florentine tricksters, a final comment on the significance of women in the patriarchal society of late medieval Florence, a society that in theory cast women as vessels of lust and perhaps of disease but in practice admired them for their ability not only to give birth and endure excessive pain but also to exercise their clever wit.

32. On Berengario, see Park, *Secrets of Women*, chaps. 3–4; Roger French, "Berengario da Carpi and the Use of Commentary in Anatomical Teaching," in *The Medical Renaissance,* ed. A. Wear, R. K. French, and I. M. Lonie, 42–74 (Cambridge: Cambridge University Press, 1985); and French, "A Note of the Anatomical Accessus of the Middle Ages," *Medical History* 23 (1979): 461–68. On iconography and Berengario, in addition to Park, see Carlino, *Books of the Body*, chap. 1.

33. Scholarship on Vesalius is extensive. See the following and their bibliographies: Charles O'Malley, *Andreas Vesalius of Brussels, 1514–1564* (Berkeley: University of California Press, 1964); Carlino, *Books of the Body*; and for an succinct introduction, Nancy Siraisi, *Medieval and Early Renaissance Medicine: An Introduction to Knowledge and Practice* (Chicago: University of Chicago Press, 1990). Falloppio is surprisingly absent in studies of anatomy. On *observationes*, see Gianna Pomata, "*Praxis Historialis*: The Uses of *Historia* in Early Modern Medicine," in *Historia: Empiricism and Erudition in Early Modern Europe*, ed. G. Pomata and N. Siraisi, 105–146 (Boston: MIT Press, 2005).

34. Maclean, *Renaissance Notion*, 28–46; and Traub, "Psychomorphology."

35. The first point is made by Mary Fissell for the English tradition in *Vernacular Bodies* and by Katharine Park for the Italian tradition in *Secrets of Women*.

36. Berengario da Carpi, *Isagogae breves* (Bologna: Benedictum Hectoris, 1522), translated in da Carpi, *A Short Introduction to Anatomy*, ed. and trans. L. R. Lind, 80–82 (Chicago: University of Chicago Press, 1959).

37. As several studies have shown, the Aristotelian model was greeted in the Renaissance by degrees of ambivalence and opposition. See n. 2.

38. Cotyledons are a conserved trait in eutherian (or placental) mammals, most evident in ungulates and primates; the structures allow menstrual blood to enter the uterus and after conception to pass to the placenta.

39. Galen continues: "It is fused with the neck of the bladder and rectum at the vagina, as well as with ovaries and the ovarian vessels, but it may be said to be attached to the other parts of the bladder and rectum to be attached to and suspended from the sacred bone, but suspended only from the spinal marrow and lumbar muscles; both suspended from, fused with, and entwined with nerves; suspended from, fused with, interwoven, and entwined with arteries and veins." Galen, "On the Dissection of the Uterus," trans. Charles Moss, in *Anatomical Record* 144 (1962): 79.

40. Ibid, 81.
41. The other illustration emphasizes the horns of the uterus.
42. The history of anatomy and of sex difference is importantly a visual one. On relationship between artists and anatomists, see (in addition to Talvacchia), William Hecksher, *Rembrandt's Anatomy of Dr. Nicolaas Tulp: An Iconological Study* (New York: New York University Press, 1958); Michelangelo Muraro, "Tiziano e le anatomie del Vesalio," in *Tiziano e Venezia: Convegno internazionale di studi, Venezia, 1976,* 307–316 (Vicenza: N. Pozza, 1980); Glenn Harcourt, "Andreas Vesalius and the Anatomy of Antique Sculpture," *Representation* 17 (1987): 28–61; and Ludmilla Jordanova, "Happy Marriages and Dangerous Liaisons: Artists and Anatomy," in *Artists and Anatomy: The Quick and the Dead* (Berkeley: University of California Press, 1997), introduction.
43. On the range of vernacular healers and the economy of health care, see the work of David Gentilcore; and William Eamon, "Plagues, Healers, and Patients in Early Modern Europe" (review essay), *Renaissance Quarterly* 52 (1999): 474–86.
44. Thomas Gemini is mentioned in the annals of the London College of Physicians in 1555; he seems to have left Flanders for London to pursue trade in print, but was, at one point, accused and penalized for practicing medicine without a license. The Annals of the College of Physicians record: "We undertook to have the letter printed by Thomas Geminus in place of his fine, which otherwise he would have had to pay in a sum of money, and this statement was printed in English in 200 copies." Charles O'Malley speculates that the restriction was one reason behind Geminus's decision to dedicate his last edition (1559) to Queen Elizabeth. T. Geminus, *Compendiosa totius anatomie delineatio: A Facsimile of the First English Edition of 1553 in the Version of Nicholas Udall*, ed. C. O'Malley (London: Dawson, 1959), 14–15, 33.
45. Thomas Raynalde, the physician, is not found in the records (incomplete) of the London College of Physicians. Before the Stationers Company was founded in 1556, there was a Thomas Raynalde living in Finsbury, 1540, at the Wardrobe in St. Andrew's Parish, 1548, and at the Star in St. Paul's Churchyard from 1549 to 1552. It is thought that he died between 1555 and 1557, when the *Birth* came into the hands of Richard Jugge and John Cawood. In addition to Jugge and Cawood, he had business relations with other well-known printers, including Nicholas Hill, connected to the printing of the second and third editions of Geminus's anatomy text; van de Berghe; and William Seres.
46. On publishing, see Adrian Johns, *The Nature of the Book: Print and Knowledge in the Making* (Chicago: University of Chicago Press, 1998); and on English translation and cultural transmission, Michael Wyatt, *The Italian Encounter with Tudor England: A Cultural Politics of Translation* (Cambridge: Cambridge University Press, 2005), 1–14.
47. S. Larkey, "The Vesalian Compendium of Geminus and Nicholas Udall's Translation: Their Relation to Vesalius, Caius, Vicary and De Mondeville," *The Library*, 4th ser., 13, no. 4 (1933): 369–94.
48. Raynalde drew from three primary sources. First, he worked closely with Richard Jonas's edition of *The Birth of Mankind* (1540), borrowing entire sections from that

earlier text on the remedies for women's diseases, infant care, and the causes of and remedies for infertility. Raynalde organized that material into the second, third, and fourth chapters, respectively. The first edition of *The Birth of Mankind* (1540) was the product of Richard Jonas, "a studious clerk" who undertook the translation of Eucharius Rösslin's *Rosengarten*. See Eucharius Rosslin, *The Rose Garden for Pregnant Women and Midwives* (1513), a translation of the German, *der Swangern frawen und hebammen rosegarten* (1513), which was translated into Latin by Rosslin's son as *De partu hominis* (1532). Second, the material in each of these chapters (in both Jonas's and Raynalde's versions) derived from ancient source material that had been in manuscript circulation for centuries. On textual transmission, see Monica Green, *The Transmission of Ancient Theories of Female Physiology and Disease through the Early Middle Ages* (Ph.D. diss., Princeton University, 1985).

49. Elizabeth Tebeaux, *The Emergence of a Tradition: Technical Writing in the English Renaissance, 1475–1640* (Amityville, NY: Baywood, 1997); S. Hull, *Chaste, Silent and Obedient: English Books for Women 1475–1640* (San Marino, CA: Huntington Library, 1982); and H. S. Bennett, *English Books and Readers 1475–1557* (Cambridge: Cambridge University Press, 1952).

50. On the ways technical knowledge served as a catalyst for change in the learned, philosophical tradition, see Pamela Long, *Openness, Secrecy, Authorship: Technical Arts and the Culture of Knowledge from Antiquity to the Renaissance* (Baltimore: Johns Hopkins University Press, 2001).

51. Geminus, *Compendiosa*, preface.

52. Thomas Raynalde, *Birth of Mankind* (London: Tho. Ray., 1598), preface.

53. Ibid.

54. Raynalde concludes that "if a man would demand to whom the child oweth most his generation: Yee may worthily make answer, that to the mother, whether you regard the pains in bearing, other else the conference of most matter in begetting." Raynalde, *Birth of Mankind*, 17.

55. Ibid., preface.

56. Geminus, *Compendiosa*, chap. 16. In the *Dissection of the Uterus*, Galen described the texture of these arms or horns as entwining, spiraling vessels.

57. Raynalde, *Birth of Mankind*, bk. 1, chap. 5.

58. Ibid., bk. 1, chap. 6.

59. Raynalde goes on to note that the cleft marks a seam in the uterus but that the uterus is "but one vault or cavity or hollowness ... as you may more evidently see in the figure." He emphasizes the critical opposition to the theory of the seven-celled uterus. Earlier anatomists claimed that the uterus had seven cells: three on the right for male fetuses, three on the left for female ones, and one in the middle for a hermaphrodite. As he turns to questions of anatomy and theories of fetal development, Raynalde incorporates the view of the uterus as a painted heart, for he makes theory conform to his heart-shaped uterus. See Raynalde, *Birth of Mankind*, vi; and Fridolf Kudlein, "The Seven Cells of the Uterus: The Doctrine and Its Roots," *Bulletin of the History of Medicine* 49 (1965): 415–23.

60. Eric Jager, *The Book of the Heart* (Chicago: University of Chicago Press, 2000), 105–19.

61. Ibid., 105–19.
62. Ibid., 120, 133–35.
63. See William W. E. Slights, "The Narrative Heart of the Renaissance," *Renaissance and Reformation/Renaissance et Réforme* 26, no. 1 (2002): 5–23.
64. As Mary Fissell has explained, Raynalde wrote in the 1540s (the first edition), when the uterus appeared marvelous more often than it appeared dangerous or diseased. Equally, fetal development is emphasized so that the female role in birth can be magnified. Menstrual blood was the nourishment that allowed the fetus to grow; the negative associations with menstrual blood are minimized. See Fissell, *Vernacular Bodies*, chap. 1.
65. The question of hospitality was first raised by Mary Fissell.
66. Raynalde, *Birth of Mankind*, preface.
67. Felicity Heal, "The Idea of Hospitality in Early Modern England," *Past and Present* 102 (1984): 74; Heal, *Hospitality in Early Modern England* (New York: Oxford University Press, 1990); and Steve Hindle, "Dearth, Fasting and Alms: The Campaign for General Hospitality in Late Elizabethan England," *Past and Present* 172 (2001): 44–86.
68. Robert Pricket, *Times Anotomie* (1606) (Cambridge: Chadwyck-Healey, 1992).
69. Although Raynalde spoke of his book as the dinner meal, the host was ambiguously figured as the author, the reader, the physician, and the patient.
70. Thomas Storer, *Wolseius triumphans,* in *Storer: The Life and Death of Thomas Wolsey* [1599] (Cambridge: Chadwyck-Healey, 1992), n.p.
71. Lazarus Riverius, *The Practice of Physick* (London: Peter Cole, 1658), 20.
72. Lanfranci, *A most excellent and learned woorke of chirurgerie, called Chirurgia parva Lanfranci ... trans. by John Halle Chirurgien* (London: Thomas Marshe, 1565).
73. It also gives added significance to Jason Moson's description of the suffocation of the womb or the ascension of the uterus, where he cites the main cause of the condition as "the great sympathy" between the uterus and the heart. *The General Practise of Physicke* (London: Richard Field,1605), 489.
74. Felix Platter, *De corporis humani structura* (1583), table viii, fig. viii. This image is featured in Michael Stolberg, "A Woman Down," 278.
75. Stolberg, "A Woman Down," 279–80. In the preface to the *Mikrokosmographia* (1615), Crooke personified the earth as one giant uterus: "or the earth, it shall be said ... it is the rich matter and Matrix, the great mother and Nurse of all creatures, the spouse of heaven, in whose onely bosom ... all the influences of the heavenly bodies do concur and unite themselves." The idea left an iconographic footprint, for maps were depicted as circular and located in the uterine space of the female body. There is also evidence of heart-shaped maps, where the entire map was shaped as a heart rather than a circle or sphere. See the Arabic example from sixteenth-century Venice: Giampiero Bellingeri and Giorgio Vercellin, "Del mappamondo turco a forma di cuore," in *Venezia e i Turchi* (Milan: Electra, 1985), 156–57.
76. The fantasy of parthogenesis pervaded the writings of Francis Bacon as well as Vesalius. See K. Park, "Dissecting the Female Body: From Women's Secrets to the

Secrets of Nature," in *Crossing Boundaries: Attending to Early Modern Women*, ed. J. Donawerth and A. Seeff (Newark, DE: University of Delaware Press, 2000), 40–43.

77. William Harvey, *The Anatomical Exercises* (New York: Dover, 1995), preface.

78. Wendy Wall, *The Imprint of Gender: Authorship and Publication in the English Renaissance* (Ithaca, NY: Cornell University Press, 1993), 175–76.

79. See Aristotle, *Gen. Animals*. II. Loeb. *The Art of Midwifery*, ed. Hilary Marland (New York: Routledge, 1993); Adrian Wilson, *The Making of Man-Midwifery: Childbirth in England, 1660–1770* (London: UCL Press, 1995); and Doreen Evenden, *The Midwives of Seventeenth-Century London* (Cambridge: Cambridge University Press, 2002).

80. Baldasar Heseler, *Andreas Vesalius' First Public Anatomy at Bologna, 1540: An Eyewitness Report*, ed. and trans. by Ruben Eriksson (Uppsala: Almquist and Wiksells, 1959).

Chapter 7

1. See the discussions of witchcraft and gender in the articles excerpted by Darren Oldridge, ed., *The Witchcraft Reader,* 2nd ed. (New York: Routledge, 2008), 247–99; and Merry E. Wiesner, ed., *Witchcraft in Early Modern Europe* (Boston: Houghton Mifflin, 2007), 149–99.

2. Peter Burke, *Popular Culture in Early Modern Europe*, 3d ed. (Farnham: Ashgate, 2009), 103.

3. Aron Gurevitch, *Medieval Popular Culture: Problems of Belief and Perception*, trans. János M. Bak and Paul A. Hollingsworth (Cambridge: Cambridge University Press, 1988), 6, 210.

4. Burke, *Popular Culture,* 104.

5. Burke, *Popular Culture*, 103, 118–30; Gurevitch, *Medieval Popular Culture,* 1–38, 78–103; Carlo Ginzburg, *The Night Battles: Witchcraft and Agrarian Cults in the Sixteenth and Seventeenth Centuries,* trans. John and Anne Tedeschi (Baltimore: Johns Hopkins University Press, 1983).

6. Carlo Ginzburg, *Clues, Myths, and the Historical Method,* trans. John and Anne Tedeschi (Baltimore: Johns Hopkins University Press, 1989), 160–64.

7. Burke, *Popular Culture,* 118 and n. 27, citing Ginzburg, *Night Battles*; Keith Thomas, *Religion and the Decline of Magic* (New York: Scribners, 1971); and Alan Macfarlane, *Witchcraft in Tudor and Stuart England: A Regional and Comparative Study* (New York: Harper Torchbooks, 1970).

8. Ginzburg, *Clues,* 164.

9. Brian P. Levack, *The Witch-Hunt in Early Modern Europe,* 3rd ed. (Harlow: Pearson Longman, 2006), 32–51.

10. Cologne, 1487. See Walter Stephens, *Demon Lovers: Witchcraft, Sex, and the Crisis of Belief* (Chicago: University of Chicago Press, 2002), 24; Martine Ostorero, "Vinet, Jean (Vineti, Johannes) (d. ca. 1470)," in *Encyclopedia of Witchcraft: The Western Tradition* (Santa Barbara, CA: ABC-CLIO, 2006), 1169–70. Henceforth, *Encyclopedia of Witchcraft* will be abbreviated as EW. Most of the authors of

these articles have written important articles or monographs on the same subjects, which are listed, along with other crucial bibliography, in the EW articles, now a fundamental resource.

11. Brian P. Levack, "Torture," EW, 1127–31.

12. Stephens, *Demon Lovers,* 277–99.

13. See John Callow, "Evans-Pritchard, Edward E. (1902–1973)," EW, 328–29; and Rainer Walz, "Douglas, Mary (1921–)," EW, 290–91, on the seminal work of these two anthropologists.

14. Allison Coudert, "Female Witches," EW, 356–59. Levack, *Witch-Hunt,* gives totals of about 45,000 executions (23) and 75–80 percent female (141).

15. Hans Peter Broedel, "The *Malleus Maleficarum* and the Construction of Witchcraft: Theology and Popular Belief," in Wiesner, *Witchcraft,* 161.

16. Éva Pócs, "Folklore," EW, 382–84.

17. Stephens, *Demon Lovers,* 1–86; David Keck, *Angels and Angelology in the Middle Ages* (New York: Oxford University Press, 1998).

18. Richard Kieckhefer, *European Witch Trials: Their Foundations in Popular and Learned Culture* (Berkeley: University of California Press, 1976), 10–26; Kieckhefer, *Magic in the Middle Ages* (Cambridge: Cambridge University Press, 1989), 1–18, 181–201.

19. Macfarlane, *Witchcraft*; Thomas, *Religion and the Decline of Magic*; Robin Briggs, *Witches and Neighbours: The Social and Cultural Context of European Witchcraft,* 2nd ed. (Oxford: Blackwell, 2002).

20. Gurevich, *Medieval Popular Culture,* chap. 3 and passim.

21. See the documents collected in Martine Ostorero, Agostino Paravicini Bagliani, and Kathrin Utz Tremp, eds., *L'Imaginaire du sabbat: Édition critique des textes les plus anciens (1430 c.–1440 c.)* (Lausanne: Université de Lausanne, 1999).

22. Text in Alan Charles Kors and Edward Peters, eds., *Witchcraft in Europe 400–1700: A Documentary History,* 2nd ed. (Philadelphia: University of Pennsylvania Press, 2001), 178.

23. See Stephens, *Demon Lovers,* 31–36.

24. I allude to the titles of Barbara Tuchman, *A Distant Mirror: The Calamitous Fourteenth Century* (New York: Ballantine, 1979); and John Aberth, *From the Brink of the Apocalypse: Confronting Famine, War, Plague, and Death in the Later Middle Ages* (New York: Routledge, 2001).

25. See Norman Cohn, *Europe's Inner Demons: An Enquiry Inspired by the Great Witch-Hunt* (New York: Basic Books, 1975).

26. Michael Bailey, *Battling Demons: Witchcraft, Heresy, and Reform in the Later Middle Ages* (University Park: Pennsylvania State University Press, 2003); Bailey, "Nider, Johannes (ca. 1380–1438)," EW, 826–28; documents in Ostorero et al., *L'Imaginaire du Sabbat.*

27. Stephens, *Demon Lovers,* 44–46.

28. Caesarius of Heisterbach, *The Dialogue on Miracles,* trans. Henry von Essen Scott and Charles Cooke Swinton Bland (London: Routledge, 1929), vol. 1, 134–35; *Malleus maleficarum,* part II, question 2, chap. 1; George Mora, ed., *Witches, Devils, and Doctors in the Renaissance: Johann Weyer, De praestigiis daemonum,* trans. John Shea (Binghamton, NY: Medieval and Renaissance Texts and Studies,

1991), 456, 716–17 (s.v. "Incubus"); Christa Tuczay, "Incubi and Succubi," EW, 546–48; Walter Stephens, "Sexual Activity, Diabolic," EW1024–27. The best edition of Heinrich Kramer's *Malleus maleficarum* is the critical edition with English translation by Christopher S. Mackay, 2 vols. (Cambridge: Cambridge University Press, 2006), but since the older, defective Montague Summers translation (1928; rpt. New York: Dover, 1971) is still widely cited, I remand to the *Malleus* by part, question, and chapter.

29. Francesco Maria Guazzo, *Compendium maleficarum: The Montague Summers Edition,* trans. E. A. Ashwin (New York: Dover, 1988), 92–93; Jean-Claude Schmitt, *Ghosts in the Middle Ages: The Living and the Dead in Medieval Society,* trans. Teresa Lavender Fagan (Chicago: University of Chicago Press, 1998), 108; Prosper Merimée's uncanny short story "La Vénus d'Ille" is based on this legend.

30. Weyer, *Witches, Devils, and Doctors,* 456; see also Guazzo, *Compendium maleficarum,* 32–33.

31. R. E. Kaske, "*Beowulf* and the Book of Enoch," *Speculum* 46 (1971): 421–31; Walter Stephens, *Giants in Those Days: Folklore, Ancient History, and Nationalism* (Lincoln: University of Nebraska Press, 1989), chap. 2.

32. St. Augustine, *The City of God,* trans. Marcus Dods et al. (New York: Modern Library, 1950), 511–12 (book 15, chap. 23); Stephens, *Demon Lovers,* 81–82.

33. Marguerite Johnson, "Lilith," EW, 651–52.

34. Reginald Scot, *The Discoverie of Witchcraft,* ed. Montague Summers (1930; rpt. New York: Dover, 1972), 49 (i.e., bk. 4, chap. 11); Marguerite Johnson, "Night Witch, or Night Hag," EW, 828–30; Owen Davies, "Nightmares," EW, 829–30; Weyer, *Witches, Devils, and Doctors,* 716–17.

35. John E. Mack, *Abduction: Human Encounters with Aliens* (New York: Scribner's, 1994); cf. Stephens, *Demon Lovers,* 367–69.

36. Lyndal Roper, *Witch Craze: Terror and Fantasy in Baroque Germany* (New Haven, CT: Yale University Press, 2004), 160–78.

37. Christa Tuczay, "Holda," EW, 501–2; Edward Peters, "Canon Episcopi," EW, 164–65.

38. Kors and Peters, *Witchcraft in Europe,* 62.

39. Kors and Peters, *Witchcraft in Europe,* 65; cf. Christa Tuczay, "Holda," 501–2.

40. Kors and Peters, *Witchcraft in Europe,* 77–78.

41. Nathaniel Hawthorne, "Young Goodman Brown," in *Young Goodman Brown and Other Tales,* ed. Brian Harding (Oxford: Oxford World's Classics, 1987), 111–24.

42. Schmitt, *Ghosts in the Middle Ages;* Kathryn A. Edwards, "Ghosts," EW, 440–42.

43. Stephens, *Demon Lovers,* 154–59.

44. Stephens, *Demon Lovers,* 146–48.

45. Stephens, *Demon Lovers,* 150; Christa Tuczay, "Flight of Witches," EW, 379–82; Walter Stephens, "Tostado, Alonso (d. 1455)," EW, 1131–32.

46. Stephens, *Demon Lovers,* 146.

47. Stephens, *Demon Lovers,* 163–64.

48. See Stephens, *Demon Lovers,* 163–64, for the male version involving sex; for witches' anointing their pudenda see Gianfrancesco Pico della Mirandola's *Strix*

(1523), ed. and trans. Alfredo Perifano as *La Sorcière: Dialogue en trois livres sur la tromperie des démons* (Turnhout: Brepols, 2007), 83–84 (Latin text); 169 (French trans.).

49. Giovanni Pizza, "Toads," EW, 1123–25.

50. Ginzburg, *The Night Battles;* Ginzburg, *Ecstasies: Deciphering the Witch's Sabbath,* trans. Raymond Rosenthal (New York: Penguin, 1992); Rune Hagen, "Shamanism," EW, 1029–31; Edward Bever, "Drugs and Hallucinogens," EW, 296–98.

51. Kieckhefer, *Magic in the Middle Ages,* 56–80; Gurevitch, *Medieval Popular Culture,* 78–103.

52. Daniela Hacke, "Love Magic," EW, 673–75.

53. Benvenuto Cellini, *My Life,* trans. Julia Conaway Bondanella and Peter Bondanella (New York: Oxford World's Classics, 2002), 109–13 (bk. 1, chaps. 63–65).

54. Richard Godbeer, "Salem," EW, 996–1000 (at 996).

55. *Malleus maleficarum,* part I, question 7; Weyer, *Witches, Devils, and Doctors,* 277–78, suggests the "dung" was merely "sexual filth"—an addiction to copulating with "the well-practiced and wanton old prostitute." Weyer opines that the "power" of the feces in a man's shoe for killing love "is abundantly clear and there is no need to refer it by tortuous reasoning to some hidden property" (393).

56. *Malleus maleficarum,* part II, question 2, chap. 3.

57. Weyer, *Witches, Devils, and Doctors,* 334; cf. Michel de Montaigne, "Of the Power of the Imagination," *The Complete Essays of Montaigne,* ed. Donald M. Frame (1958; rpt. Stanford, CA: Stanford University Press, 1992), 70–73; Edward Bever, "Impotence, Sexual," EW, 544–46.

58. Weyer, *Witches, Devils, and Doctors,* 393.

59. Stephens, *Demon Lovers,* 300–308; Stephens, "Witches Who Steal Penises: Impotence and Illusion in *Malleus maleficarum,*" *Journal of Medieval and Early Modern Studies* 28, "Body/Matter/Spirit" (Fall 1998): 495–529; Weyer, *Witches, Devils, and Doctors,* 332–35; Joe Bavier, "Penis Theft Panic Hits City [Kinshasa]," Reuters News Service, April 23, 2008. On impotence compare Natalie Zemon Davis, *The Return of Martin Guerre* (Cambridge, MA: Harvard University Press, 1983); Edward Bever, "Impotence, Sexual."

60. Weyer, *Witches, Devils, and Doctors,* 265–67; remedies for the evil eye are on 424–28; further bibliography in Weyer, 632 n. 121; and Will Ryan, "Evil Eye," EW, 332–33.

61. Oscar Di Simplicio, "Infanticide," EW, 549–50; P. G. Maxwell-Stuart, "Lamia," EW, 618; P. G. Maxwell-Stuart, "Strix, Striga, Stria," EW, 1088–89.

62. Stephens, *Demon Lovers,* 277–99, esp. 285–89; Oscar Di Simplicio, "Cats," EW, 174–75.

63. Stephens, *Demon Lovers,* 303–12; Stephens, "Witches Who Steal Penises."

64. Michel de Certeau, *The Possession at Loudun,* trans. Michael B. Smith (Chicago: University of Chicago Press, 2000); Sarah Ferber, *Demonic Possession and Exorcism in Early Modern France* (London: Routledge, 2004); Moshe Sluhovsky, *Believe Not Every Spirit: Possession, Mysticism, and Discernment in Early Modern Catholicism* (Chicago: University of Chicago Press, 2007).

65. Margaret A. Sullivan, "The Witches of Dürer and Hans Baldung Grien," *Renaissance Quarterly* 53 (2000): 332–401; Kors and Peters, *Witchcraft in Europe,* 77; Charles Zika, "Baldung [Grien], Hans (1484–1545)," EW, 80–82.

Chapter 8

1. Archivio di Stato, Venice: Sant'Ufficio, Busta 47, case of Margarita de Rossi, September 11, 1581, f. 2v–4r.
2. Pietro Fortini, *Le piacevoli e amorose notti dei novizi,* ed. Adriana Mauriello (Rome: Salerno Editrice, 1995), 2: 1155. As with Boccaccio's *Decameron,* and many later works modeled on Boccaccio, Fortini's work consisted of ten days of storytelling by characters in a frame story. Unlike Boccaccio, however, Fortini's narrators presented their narrations in the context of *veglie,* Sienese salon-like gatherings where stories, dramatic pieces, and dialogues were exchanged in an agonistic setting that significantly included women. In fact, Fortini's work is a prime example of how these gatherings supposedly worked along with the roughly contemporary and perhaps better known work of Girolamo Bargagli, *Dialogo de'giuochi che nella vegghie sanese si usano di fare* (1572), ed. P. D'Incalci Ermini (Siena: Academia Sienese degli Intronati, 1982). This comedy is atypical in many ways; most notably it lacks a title as well as the typical prologue or introduction, and it has only one act with seventeen scenes. All translations in this essay are mine unless otherwise stated.
3. For a quick overview of these points of view and this literature, see Guido Ruggiero, "Who's Afraid of Giulia Napolitana? Pleasure, Fear, and Imagining the Arts of the Renaissance Courtesan," in *The Courtesan's Arts: Cross Cultural Perspectives,* ed. Martha Feldman and Bonnie Gordan, 280–92 (Oxford: Oxford University Press, 2005).
4. Fortini, *Le piacevoli,* 1158.
5. Ibid., 1159.
6. Ibid.
7. Ibid., 1169.
8. Ibid.
9. Ibid. Italics mine.
10. Ibid. Italics mine.
11. Quoted in Guido Ruggiero, *Machiavelli in Love: Sex, Self and Society in the Italian Renaissance* (Baltimore: Johns Hopkins University Press, 2007), 85, 239 n. 1.
12. Jacques Rossiaud, *Medieval Prostitution,* trans. Lydia G. Cochrane (Oxford: Basil Blackwell, 1988), 4–9, 38–39, 59–65.
13. Ibid., 33–34.
14. Ludovico Ariosto, *La Lena,* in *Il teatro italiano II, La comedia del Cinquecento,* vol. I, ed. Guido Davico Bonino (Turin: Einaudi, 1977), 228–30.
15. Exact translations are difficult because like much of the slang used in the illicit world of the Renaissance, these terms often had multiple levels of meaning, both obscene and quite ordinary. For this discussion see Ruggiero, *Machiavelli in Love,* 96–103, and for the quote, 96.

16. Ruggiero, *Machiavelli in Love,* 103; see also there the interesting account that Machiavelli provides in a letter of the adventures of a friend of his seeking a male prostitute in this area of the city, 98–103.

17. Fortini, *Le piacevoli,* 1170.

18. Ibid.

19. Ibid., 1169.

20. Guido Ruggiero, *Binding Passions: Tales of Magic, Marriage, and Power at the End of the Renaissance* (New York: Oxford University Press, 1993), 32–33.

21. Fortini, *Le piacevoli,* 1171.

22. Ruggiero, *Machiavelli in Love,* 113, and for a more general discussion of Machiavelli's surprisingly passive approach to this passion of love that he saw as overwhelming, see 108–62.

23. The literature is immense on this topic, but for a brief sample of the issues involved see Guido Ruggiero, *The Boundaries of Eros: Sex Crime and Sexuality in Renaissance Venice* (New York: Oxford University Press, 1985).

24. Fortini, *Le piacevoli,* 1159, emphasis mine.

25. Ibid., 1179.

26. As Flavonio is leaving, however, there is a brief and allusive reference to the stereotypic male/male sexual interests of pedants that again suggests the availability of male prostitutes in the Roman baths. When in parting Doralice asks Flavonio to kiss the hands of Oresto, a servant remarks facetiously in an aside to her, "He would prefer to kiss his mouth because he is a handsome youth in the manner of pedants" (*l'arte pedantesca*). And as Flavonio remarks to himself, "I want to go to the baths of the Sun to bathe because there is a Florentine there who will please me," Doralice, overhearing the remark, exclaims, "Now this is a pedant!" (Fortini, *Le piacevoli,* 1186). The term *arte pedantesca* is used regularly in literature to refer to the sodomy of pedants with their youthful pupils, and the reference to a Florentine in the baths seems to evoke especially in this context the negative context of Florentines as sodomites, a probability underlined by the fact that this was a Sienese comedy, and jabs at Florentines and their perversities were virtually required. See, for an earlier discussion in the comedy of sodomy as the *arte* of pedants, 1152–53.

27. Fortini, *Le piacevoli,* 1198.

Chapter 9

1. For constructions of female sexuality through mythological imagery see Bette Talvacchia, "Il mercato dell'eros: Rappresentazioni della sessualità femminile nei soggetti mitologici," in *Monaca, Moglie, Serva, Cortigiana: Vita e immagine delle donne tra Rinascimento e Controriforma,* ed. Sara E. Matthews Grieco (Florence: Morgana Edizioni, 2001), 192–245.

2. For the art commissioned by Federico Gonzaga in the Palazzo del Te, see Amedeo Belluzzi, *Palazzo del Te* (Modena: Francesco Panini Editore, 1998), with full bibliography.

3. See Egon Verheyen, "Correggio's *Amori di Giove*," *Journal of the Warburg and Courtauld Institutes* 29 (1966): 160–92; for full information on Giulio Romano's work in Mantua, see the exhibition catalogue *Giulio Romano* (Milan: Electa, 1989).

4. Carl Brandon Strehlke, *Pontormo, Bronzino and the Medici: The Transformation of the Renaissance Portrait in Florence* (Philadelphia: Philadelphia Museum of Art, 2004).

5. Emma H. Mellencamp, "A Note on the Costume of Titian's *Flora*," *Art Bulletin* 51 (1969): 174–77.

6. For an indication of the arguments and lengthy bibliography around the reading of this painting see Rona Goffen, ed., *Titian's "Venus of Urbino"* (New York: Cambridge University Press, 1997).

7. Patricia Simons, "Women in Frames: The Gaze, the Eye, and the Profile in Renaissance Portraiture," in *The Expanding Discourse*, ed. Norma Broude and Mary D. Garrard, 39–57 (New York: Icon Editions, 1992).

8. Mary D. Garrard, "Leonardo da Vinci: Female Portraits, Female Nature," in Broude and Garrard, *Expanding Discourse*.

9. Giorgio Vasari, "Madonna Properzia de' Rossi, Sculptor of Bologna," in *Lives of the Painters, Sculptors and Architects*, vol. 1, trans. Gaston du C. de Vere (New York: Alfred A. Knopf, 1996), 858. The relief, dating to the 1520s, is to be found in the collection of the Museo di San Petronio, Bologna.

10. A vast literature has developed from the pioneering monograph of Mary Garrard, *Artemisia Gentileschi: The Image of the Female Hero in Italian Baroque Art* (Princeton, NJ: Princeton University Press, 1989), to the recent study by Mieke Bal, *The Artemisia Files* (Chicago: University of Chicago, 2005).

11. Recent research on Cranach and excellent reproductions of his work can be found in Bodo Brinkmann, ed., *Cranach* (London: Royal Academy Publications, 2008).

12. Hans Baldung Grien, *Judith with the Head of Holofernes* (1515) (Nuremberg: Germanisches Nationalmuseum).

13. The document is found in Charles Seymour, *Michelangelo's David: A Search for Identity* (New York, 1967), 139ff.

14. Leo Steinberg, *The Sexuality of Christ in the Renaissance and in Modern Oblivion* (Chicago: University of Chicago Press, 1983).

15. For the iconography of Mary Magdalene see Susan Haskins, *Mary Magdalen: Myth and Metaphor* (Harcourt, Brace, 1994); and Jane Dillenberger, "The Magdalen: Reflections on the Image of the Saint and Sinner in Christian Art," in *Women, Religion and Social Change*, ed. Yvonne Yazbeck Haddad and Ellison Banks Findly (Albany: State University of New York Press, 1985), 115–41.

16. See Bette Talvacchia, "The Double Life of Saint Sebastian," in *The Body in Early Modern Italy*, ed. Julia Hairston and Walter Stephens (Baltimore: Johns Hopkins University Press, 2010).

17. See Marina Warner, *Monuments and Maidens* (Atheneum, 1985), chap. 12, "The Slipped Chiton," and for a discussion in the religious context see Margaret R. Miles, "The Virgin's One Bare Breast," in Broude and Garrard, *Expanding Discourse*, 27–37.

18. Ronald Millen and Robert Erich Wolf, *Heroic Deeds and Mystic Figures: A New Reading of Rubens' Cycle of Maria de' Medici* (Princeton, NJ: Princeton University Press, 1989), 165.

19. Margit Thofner, "Helena Fourment's *Het Pelsken*," *Art History* 27 (2004): 1–33. My discussion of this painting is based on the information presented in this path-breaking article.

20. For the drawing see Carmen Bambach, ed., *Leonardo da Vinci, Master Draftsman* (New York: Metropolitan Museum of Art, 2003), catalogue number 25.

21. See Charles Dempsey, "Et nos cedamus amori: Observations on the Farnese Gallery," *Art Bulletin* 50 (1968): 363–74.

22. Sandro Botticelli, *Venus and Mars* (ca. 1485), National Gallery, London.

23. For an overview of the subject see Alison G. Stewart, *Unequal Lovers: A Study of Unequal Couples in Northern Art* (New York: Abrams, 1978).

24. Both Il Riccio and L'Antico, underappreciated for a long time, have recently had impressive exhibitions and important scholarship devoted to them. See *Rinascimento e passione per l'antico: Andrea Riccio e il suo tempo,* ed. Andrea Bacchi and Luciana Giacomelli (Trent: Soprintendenza per i beni storico-artistici, 2008); Denise Allen, ed., *Andrea Riccio: Renaissance Master of Bronzes* (New York: Frick Collection, 2008); *Bonacolsi, L'Antico. Uno scultore nella Mantova di Andrea Mantegna e di Isabella d'Este,* ed. Filippo Trevisani and Davide Gasparotto (Milan: Electa, 2008).

25. Margaret A. Sullivan, "The Witches of Albrecht Dürer and Hans Baldung Grien," *Renaissance Quarterly* 53 (2000): 332–401.

26. Ibid., 334.

27. For a reproduction and comment about the color scheme, see the entry by Gloria Fossi in *Galleria degli Uffizi: Arte, storia, collezioni* (Giunti, 2001), 249.

28. Catherine Monbeig Goguel, ed., *Francesco Salviati o La bella maniera* (Milan: Electa, 1998), catalog 71, 202–3.

29. For the binary concept *onesto/disonesto* and the *Modi* see Bette Talvacchia, *Taking Positions: On the Erotic in Renaissance Culture* (Princeton, NJ: Princeton University Press, 1999).

30. For an informative and thoughtful treatment of Agostino's *Lascivie,* see Marzia Faietti, "Carte belle, più che oneste," in *Mythologica et Erotica,* ed. Ornella Casazza and Riccardo Gennaioli, 98–103 (Florence: Sillabe, 2005).

BIBLIOGRAPHY

Abano, P. de. *Expositio problematum Aristotelis*. Paulus de Butzbach, 1475.

Abelove, H. "Some Speculations on the History of Sexual Intercourse during the Long Eighteenth Century in England." *Genders* 6 (1989): 125–30.

Aberth, J. *From the Brink of the Apocalypse: Confronting Famine, War, Plague, and Death in the Later Middle Ages*. New York: Routledge, 2001.

Adelman, J. "Making Defect Perfection: Shakespeare and the One-Sex Model." In *Enacting Gender on the English Renaissance Stage*. Edited by V. Cosmensoli and A. Russell. Urbana: University of Illinois Press, 1999.

Adelman, J. *Suffocating Mothers: Fantasies of Maternal Origin in Shakespeare's Plays, Hamlet to* The Tempest. New York: Routledge, 1992.

Afonso V. *Ordenaçoens do Senhor Rey D. Affonso V*, vol. 5. Real Imprensa da Universidade, 1792.

Alberti, L. B. *I libri della famiglia*. Edited and translated by Guido Ruggiero and Alberto Tenenti. Turin: Einaudi, 1972. English version in *The Albertis of Florence*. Translated by Guido Guarino. Lewisburg, PA: Bucknell University Press, 1971.

Allen, D., ed. *Andrea Riccio: Renaissance Master of Bronzes*. New York: Frick Collection, 2008.

"An Act for suppressing the detestable sins of Incest, Adultery and Fornication." In *Acts and Ordinances of the Interregnum, 1642–1660*, vol. 2. Edited by C. H. Firth and R. S. Rait. His Majesty's Stationery Office, 1911.

Andreadis, H. "The Sapphic-Platonics of Katherine Philips, 1632–1664." *Signs* 15 (1989): 34–60.

Andrews, R. *Scripts and Scenarios: The Performance of Comedy in Renaissance Italy*. Cambridge: Cambridge University Press, 1993.

Anonymous. *A most straunge, and true discourse, of the wonderful judgement of God: Of a monstrous, deformed infant, begotten by incestuous copulation, betweene the brothers sonne and the sisters daughter, being both vnmarried persons*. Richard Iones, 1600.

Antoninus of Florence. *Summa*. Basel: J. Amerbach, P. Froben, n.d.

Anzelewsky, F. *Dürer: Werk und Wirkung*. Erlangen: Karl Müller, 1988.

Anzelewsky, F., and S. Morét. "Drei Kriegsleute, 1489." *Dürer Holbein Grünewald: Meisterzeichnungen der deutschen Renaissance aus Berlin und Basel*. Ostfildern-Ruit: Gerd Hatje, 1997.

Aquinas, T. *Summa Theologiae*, vol. 28. Edited by T. Gilby et al. Blackfriars in conjunction with Eyre and Spottiswoode, 1966.

Aretino, P. *Lettere*, vol. 4. Edited by P. Procaccioli. Rome: Salerno, 1992.

Ariosto, L. *La Lena*. In *Il teatro italiano*, vol. II, *La comedia del Cinquecento*, vol. I. Edited by Guido Davico Bonino, 155–232. Turin: Einaudi, [1977].

Aristotle. *Gen. Animals*. II. Loeb. *The Art of Midwifery*. Edited by Hilary Marland. New York: Routledge, 1993.

Augustine. *The City of God*. Translated by Marcus Dods et al. New York: Modern Library, 1950.

Bacchi, A., and L. Giacomelli, eds. *Rinascimento e passione per l'antico: Andrea Riccio e il suo tempo*. Trent: Soprintendenza per i beni storico-artistici, 2008.

Bailey, M. *Battling Demons: Witchcraft, Heresy, and Reform in the Later Middle Ages*. University Park: Pennsylvania State University Press, 2003.

Bailey, M. "Nider, Johannes (ca. 1380–1438)." In *Encyclopedia of Witchcraft: The Western Tradition*. Edited by R. M. Golden. Santa Barbara, CA: ABC-CLIO, 2006.

Bal, M. *The Artemisia Files*. Chicago: University of Chicago Press, 2005.

Bambach, C., ed. *Leonardo da Vinci, Master Draftsman*. New York: Metropolitan Museum of Art, 2003.

Bargagli, G. *Dialogo de'giuochi che nella vegghie sanese si usano di fare* (1572). Edited by P. D'Incalci Ermini. Siena: Academia Sienese degli Intronati, 1982.

Barkan, L. *Transuming Passion: Ganymede and the Erotics of Humanism*. Stanford, CA: Stanford University Press, 1991.

Barnum, G. *Albrecht Dürer and His Legacy*. London: British Museum, 2002.

Baskins, C. *Cassone Painting, Humanism and Gender in Early Modern Italy*. Cambridge: Cambridge University Press, 1998.

Batt, B. *The Christian mans closet*. Translated by W. Lowth. Thomas Dawson and Gregorie Seton, 1581.

Bautista, J. *Confessionario en lengua mexicana y castellana*. Melchior Ocharte, 1599.

Bavier, J. "Penis Theft Panic Hits City [Kinshasa]." Reuters News Service, April 23, 2008.

Beard, T. *The theatre of God's iudgements*. Adam Islip, 1597.

Bellingeri, G., and G. Vercellin. "Del mappamondo turco a forma di cuore." In *Venezia e i Turchi*, 155–59. Milan: Electra, 1985.

Belluzzi, A. *Palazzo del Te*. Modena: Francesco Panini, 1998.

Benito Ruano, E. *Los orígenes del problema converso*. Real Academia de la Historia, 2001.

Benivieni, A. *De abditis nonnullis ac mirandis morborum et sanationum causis* [Certain Hidden and Wonderful Causes of Illness and Healing, 1507]. Edited by Giogio Weber. Florence: Olschki, 1994.

Bennett, H. S. *English Books and Readers 1475–1557*. Cambridge: Cambridge University Press, 1952.

Bennett, J. M., and A. M. Froide, eds. *Singlewomen in the European Past*. Philadelphia: University of Pennsylvania Press, 1999.

Benserade, I. de. *Iphis et Iante: Comédie*. Edited by A. Verdier. Lampsaque, 2000.

Bercé, Y.-M. *Fête et révolte: Des mentalités populaires du XVIe au XVIIe siècle*. Paris: Hachette, 1976.

Betteridge, T., ed. *Sodomy and Deviant Sex in Early Modern Europe*. Manchester: Manchester University Press, 2002.

Bever, E. "Drugs and Hallucinogens." *Encyclopedia of Witchcraft: The Western Tradition*. Edited by R. M. Golden. Santa Barbara, CA: ABC-CLIO, 2006.

Bever, E. "Impotence, Sexual." *Encyclopedia of Witchcraft: The Western Tradition*. Edited by R. M. Golden. Santa Barbara, CA: ABC-CLIO, 2006.

Bishop, J. *Beautiful blossomes*. H. Cockyn, 1577.

Bloodsworth-Lugo, M. *In-Between Bodies: Sexual Difference, Race, and Sexuality*. Albany: State University of New York, 2007.

Boaistuau, P. *Histoires prodigeuses les plus mémorables*. Iean Longis and Robert Le Mangnier, 1560.

Boccaccio, G. *Decameron*. Edited by Vittore Branca. Turin: Einaudi, 1992.

Boccaccio, G. *The Decameron*. Translated by M. Musa and P. Bondanella. New York: Penguin, 1982.

Boccaccio, G. *Famous Women*. Edited by V. Brown. Cambridge, MA: Harvard University Press, 2001.

Boissard, J. J. *Emblematum liber*. Theodorus de Bry, 1593.

Boone, Marc. "State Power and Illicit Sexuality: The Persecution of Sodomy in Late Medieval Bruges." *Journal of Medieval History* 22 (1996): 135–53.

Borgarucci, P. *Della contemplatione anatomica*. Venice: Vincenzo Valgrisi, 1564.

Borris, K., ed. *Same-Sex Desire in the English Renaissance: A Sourcebook of Sixteenth and Seventeenth-Century Texts*. New York: Routledge, 2003.

Boswell, J. *Christianity, Social Tolerance, and Homosexuality: Gay People in Western Europe from the Beginning of the Christian Era to the Fourteenth Century*. Chicago: University of Chicago Press, 1980.

Bourdeille, P. de, and S. de Brantôme. *La vie des dames galantes*. Edited by Pascal Pia and Paul Morand. Paris: Gallimard, 1981.

Bourdura, L., and A. Dunlop. *Art and the Augustinian Order in Early Renaissance Italy*. Aldershot: Ashgate, 2007.

Boyer, R. *Lives of the Bigamists: Marriage, Family, and Community in Colonial Mexico*. Albuquerque: University of New Mexico Press, 1995.

Bracciolini, P. "An seni sit uxor ducenda dialogus." In *Poggius Bracciolini: Opera omnia*, vol. 2. Edited by R. Fubin. Bottega d'Erasmo, 1966 [1437].

Brackett, J. "The Florentine *Onestà* and the Control of Prostitution, 1403–1680." *The Sixteenth Century Journal* 29 (1993): 273–300.

Bray, A. *The Friend*. Chicago: University of Chicago Press, 2003.

Bray, A. *Homosexuality in Renaissance England*. London: Gay Men's Press, 1982.

Briggs, R. *Witches and Neighbours: The Social and Cultural Context of European Witchcraft*, 2nd ed. Oxford: Blackwell, 2002.

Brinkmann, B. *Hexenlust und Sündenfall. Die seltsamen Phantasien des Hans Baldung Grien*. Petersberg: Michael Imhof Verlag, 2007.

Brinkmann, B. *Witches' Lust and the Fall of Man: The Strange Fantasies of Hans Bal-dung Grien*. Frankfurt am Main: Michael Imhof, 2007.

Brinkmann, B., ed. *Cranach*. London: Royal Academy Publications, 2008.

Broedel, H. P. "The *Malleus Maleficarum* and the Construction of Witchcraft: Theology and Popular Belief." In *Witchcraft in Early Modern Europe*. Edited by Merry E. Wiesner, 154–63. Boston: Houghton Mifflin, 2007.

Brooten, B. J. *Love Between Women: Early Christian Responses to Female Homoeroti-cism*. Chicago: University of Chicago Press, 1996.

Brown, A., ed. *Bartolomeo Scala: Humanistic and Political Writings*. Medieval & Renaissance Texts and Studies, 1997.

Brown, P. F. *Private Lives in Renaissance Venice*. New Haven, CT: Yale University Press, 2004.

Brundage, J. "Carnal Delight: Canonistic Theories of Sexuality." *Proceedings of the Fifth International Congress of Medieval Canon Law*. Edited by Stephan Kuttner and Kenneth Pennington. Vatican City: Biblioteca Apostolica Vaticana, 1980.

Brundage, J. A. *Law, Sex and Christian Society in Medieval Europe*. Chicago: University of Chicago Press, 1987.

Bullough, V. L. "Transvestites in the Middle Ages." *American Journal of Sociology* 79 (1974): 1381–94.

Bullough, V. L., and B. Bullough. *Cross Dressing, Sex, and Gender*. Philadelphia: University of Pennsylvania Press, 1993.

Burke, P. "The Courtier Abroad: Or the Uses of Italy." In *The Book of the Courtier by Baldesar Castiglione*. Edited by Daniel Javitch. New York: Norton, 2002.

Burke, P. *Popular Culture in Early Modern Europe*, 3d ed. Farnham: Ashgate, 2009.

Burnet, G. *The History of the Reformation of the Church of England*. Edited by N. Pocock. Clarendon Press, 1865.

Burns, R. I., ed. *Las siete partidas*. Philadelphia: University of Pennsylvania Press, 2001.

Butler, J. *Gender Trouble: Feminism and the Subversion of Identity*. New York: Routledge, 1990.

Butler, J. "Performative Acts and Gender Constitution: An Essay in Phenomenology and Feminist Theory." *Theater Journal* 40 (1988): 519–31.

Bylebyl, J. "Medicine, Philosophy, and Humanism in Renaissance Italy." In *Science and the Arts in the Renaissance*. Edited by J. Shirley and F. D. Hoeniger. Washington, DC: Folger Library, 1985.

Bynum, C. "The Body of Christ in the Later Middle Ages: A Reply to Leo Steinberg." *Renaissance Quarterly* 39 (1986): 399–439.

Bynum, C. W. "The Body of Christ in the Later Middle Ages: A Reply to Leo Stein-berg." In *Fragmentation and Redemption: Essays on Gender and the Human Body in Medieval Religion*. New York: Zone Books, 1991.

Caciola, N. *Discerning Spirits: Divine and Demonic Possession in the Middle Ages*. Ithaca, NY: Cornell University Press, 2003.

Cadden, J. *Meanings of Sex Difference in the Middle Ages: Medicine, Science, and Culture*. Cambridge: Cambridge University Press, 1993.

Caesarius of Heisterbach. *The Dialogue on Miracles*. Translated by Henry von Essen Scott and Charles Cooke Swinton Bland. 2 vols. London: Routledge, 1929.

Callow, John. "Evans-Pritchard, Edward E. (1902–1973)." In *Encyclopedia of Witchcraft: The Western Tradition*. Edited by R. M. Golden. Santa Barbara, CA: ABC-CLIO, 2006.

Calvi, G. "Reconstructing the Family: Widowhood and Remarriage in Tuscany in the Early Modern Period." In *Marriage in Italy, 1300–1650*. Edited by T. Dean and K.J.P. Lowe. Cambridge: Cambridge University Press, 1998.

Cantor, D., ed. *Reinventing Hippocrates*. Brookfield, VT: Ashgate, 2002.

Carlino, A. *Books of the Body: Anatomical Ritual and Renaissance Learning*. Chicago: University of Chicago Press, 1999.

Carlino, A. *Paper Bodies: A Catalogue of Anatomical Fugitive Sheets, 1538–1687*. London: Wellcome Institute for the History of Medicine, 1999.

Castiglione, B. *Il Cortegiano*. Florence: Felice Le Monnier, 1854.

Cavalli-Sforza, L., and F. Cavalli-Sforza. *Perché la scienza? L'avventura di un ricercatore*. Milan: Mondadori, 2005.

Cellini, B. *La vita*. In *Opere*. Edited by B. Maier. Milan: Rizzoli, 1968.

Cellini, B. *My Life*. Translated by Julia Conaway Bondanella and Peter Bondanella. Oxford: Oxford University Press, 2002.

Certeau, Michel de. *The Possession at Loudun*. Translated by Michael B. Smith. Chicago: University of Chicago Press, 2000.

Chartier, Roger, ed. *A History of Private Life: Passions of the Renaissance*, vol. 3. Cambridge, MA: Belknap Press, 1989.

Chaytor, M. "Husband(ry): Narratives of Rape in the Seventeenth Century." *Gender and History* 7 (1995): 378–407.

Coci, L. *Antonio Rocco: L'Alcibiade fanciullo a scola*. Salerno, 1988.

Cohen, E. "Honor and Gender in the Streets of Early Modern Rome." *Journal of Interdisciplinary History* 22 (1992): 597–625.

Cohen, E., and T. Cohen. *Daily Life in Renaissance Italy*. Westport, CT: Greenwood Press, 2001.

Cohn, N. *Europe's Inner Demons: An Enquiry Inspired by the Great Witch-Hunt*. New York: Basic Books, 1975.

Coke, E. *The third part of the Institutes of the laws of England*. W. Lee and D. Pakeman, 1644.

Collomp, A. *La maison du père: Famille et village en Haute-Provence aux XVIIe et XVIIIe siècles*. Presses universitaires de France, 1983.

Conway, M. *The Writings of Albrecht Dürer*. London: Peter Owen, 1958.

Cook, J. *A Voyage to the Pacific Ocean undertaken by Command of His Majesty for making Discoveries in the Northern Hemisphere*, vol. 1. R. Morison and Son, 1785.

Cook, J. *A Voyage to the Pacific Ocean, undertaken, by the Command of His Majesty, for making Discoveries in the Northern Hemisphere*, vol. 3. G. Nicol and T. Cadell, 1784.

Córdoba, A. de. *Quæstionarium theologicum, siue, Sylua amplissima decisionum, et variarum resolutionum casuum conscientiae*. Sumptibus Baretij Baretij, 1604.

Correll, B. "Malleable Material, Models of Power: Woman in Erasmus's 'Marriage Group' and 'Civility in Boys.'" *English Literary History* 57 (1990): 241–62.

Coryat, T. *Coryat's Crudities*. Facsimile of the 1611 edition. London: Scolar Press, 1978.

Coudert, A. "Female Witches." In *Encyclopedia of Witchcraft: The Western Tradition*. Edited by R. M. Golden. Santa Barbara, CA: ABC-CLIO, 2006.

Cowan, A. *Marriage, Manners and Mobility in Early Modern Venice*. Burlington, VT: Ashgate, 2007.

Cox, V., ed. and trans. *The Worth of Women*. Chicago: University of Chicago Press, 1997.

Crabb, A. *The Strozzi of Florence: Widowhood and Family Solidarity in the Renaissance*. Ann Arbor: University of Michigan Press, 2000.

Cressy, D. *Birth, Marriage and Death: Ritual, Religion and the Life-Cycle in Tudor and Stuart England*. Oxford: Oxford University Press, 1997.

Cunningham, A. *The Anatomical Renaissance*. Brookfield, VT: Scolar Press, 1997.

Da Carpi, B. *A Short Introduction to Anatomy [Isagogae breves, 1522]*. Edited and translated by L. R. Lind. Chicago: University of Chicago Press, 1959.

Dall'Orto, G. "'Socratic Love' as a Disguise for Same-Sex Love in the Italian Renaissance." In *Male Homosexuality in Renaissance and Enlightenment Europe*. Edited by K. Gerard and G. Hekma. New York: Harriington Park Press, 1989.

Damhouder, J. de. *Praxis rerum criminalium*. Ioannem Bellerum, 1562.

Daston, L. "Marvelous Facts and Miraculous Evidence in Early Modern Europe." *Critical Inquiry* 18 (1991): 93–124.

Daston, L., and K. Park. "The Hermaphrodite and the Orders of Nature: Sexual Ambiguity in Early Modern France." *Gay and Lesbian Quarterly* 1 (1995): 419–38.

Daston, L., and K. Park. "Hermaphrodites in Renaissance France." *Critical Matrix* 1 (1985): 1–19.

Daston, L., and K. Park. *Wonders and the Order of Nature, 1150–1750*. New York: Zone Books, 1998.

Daston, L., and F. Vidal, eds. *The Moral Authority of Nature*. Chicago: University of Chicago Press, 2004.

Davanzo Poli, D. "Le cortigiane e la moda." In *Le cortigiane di Venezia dal trecento al settecento*. Milan: Berenice Art Books, 1990.

Davidson, A. "Sex and the Emergence of Sexuality." *Critical Inquiry* 14 (1987): 16–48.

Davidson, N. "Sodomy in Early-Modern Venice." In *Sodomy and Deviant Sex in Early Modern Europe*. Edited by T. Betteridge. Manchester, UK: Manchester University Press, 2002.

Davidson, N. "Theology, Nature and the Law: Sexual Sin and Sexual Crime in Italy from the Fourteenth to the Seventeenth Century." In *Crime, Society and the Law in Renaissance Italy*. Edited by T. Dean and K.J.P. Lowe. Cambridge: Cambridge University Press, 1993.

Davies, O. "Nightmares." In *Encyclopedia of Witchcraft: The Western Tradition*. Edited by R. M. Golden. Santa Barbara, CA: ABC-CLIO, 2006.

Davis, N. "Women on Top." In *Society and Culture in Early Modern France: Eight Essays*. Stanford, CA: Stanford University Press, 1975.

Davis, N. Z. *The Return of Martin Guerre.* Cambridge, MA: Harvard University Press, 1983.

Davis, N. Z. *Society and Culture in Early Modern France: Eight Essays.* Stanford, CA: Stanford University Press, 1975.

Decker-Hauff, H., and R. Seigl. *Die Chronik der Grafen von Zimmern: Handschriften 580 und 581 der Fürstlich Fürstenbergischen Hofbibliothek Donaueschingen,* vol. 2. Constance: Jan Thorbecke, 1967.

Della Casa, G. *Galateo.* Translated by K. Eisenbichler and K. R. Bartlett. Toronto: Center for Renaissance and Reformation Studies, 1986.

Della Casa, G. *Galateo: A Renaissance Treatise on Manners.* Edited by K. Eisenbichler and K. R. Bartlett. Toronto: Centre for Reformation and Renaissance Studies, 1994.

Dempsey, C. "Et nos cedamus amori: Observations on the Farnese Gallery." *Art Bulletin* 50 (1968): 363–74.

Dillenberger, J. "The Magdalen: Reflections on the Image of the Saint and Sinner in Christian Art." In *Women, Religion and Social Changes.* Edited by Y. Yazbeck Haddad and E. B. Findly, 115–41. Albany: State University Press of New York, 1985.

Domínguez Ortiz, A. *Las clases privilegiadas en la España del antiguo régimen.* Istmo, 1973.

Douglas, M. *Purity and Danger: An Analysis of Concepts of Pollution and Taboo.* London: Routledge, 2002.

Dover, K. J. *Greek Homosexuality.* New York: Vintage, 1978.

Duits, R. "Figured Riches." *Journal of the Warburg and Courtauld Institutes* 33 (1970): 107–62.

Dülmen, R. Von. *Gesellschaft der Frühen Neuzeit: Kulturelles Handeln und sozialer Prozeß.* Vienna: Böhlau, 1993.

Dupâquier, J. *La Population française aux XVIIe et XVIIIe siècles.* Paris, 1979.

Durling, R. M., ed. and trans. *Petrarch's Lyric Poems: The Rime Sparse and Other Lyrics.* Cambridge, MA: Harvard University Press, 1976.

Dürer Holbein Grünewald: Meisterzeichnungen der deutschen Renaissance aus Berlin und Basel. Ostfildern-Ruit: Gerd Hatje, 1997.

Durkheim, E. "La prohibition de l'inceste et ses origins." *L'Année sociologique* 1 (1897): 1–70.

Eamon, W. "Plagues, Healers, and Patients in Early Modern Europe" (review essay). *Renaissance Quarterly* 52 (1999): 474–86.

Eberlein, J. K. *Albrecht Dürer.* Reinbek: Rowohlt, 2003.

Edwards, K. A. "Ghosts." In *Encyclopedia of Witchcraft: The Western Tradition.* Edited by R. M. Golden. Santa Barbara, CA: ABC-CLIO, 2006.

Epstein, S. *Inclusion: The Politics of Difference in Medical Research.* Chicago: University of Chicago Press, 2007.

Equicola, M. *Libro di natura d'amore: Di nuovo ricorretto, e con soma diligenza riformato.* Venice: G. B. Bonfadino, 1583.

Erasmus. *The Colloquies of Erasmus.* Translated by C. R. Thompson. Chicago: University of Chicago Press, 1965.

Erasmus. "The Institution of Christian Matrimony." In *Collected Works of Erasmus: Spiritualia,* vol. 69. Edited by J. W. O'Malley and L. A. Perraud. Toronto: University of Toronto Press, 1993.

Erasmus. "On Good Manners for Boys." In *Collected Works,* vol. 25. Translated by B. McGregor. Toronto: University of Toronto Press, 1985.

Erasmus. *Opera Omnia Desiderii Erasmi Roterodami.* Vol. 1, *Colloquia.* Edited by L.-E. Halkin, F. Bierlaire, and R. Hoven. Amsterdam: North Holland, 1972.

Escobar del Corro, J. *Tractatus bipartitus de puritate et nobilitate probanda.* Sumptibus Laurentij Durand, 1637.

Eser, Th., and A. Grebe. *Heilige und Hasen: Bücherschätze der Dürerzeit.* Nuremberg: Germanisches Nationalmuseum, 2008.

Evenden, D. *The Midwives of Seventeenth-Century London.* Cambridge: Cambridge University Press, 2002.

Faietti, M. "Carte belle, più che oneste." In *Mythologica et Erotica.* Edited by O. Casazza and R. Gennaioli, 98–103. Florence: Sillabe, 2005.

Fairchilds, C. *Women in Early Modern Europe, 1500–1700.* London: Pearson/Longman, 2007.

Farr, J. *Authority and Sexuality in Early Modern Burgundy, 1550–1730.* Oxford: Oxford University Press, 1995.

Feldman, M. "The Courtesan's Voice: Petrarchan Lovers, Pop Philosophy and Oral Traditions." In *The Courtesan's Arts: Cross-Cultural Perspectives.* Edited by M. Feldman and B. Gordon. Oxford: Oxford University Press, 2006.

Ferber, S. *Demonic Possession and Exorcism in Early Modern France.* London: Routledge, 2004.

Ferdinand and Isabella of Spain. *Recopilacion de las leyes destos reynos, hecha por mandado ... del rey ... Philippe Segundo.* Iuan Iniguez de Lequerica, 1592.

Fernández de Oviedo y Valdés, G. *Historia general y natural de las Indias, islas y tierrafirme del mar océano,* vol. 1. Real academia de la historia, 1851–1855.

Ferraro, J. *Marriage Wars in Late Renaissance Venice.* Oxford: Oxford University Press, 2001.

Finucci, V. *The Lady Vanishes: Subjectivity and Representation in Castiglione and Ariosto.* Stanford: Stanford University Press, 1992.

Finucci, V. *The Manly Masquerade: Masculinity, Paternity, and Castration in the Italian Renaissance.* Durham, NC: Duke University Press, 2003.

Fisher, W. "The Renaissance Beard: Masculinity in Early Modern England." *Renaissance Quarterly* 54 (2001): 155–87.

Fissell, M. *Vernacular Bodies: The Politics of Reproduction in Early Modern England.* Oxford: Oxford University Press, 2004.

Fonte, M. *Il Merito delle donne.* Venice, 1600. English version in *The Worth of Women, Wherein Is Clearly Revealed Their Nobility and Their Superiority to Men.* Edited and translated by V. Cox. Chicago: University of Chicago Press, 1997.

Fortini, P. *Le piacevoli e amorose notti dei novizi.* 2 vols. Edited by Adriana Mauriello. Rome: Salerno Edrice, 1995.

Fossi, G. *Galleria degli Uffizi: Arte, storia, collezioni.* Giunti, 2001.

Foucault, M. *The Birth of the Clinic: A Archaelogy of Medical Perception.* New York: Vintage Books, 1994.

Foucault, M. *Discipline and Punish: The Birth of the Prison.* New York: Vintage Books, 1977.

Foucault, M. *The History of Sexuality.* Vol. 1, *The Will to Knowledge.* London: Penguin, 1978.

Foucault, M. *Politics, Philosophy, Culture: Interviews and Other Writings 1977–1984.* New York: Routledge, 1988.

Franco, V. *Lettere Familiari.* Venice, 1580. Edited by Benedetto Croce. Naples: Ricciardi, 1949. English version in *The Poems and Selected Letters of Veronica Franco.* Edited and translated by A. R. Jones and M. F. Rosenthal. Chicago: University of Chicago Press, 1998.

François, E. *Protestants et catholiques en Allemagne: Identités et pluralisme, Augsbourg, 1648–1806.* A. Michel, 1993.

French, R. "Berengario da Carpi and the Use of Commentary in Anatomical Teaching." In *The Medical Renaissance.* Edited by A. Wear, R. K. French, and I. M. Lonie. Cambridge: Cambridge University Press, 1985.

French, R. "A Note of the Anatomical Accessus of the Middle Ages." *Medical History* 23 (1979): 461–68.

Freud, S. *Totem and Taboo: Some Points of Agreement between the Mental Lives of Savages and Neurotics.* New York: Routledge and Kegan Paul, 1950.

Frick, C. *Dressing Renaissance Florence.* Baltimore: Johns Hopkins University Press, 2002.

Friedberg, A., ed. *Corpus juris canonici,* vol. 1. Tauchnitz, 1879.

Frutta, E. "Limpieza de sangre y nobleza en el México colonial: La formackas 3ión de un saber nobiliario (1571–1700)." *Jahrbuch für Geschichte Lateinameri* 9 (2002): 217–35.

Gainsford, T. *The rich cabinet furnished with varietie of excellent discriptions.* R. Iackson, 1616.

Galen. "On the Dissection of the Uterus." Translated by Charles Moss. In *Anatomical Record* 144 (1962): 77–83.

Gallucci, M. A. *Benvenuto Cellini: Sexuality, Masculinity, and Artistic Identity in Renaissance Italy.* New York: Palgrave, 2003.

Garrard, M. *Artemisia Gentileschi: The Image of the Female Hero in Italian Baroque Art.* Princeton, NJ: Princeton University Press, 1989.

Garrard, M. "Here's Looking at Me: Sofonsiba Anguissola and the Problem of the Woman Artist." *Renaissance Quarterly* 47 (1994): 556–622.

Garrard, M. "Leonardo da Vinci: Female Portraits, Female Nature." In *The Expanding Discourse.* Edited by Norma Broude and Mary D. Garrard. New York: Icon Editions, 1992.

Geminus, T. *Compendiosa totius anatomie delineatio: A Facsimile of the First English Edition of 1553 in the Version of Nicholas Udall.* Edited by C. O'Malley. London: Dawson, 1959.

Gentilcore, D. *Healers and Healing in Early Modern Italy.* New York: Manchester University Press, 1998.

Gentilcore, D. *Medical Charlatanism in Early Modern Italy.* Oxford: Oxford University Press, 2007.

Gilbert, R. *Early Modern Hermaphrodites: Sex and Other Stories.* New York: Palgrave, 2002.

Ginzburg, C. *Clues, Myths, and the Historical Method.* Translated by J. Tedeschi and A. Tedeschi. Baltimore: Johns Hopkins University Press, 1989.

Ginzburg, C. *Ecstasies: Deciphering the Witch's Sabbath.* Translated by R. Rosenthal. New York: Penguin, 1992.

Ginzburg, C. *The Night Battles: Witchcraft and Agrarian Cults in the Sixteenth and Seventeenth Centuries.* Translated by J. Tedeschi and A. Tedeschi. Baltimore: Johns Hopkins University Press, 1983.

Godbeer, R. "Salem." In *Encyclopedia of Witchcraft: The Western Tradition.* Edited by R. M. Golden. Santa Barbara, CA: ABC-CLIO, 2006.

Goddard, S. H., ed. *The World in Miniature Engravings by the German Little Masters 1500–1550.* Kansas: The Spencer Museum of Art, 1988.

Goffen, R., ed. *Titian's "Venus of Urbino."* New York: Cambridge University Press, 1997.

Goldberg, J. *Sodomites: Renaissance Texts, Modern Sexualities.* Stanford, CA: Stanford University Press, 1992.

Gomez, A. *Opus præclarum ... super legibus Tauri.* Andreas à Portonarijs, 1575.

Goody, J. "A Comparative Approach to Incest and Adultery." *British Journal of Sociology* 7 (1956): 286–305.

Green, M. *The Transmission of Ancient Theories of Female Physiology and Disease through the Early Middle Ages.* Ph.D. diss., Princeton University, 1985.

Grieco, S.F.M. "Pedagogical Prints: Moralizing Broadsheets and Wayward Women in Counter Reformation Italy." In *Picturing Women in Renaissance and Baroque Italy.* Edited by G. A. Johnson and S.F.M. Grieco. Cambridge: Cambridge University Press, 1997.

Grien, H. B. *Judith with the Head of Holofernes.* Nuremberg: Germanisches Nationalmuseum, [1515].

Grote, L. *Albrecht Dürer: Reisen nach Venedig.* Munich: Prestel, 1998.

Grotius, H. *De iure praedae commentarius: Commentary on the Law of Prize and Booty.* Edited by M. J. van Ittersum. Indianapolis: Liberty Fund, 2006.

Grotius, H. *The Rights of War and Peace.* Edited by R. Tuck. Indianapolis: Liberty Fund, 2005.

Guazzo (Guaccio), F. M. *Compendium maleficarum: The Montague Summers Edition.* Translated by E. A. Ashwin. New York: Dover, 1988.

Gurevitch, A. *Medieval Popular Culture: Problems of Belief and Perception.* Translated by J. M. Bak and P. A. Hollingsworth. Cambridge: Cambridge University Press, 1988.

Hacke, D. *Women, Sex and Marriage in Early Modern Venice.* Burlington, VT: Ashgate, 2004.

Hacke, D. "Love Magic." In *Encyclopedia of Witchcraft: The Western Tradition.* Edited by R. M. Golden. Santa Barbara, CA: ABC-CLIO, 2006.

Hagen, R. "Shamanism." In *Encyclopedia of Witchcraft: The Western Tradition.* Edited by R. M. Golden. Santa Barbara, CA: ABC-CLIO, 2006.

Halperin, D. *How to Do the History of Male Homosexuality.* Chicago: University of Chicago Press, 2002.

Hanning, R. W., and D. Rosand, eds. *Castiglione: The Ideal and the Real in Renaissance Culture.* New Haven, CT: Yale University Press, 1983.

Häring, N. M. "Alain of Lille, 'De planctu naturae.'" *Studi Medievali* 19 (1978): 797–879.

Harcourt, G. "Andreas Vesalius and the Anatomy of Antique Sculpture." *Representation* 17 (1987): 28–61.

Harvey, W. *The Anatomical Exercises.* New York: Dover, 1995.

Haskins, S. *Mary Magdalen: Myth and Metaphor.* New York: Harcourt Brace, 1994.

Hawthorne, N. "Young Goodman Brown." In *Young Goodman Brown and Other Tales.* Edited by B. Harding. Oxford: Oxford World's Classics, 1987.

Heal, F. *Hospitality in Early Modern England.* New York: Oxford University Press, 1990.

Heal, F. "The Idea of Hospitality in Early Modern England." *Past and Present* 102 (1984): 66–93.

Hecksher, W. *Rembrandt's Anatomy of Dr. Nicolaas Tulp: An Iconological Study.* New York: New York University Press, 1958.

Heikamp, D. *L'Antico.* Milan: Fabbri, 1966.

Hejden, M. van der. "Women as Victims of Sexual and Domestic Violence in Seventeenth-Century Holland: Criminal Cases of Rape, Incest, and Maltreatment in Rotterdam and Delft." *Journal of Social History* 33 (2000): 623–44.

Henry VIII. *Acte for the punyshment of the Vice of Buggery.* In *The Statutes of the Realm*, vol. 3. The Record Commission, 1817.

Heseler, B. *Andreas Vesalius' First Public Anatomy at Bologna, 1540: An Eyewitness Report.* Edited and translated by Ruben Eriksson. Uppsala: Almquist and Wiksells, 1959.

Hewlett, M. "The French Connection: Syphilis and Sodomy in Late-Renaissance Lucca." In *Sins of the Flesh: Responding to Sexual Disease in Early Modern Europe.* Edited by K. Siena. Toronto: Centre for Reformation and Renaissance Studies, 2005.

Hillman, D., and C. Mazzio, eds. *The Body in Parts: Fantasies of Corporeality in Early Modern Europe.* London: Routledge, 1997.

Hindle, S. "Dearth, Fasting and Alms: The Campaign for General Hospitality in Late Elizabethan England." *Past and Present* 172 (2001): 44–86.

Hinz, B. "Nackt/Akt: Dürer und der Prozess der Zivilisation." *Städel Jahrbuch* N.F. 14 (1993): 199–230.

Hollander, A. *Sex and Suits: The Evolution of Modern Dress.* New York: Kodansha International, 1994.

Holman, B. *Disegno: Italian Renaissance Designs for the Decorative Arts.* Dubuque, IA: Kendall, 1997.

Holzberg, N. *Willibald Pirckheimer: Griechischer Humanismus in Deutschland.* Munich: Wilhelm Fink, 1981.

Howard, J. E. "Crossdressing, the Theatre, and Gender Struggle in Early Modern England." *Shakespeare Quarterly* 39 (1988): 418–40.

Howard, J. E. *The Stage and Social Struggle in Early Modern England*. London: Routledge, 1994.

Hufton, O. "Istruzione, Lavoro e Povertà." In *Monaca, Moglie, Serva, Cortigiana: Vita e imagine delle donne tra Rinascimento e Controriforma*. Edited by S. F. Matthews-Grieco. Florence: Morgana Edizioni, 2001.

Hughes, D. "Sumptuary Law and Social Relations in Renaissance Italy." In *The Italian Renaissance: The Essential Readings*. Edited by P. Findlen. Oxford: Blackwell, 2002.

Hull, I. V. *Sexuality, State and Civil Society in Germany, 1700–1815*. Ithaca, NY: Cornell University Press, 1996.

Hull, S. *Chaste, Silent and Obedient: English Books for Women 1475–1640*. San Marino, CA: Huntington Library, 1982.

Institoris, H. *The Hammer of Witches: A Complete Translation of the Malleus Maleficarum*. Translated by Christopher S. Mackay. Cambridge: Cambridge University Press, 2009.

Institoris, H. *Malleus Maleficarum von Heinrich Institoris (alias Kramer) unter Mithilfe Jakob Sprengers aufgrund der dämonologischen Tradition zusammengestellt: Wiedergabe des Erstdrucks von 1487 (Hain 9238)*. Edited by A. Schnyder. Göppingen: Kümmerle, 1991.

Ivory, Y. *The Homosexual Revival of Renaissance Style, 1850–1930*. New York: Palgrave Macmillan, 2009.

Jacobs, F. H. "Aretino and Michelangelo, Dolce and Titian, *Femmina, Masculo, Grazia*." *Art Bulletin* 82 (2000): 51–67.

Jaeger, S. *Ennobling Love: In Search of a Lost Sensibility*. Philadelphia: University of Pennsylvania Press, 1999.

Jager, E. *The Book of the Heart*. Chicago: University of Chicago Press, 2000.

Jayne, S. R. *Marsilio Ficino's Commentary on Plato's Symposium*. Columbia: University of Missouri Press, 1944.

Jevons, F. B. *An Introduction to the History of Religion*. Methuen, 1902.

Johns, A. *The Nature of the Book: Print and Knowledge in the Making*. Chicago: University of Chicago Press, 1998.

Johnson H., and F. A. Dutra, eds. *Pelo Vaso Traseiro: Sodomy and Sodomites in Luso-Brazilian History*. Tucson: Fenestra Books, 2006.

Johnson, M. "Lilith." In *Encyclopedia of Witchcraft: The Western Tradition*. Edited by R. M. Golden. Santa Barbara, CA: ABC-CLIO, 2006.

Johnson, M. "Night Witch, or Night Hag." In *Encyclopedia of Witchcraft: The Western Tradition*. Edited by R. M. Golden. Santa Barbara, CA: ABC-CLIO, 2006.

Jones, A. R., and P. Stallybrass. "Fetishizing Gender: Constructing the Hermaphrodite in Renaissance Europe." In *Body Guards: The Cultural Politics of Gender Ambiguity*. Edited by J. Epstein and K. Straub. New York: Routledge, 1991.

Jones, A. R., and P. Stallybrass. *Renaissance Clothing and the Materials of Memory*. Cambridge: Cambridge University Press, 2000.

Jordanova, L. "Happy Marriages and Dangerous Liasons: Artists and Anatomy." In *Artists and Anatomy: The Quick and the Dead*. Berkeley: University of California Press, 1997.

Kaiser, D. H. "'Whose Wife Will She Be at the Resurrection?' Marriage and Remarriage in Early Modern Russia." *Slavic Review* 62 (2003): 304–14.

Karras, R. M. *Sexuality in Medieval Europe: Doing Unto Others.* London: Routledge, 2005.

Kaske, R. E. "*Beowulf* and the Book of Enoch." *Speculum* 46 (1971): 421–31.

Keck, D. *Angels and Angelology in the Middle Ages.* New York: Oxford University Press, 1998.

Keller, E. *Generating Bodies and Gendered Selves: The Rhetoric of Reproduction in Early Modern England.* Seattle: University of Washington Press, 2007.

Kent, D. *Friendship, Love, and Trust in Renaissance Florence.* Cambridge, MA: Harvard University Press, 2009.

Kieckhefer, R. *European Witch Trials: Their Foundations in Popular and Learned Culture.* Berkeley: University of California Press, 1976.

Kieckhefer, R. *Magic in the Middle Ages.* Cambridge: Cambridge University Press, 1989.

King, H. *Hippocrates' Women: Reading the Female Body in Ancient Greece.* London: Routledge, 1998.

King, H. "The Mathematics of Sex: One to Two, or Two to One?" In *Studies in Medieval and Renaissance History: Sexuality and Culture in Medieval and Renaissance Europe*, third series, vol. 2. Edited by P. Soergel. New York: AMS Press, 2005.

Kirkham, V. ed. and trans. *Laura Battiferra and Her Literary Circle: An Anthology.* Chicago: University of Chicago Press, 2006.

Klapisch-Zuber, C. *Women, Family and Ritual in Renaissance Italy.* Chicago: University of Chicago Press, 1985.

Klestinec, C. "Civility, Comportment, and the Anatomy Theater: Girolamo Fabrici and His Medical Students in Renaissance Padua." *Renaissance Quarterly* 60 (2007): 434–63.

Knox, D. *Ironia: Medieval and Renaissance Ideas on Irony.* Leiden: Brill, 1989.

Koerner, J. L. *The Moment of Self-Portraiture in German Renaissance Art.* Chicago: University of Chicago Press, 1993.

Kors, A. C., and E. Peters, eds. *Witchcraft in Europe 400–1700: A Documentary History*, 2nd ed. Philadelphia: University of Pennsylvania Press, 2001.

Kramer, H., and J. Sprenger, attributed. *Malleus maleficarum.* 2 vols. Edited and translated by C. S. Mackay. Cambridge: Cambridge University Press, 2006.

Krekić, B. "'Abominandum crimen': Punishment of Homosexuals in Renaissance Dubrovnik." *Viator: Medieval and Renaissance Studies* 18 (1987): 339–42.

Kudlein, F. "The Seven Cells of the Uterus: The Doctrine and Its Roots." *Bulletin of the History of Medicine* 49 (1965): 415–23.

Lanfranci. *A most excellent and learned woorke of chirurgerie, called Chirurgia parva Lanfranci ... trans. by John Halle Chirurgien.* London: Thomas Marshe, 1565.

Laqueur, T. *Making Sex: Body and Gender from the Greeks to Freud.* Cambridge, MA: Harvard University Press, 1990.

Laqueur, T. "Orgasm, Generation and the Politics of Reproductive Biology." In *The Making of the Modern Body: Sexuality and Society in the Nineteenth Century.* Edited by C. Gallagher and T. Laqueur. Berkeley: University of California Press, 1987.

Larkey, S. "The Vesalian Compendium of Geminus and Nicholas Udall's Translation: Their Relation to Vesalius, Caius, Vicary and De Mondeville." *The Library*, 4th ser., 13, no. 4 (1933): 369–94.

Lavan, M. *Virgins of Venice: Broken Vows and Cloistered Lives in the Renaissance Convent*. New York: Viking, 2002.

Lawler, T., G. Marc'hadour, and R. C. Marius, eds. *A Dialogue Concerning Heresies*. New Haven, CT: Yale University Press, 1981.

Lemay, H. "The Stars and Human Sexuality: Some Medieval Scientific Views." *Isis* 71 (1980): 127–35.

Lemnius, L. *De occultis naturae miraculis*. Apud Ioannem Birckmanum, 1573.

Levack, B. P. "Torture." In *Encyclopedia of Witchcraft: The Western Tradition*. Edited by R. M. Golden. Santa Barbara, CA: ABC-CLIO, 2006.

Levack, B. P. *The Witch-Hunt in Early Modern Europe*, 3rd ed. Harlow: Pearson Longman, 2006.

Levine, L. *Men in Women's Clothing: Anti-Theatricality and Effeminization 1579–1642*. Cambridge: Cambridge University Press, 1994.

Lévi-Strauss, C. *The Elementary Structures of Kinship*. London: Eyre and Spottiswoode, 1969.

Levy, A. *Re-Membering Masculinity in Early Modern Florence: Widowed Bodies, Mourning and Portraiture*. Burlington, VT: Ashgate, 2006.

Levy, J. L. "The Erotic Engraving of Sebald and Barthel Beham: A German Interpretation of a Renaissance Subject." In *The World in Miniature Engravings by the German Little Masters 1500–1550*. Edited by St. H. Goddard. Lawrence, KS: The Spencer Museum of Art, 1988.

Levy, S. *Elizabethan Treasures: The Hardwick Hall Textiles*. London: National Trust/ Harry Abrams, 1998.

Liceti, F. *De monstrorum causis, natura, et differentiis*. Apud Paulum Frambottum, 1616.

Lloyd, G.E.R. *Two Types of Argumentation in Early Greek Thought*. Cambridge: Cambridge University Press, 1971.

Löcher, K. *Barthel Beham: Ein Maler aus dem Dürerkreis*. Munich: Deutscher Kunstverlag, 1999.

Löcher, K. "Madonna und Kind (Haller-Madonna)." In *Nürnberg 1300–1550: Kunst der Gotik und der Renaissance*. Munich: Prestel, 1986.

Long, K. P. *Hermaphrodites in Renaissance Europe*. Aldershot: Ashgate, 2006.

Long, P. *Openness, Secrecy, Authorship: Technical Arts and the Culture of Knowledge from Antiquity to the Renaissance*. Baltimore: Johns Hopkins University Press, 2001.

Lowe, K.J.P. *Nuns' Chronicles and Convent Culture in Renaissance and Counter-Reformation Italy*. Cambridge: Cambridge University Press, 2003.

Luther, M. *Luther's Works*, vol. 39. Edited by H. T. Lehmann. Minneapolis, MN: Fortress Press, 1970.

Luther, M. *Werke: Kritische Gesammtausgabe. Tischreden*. Weimar: Böhlau, 1912–1921.

Macfarlane, A. *Witchcraft in Tudor and Stuart England: A Regional and Comparative Study*. New York: Harper Torchbooks, 1970.

Maclachlan, E., ed. and trans. *Chiara Matraini: Selected Poetry and Prose.* Chicago: University of Chicago Press, 2007.

Mack, J. E. *Abduction: Human Encounters with Aliens.* New York: Scribner's, 1994.

Maclean, I. *The Renaissance Notion of Woman: A Study in the Fortunes of Scholasticism and Medical Science in European Intellectual Life.* Cambridge: Cambridge University Press, 1980.

Maggi, A. *The Rhetoric of Satan.* Chicago: University of Chicago Press, 2000.

Magistris, M. de. *Questiones morales … de fortitudine.* Johan Petit, 1511.

Major, J. *In quartum Sententiarum quæstiones vtilissimæ.* In officina Iodoci Badii, 1519.

Malinowski, B. *The Sexual Life of Savages in North-Western Melanesia: An Ethnographic Account of Courtship, Marriage and Family Life among the Natives of the Trobriand Islands, British New Guinea.* New York: Routledge, 1929.

Marinella, L. *La Nobiltà e excellenza delle donne coi' difetti e mancamenti degli huomeni.* Venice: Ciotti, 1600, 1601, 1621. English version in *The Nobility and Excellence of Women and the Defects and Vices of Men.* Edited and translated by L. Panizzi and A. Dunhill. Chicago: University of Chicago Press, 1999.

Martines, L. "Poetry as Politics and Memory in Renaissance Florence and Italy." In *Art, Memory and Family in Renaissance Florence.* Edited by G. Ciapelli and P. L. Rubin. Cambridge: Cambridge University Press, 2000.

Maus, K. "A Womb of His Own: Male Renaissance Poets in the Female Body." In *Sexuality and Gender in Early Modern Europe: Institutions, Texts, and Images.* Edited by J. Turner. Cambridge: Cambridge University Press, 1993.

Maxwell-Stuart, P. G. "Lamia." In *Encyclopedia of Witchcraft: The Western Tradition.* Edited by R. M. Golden. Santa Barbara, CA: ABC-CLIO, 2006.

Maxwell-Stuart, P. G. "Strix, Striga, Stria." In *Encyclopedia of Witchcraft: The Western Tradition.* Edited by R. M. Golden. Santa Barbara, CA: ABC-CLIO, 2006.

Medina, B. de. *Breve instruction de como se ha de administrar el sacramento de la penitencia.* Herederos de Mathias Gast, 1579.

Melanchthon, P. *Opera quae supersunt omnia,* vol. 23. Edited by H. E. Bindseil. C. A. Schwetschke, 1855.

Mellencamp, E. H. "A Note on the Costume of Titian's *Flora.*" *Art Bulletin* 51 (1969): 174–77.

Mende, M. "Wer war Dürers Kuschelhase?" *Die Welt,* February 26, 2003. www.welt.de/printwelt/article420380/Wer_war_Duerers_Kuschelhase.html.

Mérimée, P. "The Venus of Ille." In *Carmen and Other Stories.* Translated by N. Jotcham, 132–61. Oxford: Oxford World's Classics, 1989.

Miles, M. R. "The Virgin's One Bare Breast." In *The Expanding Discourse.* Edited by N. Broude and M. D. Garrard. New York: Icon Editions, 1992.

Millen, R., and R. Wolf. *Heroic Deeds and Mystic Figures: A New Reading of Rubens' Cycle of Maria de' Medici.* Princeton, NJ: Princeton University Press, 1989.

Miller, M. *Material Friendship: Service and Amity in Early Modern French Literature.* Ph.D. diss., University of Michigan, 2008.

Milton, J. *Eikonoklastes.* London: Thomas Brewster and George Moule, 1650.

Monbeig Goguel, C., ed. *Francesco Salviati o La bella maniera.* Milan: Electa, 1998.

Montaigne, M. de. *The Complete Essays*. Translated and edited by M. A. Screech. New York: Penguin, 2004.

Montaigne, M. de. *The Diary of Montaigne's Journey to Italy in 1580 and 1581*. Translated and edited by E. J. Treichmann. New York: Harcourt Brace, 1929.

Montaigne, M. de. "Of the Power of the Imagination." In *The Complete Essays of Montaigne*. Translated by D. M. Frame. Stanford, CA: Stanford University Press, 1992 [1958].

Mora, G., ed. *Witches, Devils, and Doctors in the Renaissance: Johann Weyer, De praestigiis daemonum*. Translated by J. Shea. Binghamton, NY: Medieval and Renaissance Texts and Studies, 1991.

Moson, J. *The General Practise of Physicke*. London: Richard Field, 1605.

Mott, L. "Meu menino lindo: Cartas de amor de um frade sodomita, Lisboa (1690)." *Luso-Brazilian Review* 38 (2001): 97–115.

Mortimer, A., trans. *Petrarch: Selected Poems*. Tuscaloosa: University of Alabama Press, 1977.

Mülleder, G. "Unterschiedliche Deliktvorstellungen bei Ober- und Unterbehörden am Beispiel der Salzburger Zauberer-Jackl-Prozesse (1675-1679)." In *Hexenprozesse und Gerichtspraxis*. Edited by H. Eiden and R. Volmer. Trier: Spee, 2002.

Muller, J. *Barthel Beham: Kritischer Katalog*. Baden-Baden: Heitz, 1958.

Muraro, M. "Tiziano e le anatomie del Vesalio." In *Tiziano e Venezia: Convegno internazionale di studi, Venezia, 1976*. Vicenza: N. Pozza, 1980.

Nagl, H. "Der Zauberer-Jackl-Prozeß: Hexenprozesse im Erzstift Salzburg 1675-1690." *Mitteilungen der Gesellschaft für Salzburger Landeskunde* 112/113 (1972/73): 385–540, and 114 (1974): 79–21.

Naphy, W. *Sex Crimes from Renaissance to Enlightenment*. Stroud: Tempus, 2002.

Navarre, M. de. *L'Heptaméron, Nouvelle 48*. In *The Heptameron*. Translated by P. A. Chilton. Harmondsworth, Middlesex: Penguin, 1984.

Nürnberg 1300–1550: Kunst der Gotik und der Renaissance. Munich: Prestel, 1986.

Oakley, F. *Natural Law, Laws of Nature, Natural Rights: Continuity and Discontinuity in the History of Ideas*. New York: Continuum, 2005.

Oldridge, D., ed. *The Witchcraft Reader*, 2nd ed. New York: Routledge, 2008.

O'Malley, C. *Andreas Vesalius of Brussels, 1514–1564*. Berkeley: University of California Press, 1964.

Ordonnantie van de polityen binnen Hollandt. Aelbert Heyndricsz, 1586.

Orgel, S. *Impersonations: The Performance of Gender in Shakespeare's England*. Cambridge: Cambridge University Press, 1996.

Orgel, S. "Ganymede Agonistes." *GLQ: A Journal of Lesbian and Gay Studies* 10 (2004): 485–501.

Osiander, A. *Von den verbotenen Heiraten*. In *Gesamtausgabe*. Edited by G. Müller and G. Seebaß. Gütersloher Verlagshaus Mohn, 1985.

Ostorero, M. "Vinet, Jean (Vineti, Johannes) (d. ca. 1470)." In *Encyclopedia of Witchcraft: The Western Tradition*. Edited by R. M. Golden. Santa Barbara, CA: ABC-CLIO, 2006.

Ostorero, M., A. P. Bagliani, and K. Utz Tremp, eds. *L'Imaginaire du sabbat: Édition critique des textes les plus anciens (1430 c.–1440 c.).* Lausanne: Université de Lausanne, 1999.

Otis, L. *Prostitution in Medieval Society: The History of an Urban Institution in Languedoc.* Chicago: University of Chicago Press, 1985.

Ovid. *Metamorphoses IX–XII.* Edited by D. E. Hill. Warminster: Aris and Phillips, 1999.

Ozment, S. *Magdalena and Balthasar: An Intimate Portrait of Life in Sixteenth-Century Europe Revealed in the Letters of a Nuremberg Husband and Wife.* New Haven, CT: Yale University Press, 1986.

Palmieri, M. *Della vita civile.* Edited by F. Battaglia. Bologna: Zanichelli, 1944 [1529].

Papon, I. *Recueil d'arrests notables des cours souveraines de France.* Nicolas Buon, 1601.

Park, K. "Dissecting the Female Body: From Women's Secrets to the Secrets of Nature." In *Crossing Boundaries: Attending to Early Modern Women.* Edited by J. Donawerth and A. Seeff, 29–47. Newark: University of Delaware Press, 2000.

Park, K. *Doctors and Medicine in Early Renaissance Florence.* Princeton, NJ: Princeton University Press, 1985.

Park, K. *Secrets of Women: Gender, Generation, and the Origins of Human Dissection.* New York: Zone Books, 2006.

Park, K. "Medicine and Magic: The Healing Arts." In *Gender and Society in Renaissance Italy.* Edited by J. C. Brown and R. C. Davis. New York: Longman, 1998.

Park, K. "Was There a Renaissance Body?" In *The Italian Renaissance in the Twentieth Century.* Edited by A. Grieco, M. Rocke, and F. G. Superbi, 321–35. Florence: Olschki, 1999.

Park, K., and R. Nye. "Destiny Is Anatomy." *The New Republic* (February 18, 1991), 53–57.

Parker, Archbishop Matthew. *An admonition. To all suche as shall intende hereafter to enter the state of matrimony godly, and agreably to lawes.* R. Wolfe, 1571.

Parker, P. "Gender Ideology, Gender Change: The Case of Marie Germain." *Critical Inquiry* 19 (1993): 337–64.

Parsons, T. "The Incest Taboo in Relation to Social Structure and the Socialisation of the Child." *British Journal of Sociology* 5 (1954): 101–17.

Passi, G. *Dei Donneschi difetti.* Venice: Scamorza, 1599, 1601, 1618; Latin edition, 1612.

Pastoureau, M. *The Devil's Cloth: A History of Stripes.* New York: Washington Square Press, 1991.

Patrick, J. M. "A Consideration of La Terre Australe Connue by Gabriele de Figny." *PMLA* 61 (1964): 739–51.

Pelling, M. "Medical Practice in Early Modern England: Trade or Profession?" In *The Professions in Early Modern England.* Edited by W. Prest. New York: Croom Helm, 1987.

Pelling, M. *The Common Lot: Sickness, Medical Occupations and the Urban Poor in Early Modern England.* London: Longman, 1998.

Pepys, S. *The Diary of Samuel Pepys: A New and Complete Transcription,* vol. 9. Edited by R. Latham and W. Matthews. London: Bell, 1976 [1668].

Pérez Sánchez, A. E., and N. Spinosa. *Ribera 1591–1652* Madrid: Museo del Prado, 1992.

Peters, E. "Canon Episcopi." In *Encyclopedia of Witchcraft: The Western Tradition.* Edited by Richard M. Golden. Santa Barbara, CA: ABC-CLIO, 2006. 164–65.

Pettitt, T. "'Here Comes I, Jack Straw': English Folk Drama and Social Revolt." *Folklore* 95 (1984): 3–20.

Pico della Mirandola, G. F. "Oration on the Dignity of Man." In *The Renaissance Philosophy of Man: Selections in Translation.* Edited by E. Cassirer, P. O. Kristeller, and J. H. Randall. Chicago: University of Chicago Press, 1948.

Pico della Mirandola, G. *La Sorcière: Dialogue en trois livres sur la tromperie des démons.* Edited and translated by A. Perifano. Turnhout: Brepols, 2007.

Pius V. "Cum primum." In *Bullarum privilegiorum ac diplomatum Romanorum Pontificum amplissima collection,* vol. 4. Edited by C. Cocquelines. Sumptibus Hieronymi Mainardi, 1745.

Pizza, G. "Toads." In *Encyclopedia of Witchcraft: The Western Tradition.* Edited by R. M. Golden. Santa Barbara, CA: ABC-CLIO, 2006.

Plato. *The Symposium.* Translated by C. Gill. London: Penguin, 1999.

Platter, F. *De corporis humani structura.* Basel: Frobiniana, 1583.

Pliny. *Natural History.* Edited by H. Rackman. Cambridge, MA: Harvard University Press, 1952.

Pócs, É. "Folklore." In *Encyclopedia of Witchcraft: The Western Tradition.* Edited by R. M. Golden. Santa Barbara, CA: ABC-CLIO, 2006.

Poirier, G. *L'homosexualité dans l'imaginaire de la Renaissance.* Paris: Champion, 1996.

Pomata, G. *Contracting a Cure: Patients, Healers, and the Law in Early Modern Bologna.* Baltimore: Johns Hopkins University Press, 1998.

Pomata, G. "Menstruating Men: Similarity and Difference of the Sexes in Early Modern Medicine." In *Generation and Degeneration: Tropes of Reproduction in Literature and History from Antiquity through Early Modern Europe.* Edited by V. Finucci and K. Brownlee, 109–52. Durham, NC: Duke University Press, 2001.

Pomata, G. "*Praxis Historialis*: The Uses of *Historia* in Early Modern Medicine." In *Historia: Empiricism and Erudition in Early Modern Europe.* Edited by G. Pomata and N. Siraisi. Boston: MIT Press, 2005.

Price, D. H. *Albrecht Dürer's Renaissance: Humanism, Reformation, and the Art of Faith.* Ann Arbor: University of Michigan Press, 2003.

Pricket, R. *Times Anotomie* (1606). Cambridge: Chadwyck-Healey, 1992.

Pseudo-Lucian. "Affairs of the Heart." In *Lucian,* vol. 8. Translated by M. D. Macleod. Cambridge, MA: Harvard University Press, 1967.

Pufendorf, S. *De jure naturae et gentium.* Sumtibus Adami Junghans, 1672.

Puff, H. "The Death of Orpheus (according to Albrecht Dürer)." In *Dead Lovers: Erotic Bonds and the Study of Premodern Europe.* Edited by B. Dufallo and P. Mc-Cracken. Ann Arbor: University of Michigan Press, 2006.

Puff, H. "Female Sodomy: The Trial of Katherina Hetzeldorfer (1477)." *Journal of Medieval and Early Modern Studies* 30 (2000): 41–61.

Puff, H. "Nature on Trial: Acts 'Against Nature' in the Law Courts of Early Modern Germany and Switzerland." In *The Moral Authority of Nature.* Edited by L. Daston and F. Vidal. Chicago: University of Chicago Press, 2004.

Puff, H. "Sodomie und Herrschaft: Eine Problemskizze." In *Liebe und Widerstand: Ambivalenzen historischer Geschlechterbeziehungen*. Edited by I. Bauer, C. Ehrmann-Hämmerle, and G. Hauch. Vienna: Böhlau, 2005.

Puff, H. *Sodomy in Reformation Germany and Switzerland, 1400–1600*. Chicago: University of Chicago Press, 2003.

Quaife, G. *Wanton Wenches and Wayward Wives: Peasants and Illicit Sex in Early Seventeenth Century England*. New Brunswick, NJ: Rutgers University Press, 1979.

Quilligan, M. *Incest and Agency in Elizabethan England*. Philadelphia: University of Pennsylvania Press, 2005.

Radbruch, G., ed. *Die Peinliche Gerichtsordnung Kaiser Karls V. von 1532 (Carolina)*. Reclam, 1962.

Radcliff-Umstead, D. *The Birth of Modern Comedy in Renaissance Italy*. Chicago: University of Chicago Press, 1969.

Raynalde, T. *Birth of Mankind*. London: Tho. Ray., 1598.

Recopilacion de leyes de los Reynos de las Indias. Consejo de las Indias, 1681.

Reiche, I., et al. "Spatially Resolved Synchroton-Induced X-Ray Fluorescence Analyses of Metal Point Drawings and Their Mysterious Inscriptions." *Spectrochimica Acta Part B: Atomic Spectroscopy* 59 (2004): 1657–62.

Reiffenberg, F., ed. *Mémoires de Jacques Du Clercq*. In *Collection des chroniques nationals françaises*. Paris: Dondey-Dupre, 1826–1827.

Riverius, L. *The Practice of Physick*. London: Peter Cole, 1658.

Roberts, B., and L. Groenendijk. "'Wearing Out a Pair of Fool's Shoes': Sexual Advice for Youth in Holland's Golden Age." *Journal of the History of Sexuality* 13, no. 2 (2004): 139–56.

Robinson, O. F. *Criminal Law of Ancient Rome*. London: Duckworth, 1995.

Rocke, M. *Forbidden Friendships: Homosexuality and Male Culture in Renaissance Florence*. Oxford: Oxford University Press, 1996.

Rocke, M. "Gender and Sexual Culture in Renaissance Italy." In *Gender and Society in Renaissance Italy*. Edited by J. Brown and R. Davis. London: Longman, 1998.

Roper, L. *The Holy Household: Women and Morals in Reformation Augsburg*. Oxford: Clarendon Press, 1989.

Roper, L. *Oedipus and the Devil: Witchcraft, Sexuality, and Religion in Early Modern Europe*. London: Routledge, 1994.

Roper, L. "Tokens of Affection: The Meanings of Love in Sixteenth-Century Germany." In *Dürer and His Culture*. Edited by D. Eichberger and C. Zika. Cambridge: Cambridge University Press, 1998.

Roper, L. *Witch Craze: Terror and Fantasy in Baroque Germany*. New Haven, CT: Yale University Press, 2004.

Rosenthal, M. *The Honest Courtesan: Veronica Franco as Citizen and Poet in Sixteenth-Century Venice*. Chicago: University of Chicago Press, 1992.

Rossiaud, J. *Medieval Prostitution*. Translated by L. G. Cochrane. Oxford: Basil Blackwell, 1988.

Rothstein, M. "Mutations of the Androgyne: Its Function in Early Modern French Literature." *Sixteenth Century Journal* 34 (2003): 409–37.

Röver-Kann, A. *Albrecht Dürer: Das Frauenbad von 1496*. Bremen: Kunstverein, 2001.

Rowland, I. "Revenge of the Regensburg Humanists, 1493." *Sixteenth Century Journal* 25 (1994): 307–22.

Rublack, U. "Sexual Difference, Law and Subjectivity in Early Modern Germany." In *After the History of Sexuality: German Interventions*. Edited by D. Herzog, H. Puff, and S. Spector. New York: Berghahn, forthcoming.

Ruggiero, G. *Binding Passions: Tales of Magic, Marriage, and Power at the End of the Renaissance*. New York: Oxford University Press, 1993.

Ruggiero, G. *The Boundaries of Eros: Sex Crime and Sexuality in Renaissance Venice*. New York: Oxford University Press, 1985.

Ruggiero, G. *Machiavelli in Love: Sex, Self and Society in the Italian Renaissance*. Baltimore: Johns Hopkins University Press, 2007.

Ruggiero, G. "Who's Afraid of Giulia Napolitana? Pleasure, Fear, and Imagining the Arts of the Renaissance Courtesan." In *The Courtesan's Arts: Cross Cultural Perspectives*. Edited by M. Feldman and B. Gordan, 280–92. Oxford: Oxford University Press, 2005.

Rupprich, H., ed. *Dürer: Schriftlicher Nachlass*. Vol. 1, *Autobiographische Schriften/ Briefwechsel/Dichtungen*. Berlin: Deutscher Verein für Kunstwissenschaft, 1956.

Ryan, W. "Evil Ey." In *Encyclopedia of Witchcraft: The Western Tradition*. Edited by R. M. Golden. Santa Barbara, CA: ABC-CLIO, 2006.

Sahm, H. *Dürers kleinere Texte: Konventionen als Spielraum für Individualität*. Tübingen: Niemeyer, 2002.

Sales, F. De. "Introduction a la vie devote." In *Œuvres*. Edited by A. Ravier and R. Devos. Gallimard, 1969.

Sánchez, T. *Disputationum de sancto matrimonii sacramento*. Apud Martinum Nutium, 1607.

Sánchez Ortega, M. H. *La mujer y la sexualidad en el antiguo régimen: La perspectiva inquisitorial*. Akal, 1992.

Saslow, J. M. *Ganymede in the Renaissance: Homosexuality in Art and Society*. New Haven, CT: Yale University Press, 1986.

Sawday, J. *The Body Emblazoned: Dissection and the Human Body in Renaissance Culture*. London: Routledge, 1995.

Schade, S. "Zur Genese des voeyuristischen Blicks: Das Erotische in den Hexenbildern Hans Baldung Griens." In *Frauen, Kunst, Geschichte: Zur Korrektur des herrschenden Blicks*. Edited by C. Bischoff. Marburg: Anabas, 1984.

Schiebinger, L. "Skeletons in the Closet: The First Illustrations of the Female Skeleton in Eighteenth-Century Anatomy." In *The Making of the Modern Body: Sexuality and Society in the Nineteenth Century*. Edited by C. Gallagher and T. Laqueur. Berkeley: University of California Press, 1987.

Schilling, M. *Bildpublizistik der frühen Neuzeit: Aufgaben und Leistungen des illustrierten Flugblatts in Deutschland bis um 1700*. Tübingen: Niemeyer, 1990.

Schleiner, W. "Cross-Dressing, Gender Errors, and Sexual Taboos in Renaissance Literature." In *Gender Reversals and Gender Cultures: Anthropological and Historical Perspectives*. Edited by S. P. Ramet. London: Routledge, 1996.

Schmitt, J.-C. *Ghosts in the Middle Ages: The Living and the Dead in Medieval Society*. Translated by T. L. Fagan. Chicago: University of Chicago Press, 1998.

Schröder, K.-A., and M. L. Sternath, eds. *Albrecht Dürer*. Vienna: Albertina, 2003.

Schultz, B. *Art and Anatomy in Renaissance Italy*. Ann Arbor, MI: UMI Research Press, 1985.

Scot, R. *The Discoverie of Witchcraft*. Edited by M. Summers. New York: Dover, 1972 [1930].

Scherbaum, A. "Madonna mit Kind (Haller-Madonna)." In *Albrecht Dürer*. Edited by K.-A. Schröder and M. L. Sternath. Vienna: Albertina, 2003.

Schwartz, S. B. "Brazilian Ethnogenesis: *Mestiços, mamelucos*, and *pardos*." In *Le Nouveau Monde, Mondes nouveaux: L'expérience américaine*. Edited by S. Gruzinski and N. Wachtel. Éditions de l'École des hautes études en sciences sociales, 1996.

Scribner, R. "Vom Sakralbild zur sinnlichen Schau: Sinnliche Wahrnehmung und das Visuelle bei der Objektivierung des Frauenkörpers in Deutschland im 16. Jahrhundert." In *Gepeinigt, begehrt vergessen*. Edited by K. Schreiner and N. Schnitzler. Munich: W. Fink, 1992.

Sedgwick, E. K. *Between Men: English Literature and Male Homosocial Desire*. New York: Columbia University Press, 1985.

Sepúlveda, J. G. de. *Opera*. Ex typographia regia de la gazeta, 1780.

Sercambi, G. *Novelle*, vol. 1. Edited by G. Sinicropi. Bari: G. Laterza, 1972.

Seymour, C. *Michelangelo's David: A Search for Identity*. New York, 1967.

Shakespeare, W. *William Shakespeare: The Complete Works*. Edited by A. Harbage. Baltimore: Penguin, 1971.

Shapiro, M. "The Introduction of Actresses in England: Delay or Defensiveness?" In *Enacting Gender on the English Renaissance Stage*. Edited by V. Comensoli and A. Russell. Urbana: University of Illinois Press, 1999.

Siena, K. "Pollution, Promiscuity, and the Pox: English Venereology and the Early Modern Medical Discourse on Social and Sexual Danger." *Journal of the History of Sexuality* 8 (1998): 553–74.

Simon-Muscheid, K. "Frauen in Männerrollen." In *Arbeit—Liebe—Streit: Texte zur Geschichte des Geschlechterverhältnisses und des Alltags*. Edited by D. Rippmann et al. Liestal: Verlag des Kantons Basel-Landschaft, 1996.

Simons, P. "Images of Bathing Women in Early Modern Europe and Turkey." In *Crossing Cultures: Conflict, Migration and Convergence*. Edited by J. Anderson. Melbourne: Miegunyah Press, 2009.

Simons, P. "Lesbian (In)Visibility in Italian Renaissance Culture: Diana and Other Cases of *donna con donna*." In *Gay and Lesbian Studies in Art History*. Edited by W. Davis. New York: Harrington Park Press, 1994.

Simons, P. "Women in Frames: The Gaze, the Eye, and the Profile in Renaissance Portraiture." In *The Expanding Discourse*. Edited by N. Broude and M. D. Garrard. New York: Icon Editions, 1992.

Simons, P., and M. Kornell. "Annibal Caro's After-Dinner Speech (1536) and the Question of Titian as Vesalius's Illustrator." *Renaissance Quarterly* 61 (2008): 1069–93.

Simplicio, O. Di. "Cats." In *Encyclopedia of Witchcraft: The Western Tradition*. Edited by R. M. Golden. Santa Barbara, CA: ABC-CLIO, 2006.

Simplicio, O. Di. "Infanticide." In *Encyclopedia of Witchcraft: The Western Tradition*. Edited by R. M. Golden. Santa Barbara, CA: ABC-CLIO, 2006.

Singer, C. *A Short History of Medicine.* New York: Oxford University Press, 1928.

Siraisi, N. *Medieval and Early Renaissance Medicine: An Introduction to Knowledge and Practice.* Chicago: University of Chicago Press, 1990.

Slights, W. E. "The Narrative Heart of the Renaissance." *Renaissance and Reformation/Renaissance et Réforme* 26, no. 1 (2002): 5–23.

Sluhovsky, M. *Believe Not Every Spirit: Possession, Mysticism, and Discernment in Early Modern Catholicism.* Chicago: University of Chicago Press, 2007.

Smith, B. *Homosexual Desire in Shakespeare's England.* Chicago: University of Chicago Press, 1991.

Smith, J. C. *Nuremberg: A Renaissance City, 1500–1618.* Austin: University of Texas Press, 1983.

Smith, W. *The Hippocratic Tradition.* Ithaca, NY: Cornell University Press, 1979.

Sonnabend, M. *Albrecht Dürer: Die Druckgraphiken im Städel Museum.* Frankfurt am Main: Städel Museum, 2007.

Spenser, E. "A View of the Present State of Ireland." In *The Works of Edmund Spenser.* Edited by E. Greenlaw, C. G. Osgood, F. M. Padelford, and R. Heffner. Baltimore: Johns Hopkins University Press, 1932–1957.

Speroni, S. *Dialogo della dignità delle donne.* In *Trattatisti del Cinquecento.* Edited by M. Pozzi. Milan-Naples: Ricciardi, 1978.

Stallybrass, P. "Worn Worlds: Clothes and Identity on the Renaissance Stage." In *Subject and Object in Renaissance Culture.* Edited by M. de Grazia, M. Quilligan, and P. Stallybrass. Cambridge: Cambridge University Press, 1996.

Steinberg, L. *The Sexuality of Christ in the Renaissance and in Modern Oblivion.* Chicago: University of Chicago Press, 1983.

Steinhausen, G., ed. *Briefwechsel Balthasar Paumgartners des Jüngeren mit seiner Gattin Magdalena, geb. Behaim (1592–1598).* Tübingen: Litterarischer Verein, 1895.

Stephens, W. *Demon Lovers: Witchcraft, Sex, and the Crisis of Belief.* Chicago: University of Chicago Press, 2002.

Stephens, W. *Giants in Those Days: Folklore, Ancient History, and Nationalism.* Lincoln: University of Nebraska Press, 1989.

Stephens, W. "Sexual Activity, Diabolic." In *Encyclopedia of Witchcraft: The Western Tradition.* Edited by R. M. Golden. Santa Barbara, CA: ABC-CLIO, 2006.

Stephens, W. "Tostado, Alonso (d. 1455)." In *Encyclopedia of Witchcraft: The Western Tradition.* Edited by R. M. Golden. Santa Barbara, CA: ABC-CLIO, 2006.

Stephens, W. "Witches Who Steal Penises: Impotence and Illusion in *Malleus maleficarum.*" *Journal of Medieval and Early Modern Studies* 28, "Body/Matter/Spirit" (Fall 1998): 495–529.

Steward, P. D. "A Play on Doubles: The 'Calandria.'" *Modern Language Studies* 14 (1984): 22–32.

Stewart, A. *Unequal Lovers: A Study of Unequal Couples in Northern Art.* New York: Abrams, 1978.

Stewart, A. G. *Before Bruegel: Sebald Beham and the Origins of Peasant Festival Imagery.* Aldershot: Ashgate, 2008.

Stolberg, M. "A Woman Down to the Bones: The Anatomy of Sexual Difference in the Sixteenth and Early Seventeenth Centuries." *Isis* 94 (2003): 274–99.

Stone, L., and P. F. Lurquin. *A Genetic and Cultural Odyssey: The Life and Work of L. Luca Cavalli-Sforza*. New York: Columbia University Press, 2005.

Storer, T. *Wolseius triumphans*. In *Storer: The Life and Death of Thomas Wolsey*. Cambridge: Chadwyck-Healey, 1992 [1599].

Strauss, G. *Nuremberg in the Sixteenth Century: City Politics and Life between Middle Ages and Modern Times*. Bloomington: Indiana University Press, 1976.

Strehlke, C. *Pontormo, Bronzino and the Medici: The Transformation of the Renaissance Portrait in Florence*. Philadelphia: Philadelphia Museum of Art, 2004.

Strocchia, S. T. "Gender and the Rites of Honour in the Italian Renaissance Cities." In *Gender and Society in Renaissance Italy*. Edited by J. C. Brown and R. C. Davis, 39–60. New York: Longman, 1998.

Stubbes, P. *The Anatomie of Abuses in Ailgna: Containing a Discoverie or Briefe Summarie of Such Notable Vices and Corruptons, as now raigne in many Christian Countreyes of the World*. London: Richard Jones, 1585.

Sugg, R. *Murder After Death: Literature and Anatomy in Early Modern England*. Ithaca, NY: Cornell University Press, 2007.

Sullivan, M. "The Witches of Dürer and Hans Baldung Grien." *Renaissance Quarterly* 53 (2000): 332–401.

Talvacchia, B. "The Art of Courting Women's Laughter." In *New Perspectives on Women and Comedy*. Edited by R. Barreca. Philadelphia: Gordon and Breach, 1992.

Talvacchia, B. "The Double Life of Saint Sebastian." In *The Body in Early Modern Italy*. Edited by J. Hairston and W. Stephens. Baltimore: Johns Hopkins University Press, 2010.

Talvacchia, B. "Il mercato dell Eros: Rappresentazioni della sessualità femminile nei soggetti mitologici." In *Monaca, moglie, serva, cortigiana: Vita e immagine delle donne tra Rinascimento e Controriforma*. Edited by S.F.M. Grieco, 192–245. Florence: Morgana Edizioni, 2001.

Talvacchia, B. *Taking Positions: On the Erotic in Renaissance Culture*. Princeton, NJ: Princeton University Press, 1999.

Tanner, N. P., ed. *Decrees of the Ecumenical Councils*, vol. 1. Sheed and Ward, 1990.

Tebeaux, E. *The Emergence of a Tradition: Technical Writing in the English Renaissance, 1475–1640*. Amitville, NY: Baywood, 1997.

Theweleit, K. *Male Fantasies*. Translated by S. Conway. Minneapolis: University of Minnesota Press, 1987.

Thofner, M. "Helena Fourment's *Het Pelsken*." *Art History* 27 (2004): 1–33.

Thomas, K. *Religion and the Decline of Magic*. New York: Scribners, 1971.

Thomasius, C. *Dissertationem juridicam de crimine bigamiæ*. Georgius Beyer, 1685.

Thomasius, C. *Institutionum jurisprudentiæ divinæ*. Sumptibus et Typis Viduae Christophori Salfeldii, 1717.

Traub, V. "The Psychomorphology of the Clitoris, or, the Reemergence of the *Tribade* in English Culture." In *Generation and Degeneration: Tropes of Reproduction in Literature and History from Antiquity through Early Modern Europe*. Edited by V. Finucci and K. Brownlee, 153–88. Durham, NC: Duke University Press, 2001.

Traub, V. *The Renaissance of Lesbianism in Early Modern England*. Cambridge: Cambridge University Press, 2002.

Trevisani, F., and D. Gasparotto, eds. *Bonacolsi, L'Antico. Uno scultore nella Mantova di Andrea Mantegna e di Isabella d'Este*. Milan: Electa, 2008.

Tuchman, B. *A Distant Mirror: The Calamitous Fourteenth Century*. New York: Ballantine, 1979.

Tuczay, C. "Flight of Witches." In *Encyclopedia of Witchcraft: The Western Tradition*. Edited by R. M. Golden. Santa Barbara, CA: ABC-CLIO, 2006.

Tuczay, C. "Holda." In *Encyclopedia of Witchcraft: The Western Tradition*. Edited by R. M. Golden. Santa Barbara, CA: ABC-CLIO, 2006.

Tuczay, C. "Incubi and Succubi." In *Encyclopedia of Witchcraft: The Western Tradition*. Edited by R. M. Golden. Santa Barbara, CA: ABC-CLIO, 2006.

Vasari, G. *The Lives of the Painters, Sculptors and Architects*. 2 vols. Translated by G. du C. de Vere. New York: Alfred A. Knopf, 1996.

Vecellio, C. *Costumes Anciens et Modernes/Habiti antichi e moderni di tutto il mondo*. Paris: Didot Frères Fils, 1980.

Velasco, S. *Male Delivery: Reproduction, Effeminacy, and Pregnant Men in Early Modern Spain*. Nashville, TN: Vanderbilt University Press, 2006.

Venette, N. *De la generation de l'homme, ou tableau de l'amour conjugale*. Claude Joly, 1716.

Verheyen, E. "Correggio's *Amori di Giove*." *Journal of the Warburg and Courtauld Institutes* 29 (1966): 160–92.

Vignali, A. *La cazzaria: The Book of the Prick*. Edited by I. F. Moulton. New York: Routledge, 2003.

Vincent, S. *Dressing the Elite: Clothes in Early Modern England*. Oxford: Berg, 2003.

Vinet, J. *Tractatus contra daemonum invocatores*. Cologne, 1487 (composed ca. 1450).

Vives, J. L. *De institutione foeminae Christianae*. 1529. English version in *The Education of a Christian Woman*. Edited and translated by C. Fantazzi. Chicago: University of Chicago Press, 2000.

Wack, M. F. *Lovesickness in the Middle Ages: The Viaticum and its Commentaries*. Philadelphia: University of Pennsylvania Press, 1990.

Wall, W. *The Imprint of Gender: Authorship and Publication in the English Renaissance*. Ithaca, NY: Cornell University Press, 1993.

Walz, R. "Douglas, Mary (1921–)." In *Encyclopedia of Witchcraft: The Western Tradition*. Edited by R. M. Golden. Santa Barbara, CA: ABC-CLIO, 2006.

Warner, M. *Monuments and Maidens*. New York: Atheneum, 1985.

Wear, A., R. K. French, and I. M. Lonie, eds. *The Medical Renaissance*. Cambridge: Cambridge University Press, 1985.

Weigert, L. "Autonomy as Deviance: Sixteenth-Century Images of Witches and Prostitutes." In *Solitary Pleasures: The Historical, Literary, and Artistic Discourses of Autoeroticism*. Edited by P. Bennett and V. A. Rosario. New York: Routledge, 1995.

Weyer, J. *Witches, Devils, and Doctors in the Renaissance: Johann Weyer, De praestigiis daemonum*. Edited by G. Mora et al. Translated by J. Shea. Medieval and Renaissance Texts and Studies, 1991.

Wickram, G. *Das Rollwagenbüchlin*. Edited by J. Bolte. Stuttgart: Reclam, 1968.

Wiesner, M. E. *Women and Gender in Early Modern Europe*, 2nd ed. Cambridge: Cambridge University Press, 2000.

Wiesner, M. E. "Women's Defence of Their Public Role." In *Gender, Church and State in Early Modern Germany.* London: Longman, 1998.

Wiesner, M. E., ed. *Witchcraft in Early Modern Europe.* Boston: Houghton Mifflin, 2007.

Wiesner-Hanks, M. E. *Christianity and Sexuality in the Early Modern World: Regulating Desire, Reforming Practice.* London: Routledge, 2000.

William of Worcester. *The Boke of Noblesse: Addressed to King Edward IV on his Invasion of France.* London: J. B. Nichols, 1860.

Williams, G. *A Dictionary of Sexual Language and Imagery in Shakespearean and Stuart Literature.* London: Athlone Press, 1994.

Wilson, A. *The Making of Man-Midwifery: Childbirth in England, 1660–1770.* London: UCL Press, 1995.

Wind, E. "Dürer's 'Männerbad': A Dionysian Mystery." *Journal of the Warburg and Courtauld Institute* 2 (1938): 269–71.

Wölfflin, H. *The Art of Albrecht Dürer.* Translated by A. Grieve and H. Grieve. London: Phaidon, 1971.

Wrigley, E. A., and R. S. Scofield. *The Population History of England 1541–1871: A Reconstruction.* London, 1982.

Wyatt, M. *The Italian Encounter with Tudor England: A Cultural Politics of Translation.* Cambridge: Cambridge University Press, 2005.

Zapperi, R. *The Pregnant Man.* Translated by B. Williams. Chur: Harwood Academic, 1991.

Zika, C. "She-Man: Visual Representations of Witchcraft and Sexuality." In *Exorcizing Our Demons: Magic, Witchcraft and Visual Culture in Early Modern Europe.* Leiden: Brill, 2003.

Zika, C. "Baldung [Grien], Hans (1484–1545)." In *Encyclopedia of Witchcraft: The Western Tradition.* Edited by R. M. Golden. Santa Barbara, CA: ABC-CLIO, 2006.

Zimmerman, S. "Disruptive Desire, Artifice and Indeterminacy in Jacobean Comedy." In *Erotic Politics: Desire on the Renaissance Stage.* Edited by S. Zimmerman. New York: Routledge, 1992.

Zuñiga, J. P. "La voix du sang: Du métis á l'idée de métisage en Amérique espagnole." *Annales: Histoire, Sciences Sociales* 54 (1999): 432.

CONTRIBUTORS

N. S. Davidson is Tutor in Modern History, St Edmund Hall, University of Oxford. He is author of *The Counter-Reformation* and many essays on Early Modern topics, including "Theology, Nature and the Law: Sexual Sin and Sexual Crime in Italy from the 14th to the 17th Centuries," and "Sexual Abuse in Renaissance and Early-Modern Italy."

Fredrika Jacobs is Professor in the Department of Art History at Virginia Commonwealth University. She is author of *Defining the Renaissance Virtuosa: Women Artists and the Language of Art History and Criticism* and *The Living Image in Renaissance Art*.

Ann Rosalind Jones is Esther Cloudman Dunn Professor of Comparative Literature at Smith College. She is the author of *The Currency of Eros: Women's Love Lyric in Europe, 1540–1600*; editor and translator, with Margaret Rosenthal, of *The Poems and Selected Letters of Veronica Franco*; with Peter Stallybrass, author of *Renaissance Clothing and the Materials of Memory*; and, with Margaret Rosenthal, an illustrated translation of Cesare Vecellio's *Habiti antichi et moderni di diverse parti del mondo*.

Cynthia Klestinec is Assistant Professor in the Department of English at Miami University, Ohio. Among her publications is "Civility, Comportment and the Anatomy Theater: Girolamo Fabrici and His Medical Students in Renaissance Padua." She has just completed a book-length manuscript, *Theaters of Anatomy*, forthcoming, Johns Hopkins University Press, 2011.

Helmut Puff is Associate Professor in the Departments of History and of Germanic Languages at the University of Michigan in Ann Arbor. He is author of *Deutsch in lateinischen Grammatikunterricht, 1480–1560* and *Sodomy in Reformation Germany and Switzerland*. He was co-editor of the journal *Gender and History* from 2002 to 2005.

Guido Ruggiero is College of Arts and Sciences Cooper Fellow and Professor and Chair of the Department of History at the University of Miami. He is author of *Violence in Early Renaissance Venice*; *The Boundaries of Eros: Sex Crime and Sexuality in Renaissance Venice*; *Binding Passions: Tales of Magic, Marriage and Power from the End of the Renaissance*; *Machiavelli in Love: Sex, Self and Society in Renaissance Italy*; as well as *Sex and Gender in Historical Perspective*; *Microhistory and the Lost Peoples of Europe*; and *History from Crime*; edited with Edward Muir. In addition he has edited *The Blackwell Companion to the Worlds of the Renaissance*, and *Five Comedies from the Italian Renaissance*, edited and translated with Laura Giannetti. He also edited the series *Studies in the History of Sexuality* for Oxford University Press and was a co-editor of the six-volume *Encyclopedia of European Social History* for Scribner's.

Walter Stephens is the Charles S. Singleton Professor of Italian Studies at the Johns Hopkins University. He is author of *Giants in Those Days: Folklore, Ancient History and Nationalism* and *Demon Lovers: Witchcraft, Sex, and the Crisis of Belief*, and co-editor of *Discourses of Authority in Medieval Literature* and *The Body in Early Modern Italy*. He co-edits *MLN Italian Issue* and sits on the editorial boards of *Renaissance Quarterly* and *Magic, Ritual, and Witchcraft*.

Bette Talvacchia is Board of Trustees Distinguished Professor of Art History in the Department of Art and Art History at the University of Connecticut. She is author of *Raphael* and *Taking Positions: On the Erotic in Renaissance Culture*.

INDEX

Italic numbers denote reference to illustrations.